praise for chef's night out

"*Chef's Night Out answers, beautifully, my favorite question for fellow chefs: where do you like to eat, and why?*"

MARIO BATALI, CHEF/CO-OWNER, BABBO, ESCA, AND LUPA RESTAURANTS

"*In New York, I run into many of my fellow chefs at our various hangouts, so I feel that I am definitely in the know as far as my city is concerned. It will be exciting to take this book with me on my next trip, and I look forward to seeing more local color, based on my reading, than I might normally get a chance to. After all, who knows better where to go than the professionals! What a wonderful idea and what a good read this book is—kudos, as usual, to the Page—Dornenburg team.*"

DANIEL BOULUD, CHEF OWNER, DANIEL AND CAFÉ BOULUD

"*Anyone with a taste for good food will appreciate this comprehensive publication. From San Francisco to Boston, Andrew Dornenburg and Karen Page have created a must-have guide for the most discriminating palates. Featuring some of the country's most prominent chefs, Chef's Night Out is a great resource to keep handy in your hometown and to pack when traveling.*"

MAYOR WILLIE L. BROWN, JR., MAYOR OF SAN FRANCISCO

"*I suggest you find room in your luggage for this brimming-with-insider-information tome on the best eating out venues in America. I wouldn't leave home without it.*"

MARCEL DESAULNIERS, CHEF-OWNER, THE TRELLIS

"*Of all of Andrew and Karen's works, this is the most mouth-watering! Reading the many tantalizing descriptions of so many wonderful restaurants by all of these chefs I admire so much, I kept developing an urge to travel and eat! This book will become my new reference for dining out around the country. If you love eating out, get this book!*"

CHARLIE TROTTER, CHEF-OWNER, CHARLIE TROTTER'S

"*Everything they write reflects Karen and Andrew's passion for great food and their affection for the people who create and celebrate it. Where do chefs eat? Of course I want to know....Chef's Night Out is studded with tips I need when I'm on the road—Raji Jallepalli's favorite BBQ joints in Memphis. The taco truck on Bertolli's Oakland hit list. And the Miami spot Norman Van Aken rates tops for a Cuban 'midnight' sandwich.*"

GAEL GREENE, LONG-TIME RESTAURANT CRITIC, *NEW YORK MAGAZINE*

"*I'm lucky: whenever I want an insightful restaurant recommendation, I call Karen Page. With the publication of Chef's Night Out, I can save on my phone bill. No one has a better perspective on the culinary scene than Karen and Andrew. Chef's Night Out is a must-have for any food enthusiast (and that's everyone, isn't it?). Buy this book!*"

TERRI DIAL, PRESIDENT AND CEO, WELLS FARGO BANK

"*What a fantastic resource! These are the kinds of places where we get all our inspiration. We can hardly wait to start tasting!*"

MARY SUE MILLIKEN AND **SUSAN FENIGER**, CHEFS-OWNERS, BORDER GRILL AND CIUDAD

"*This book may be the ultimate insider's guide to eating out. There's no better guide to finding a great hot dog or incredible geoduck clams than a talented local chef. A copy will live in my carry-on to dip into while in transit and to feast from when I arrive.*"

LYNNE ROSSETTO KASPER, HOST OF PUBLIC RADIO'S NATIONAL FOOD SHOW *THE SPLENDID TABLE*™

"Chef's Night Out *is also a winemaker's delight—proving that often the best wine lists are where the best food is.*"

ROBERT MONDAVI,
OWNER, ROBERT MONDAVI WINERY

"*An utterly engaging and comprehensive view of dining for pleasure. The innovative Andrew Dornenburg and Karen Page have a tremendous capacity for penning cover-to-cover reading—*Chef's Night Out *is a must for every discerning diner.*"

ALAIN DUCASSE, CHEF-OWNER, ALAIN DUCASSE
AU PLAZA ATHÉNÉE (PARIS), ALAIN DUCASSE AT
THE ESSEX HOUSE (NEW YORK CITY), AND LE
LOUIS XV–ALAIN DUCASSE (MONTE CARLO)

"*You'll want to get out a notebook as you read* Chef's Night Out, *and make a list of restaurant finds. Andrew Dornenburg and Karen Page have once again unearthed the secrets of the restaurant business and made every reader an insider. It's fascinating to hear chefs talk about how they taste and evaluate others' restaurants, and it will be irresistible to track down their favorites and try them yourself.*"

PHYLLIS RICHMAN, LONG-TIME RESTAURANT
CRITIC OF *THE WASHINGTON POST,* AND
AUTHOR OF *THE BUTTER DID IT,
MURDER ON THE GRAVY TRAIN,* AND
WHO'S AFRAID OF VIRGINIA HAM?

"*Karen and Andrew have done it again! Their work is delicious—what fun to learn where great chefs eat. The only thing better than reading about leading chefs' favorite restaurants in* Chef's Night Out *is to visit them with Dornenburg and Page.*"

RIKKI KLIEMAN, COURT TV ANCHOR,
AND **WILLIAM BRATTON,** FORMER
NEW YORK POLICE COMMISSIONER

"*Who else can tell you where to eat in town? From burgers to foie gras, this book of chef recommendations is a must for any food lover.*"

CAPRIAL PENCE,
CHEF-OWNER, CAPRIAL'S BISTRO

"*For a man from out of town,* Chef's Night Out *is exactly the book I would look for—an easy, friendly, concise guide to the right places to eat, with the authority of professionals behind it.*"

GORDON RAMSAY, CHEF-OWNER,
RESTAURANT GORDON RAMSAY (LONDON)

"*You're visiting a city. You want some good food. But how to get the inside skinny on where to eat? You dread having to rely on the counsel of the hotel concierge—or worse yet, the 'where to dine' section of the hotel magazine, which is how you just end up where everyone else is. Now Andrew Dornenburg and Karen Page have solved the problem. In 28 cities across the U.S., you can eat where the people who really know food love to dine.* Chef's Night Out *is my new secret weapon in the traveling world. Thank you, Andrew and Karen!*"

SHOSHANA ZUBOFF, PROFESSOR,
HARVARD BUSINESS SCHOOL

"*Andrew Dornenburg and Karen Page are perhaps the most serious and discriminating of the younger food writers. Nobody could have done it better and nobody will be able to do it so well again. This is a book not to be missed.*"

DIETER G. SCHORNER,
PROFESSOR OF PASTRY AND BAKING STUDY, THE CULINARY INSTITUTE OF AMERICA

"*Sometime around 1985, chef's finally started to learn a way to both cook and still see a bit of the world. It was a slow process, like learning to live "on the outside," in certain vernaculars. Stop worrying about looking to just the journalists (the guards!) to talk about the world of food—the inmates are running the asylum, and they know just where to get anything you want! Here it is:* Chef's Night Out. *Make a break for it!*"

NORMAN VAN AKEN,
CHEF-OWNER, NORMAN'S

To Joey,
My world traveler~
may you always eat
well on the road!
I love you, Frog

Chef's Night Out

Rocco DiSpirito at Katz's Delicatessen (New York City)

★ ★ ★ ★

FROM four-star RESTAURANTS

TO NEIGHBORHOOD FAVORITES:

100 top chefs TELL YOU WHERE

(AND HOW!) TO ENJOY AMERICA'S BEST

Chef's Night Out

Andrew Dornenburg and Karen Page

PHOTOGRAPHY BY MICHAEL DONNELLY

JOHN WILEY & SONS, INC.

New York · Chichester · Weinheim · Brisbane · Singapore · Toronto

Library of Congress Cataloging-in-Publication Data

ISBN 0-471-36345-6

Printed in the United States of America.
10 9 8 7 6 5 4 3 2 1

FOR MOM

Patricia C. Dornenburg (1928–2000)
in a 1930s ad for a coal-oil stove

THE BEST CHEFS, LIKE THE BEST restaurants, continue to evolve and grow. Nothing is stagnant; everything changes, either for the better or for the worse. If chefs are to change for the better, then their influences must be positive. There are three things that can provide nourishment and energy for positive change: the air you breathe, the food you eat, and the ideas you ponder.

Leading chefs never stop learning about food. They are always seeking out opportunities to learn more about food and to expand the way they think about food. Food becomes the lens through which they often see, experience, think about, and talk about the world. On a Sunday or Monday night (chefs' most frequent nights off), you'll often find a chef "researching" a friend or colleague's restaurant over dinner.

It's hard to describe the exact ways in which this knowledge manifests itself; the benefits accrue to the chef in a much more holistic manner than they do in any single, identifiable way, such as in improving technique or seasoning. Somehow, everything a chef has ever tasted, smelled, touched, seen, heard, read, or otherwise experienced is translated through the chef's hands and finds its way onto a plate. The greater these experiences, both in quality and quantity, the more the chef is able to bring to the kitchen.

Aspiring chefs shouldn't stint on seeking out such experiences. Rather, they should view spending on travel, eating, and reading as an investment in themselves, their educations, and their personal and professional development.

—ANDREW DORNENBURG and KAREN PAGE,
Becoming a Chef

Rick Bayless and Nobu Matsuhisa

CONTENTS

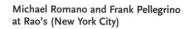

Michael Romano and Frank Pellegrino at Rao's (New York City)

Arthur Manjourides and Gordon Hamersley at Charlie's Sandwich Shoppe (Boston)

Anne Rosenzweig and her daughter, Lily, at Shanghai Cuisine (New York City)

Daniel Boulud with his daughter, Alix

preface

SINCE RESEARCHING AND WRITING OUR FIRST BOOK, *Becoming a Chef*, five years ago, we have been on a mission to help educate and inspire the next generation of professional chefs—not to mention the growing legion of serious food and restaurant enthusiasts—by sharing the wisdom and experiences of some of America's leading palates.

Chronicling the paths to success of America's leading chefs has taken us through some of the best restaurant kitchens across the country. However, we have come to realize that we may have been remiss in not stopping longer to speak with chefs in restaurant dining rooms, which is where many report their key learning experiences have taken place. In researching and writing *Chef's Night Out*, we spoke with chefs for the first time "on the record" about eating, as opposed to cooking.

Of course, we've been talking with many of them for years about eating; it's just been "off the record." In traveling across America to interview chefs, we often made it a point to eat at their restaurants whenever we could as a way of getting to understand them and their approach to cuisine. However, during those times of day or on those days of the week when their restaurants weren't open, we'd ask them where they'd recommend we go for lunch or for dinner. We got turned on to some of our favorite restaurants this way.

Our conversations with Anne Rosenzweig of the Lobster Club in New York led us to check out Campanile on an early visit to Los Angeles. Subsequently, our conversations with Nancy Silverton and Mark Peel of Campanile led us to a fabulous Mexican joint in a colorful part of L.A. (see p. 117). At the time, the restaurant wasn't in any guidebooks. As we were heading out the door to drive there, Mark assured us, "Don't worry about the armed guard at the door—the place is safe."

Johanne Killeen and George Germon of Al Forno in Providence sent us to a place that's become our second-favorite destination when in their area: Mike's Kitchen, which is located in the VFW Hall in Cranston, RI (see pp. 227, 230). It's frequented by locals and serves terrific home-style Italian food, including wonderful sausages and what Johanne and George argue (with our concurrence) is some of the world's best soft polenta.

Realizing the treasure trove of culinary knowledge and hot restaurant tips that resided within America's outstanding chefs, we set out to interview one hundred of them to find out where they ate on their nights off. If a chef was willing to spend his or her own precious dollars (and free time, which is just as precious) at a restaurant, that certainly spoke highly of it to us! So, over breakfast, lunch, coffee, and drinks—as well as over the phone—we persuaded chefs to tell us about their favorite restaurants, as well as their favorite spots for dishes ranging from ubiquitous classics (such as hamburgers, oysters, and pizza) to regional specialties (barbecue, cheese steaks, pastrami sandwiches, and the like).

We learned more than we ever dreamed. Not only did we compile a food lover's guide to some of the most interesting restaurants across the country (Part IV), but we were both entertained and educated by learning what professional chefs get from the experience of dining out, which comprises the first three sections of this book.

In Part I, you'll learn why leading chefs believe that dining out is even more important to an aspiring chef's culinary education than culinary school itself.

Part II will share leading chefs' guidelines on educating the palate as the route to becoming a better cook.

And in Part III, you'll discover how to eat like a chef—with the discrimination of a restaurant critic, yet the appreciation of a zealous foodie.

Finally, in Part IV you'll be introduced to some of the very special restaurants that have won the hearts of leading chefs in America today. When perusing it, the reader should keep in mind that professional chefs are different from restaurant critics in that they do not describe food and the restaurant experience for a living—they please people for a living. Thus, they come at their recommendations from their hearts first, and then their heads. That is to say, chefs may recommend a restaurant that serves one dish that they particularly love or that is a favorite of their entire family. Not surprisingly, chefs often recommend restaurants that are headed by talented chefs with whom they used to cook—preferences that come from enjoying their colleagues' food in the dining room and respecting their integrity in the heat of the kitchen.

Chefs, like us and perhaps like you, are looking for quality and comfort in a restaurant. They aren't always looking for a place that's fancy or an intellectual exercise. Because they spend six days a week composing flavors, on a night off they often don't want to spend too much time thinking about the food. Nor do they want to be tasting flavors that are too similar to the ones they work with day in and day out, so variety is important to them as well. Yet since leading chefs spend their time around the best ingredients, quality is very important to them. Freshness is always paramount, as is good technique. They want their steaks prime, dry-aged, and rare. They want their flavors bright, balanced, and clean. While they try to "turn it off," as they say, and look the other way when the service or ambiance isn't perfect, they can't turn off their palates. They know all too well what is in the market, and can taste in an instant when ingredients have been mishandled or served past their prime.

So while you will find a wide variety of restaurants recommended in the pages that follow—from those offering some of the best fine-dining experiences available in the world today to others in much more humble settings offering perhaps only a single signature dish—you can bet there is something special about each that is worth discovering for yourself. We wish you a delicious journey!

Bon appétit,

ANDREW DORNENBURG and KAREN PAGE
DECEMBER 2000

acknowledgments

We would like thank the many people who helped this book come together so beautifully. It doesn't take a village to complete a book—it takes a *city!* From our hearts, we thank:

All the chefs who managed to find a way to make time for us to interview them, and who were so generous with their experiences, insights, and even their friendship.

Our great team at John Wiley & Sons: associate managing editor Eileen Chetti, publicist Lucy Kenyon, and editorial assistant Tia Prakash, and especially our dedicated editor Pam Chirls and ace marketing director Valerie Peterson. And, with great anticipation, Gail Rentsch and Jeany Wolf of Rentsch Associates.

The very talented designers at Vertigo Design (and especially Rob Smith!).

Our literary agent Doe Coover.

Our right-arm (yet left-handed) research associate Meeghan Truelove, an awesome proofreader and talented writer in her own right, who is always up for every wacky assignment that comes her way (from testing recipes to tasting her fair share of everything from pie to popcorn!); transcriptionist *extraordinaire* Barbara Linder Millard (blmill6267@ aol.com, whom we also thank for barbecuing all those Usinger's sausages!); and Linda Thompson, for her thoughtful review and generous feedback.

Our photographer Michael Donnelly—for capturing such beautiful photos that truly make the words in this book come to life! We join Mike in thanking his ace assistants Karen Stead and Burçu Avsar, as well as the following establishments for so generously letting our photography team get the best angle and light to shoot the beautiful photographs for this book: Café Boulud (New York City), Charlie's Sandwich Shoppe (Boston), Casablanca (Cambridge), Cello (New York City), Chibi's Sake Bar (New York City), Daniel (New York City), Etats-Unis (New York City), Frank's Steak House (Cambridge), Gray's Papaya (New York City), H&H Bagels (New York City), John's Pizzeria (New York City), Katz's Delicatessen (New York City), The King Cole Bar (New York City), Krispy Kreme (New York City), La Maison du Chocolat (New York City), Larry Burdick Chocolates (Cambridge), Le Pain Quotidien (New York City), Lombardi's (New York City), Oyster Bar (New York City), Pacific Time (Miami), Payard Pâtisserie (New York City), Pearl Oyster Bar (New York City), Petrossian (New York City), Pho Bang (New York City), Rao's (New York City), Shanghai Cuisine (New York City), Seoul Food (Cambridge), Triple Eight Palace (New York City), Richart Design et Chocolat (New York City), and Woodman's (Essex, Massachusetts). A special thank-you to Frank Pellegrino of Rao's for making our photo shoot there such a delicious memory!

All our friends and family members who have been so supportive during our work on this book, especially Melissa Balmain and Bill Fitz-Patrick, Sharon and Stephen Baum, Lucinda and Av Bhavsar, Susan Butler, Fiona and Mike Donnelly, Mark and Meredith (and Gail and Kristen) Dornenburg, Robert Dornenburg, Bunny Ellerin and Geoff Vincent, Marie Ellyn, Heather Evans and Matt Baumgardner, Ashley Garrett and Alan Jones, Donna Hage, Mary Ann Halford and Kevin Meaney, Rikki Klieman and Bill Bratton, Laura Lau, Lee and John Logan, Lori Ludwig and John Broussard, Marilynn Scott Murphy, Jody Oberfelder and Juergen Riehm, Heidi Olson and Roger Duffy, Kelley and Scott Olson, Kevin and Julie (and Jessica) Page, Chris and Erik (and Wendy) Pearson, Cynthia and Jeff Penney, Anthony Pulgram, Cynthia and Leo Russell, Barry Salzman, Tony Schwartz and Deborah Pines, Kimberly Brown Seely, Jeri Slavin and Marty Gottlieb, Karen Springen and Mark Kerber, Kessa and Mark (and Alexis) Stevens, Kathy and Michael Takata, Linda Thompson, Jane Umanoff, Valerie Vigoda and Brendan Milburn, Steve Wilson, Trey Wilson, Stephanie Winston, and George and Karin Young.

Finally, we would like to thank each other, for persevering and for being there during a year filled with everything from great challenges to great meals. . . .

ANDREW DORNENBURG AND KAREN PAGE
DECEMBER 2000

Chef's Night Out

The dozens of professional chefs surveyed
for *Chef's Night Out* include:

FERRÁN ADRIÀ, EL BULLÍ (BARCELONA)

JOSE ANDRES, JALEO (WASHINGTON, DC)

PAUL BARTOLOTTA, FORMERLY OF SPIAGGIA (CHICAGO)

MARIO BATALI, BABBO, ESCA, AND LUPA (NEW YORK)

RICK BAYLESS, FRONTERA GRILL AND TOPOLOBAMPO (CHICAGO)

FRANKLIN BECKER, LOCAL (NEW YORK)

JIM BECKER, RAUXA (SOMERVILLE, MA)

PAUL BERTOLLI, OLIVETO (OAKLAND, CA)

CHRIS BIANCO, PIZZERIA BIANCO (PHOENIX)

DANIEL BOULUD, CAFÉ BOULUD AND RESTAURANT DANIEL (NEW YORK)

TERRANCE BRENNAN, PICHOLINE AND ARTISANAL (NEW YORK)

FRANK BRIGTSEN, BRIGTSEN'S (NEW ORLEANS)

ANDREW CARMELLINI, CAFÉ BOULUD (NEW YORK)

REBECCA CHARLES, PEARL OYSTER BAR (NEW YORK)

STEVEN CHIAPPETTI, MOSSANT BISTRO (CHICAGO)

PHILIPPE CHIN, CHIN CHIN RESTAURANT AND BAR (PHILADELPHIA)

JIM COLEMAN, TREETOPS AT THE RITTENHOUSE HOTEL (PHILADELPHIA)

TOM COLICCHIO, GRAMERCY TAVERN AND CRAFT (NEW YORK)

SANFORD D'AMATO, SANFORD (MILWAUKEE)

GARY DANKO, GARY DANKO (SAN FRANCISCO)

ROBERT DEL GRANDE, CAFÉ ANNIE (HOUSTON)

TRACI DES JARDINS, JARDINIÈRE (SAN FRANCISCO)

MARCEL DESAULNIERS, THE TRELLIS (WILLIAMSBURG, VA)

ROCCO DISPIRITO, UNION PACIFIC (NEW YORK)

JONATHAN EISMANN, PACIFIC TIME (MIAMI)

TODD ENGLISH, OLIVES AND FIGS (BOSTON)

BOBBY FLAY, BOLO AND MESA GRILL (NEW YORK)

DIANE FORLEY, VERBENA (NEW YORK)

GALE GAND AND RICK TRAMONTO, BRASSERIE T AND TRU (CHICAGO)

GEORGE GERMON AND JOHANNE KILLEEN, AL FORNO (PROVIDENCE)

SUZANNE GOIN, LUCQUES (LOS ANGELES)

JOYCE GOLDSTEIN, FORMERLY OF SQUARE ONE (SAN FRANCISCO)

CHRISTOPHER GROSS, CHRISTOPHER'S FERMIER BRASSERIE (PHOENIX)

GORDON HAMERSLEY, HAMERSLEY'S BISTRO (BOSTON)

DAVID HOLBEN, SEVENTEEN SEVENTEEN (DALLAS)

RAJI JALLEPALLI, RESTAURANT RAJI (MEMPHIS)

JEAN JOHO, EVEREST AND BRASSERIE JO (CHICAGO)

CHRISTINE KEFF, FLYING FISH (SEATTLE)

LORETTA KELLER, BIZOU (SAN FRANCISCO)

SEAN KELLY, AUBERGINE CAFÉ (DENVER)

ROBERT KINKEAD, KINKEAD'S (WASHINGTON, DC)

RIS LACOSTE, 1/89 (WASHINGTON, DC)

JEAN-MARIE LACROIX, THE FOUNTAIN AT THE FOUR SEASONS (PHILADELPHIA)

EMILY LUCHETTI, FARALLON (SAN FRANCISCO)

LESLIE MACKIE, MACRINA BAKERY (SEATTLE)

MARK MILLER, COYOTE CAFÉ (SANTA FE AND LAS VEGAS)

MARY SUE MILLIKEN AND SUSAN FENIGER, BORDER GRILL AND
     CIUDAD (LOS ANGELES)

CARRIE NAHABEDIAN, RESTAURANT NAHA (CHICAGO)

PATRICK O'CONNELL, THE INN AT LITTLE WASHINGTON (WASHINGTON, VA)

PAUL O'CONNELL, CHEZ HENRI (CAMBRIDGE, MA)

BRADLEY OGDEN, LARK CREEK INN (LARKSPUR, CA)

CINDY PAWLCYN, MUSTARDS GRILL (NAPA)

FRANÇOIS PAYARD, PAYARD PÂTISSERIE (NEW YORK)

MARK PEEL AND NANCY SILVERTON, CAMPANILE (LOS ANGELES)

JERRY PELLEGRINO, CORKS (BALTIMORE)

CAPRIAL PENCE, CAPRIAL'S BISTRO AND WINE (PORTLAND, OR)

MONICA POPE, BOULEVARD BISTROT (HOUSTON)

NORA POUILLON, RESTAURANT NORA AND ASIA NORA (WASHINGTON, DC)

STEPHAN PYLES, AQUAKNOX AND FISHBOWL (DALLAS)

ANNE QUATRANO AND CLIFFORD HARRISON,
     BACCHANALIA AND FLOATAWAY CAFE (ATLANTA)

KENT RATHBUN, ABACUS (DALLAS)

THIERRY RAUTUREAU, ROVER'S (SEATTLE)

SUSAN REGIS, BIBA (BOSTON)

MICHEL RICHARD, CITRONELLE (WASHINGTON, DC)

ERIC RIPERT, LE BERNARDIN (NEW YORK)

HANS RÖCKENWAGNER, RÖCK AND RÖCKENWAGNER (LOS ANGELES)

MICHAEL ROMANO, UNION SQUARE CAFE (NEW YORK)

ANNE ROSENZWEIG, THE LOBSTER CLUB (NEW YORK)

AMY SCHERBER, AMY'S BREAD (NEW YORK)

CHRIS SCHLESINGER, EAST COAST GRILL (CAMBRIDGE, MA)

JIMMY SCHMIDT, THE RATTLESNAKE CLUB (DETROIT)

CORY SCHREIBER, WILDWOOD (PORTLAND, OR)

GUENTER SEEGER, SEEGER'S (ATLANTA)

JAMIE SHANNON, COMMANDER'S PALACE (NEW ORLEANS)

CRAIG SHELTON, THE RYLAND INN (WHITEHOUSE, NJ)

LYDIA SHIRE, BIBA AND PIGNOLI (BOSTON)

MICHAEL SMITH AND DEBBIE GOLD, AMERICAN RESTAURANT
    (KANSAS CITY)

ANDRÉ SOLTNER, FORMERLY OF LUTÈCE (NEW YORK)

HIRO SONE AND LISSA DOUMANI, TERRA (ST. HELENA, CA)

SUSAN SPICER, BAYONA AND HERBSAINT (NEW ORLEANS)

ALLEN SUSSER, CHEF ALLEN'S (MIAMI)

ELIZABETH TERRY, ELIZABETH ON 37TH (SAVANNAH)

JACQUES TORRES, FORMERLY OF LE CIRQUE 2000 (NEW YORK)

LAURENT TOURONDEL, CELLO (NEW YORK)

BARBARA TROPP, FORMERLY OF CHINA MOON CAFE (SAN FRANCISCO)

CHARLIE TROTTER, CHARLIE TROTTER'S (CHICAGO)

NORMAN VAN AKEN, NORMAN'S (MIAMI)

JEAN-GEORGES VONGERICHTEN, JEAN GEORGES , JO JO,
    MERCER KITCHEN, AND VONG (NEW YORK)

DAVID WALTUCK, CHANTERELLE AND LE ZINC (NEW YORK)

JANOS WILDER, JANOS (TUCSON)

CINDY WOLF, CHARLESTON (BALTIMORE)

TAKASHI YAGIHASHI, TRIBUTE (FARMINGTON HILLS, MI)

ROY YAMAGUCHI, ROY'S (HONOLULU)

restaurants mentioned in

Chef's Night Out

Aspen
MATSUHISA

Atlanta
ALON'S BAKERY
ANDALUZ BAR DE TAPAS
BACCHANALIA
BIEN THUY
BONE'S
CHOPS
CORNER BAKERY
THE DINING ROOM
FAT MATT'S RIB SHACK
FLOATAWAY CAFÉ
MAJOR MCGILL'S FISH HOUSE
OK CAFÉ
SEEGER'S
SOTO
THELMA'S RIB SHACK
ZOCALO MEXICAN TAQUERIA

Austin
JEFFREY'S
ROYERS ROUND TOP CAFÉ (Round Top)

Baltimore
BANJARA
BIRDS OF A FEATHER
B.O.P.
CHARLESTON
CORKS
JIMMY'S
KOOPER'S TAVERN
MARIA D'S
MATSURI
MOTHER'S FEDERAL HILL GRILLE
NICHIBAN
ONE WORLD CAFÉ
PIERPOINT
PRIME RIB
TAMBER'S NIFTY FIFTIES DINER
TEN-O-SIX
VESPA

Boston
ANTHONY'S PIER 4 RESTAURANT
BACK EDDY (Westport)
THE BARKING CRAB RESTAURANT

BIBA
BLUE FIN (Cambridge)
BLUE ROOM (Cambridge)
BOSTON SPEED'S
B-SIDE LOUNGE (Cambridge)
BUTLER'S COLONIAL DOUGHNUTS
   (Westport)
CAFE LOUIS
CAFÉ MAMI (Cambridge)
CAPITAL GRILLE
CASABLANCA (Cambridge)
CHARLIE'S SANDWICH SHOPPE
CHATHAM SQUIRE (Chatham)
CHEZ HENRI (Cambridge)
CHINA PEARL RESTAURANT
CHRISTINA'S ICE CREAM (Cambridge)
DALI RESTAURANT AND TAPAS BAR
   (Somerville)
DURGIN PARK
EAST COAST GRILL AND RAW BAR
   (Cambridge)
EAST OCEAN CITY
EMMA'S PIZZA (Cambridge)
FIGS (Charlestown)
FLORA (Arlington)
FORMAGGIO KITCHEN (Cambridge)
FRANKLIN CAFÉ
FRANK'S STEAK HOUSE (Cambridge)
GINZA
GRILL 23 AND BAR
HAMERSLEY'S BISTRO
HANA SUSHI (Cambridge)
INDIAN SAMRAAT RESTAURANT
JAKE'S BOSS BARBECUE (Jamaica
   Plain)
JP SEAFOOD CAFÉ (Jamaica Plain)
KELLY'S (Quincy)
KING FUNG GARDEN
LEGAL SEA FOODS
LOCKE-OBER
LUMIERE (W. Newton)
MR. BARTLEY'S BURGER COTTAGE
   (Cambridge)
NEW PARIS BAKERY (Brookline)
NEW SHANGHAI RESTAURANT
OLIVES (Charlestown)
PATE'S (Chatham)
PEACH FARM

PIGNOLI
PIZZERIA REGINA
PORTER SQUARE MALL NOODLE
   SHOPS (Cambridge)
RAUXA CAVA BAR AND RESTAURANT
   (Somerville)
SANTARPIO'S
SEOUL FOOD (Cambridge)
SHANGHAI CAFÉ
SULTAN'S KITCHEN
TABERNA DE HARO (Brookline)
TERRAMIA RISTORANTE
1369 COFFEE HOUSE (Cambridge)
TORCH
TRUC
TUSCAN GRILL (Waltham)
UMBERTO GALLERIA
WOODMAN'S (Essex)

Chicago
AL'S NUMBER 1 ITALIAN BEEF
ARUN'S
THE BERGHOFF
BIG BOWL
BILL'S PIZZA (Mundelein)
BITTERSWEET
BLACKBIRD
BOB CHINN'S CRAB HOUSE (Wheeling)
BRASSERIE JO
BRASSERIE T (Northfield)
CAFÉ BA-BA REEBA!
CHARLIE TROTTER'S
CHICAGO KALBI KOREAN
   RESTAURANT
DAVE'S ITALIAN KITCHEN
THE DINING ROOM
EVEREST
FRONTERA GRILL
GARRETT'S POPCORN SHOP
GIBSONS BAR AND STEAKHOUSE
GINO'S
GYROS ON THE SPIT
HEAVEN ON SEVEN
HOUSTON'S RESTAURANT
JIM'S HOT DOG STAND
JOHNNY ROCKETS
KOREAN RESTAURANT
LE FRANÇAIS (Wheeling)

LULU'S (Evanston)
MARGIE'S CANDIES
MATSUYA
MAXWELL STREET MARKET
MON AMI GABI
MOSSANT
MR. BEEF
NANIWA
N.N. SMOKEHOUSE
PAPAGUS
PHOENIX RESTAURANT
PIZZERIA DUE
PORTILLO'S HOT DOGS
PS BANGKOK
ROBINSON'S NO. 1 RIBS
SAI CAFÉ
SEASONS
SPAGO
SPIAGGIA
SUSHI WABI
TONY'S SUBMARINE SANDWICH
  (Deerfield)
TOPOLOBAMPO
TRU
WILDFIRE

CINCINNATI
CAMP WASHINGTON CHILI

CLEVELAND
HONEY HUT ICE CREAM
WEST SIDE MARKET

DALLAS
ABACUS
ADAM'S MARK HOTEL
AMICI SIGNATURE ITALIAN
  (Carrollton)
AQUAKNOX
ARC-EN-CIEL (Garland)
BALLS HAMBURGERS
BISTRAL
BROTHERS PIZZA
BUBBA'S CHICKEN
CANTINA LAREDO
CAPITAL GRILLE
CHAMBERLAIN'S (Addison)
CUQUITA'S
DADDY JACK'S LOBSTER AND
  CHOWDER HOUSE
DALLAS FARMERS' MARKET
DREAM CAFÉ
DUCK INN (Lake Dallas)
THE FAIRMONT HOTEL
FISHBOWL
GOOD EATS
GREEN PAPAYA
THE GREEN ROOM
JAVIER'S
KEL'S

LEFTY'S LOBSTER AND CHOWDER
  HOUSE (Addison)
LIBERTY
MAMA'S DAUGHTER'S DINER
THE MANSION ON TURTLE CREEK
MIA'S TEX MEX
MOTHER'S
THE ORIGINAL SONNY BRYAN'S
PAPPAS BROTHERS STEAKHOUSE
PRIMO'S BAR AND GRILL
THE RIVIERA
SEVENTEEN SEVENTEEN
SNUFFER'S
SONNY BRYAN'S SMOKEHOUSE
STAR CANYON
THAI NIPA RESTAURANT
VICTOR'S TAQUERIA
YAMAGUCHI

DENVER
ANNIE'S CAFÉ AND BAKERY (Nederland)
AUBERGINE CAFÉ
BISCUIT
DENVER BREAD COMPANY
EL TACO DE MEXICO
ENZO'S END PIZZERIA
GELATO D'ITALIA
JAX FISH HOUSE
LA PASADITA INN
NEW SAIGON RESTAURANT
POTAGER

DETROIT
ANNAM RESTAURANT VIETNAMESE
  (Dearborn)
CHERRY BLOSSOM JAPANESE
  RESTAURANT (Novi)
CHUCK MUER RESTAURANTS
  (W. Bloomfield)
DUNKIN' DONUTS
EMILY'S RESTAURANT (Northville)
FORTE (Birmingham)
FRANKLIN CIDER MILL (Bloomfield
  Hills)
LAFAYETTE CONEY ISLAND
MAMA ROSA'S
THE MINI RESTAURANT (Windsor,
  Ontario)
MON JIN LAU (Troy)
THE RATTLESNAKE CLUB
STONE HOUSE BREAD (Leland)
TAPAWINGO (Ellsworth)
TRIBUTE (Farmington Hills)
VILLAGE GRILLE (Grosse Point)
YATES CIDER MILL (Rochester)
ZINGERMAN'S (Ann Arbor)

FORT WORTH
JOE T. GARCIA'S MEXICAN FOOD
  RESTAURANT

HONOLULU
ALAN WONG'S
DYNASTY
HELENA'S HAWAIIAN FOODS
IMANAS IZAKAYA NOMBEI
LEUNG'S CAFÉ
ROY'S
SIDE STREET INN

HOUSTON
ASHIANA
BECK'S PRIME HAMBURGER PLACE
BOULEVARD BISTROT
CAFÉ ANNIE
CAFÉ EXPRESS
EL MESON
FUSION CAFÉ
FUZZY'S PIZZAS (Katy)
GOODE COMPANY BARBEQUE
LA VISTA PIZZERIA AND ITALIAN
  CUISINE
MAI'S RESTAURANT
NINFA'S
NIT NOI THAI RESTAURANT
OTILIA'S MEXICAN RESTAURANT
OTTO'S BARBECUE AND HAMBURGERS
PALM
PAULIE'S
RIO RANCH
TACO MILAGRO HANDMADE FOOD
  AND TEQUILA BAR

KANSAS CITY
THE AMERICAN RESTAURANT
BOULEVARD BREWING COMPANY
D'BRONX
JACK'S STACK BARBECUE OF MARTIN
  CITY
LAMAR'S DONUTS
LC'S BAR-B-QUE
ORTEGA'S MINI MARKET AND
  RESTAURANTE
THE PEANUT
SAIGON 39
STROUD'S

LAS VEGAS
BORDER GRILL
THE JOYFUL HOUSE

LOS ANGELES
ANGELI CAFFÉ
APPLE PAN (W. Los Angeles)
AUTHENTIC CAFÉ
BARNEY GREENGRASS (Beverly Hills)
BAY CITIES ITALIAN DELI (Santa
  Monica)
THE BEACH HOUSE (Santa Monica)
BOB BURNS (Santa Monica)
BORDER GRILL (Santa Monica)

C&K IMPORTING
CALIFORNIA PIZZA KITCHEN
CAMPANILE
CHAN DARA
CHAN DARA—HOLLYWOOD
CHARMING GARDEN (Monterey Park)
CITRONELLE (Santa Barbara)
CITRUS
CIUDAD
DIDIO'S ITALIAN ICE (Santa Monica)
DU-PAR'S
EAT-A-PITA
EL CHOLO MEXICAN RESTAURANT
EL TAURINO
FRED'S 62
GINZA SUCHI-KO (Beverly Hills)
GRAND CENTRAL MARKET
HARBOR SEAFOOD (San Gabriel)
HOLLYWOOD FARMERS' MARKET
 (Hollywood)
HOLLYWOOD HILLS COFFEE SHOP
IKE SUSHI
IN-N-OUT BURGERS
ITACHO (W. Hollywood)
THE IVY (W. Hollywood)
IZZY'S DELI (Santa Monica)
JAY'S JAYBURGERS (Silverlake)
JODY MARONI SAUSAGE KINGDOM
 (Venice)
JOHN O'GROATS (W. Los Angeles)
LA BREA BAKERY
LA SERANATA GARIBALDI
LA SUPER-RICA TAQUERIA (Santa
 Barbara)
LOCONDA VENETA (W. Hollywood)
LOS ANGELES FARMERS' MARKET
 (Santa Monica)
LUCQUES (W. Hollywood)
MAKO (Beverly Hills)
MANPUKU (W. Los Angeles)
MAROUCH
MATSUHISA (Beverly Hills)
MEILONG VILLAGE (San Gabriel)
MICHAEL'S (Santa Monica)
MILLIE'S (Silverlake)
MO BETTER MEATTY MEAT BURGERS
MORTONS (W. Hollywood)
MUSSO AND FRANK'S GRILL
 (Hollywood)
NAWAB OF INDIA (Santa Monica)
ORIGINAL PANTRY
PALERMO
THE PALM (W. Hollywood)
PANE E VINO (Santa Barbara)
PAPA CRISTOS
PHILIPPE'S—THE ORIGINAL
PIZZA BUONO
RENU NAKORN (Norwalk)
RÖCK (Marina del Rey)
RÖCKENWAGNER (Santa Monica)

RÖCKENWAGNER BAKERY (Santa
 Monica)
ROSCOE'S HOUSE OF CHICKEN 'N'
 WAFFLES
SANTA MONICA FARMERS' MARKET
 (Santa Monica)
SO KONG DONG
SOOT BULL JEEP
SPAGO BEVERLY HILLS (Beverly Hills)
SUSHI GEN
SUSHI SASABUNE
TACO DELTA
TACOS MEXICO
TAVERNA TONY (Malibu)
THAI HOUSE
TLAPAZOLA GRILL (W. Los Angeles)
TOMBO (Torrance)
VINCENTI RISTORANTE
VIP HARBOR SEAFOOD (W. Los Angeles)
YABU

Memphis
AUBERGINE
BOSCO'S PIZZA KITCHEN AND
 BREWERY (Germantown)
CAFÉ ESPRESSO AT THE RIDGEWAY
 INN
CITY BREAD
CORKY'S B-B-Q RESTAURANT
HOUSE OF INDIA
INDIA PALACE
LA BAGUETTE FRENCH BREAD SHOP
LE CHARDONNAY
PAYNE'S BBQ
RESTAURANT RAJI
SAIGON LE
TSUNAMI

Miami
BALEEN (Coconut Grove)
CAFÉ ABBRACCI (Coral Gables)
CAPTAIN'S TAVERN
CHEF ALLEN'S (Aventura)
DARREL AND OLIVER'S É MAXX
 (Pompano Beach)
DELI DEN (Fort Lauderdale)
EL PALACIO DE LOS JUGOS
GARCIA'S SEAFOOD GRILL AND FISH
 MARKET
HY VONG
ISLAMORADA FISH COMPANY
 (Islamorada)
JAXON'S ICE CREAM (Dania)
JOE'S STONE CRAB (Miami Beach)
LATIN AMERICAN CAFETERIA
L.C.'S (N. Miami)
LINCOLN ROAD CAFÉ (Miami Beach)
MARK'S LAS OLAS (Fort Lauderdale)
NEMO (Miami Beach)
NENA'S KITCHEN

NEWS CAFÉ (Miami Beach)
NORMAN BROTHERS PRODUCE
NORMAN'S (Coral Gables)
PACIFIC TIME (Miami Beach)
PANINI OTECA
PUERTO SAGUA (South Beach)
RASCAL HOUSE (Miami Beach)
ROD AND GUN CLUB (Everglades City)
S&S DINER
TAKEYAMA (Plantation)
TAP-TAP HAITIAN RESTAURANT
 (Miami Beach)

Milwaukee
BEANS AND BARLEY MARKET AND
 CAFÉ
COQUETTE CAFÉ
DENTICE BROTHERS ITALIAN
THE HILTON
JACK PANDL'S ORIGINAL WHITE FISH
 BAY INN
JOHN ERNST
LAKE FRONT BREWERY
LEON'S FROZEN CUSTARD
PETER SCIORTINO'S BAKERY
POLENEZ
SANFORD
SENTRY FOOD STORE
SHAHRAZAD
SPEED QUEEN BAR-B-Q
USINGER'S
ZAFFIRO'S PIZZA AND BAR

Napa Valley
BISTRO JEANTY (Yountville)
BOUCHON (Yountville)
THE DINER (Yountville)
THE FRENCH LAUNDRY (Yountville)
GORDON'S CAFÉ AND WINE BAR
 (Yountville)
THE GRILL AT MEADOWOOD
 (St. Helena)
HANA JAPANESE RESTAURANT
 (Rohnert Park)
MUSTARDS GRILL (Napa)
NAPA VALLEY OLIVE OIL COMPANY
 (St. Helena)
SCHRAMSBURG WINERY (Calistoga)
TAYLOR'S REFRESHER (St. Helena)
TERRA (St. Helena)
TRA VIGNE (St. Helena)
TRIPLE-S RANCH RESORT

New Haven
FRANK PEPE PIZZERIA NAPOLETANA
LOUIS' LUNCH

New Jersey
DORIS AND ED'S SEAFOOD
 RESTAURANT (Highlands)

HILTON AT SHORT HILLS (Short Hills)
RESTAURANT SERENADE (Chatham)
THE RYLAND INN (Whitehouse)
SHUMI JAPANESE RESTAURANT
   (Somerville)
SPIRITO'S (Elizabeth)
STAGE HOUSE INN (Scotch Plains)
STAGE LEFT (New Brunswick)
STATE LINE DINER (Mahwah)
WHITE HOUSE SUB SHOP (Atlantic City)

New Orleans

ACME OYSTER AND SEAFOOD
   HOUSE
BAYONA
BRIGTSEN'S
CAFÉ DU MONDE
CAMELIA GRILL
CASAMENTO'S RESTAURANT
CENTRAL GROCERY
CHINAMAN'S BAYOU
CLANCY'S
COMMANDER'S PALACE
COMMUNITY COFFEE WITH CHICORY
CRESCENT CITY STEAK HOUSE
DRAGO'S
DUNBAR'S
EMERIL'S
FELIX'S RESTAURANT AND OYSTER BAR
FOODIES KITCHEN (Metairie)
FRANKY AND JOHNNY'S
GUMBO SHOP
HERBSAINT
KIM SON
K-PAUL'S
MONA'S CAFÉ
MOSCA'S (Avondale)
MOTHER'S
MR. B'S BISTRO
P&J'S
PORT OF CALL
SAMURAI SUSHI
TAQUERIA CORONA
UGLESICH RESTAURANT AND BAR
ZEA (Harahan)

New York

ACADIA PARISH CAJUN CAFÉ
   (Brooklyn)
ADELMAN'S (Brooklyn)
AN AMERICAN PLACE
AMY'S BREAD
AQUAGRILL
ARTISANAL
BABBO
BALDUCCI'S
BALTHAZAR
BAMONTE'S (Brooklyn)
BAR DEMI
BELLA BLU

BIG NICK'S BURGER JOINT
BLUE RIBBON
BLUE RIBBON BAKERY
BLUE RIBBON SUSHI
BOLO
BOND STREET
CAFÉ BOULUD
CAFÉ FÈS
CAFE MEZÉ (Hartsdale)
CARNEGIE DELI
CELLO
CENT'ANNI
CHANTERELLE
CHEZ LAURENCE
CHIBI'S SAKE BAR
CHIN CHIN
CITY HALL
CITY LIMITS DINER (White Plains)
CORNER BISTRO
CRAFT
CUSTARD BEACH
CYCLO
DA CIRO
DAILY CHOW
DA SILVANO
DEAN AND DELUCA
DELLA FEMINA (East Hampton)
DESTINÉE
DOMINICK'S (Bronx)
ECCE PANIS
EJ'S LUNCHEONETTE
EL AZTECA MEXICAN RESTAURANT
ESCA
ESS-A-BAGEL
ETATS-UNIS
FATOOSH (Brooklyn)
FLORENT
FOUR SEASONS
GABRIELA'S
GAGE AND TOLLNER (Brooklyn)
GAM MEE OK
GENNARO
GOLDEN UNICORN
GOSMAN'S DOCK (Montauk)
GOTHAM BAR AND GRILL
GRAMERCY TAVERN
GRAY'S PAPAYA
H&H
HANGAWI
HARU
HENRY'S IN BRIDGEHAMPTON
   (Bridgehampton)
HONMURA-AN
IL BAGATTO
INDOCHINE
'INO
JACQUES TORRES CHOCOLATE
   (Brooklyn)
JAI YA THAI (Queens)
JEAN GEORGES

J.G. MELON
JOE'S SHANGHAI
JOHN'S PIZZERIA
JO JO
KATZ'S
KEENS STEAK HOUSE
THE KING COLE BAR
KNISH NOSH (Queens)
KURUMA ZUSHI
L&B SPUMONI GARDENS (Brooklyn)
L'ABSINTHE
LA CÔTE BASQUE
LA MAISON DU CHOCOLAT
LE BERNARDIN
LE CIRQUE 2000
L'ECOLE AT THE FRENCH CULINARY
   INSTITUTE
LE PAIN QUOTIDIEN
LES HALLES
LESPINASSE
LEXINGTON RIB CO.
L'EXPRESS
LE ZINC
THE LOBSTER CLUB
LOCAL
LOMBARDI'S
LUPA
MARIO'S (Bronx)
MARKT
MAVALLI PALACE
MENCHANKO-TEI
MERCER KITCHEN
MESA GRILL
MEZZALUNA
MICHAEL JORDAN'S STEAK HOUSE
MONSOON
MOOSEWOOD (Ithaca)
MRS. STAHL'S KNISHES (Brooklyn)
NATURAL RESTAURANT
NEW SILVER PALACE RESTAURANT
NEW YORK NOODLE TOWN
NEXT DOOR NOBU
NHA TRANG
NICK AND TONI'S (East Hampton)
NOBU
OCEAN PALACE SEAFOOD
   RESTAURANT (Brooklyn)
THE OYSTER BAR
PAOLA'S
PATOIS (Brooklyn)
PATSY'S PIZZA
PAYARD PÂTISSERIE AND BISTRO
PEACOCK ALLEY
PEARL OYSTER BAR
PENANG (Queens)
PETER LUGER (Brooklyn, Long Island)
PETROSSIAN
PHO BANG
PHO VIET HUONG
PICHOLINE

PICK-A-BAGEL
PIO PIO (Queens)
PONGAL
RAO'S
RATNER'S
RECTANGLES
THE RED CAT
RENÉ PUJOL
REPUBLIC
RESTAURANT DANIEL
RICHART DESIGN ET CHOCOLAT
RIVER CAFÉ
ROLF'S
ROSA MEXICANO
RUTH'S CHRIS STEAK HOUSE
SACHI
SAHADI (Brooklyn)
SAHARA (Brooklyn)
SAKAGURA
SAMMY'S ROUMANIAN
SAPPORO
SARABETH'S
SCOPA
SECOND AVENUE DELI
SEPPI'S
SERAFINA FABULOUS PIZZA
SERENDIPITY 3
SHANGHAI CUISINE
SHUN LEE WEST
SOUP KITCHEN INTERNATIONAL
SPARKS STEAK HOUSE
SRIPRAPHAI (Queens)
SUGIYAMA
SULLIVAN STREET BAKERY
SUSHIHATSU
SUSHIKO (Queens)
SUSHISAY
TABLA
TAKA
THE TEA BOX
TERESA'S (Brooklyn)
TOTONNO PIZZERIA NAPOLITANO
  (Brooklyn)
TRIPLE EIGHT PALACE
20 MOTT STREET RESTAURANT
UMBERTO'S (New Hyde Park)
UNCLE GEORGE'S GREEK TAVERN
  (Queens)
UNION PACIFIC
UNION SQUARE CAFE
UNION SQUARE GREENMARKET
VARSANO'S CHOCOLATES
VERBENA
VIA QUADRONNO
VICTOR'S CAFÉ
VIET-NAM
VONG
WONDEE SIAM
YONAH SCHIMMELL'S KNISHES
ZUTTO

PHILADELPHIA
BARD'S
BISTRO ST. TROPEZ
BLUE ANGEL
BONK'S BAR
BRASSERIE PERRIER
CENT'ANNI
CHIN CHIN RESTAURANT AND BAR
DMITRI'S
DOCK STREET BRASSERIE
FELICIA'S
THE FOUNTAIN RESTAURANT (at the
  Four Seasons Hotel)
FRANKIE'S SEAFOOD ITALIANO
GENJI JAPANESE RESTAURANT
GENO'S STEAKS
L. SARCONE AND SON
LA COLOMBE TORREFACTION
  RESTAURANT AND COFFEEHOUSE
MORTON'S OF CHICAGO
NICK'S ROAST BEEF
PAT'S KING OF STEAKS
PIETRO'S COAL OVEN PIZZERIA
THE PRIME RIB
THE READING TERMINAL MARKET
ROSE TATTOO CAFÉ
ROUGE
RUTH'S CHRIS STEAK HOUSE
SASSAFRAS INTERNATIONAL CAFÉ
SHANK & EVELYN'S LUNCHEONETTE
SOM SAK
STRIPED BASS
TACCONELLI'S PIZZA
TREETOPS AT THE RITTENHOUSE
  HOTEL
VIETNAM

PHOENIX
BAR BIANCO
BARMOUCHE
BISTRO 24 AT THE RITZ-CARLTON
  HOTEL
CHINA CHILI
CHRISTOPHER'S FERMIER BRASSERIE
DUCK & DECANTER
LECCABAFFI (Scottsdale)
LOS DOS MOLINOS
PIZZERIA BIANCO
RANCHO PINOT GRILL (Scottsdale)
RESTAURANT HAPA (Scottsdale)
RITO'S MARKET AND MEXICAN TAKE-
  OUT

PORTLAND (OREGON)
BRIDGEPORT BREW PUB
CAFÉ AZUL
CAPRIAL'S BISTRO AND WINE
FULLER'S RESTAURANT
GRAND CENTRAL BAKING CO.
HIGGINS RESTAURANT AND BAR

HOUSE OF LOUIE
LA IGUANA FELIZ
LEGIN
LEMONGRASS
MCMENAMINS PUB
NICHOLAS RESTAURANT
ORIGINAL PANCAKE HOUSE
PEARL BAKERY
STANICH'S WEST
WILDWOOD RESTAURANT AND BAR

PROVIDENCE
AL FORNO
BASTA! CAFÉ (Cranston)
EMPIRE RESTAURANT
GRAY'S ICE CREAM (Tiverton)
LEGAL SEA FOODS (Warwick)
LISBON AT NIGHT (Pawtucket)
LUCKY GARDEN DIM SUM
MIKE'S KITCHEN (Cranston)
NEATH'S NEW AMERICAN BISTRO
NEW JAPAN
NEW RIVERS
OLGA'S CUP AND SAUCER
STANLEY'S RESTAURANT (Central Falls)
YE OLDE ENGLISH FISH AND CHIPS
  SHOP (Woonsocket)

SAN FRANCISCO
ACME BREAD (Berkeley)
ALEMANY FARMERS' MARKET
ARAWAN (Sausalito)
BALBOA CAFÉ
BAY BREAD
BAY VILLAGE BAKERS (Point Reyes
  Station)
BERKELEY FARMERS' MARKET
BIX
BIZOU
BOLINAS BAY BAKERY AND CAFÉ
  (Bolinas)
BOULEVARD
CAFFÈ GRECO
CAMPTON PLACE HOTEL
CHARLOTTE'S CONFECTIONS
  (Millbrae)
CHAVA'S MEXICAN RESTAURANT
CHEESE BOARD COLLECTIVE
  (Berkeley)
CHEZ PANISSE (Berkeley)
COWGIRL CREAMERY (Point Reyes
  Station)
DELFINA
E&O TRADING CO.
FARALLON
FENG NIAN (Sausalito)
GARY DANKO
GLOBE RESTAURANT
HAWTHORNE LANE
HAYES STREET GRILL

INDIAN OVEN
JARDINIÈRE
KHAN TOKE THAI HOUSE
KLEIN'S DELICATESSEN
KOI PALACE (Daly City)
LA FOLIE
THE LARK CREEK INN (Larkspur)
LA TAQUERIA
MAKI
MARIN FARMERS' MARKET (San Rafael)
MR. ESPRESSO (Oakland)
MULBERRY STREET (San Rafael)
NOE VALLEY BAKERY AND BREAD CO.
OLIVETO (Oakland)
ONE MARKET RESTAURANT
PHO LAM VIEN (Oakland)
POSTRIO
RISTORANTE MILANO
RIVOLI (Berkeley)
SAM'S GRILL
THE SLANTED DOOR
STARS
SWAN OYSTER DEPOT
TACO TRUCK (Oakland)
TADICH GRILL
TAQUERIA SAN JOSE #2
THEP PHANOM
TIMO'S
TOMMASO'S
TOMMY'S JOYNT
TON KIANG
YANK SING
YUET LEE SEAFOOD RESTAURANT
ZARZUELA
ZUNI CAFÉ

santa fe
CAFÉ PASQUAL'S

savannah
CAFÉ METROPOLE
DESPOSITO'S (Thunderbolt)
ELIZABETH ON 37TH
JOHNNY HARRIS
MAI WAI
MRS. WILKES DINING ROOM
NORTH BEACH GRILL (Tybee)
VINNIE VAN GO GO'S

seattle
ANTHONY'S
ANTHONY'S PIER 66
AROSA CAFÉ
CACTUS
CAFÉ CAMPAGNE
CAFÉ LAGO
CAFFÈ LADRO
CHINOOKS AT SALMON BAY
CHINOOK WINES
ELLIOTT'S OYSTER HOUSE

EMMETT WATSON'S OYSTER BAR
ETTA'S SEAFOOD
FLYING FISH
FRAN'S CHOCOLATES
GRAND CENTRAL BAKING CO.
HANA RESTAURANT
HARVEST VINE
IL FORNAIO
LA PANZARELLA
LA MEDUSA
LE PANIER
LITTLE CHINOOK'S FISH AND CHIPS
LUSH LIFE
MCCORMICK & SCHMICK'S
MACRINA BAKERY AND CAFÉ
MAD PIZZA
MAGGIE BLUFF'S GRILL
MALENA'S TACO SHOP
NISHINO
THE PAINTED TABLE
PALACE KITCHEN
PARK DELI
PASEO CARIBBEAN RESTAURANT
PEGASUS PIZZA
PHO BAC
PIECORA'S
PIKE PLACE MARKET
RED MILL BURGERS
ROVER'S
SALUMI
SAZERAC RESTAURANT
SCOOP DU JOUR ICE CREAMERY
SEA GARDEN
TULLY'S
UNIVERSITY DISTRICT FARMERS
    MARKET

tucson
CAFÉ POCA COSA
MARISCO'S CHIHUAHUA
RESTAURANT JANOS AND J-BAR
SUSHI HAMA
TACQUERIA PICO DE GALLO
VIVACE

washington, DC
ASIA NORA
ATYLACYL (Gaithersburg, MD)
BIS
BISTRO FRANÇAIS
BISTROT LEPIC
BREAD LINE
CANTLER'S RIVERSIDE INN
    (Annapolis, MD)
CAPITAL Q
CASHION'S EAT PLACE
CESCO TRATTORIA
CITRONELLE
CLYDE'S OF GEORGETOWN
CRISP AND JUICY (Arlington, VA)

DC COAST
EL POLLO RICO (Arlington, VA)
FACCIA LUNA PIZZERIA
FIO'S
FIREHOOK BAKERY & COFFEE HOUSE
FULL KEE
GABRIEL
GALILEO RESTAURANT
GÉRARD'S PLACE
HUONG QUE/THE FOUR SISTERS
    (Falls Church, VA)
THE INN AT LITTLE WASHINGTON
    (Washington, VA)
JALEO
JOHNNY'S HALF SHELL
KAZ SUSHI BISTRO
KINKEAD'S
LEBANESE TAVERNA
MAKOTO RESTAURANT
MARCEL'S
MARVELOUS MARKET
MESKEREM ETHIOPIAN RESTAURANT
MIXTEC
MORTON'S
OBELISK
OLD EBBITT GRILL
PEKING GOURMET INN (Falls Church,
    VA)
PESCE
PIZZERIA PARADISO
THE PRIME RIB
RAKU, AN ASIAN DINER
RESTAURANT NORA
ROCKLANDS WASHINGTON'S
    BARBECUE
SAM AND HARRY'S
1789
SUSHI-KO
TABERNA DEL ALABARDERO
TEAISM
TOMBS
TONY CHENG'S SEAFOOD
    RESTAURANT AND MONGOLIAN
    BARBECUE
ZED'S ETHIOPIAN RESTAURANT

williamsburg (virginia)
ACACIA (Richmond)
BOBBYWOOD (Norfolk)
DOUMAR'S CONES AND BARBECUE
    (Norfolk)
THE FROG AND THE REDNECK
    (Richmond)
LE YACA
PIERCE'S PITT BAR-B-QUE
RIVER'S INN (Gloucester Point)
SUSHI YAMA (Newport News)
TODD JURICH'S BISTRO (Norfolk)
THE TRELLIS
THE WILLIAMSBURG INN
YORKTOWN PUB

WHY EAT OUT?

PART I

YOU ARE WHAT YOU EAT: THE IMPORTANCE OF DINING OUT

Amy Scherber and François Payard

AQUAKNOX AND FISHBOWL (DALLAS)

"It's very important to eat out, and to train your palate. For a professional chef, it's as important as culinary school and textbook study."

"Understanding what it's like to dine in the kind of place where you want to work needs to become part of an aspiring chef's experience. If you lose sight of that, your food gets off track and loses its punch."

RICK BAYLESS

FRONTERA GRILL AND TOPOLOBAMPO
(CHICAGO)

WHAT DOES IT TAKE TO BECOME A GREAT CHEF IN America today? Certainly education—either as an apprentice or, more than ever before, in professional cooking schools—and experience in the kitchen are important. A profound understanding of ingredients, and the flavors and techniques that will best enhance their taste, is vital—along with a commitment to excellence at every step of the way.

But leading professional chefs across America agree that the most important aspect of a professional chef's development is eating out. What most of the general public do for sustenance, and many restaurant lovers do for entertainment, is the lifeblood of an ambitious chef's professional development.

"I am a huge advocate of chefs learning to cook by eating in good restaurants," says Rick Bayless of Frontera Grill and Topolobampo (Chicago). "I recommend that constantly. The first thing that anyone who's serious about becoming a chef should do is save up every penny they've got and eat at the best restaurants in the country. And not just once—they need to go regularly."

Bob Kinkead, chef-owner of Kinkead's (Washington, DC), agrees. "I have always been of the opinion that I learn a lot more by dining in restaurants than by working in them," says Kinkead. "That's how I saw the big picture of what a restaurateur aims to achieve. A lot of the time, people get stuck in the restaurant kitchen or in the dining room and they don't get to see what the rest of the picture is all about. For chefs and cooks, it's important to see the context in which food is presented. The whole dining experience is not just about the food, the service, or the décor—great restaurants pull everything together into a great package."

Eating out offers professional chefs a chance to experience a taste of history; to learn the best practices of those restaurants that excel at one or more aspects of the restaurant experience, such as food, service, and/or ambiance; and to develop a sense of their own place within the context of the contemporary restaurant culture.

Suzanne Goin of Lucques (Los Angeles) believes that it's absolutely essential for young cooks to eat out. "I can't think of anything that is more important," she insists. "When I interview a cook, I always ask, 'Where do you eat? What are your favorite restaurants? Have you eaten here?' That is how I figured out where to work—I wanted to work where I wanted to eat! When I walked into Al Forno [in Providence], I smelled the aromas, tasted the food, and just knew I had to work there!"

Despite the importance of dining out as part of a culinary professional's education, it's something that is not part of a typical cooking school's curriculum—underscoring the need for the book you're now holding. "In cooking school, we were never taught how to dine," recalls Rocco DiSpirito of Union Pacific (New York). "In fact, I don't think there's enough emphasis placed on the notion that you need to dine as much as you cook in order to really have a full understanding of the two sides of the experience."

Rick Tramonto and Gale Gand of Tru and Brasserie T (Chicago) concur. "Young kids should spend more money on travel and eating," argues Tramonto. Gand adds, "We think dining out is so important that we even recommend that cooks invest in themselves by maxing out their credit cards on restaurants instead of clothes!"

Investing in this book is an excellent place to start, to point you on your journey.

Eating Out as a Life-Changing Experience

In the best of circumstances, dining in restaurants can literally be a life-changing experience. In fact, it was in this way that several leading chefs found their calling.

"My dad was a total Francophile, and took us to lunch at Roger Vergé when I was around twelve," recalls Suzanne Goin of Lucques. "I was served a whole fish, with slices of cucumber on top as the scales. As a kid, that fish completely blew me away! We had a cheese plate, and the waiter was so great to me and my sister as he showed us all the different goat cheeses, which I loved. Plus, the restaurant is a beautiful stone mill in a dreamy, fantasy setting. It felt like we were members of a little club.

"My dad had a rule when I was growing up: If we were willing to try something new and it turned out we didn't like it, we could always get a cheeseburger. So, as a kid, I would order everything from blood sausage and head cheese to oysters on the half shell and Oysters Rockefeller. And I found that I liked them all!"

CINDY PAWLCYN

MUSTARDS GRILL
(NAPA)

"The experience was not just about the food, but about the restaurant—the whole magical world of it," says Goin. "It made me want to get closer to that world, not only by becoming a chef, but by opening a restaurant—so I could really be creating something, as opposed to just cooking something."

A visit to the Drake Hotel when she was sixteen was a turning point for Cindy Pawlcyn of Mustards Grill (Napa). "I had soft-shell crabs, which were sautéed tableside with sherry, and I remember thinking, 'This is so cool—*I* want to be a chef!' I had already been thinking of becoming a chef, but this was the experience that really convinced me. It was every single element of it, from the exotic aromas, flavors, and

RICK BAYLESS OF FRONTERA GRILL AND TOPOLOBAMPO (CHICAGO)

Learning the Potential of the Dining Experience at Age Twelve

I WAS DEDICATED TO GOOD RESTAURANT EATING FROM A VERY EARLY AGE. But I didn't have a lot of family support, despite the fact that I came from a family that owned and operated a restaurant. The notion of eating in a really fine restaurant was beyond the scope of my immediate family.

A couple of years after Julia Child had started cooking on television, when I was twelve years old, I got her book *Mastering the Art of French Cooking* and cooked my way through the volume, week by week by week. I was familiar with the dishes and really excited to go to a restaurant that knew how to make them. I had saved up my money, so I made my own reservation and took the bus downtown to Oklahoma City for lunch at the High Tower Restaurant. It had been there for a long time and was very sophisticated, with lots of tableside service.

I sat down and told them what I wanted, because I knew what the dishes were. I think at first they didn't know what to make of me—a twelve-year-old dining alone. But they were very nice. I can still tell you everything I had: I started with a bowl of vichyssoise, then I had broiled flank steak, which was laid on a wooden platter, surrounded by browned piped potatoes. Then they brought an enormous silver punch bowl filled with chocolate mousse to the table, and I had a scoop of chocolate mousse to finish my meal. It was, without a doubt, the most dramatic moment of my life.

I felt like a million dollars when I walked out of there, and that feeling set a benchmark for me.

textures to the beauty of the dining room and their treating us like ladies—the whole nine yards."

Paul Bartolotta, formerly of Spiaggia (Chicago), found himself working in restaurants in Milwaukee as a teenager, but his job developed into a calling. "I ended up working for a Florentine chef," he remembers, "and I would sit around late at night, listening to his stories about growing up in Italy. I was enamored with all the folklore. He told me, 'If you want to get closest to real Italian food, you need to go to Doro's in Chicago.'

"So, when I was seventeen, I put on my white polyester suit and took the train to Chicago for the first meal I had ever had by myself. Doro's had white leather chairs, white linen and fine silver, and served northern Italian food. They were wondering what this kid was doing eating by himself in a restaurant, but I was totally excited by the whole experience. At the end of the meal, I asked to thank the chef. When it was explained to me that the chef didn't come into the dining room, I asked to go into the kitchen. At that time, diners weren't allowed in the kitchen, but I finally got back there, where I found all these cooks speaking Italian. The chef was a big burly guy with a waxed handlebar mustache, a floppy chef's hat, and a little tie around his neck. He looked like the quintessential Italian chef.

"I asked if I could watch for a few minutes, and just stood by the wall, watching him call orders. It was an epiphany for me—that's when I knew that I wanted to cook," says Bartolotta. "I subsequently went back several times, ultimately becoming friends with the chef. I would come in and watch them cook in the morning, then go sit and eat lunch, and then take the bus and train back to Milwaukee."

Allen Susser of Chef Allen's (Miami) recalls eating at La Grenouille in New York when he was seventeen. "It was very classic, fabulous French cuisine. It was the first time I ate frogs' legs and had the adventure of eating something new and different. The whole combination of food, wine, and service was transformational. The experience at La Grenouille showed me what classic cuisine could be like, and it brought together all the information I was learning in school [New York City Technical College]. That meal compelled me to go to France to work."

A fellow student at New York City Technical College, Michael Romano of Union Square Café (New York), befriended an instructor who nurtured his interest in the field. "Tom Arends, who taught a wine course, and I became good friends. He saw a real spark for this profession in me. He was influential in getting me a job in Paris at the Hotel Bristol, and while I was there, he visited and we had many meals together.

"One was at the Bath Hotel in England. It was like one of those meals you read about in the old books. We were drinking Burgundy from the thirties and eating roasted grouse—in England they hang grouse, and they get pretty ripe. The experience of having all this food that I had read and heard about, accompanied by forty-year-old Burgundies, was a great education.

"He also took me to most of the three-star restaurants in Paris at that time. Those meals were very classic, and they brought to life in a spectacular way the things I was learning about in school. If you've never had that kind of experience, you just don't know it exists. It doesn't matter what you're cooking if you've never seen what it can be. I am very grateful for those experiences. Knowing how much they influenced me, I encourage aspiring chefs to seek them out," says Romano.

Dining as Professional Development

Any serious creative professional must first devote time and effort to mastering his or her creative domain. While it's possible to simply pick up a paintbrush and start painting, the serious study of painting involves not only learning the basics of paint, paintbrushes, and canvases, but examining and analyzing the techniques and philosophies of great painters in history.

"No professional operates in a vacuum," observes Robert Del Grande of Café Annie (Houston). "If you look back, Mozart knew Haydn's music backward and forward, and Beethoven knew Mozart's music backward and forward, and all three of them studied Bach's music. You always want to study those who came before you, and then your peers."

The same is true for professional chefs. Their concerted efforts to learn from those who came before them send them not only to books but to the restaurants in whose hallowed halls cuisine came—and is coming—into its own.

"Reading good art criticism will allow you to develop a sense of how a certain piece of art fits into the whole world of art, both historically and conceptually," says Rick Bayless. "In terms of cuisine, I think it's very hard for young chefs to get that perspective. You can't get it in the kitchen—you've got to be in the dining room."

A Taste of History

A generation ago, any self-respecting professional chef in America needed to make a pilgrimage to Europe to learn from some of the world's best restaurants. Today, many of the world's best restaurants can be found in the United States, but still, because of the importance of particular European restaurants and chefs in culinary history, many of the most serious professionals with the resources to do so still make it a point to visit these restaurants.

"My most formative experiences were during the 1980s, when I started going to France and experiencing the three-star restaurants. They were so different from anything I'd ever encountered in the United States. That has changed in the last fifteen years, and we now have restaurants that are at that level. But back then, we didn't have chefs the caliber of today's Daniel Bouluds."

TRACI DES JARDINS
JARDINIÈRE (SAN FRANCISCO)

The anecdotes that follow in this section are representative of story after story we heard from leading chefs across the country. While the specific details differ, we suspect that the other chefs who have made pilgrimages to the same restaurants will nod in recognition of their own similar experiences.

LA PYRAMIDE

La Pyramide is one of the most influential restaurants in France's restaurant history, as it is in many ways the "grandfather" of several of the country's other most important restaurants. Some of the cooks who once worked under the restaurant's legendary chef-owner Fernand Point include Paul Bocuse, Alain Chapel, Louis Outhier, and the Troisgros brothers, all of whom went on to become Michelin three-star chefs in their own right. The restaurant is also credited with giving rise to nouvelle cuisine.

Fernand Point was succeeded after his death by his wife, Marie-Louise, who continued to run the restaurant and maintain its Michelin three-star rating. Point's book *Ma Gastronomie* is considered a classic. It was published posthumously in 1969 as a colorful history of La Pyramide, Point's culinary philosophy, and his signature recipes. Its broad influence—as well as the restaurant's reputation—naturally led chefs from around the world to make pilgrimages to La Pyramide.

"When I was younger, I read a lot and was very taken with Fernand Point and La Pyramide," remembers David Waltuck of Chanterelle and Le Zinc (New York). "When I graduated from college I went to Europe to travel by myself, and I had to have lunch at La Pyramide. Fernand had already passed away, but his wife was still there, as were many of the staff members I had read about.

"It was extraordinary. I had built my expectations up so much, but the experience didn't let me down. I still remember everything I ate. I started with a crayfish gratin, one of La Pyramide's signature dishes, then had trout mousse with a black truffle sauce, followed by beef with red wine and marrow, and finally dessert. I remember being very, very full—I didn't eat for a day afterward!

"I drank a half bottle of white wine and a half bottle of red wine, and I was struck that the sommelier treated wine without any kind of pretension. He had a workingman's hands, which wrapped around each bottle. I saw him open a very expensive bottle of wine at another table; he poured a little wine right onto the floor because he thought there was some cork in it, and then he just continued to pour it into the glasses.

"I feel that a lot of what we do at Chanterelle was influenced by La Pyramide," acknowledges Waltuck. "I did not work with Point and make no claims to be Paul Bocuse, who did, but reading *Ma Gastronomie* and understanding what the place was like in the thirties and forties definitely influenced us. Chanterelle has a handwritten menu, like La Pyramide. And we too believe that food can be done in a careful and special way without being pretentious."

Carrie Nahabedian of Restaurant Naha (Chicago) recalls backpacking through France on her first visit to Europe, at age nineteen. "The only place I really wanted to go was La Pyramide," she recalls. "It was a big escapade—we took the train from Paris to Lyon, and then to the sleepy town of Vienne. In the train station we changed from our T-shirts and grubby jeans into nicer clothes, and gave a kid a dollar to watch our backpacks. We walked over to La Pyramide, all dressed up, and there was Madame Point, writing the menus by hand. I felt like I was walking back in time.

"The experience was incredible," she remembers. "The dining room was amazing. The women were dressed as if it was their last day on earth; they were in Chanel suits, with all their pearls. The restaurant had stools for their purses and stools for their dogs. I still remember the butter—it was shaped like La Pyramide, the statue in the middle of town. The sommelier, who had been there since the restaurant's opening, presented me with the wine list. When I opened it, it smelled like the 1800s! He told me that they kept the wine lists in the cellar.

"I ate all the classic dishes, like the gratin of crayfish. Whereas a chef today might create a dish in an hour and just play around with it a little bit, Fernand Point worked *seven years* perfecting that dish. We had Bresse chicken with truffles stuffed under the skin, and potatoes swathed in cream. I even remember how crusty the bread was. We had a bit of an introduction from Jean Banchet [the founding chef of Le Français in Wheeling, IL], who used to work at La Pyramide and for whom I had worked, and they sent us every dessert on the menu, including the signature gâteau Marjolaine, which was named after Point's daughter. Then they sent us after-lunch drinks! The chef came out and spoke to us, and everyone could not have been nicer. I still recall signing the American Express bill after the meal. I figured out that it cost a hundred and forty-five dollars—and that was twenty years ago! I sweated that one out, wondering how I was going to pay for it after having spent three months in Europe!

"After all this, we still had to get back on the train. I remember feeling like Cinderella after the ball, because we had to convert back to the traveling fools that we were. We stumbled back to the train station to the laughs of the kids who were watching our bags. The restaurant had given us a bag of macaroons and cookies for the train, and I remember skipping meals until the next day.

"I still have the menu Madame Point gave me, written in her big, flowing handwriting," Nahabedian muses. "And I still have my travel diary, tied with ribbon, with all the details written in it."

> "Visiting La Pyramide, I was overwhelmed by the aura and all the history. All the components—from the food to the service—were impeccable."
>
> CHARLIE TROTTER
>
> CHARLIE TROTTER'S (CHICAGO)

TAILLEVENT

Taillevent is one of the most legendary Michelin three star restaurants in Paris, renowned not only for its cuisine, but also for its extraordinary hospitality. Several chefs point to the level of service they experienced at Taillevent as an ideal they strive for in their own restaurants.

"We went to Taillevent on our first trip to Paris," recalls Patrick O'Connell of the Inn at Little Washington (Washington, VA). "We saved it until the end of our visit, because even then it was considered by most people to be one of the three greatest restaurants. There was a taxi strike in Paris, and we were late because we'd taken the Métro and had gotten off at the wrong station. We were having a fight on opposite sides of the Champs-Elysées, hollering at each other, and I said, 'Well, we might as well not even go—we're forty-five minutes late already! You know how they are in fancy restaurants—they throw you out if you're five minutes late. They're haughty and mean and horrible.' But we decided that instead of blaming each other, we'd sullenly skulk in there anyway.

"We got there expecting one of those haughty greetings—you know, 'What do you mean, you are forty-five minutes late for your reservation?' But instead, Monsieur Jean-Claude Vrinat came running to the door saying, 'I'm so sorry, I'm so sorry—will you forgive us?' He knew there had been a taxi strike and after seeing that we were not in the best of moods, he just kept bowing and assuring us, 'We'll make it up to you!' He was keenly aware of what it might be like to be a visitor in a foreign country, all geared up for this grand experience, and then coming up against this frustration.

"We ended up having an amazing evening there. Afterward he had someone drive us back to our hotel in his car. We were astounded by such a thoughtful gesture, but for him it was just part of business as usual," recalls O'Connell.

Bob Kinkead of Kinkead's (Washington, DC) had been working in France and recalls, "My then-girlfriend, who's now my wife, came over to meet me in Paris, and I was dying to go to Taillevent. The only time we could go was for lunch the day she arrived. I picked her up from the airport, ran her to the hotel to change, and showed up to the restaurant at one-fifteen for our one o'clock reservation. We were worried because we were late, yet we were the first there. The owner, Jean-Claude Vrinat, is one of the great restaurateurs of this or any century, and he said to us, in perfect English, 'Because monsieur and madame are here before the rest of our guests have arrived, we would like to offer you our house special pear cocktail.' We, of course, accepted.

"We ordered the tasting menu, and when the second course came out—a seafood mousse—it was ammoniated. As this was a three-star restaurant, it meant that somebody had screwed up in spades! I called the waiter over and he could smell it right away, so he apologized and took it away. Then literally every waiter and bus boy, and even the owner and chef, came out and apologized. They sent us an escargot course that was sensational.

"The rest of the meal was terrific, but as the meal progressed, I was reminded that Diane does very poorly with being overtired. As the adrenaline wore off and the time change and jet lag set in, she went from nodding out to literally crying from exhaustion. My grasp of French was enough to order, but not enough to explain the concept of jet lag.

"They came over and apologized again, making sure it was not the food that had us upset. Then Mr. Vrinat walked over with a shawl and draped it over Diane's shoulders, saying, 'Madame might have a chill?' He asked if there was anything he could do or if there was any problem. Then he came over again and said, 'Because madame is upset, in addition to the dessert, we are going to serve you apricot soufflés.' After that, he came over with the cognac cart. Their cart is one of the finest collections in the world, with some over a hundred years old, and he basically said, 'Take your best shot!'

"I came to realize that these people were willing to do anything they possibly could to ensure that we were not going to have a bad time. It is a three-star restaurant, so you are paying for an over-the-top experience, but none of the other three-star restaurants I have ever been to has ever gone to that extreme. It set the standard for service by which I judge every other restaurant that I visit," says Kinkead.

"The first time I was ever in Europe, Deann and I went to Paris for a week," says Rick Bayless. "Having done a lot of reading, I wanted to eat at Taillevent. We made a lunch reservation, and I can tell you exactly how much we spent, because it seemed so outrageously expensive: a hundred and thirty dollars for lunch. Here we were, staying in a place that cost twenty dollars a night, and we spent a hundred and thirty dollars for lunch!

"We walked in the door as young people, wet behind the ears, and we obviously didn't know what to expect or what to do, but we were still treated like the king and queen. We had been out shopping, so we had all our bags with us. They whisked them away, took off our coats, and immediately started catering to every need we could ever imagine. It was the most magical dining experience I have ever had. I have been to a lot of those kinds of restaurants since then, but to this day, I still have never had service that was so caring and luxurious. When they came around to the table at the end of our meal—and, of course, we were thinking about money all the way through the meal, because it was very expensive for us—they offered us a *digestif* on the house. I thought I had died and gone to heaven! It meant so much. I don't know whether they were bemused by us because we loved everything that they did for us or whether they would just normally have done that for everyone, but I felt like they were doing it only for me."

Bayless says he recalls that experience constantly at Frontera Grill and Topolobampo. "When people come in, we try to be aware of those extra little touches. Sometimes it's just a matter of saying to an out-of-towner,

'Oh, have you gone to the Terra Museum of American Art? There's a great show over there.' Or 'Catch the Maxwell Street Market on Sunday morning—you'll never forget it'—anything we can do to let them know that we're concerned about them as individuals, not just as a number," he says. "That meal at Taillevent really focused us, and it's why we are dedicated to having only one restaurant: because we know we can't do that with multiple restaurants."

A Few Great Restaurants in France's Culinary History

LA TOUR D'ARGENT (1582–)

15, quai de la Tournelle
75005 Paris
Phone: (33) 01 43 54 23 31
Fax: (33) 01 44 07 12 04
www.tourdargent.com

Considered a national institution, La Tour d' Argent is famed for numbering orders of its specialty, *caneton* (duck). The first one was served to Edward VII in 1890, and about a million have been sold in the 110 years since.

LUCAS-CARTON (1851–)

9, place de la Madeleine
75008 Paris
Phone: (33) 01 42 65 22 90
Fax: (33) 01 42 65 06 23

A landmark restaurant whose kitchen is headed by Alain Senderens. His signature dish of Canard Apicius, duck roasted with honey and spices, was inspired by the ancient Roman gastronome.

LA PYRAMIDE (1924–)

14, boulevard Fernand Point
38200 Vienne (Isère)
Phone: (33) 04 74 53 01 96
Fax: (33) 04 74 85 69 73
E-mail: pyramide@relaischateaux.fr
www.relaischateaux.fr/pyramide

This restaurant was run for many years by the venerable Fernand Point (1897–1955), who trained some of France's leading chefs, including Paul Bocuse, Alain Chapel, and Jean and Pierre Troisgros.

TAILLEVENT (1946–)

15, rue Lamennais
75008 Paris
Phone: (33) 01 44 95 15 01
Fax: (33) 01 42 25 95 18

Named for a famous chef who authored one of the oldest French cookbooks, Taillevent is considered by many to be the best restaurant in Paris.

LA MAISON TROISGROS (1957–)

Place de la Gare
42300 Roanne (Loire)
Phone: (33) 04 77 71 66 97
Fax: (33) 04 77 70 39 77
E-mail: troisgros@relaischateaux.fr
www.troisgros.fr

In 1998, the family-run Troisgros celebrated thirty consecutive years of holding Michelin's three-star rating.

PAUL BOCUSE (1959–)

69660 Collonges-au-Mont-d'Or
Phone: (33) 04 72 42 90 90
Fax: (33) 04 72 27 85 87
E-mail: paul.bocuse@bocuse.fr
www.bocuse.com

This eponymous restaurant is overseen by the esteemed Paul Bocuse, whose rise along with modern communications led him to become in his lifetime one of the world's best-known chefs.

LES PRÉS D'EUGÉNIE (1963–)

40320 Eugénie-les-Bains
Phone: (33) 05 58 05 06 07
Fax: (33) 05 58 51 10 10
E-mail: guerard@relaischateaux.fr
www.relaischateaux.fr/guerard

Michel Guérard and his wife, Christine, run this elegant restaurant in a spot that was favored by the nineteenth-century French empress Eugénie.

LE MOULIN DE MOUGINS (1969–)

Quartier Notre-Dame-de-Vie
06250 Mougins (Alpes-Maritimes)
Phone: (33) 04 93 75 78 24
Fax: (33) 04 93 90 18 55
E-mail: mougins@relaischateaux.fr
www.relaischateaux.fr/mougins

The chef, Roger Vergé, and his wife, Denise, established their restaurant and seven-room hotel in a picturesque sixteenth-century olive mill on a hill above the French Riviera.

UNDERSTANDING THE CUSTOMER'S PERSPECTIVE

Time and again, leading chefs stressed that dining out is not just important for learning about food. The insights they gain into the customer's perspective are invaluable in their development as restaurant professionals.

"Cooks need to realize that the plate they put together in forty-two seconds is going to be scrutinized for half an hour as a diner eats it and picks it apart," says Michael Romano of Union Square Cafe (New York). "Cooks tend to lose sight of the fact that this is *food* they're working with, food that people are going to put in their bodies. Too often, it becomes a routine for them.

"There are many fields of endeavor in life that bring pleasure to people's lives, from music to painting to dancing to cooking, but cooking is different from all the rest in one critical aspect: If you don't like a concert or a painting, you can just walk away, but if something is wrong with your food, it can make you ill or even kill you. As cooks, we are the only ones who get that intimacy with people. That is a very special trust that we have. No other field has that. You'll forget about a bad play the next day, but what we do *becomes* you, very literally. That's something that I want my cooks to think about. It's important for them to have that respect for themselves and for their craft," Romano says.

"I always tell people that the reason our restaurant is good isn't because we're strong in the kitchen; it's because we know what it's like to be in the dining room," asserts Rick Bayless. "We have a really firm policy that our staff has to eat in our restaurant regularly as guests. We don't think that they can understand what it's like to *be* a customer unless they *are* one. We focus very strongly on that: what it's like to walk in the front door, sit down, and have a meal here."

Developing the critical eye of a customer is very important to a chef, according to Eric Ripert of Le Bernardin (New York). "When you create a new dish, you put so much of your heart into it that you become unable to critique it objectively. Because you did it, it's your baby. Technically, it was difficult to make, and you are so proud of it, it feels as though it's a miracle," he admits. "But the customer doesn't care how difficult it was to put together. What the customer cares about is how it looks and tastes. So I think it is very important to get some distance, and to see things through a customer's eyes."

Jean-Georges Vongerichten of Jean Georges (New York) agrees. "Pierre, my chef, and I will never put a dish on the menu if we don't first sit down and eat the whole dish," he says. "When you compose a dish and try it in the kitchen, you don't know what's missing. But if you sit down to eat your dish, you'll know after a few bites whether the balance is right or whether there's something that needs adjusting.

"My cooks will say a new dish tastes great, and I will ask them if they have tried it in the dining room. The inexperienced ones will ask, "Does that make a difference?" Cooks are surprised to learn that food tastes different in the dining room. In addition to getting aromas you don't get in the kitchen, food tastes different when you're seated with a napkin in your lap, holding a nice fork and a glass of wine."

ELIZABETH TERRY
ELIZABETH ON 37TH (SAVANNAH)

"Also, once food leaves your kitchen, it is experienced in the dining room in a totally different way," he explains. "In the kitchen, you work under intense fluorescent light, and you might only glance at a plate. In the dining room, the customer literally sees it in an entirely different light."

Rocco DiSpirito of Union Pacific (New York) recalls, "I was working at Adrienne as a *commis* on the fish station, and one night I decided to come in for dinner. That's when it first occurred to me that what we feel in the kitchen is completely different from what the guest feels in the dining room. The environments are so different, even though it's just a thin wall separating the two. I was amazed that the food I was eating was the same food I knew from the kitchen. It struck me at that point that it's truly amazing how this all comes together in the package we call a dining experience. Up until then, I had a one-dimensional view of dining based solely on what I did in the kitchen. I didn't really understand that there are so many other components that make up a great dining experience."

EXPERIENCE THE INDUSTRY'S BEST PRACTICES

Jeremiah Tower, the legendary founder of Stars (San Francisco), would always press the point that "you can't create for others what you haven't yet experienced yourself." It was for this reason that he took his staff to the finest restaurants and hotels to experience the best. Understanding why a restaurant excels—and experiencing that excellence—helps chefs critique their own performances and readjust their standards.

While you should trust your judgment and form your own opinions, it is instructive to dine in restaurants that leading chefs agree are great. Perfection is next to impossible, but experiencing the best restaurants helps clarify the standards to which leading chefs hold themselves.

FOOD

While flavors and textures frequently command the most attention during a dining experience, it is often the more subtle care taken with food that sets great restaurants apart from good restaurants. Exquisite products and the extraordinary treatment of those products can escape the average diner, but they make chefs sit up and take note.

Mario Batali of Babbo, Esca, and Lupa (New York) recalls his first meal at Marc Meneau's L'Espérance. "It was the week before I went there to work as an extern, and I had a meal there that—from the very first bite to the very last drop of Armagnac—was, without a doubt, a goose-bump

"The difference between a great restaurant and a good one is that the great ones are the ones you want to emulate. I've always said you can tell a great restaurant because you want to steal every idea!"

ROBERT DEL GRANDE
CAFÉ ANNIE (HOUSTON)

experience. It was an eye-opener. All the details of a dining experience that I'd never thought about became crystal clear. I had just worked with Marco Pierre White [a London three-star chef], who was the first to open my eyes to what food could be besides just something to eat on a plate, but Marc Meneau did it all—food, service, everything.

"It cost a great deal of money, but it was a worthwhile investment. I got out of it what could be the perfect meal. His food was harmonious, like a concert. I didn't think of it as simple at the time, but it really was. The first course was raw mushrooms, then there were two fish courses, then a game course, then a meat course, then a cheese course, then a series of desserts followed by hot chocolate cookies. It was such a superior experience; every single thing was perfect and very visually appealing. I remember thinking, 'Wow, look at these beautiful paintings that someone drew in my sauce' and 'These guys are crocheting things that look like my grandmother's afghan in the sauce . . . it's amazing!' It was a turning point for me," says Batali.

Patrick O'Connell still recalls the smallest details of his earliest trips to Europe's three-star restaurants. "On a trip to Girardet [in Switzerland], I noticed that the tiny little greens that garnished the plate were dressed," says O'Connell. "I realized, 'Ah, of course, how could I have been so stupid not to have thought of this myself?' It was a revelation that anything on the plate had to be the best of its kind, and had to be able to stand alone."

service

Most customers overlook the particular character of a restaurant's service. But all the subtleties of good service add up; it's so much more than a warm greeting, a nice waiter, and a thank you when you leave. Good service makes a customer feel comfortable, but great service makes him feel engaged and exhilarated.

"I'm always struck by the coat-check person in great restaurants," muses Patrick O'Connell. "Instead of standing passively by, waiting for you to undo your coat, they approach you, help you off with your coat, and begin to brush you off, the way an attendant would do—which immediately makes you feel like a royal personage."

Michael Romano of Union Square Cafe (New York) believes that when cooks go to a great place for dinner, they should watch the nuances of everything that happens once they sit down. He recalls, "Danny [Meyer, Union Square Cafe's owner] and I were at a restaurant in Paris, and the [sommelier] was showing us the wine list. He started to talk about a couple of interesting things he had that were not on the list. Now, that's a

"With as long as I've been involved in this business, I've still not grown jaded about the dining experience. I'm into dining because I really enjoy trying to understand the layers of things that happen and the subtlety of how they happen. That is still a big thrill to me."

CHARLIE TROTTER
CHARLIE TROTTER'S (CHICAGO)

wonderful thing, because you feel like he's bringing you into this private club or whatever. But the tricky part with that is, how do you let the guest know how much the wine is? It can be sort of crude to say, 'Oh, that'll run you five hundred dollars.'

"What he did was really exquisite and showed real class. He would say, 'We have Château Blah-blah-blah,' and add, 'And that is in *this* range,' while pointing to the price of another bottle on the list. So he didn't overtly mention money, but you got the idea. It's very subtle," admits Romano. "But that's an example of the kind of thing that you'll miss if you're not paying attention. And it's something you can easily incorporate into your own business."

"I still think you're hard pressed to find service that surpasses what you're going to get at a three-star restaurant in France," says Traci Des Jardins of Jardinière (San Francisco). "The attention to detail is incredible—you never want for anything. Once you order, you never have to ask for anything else. It is all just there at your fingertips, even to the point of having your glass always full to the same level."

AMBIANCE

The synergy of food, service, and décor coming together in a restaurant supports the intangible quality known as ambiance. Every restaurant has its own ambiance, but when all the elements that go into it are in concordance, a dining experience can be transformed from unique into extraordinary.

Sanford D'Amato of Sanford Restaurant (Milwaukee) credits ambiance as an integral part of the best overall restaurant experiences he's ever had. "They were all at Georges Blanc, where it was not only the food and the service, but the way the room was set up and the whole ambiance of the place," he says. "There was not a bad table in the room.

"My first time in France, there was a definite intimidation factor walking into a place like that," recalls D'Amato. "You walk into a three-star restaurant and think you are going to see God. But at Georges Blanc, they make you feel as though they are truly happy to see you. You sit down and feel like you belong, that this is where you should be. It really transformed what my wife, Angie, and I wanted to do at our place. People who come to Sanford might be intimidated at first, but by the time they leave, they feel like they've been in someone's home."

For Charlie Trotter, eating at the Michelin three-star restaurant Girardet in Switzerland for the first time was a transcendent experience brought about by the way all elements of the dining experience worked together. "Everything about it—the service, the ambiance, the

"I can have perfect food in a place where the service is just okay and still love it, and I can have really great service in a place where the food is just okay and still love it, but when it all hits, that's when you get the extra ten percent. The most important thing that I would tell cooks is to understand that the ultimate objective is guest satisfaction. It's not an us-versus-them thing—it's an us-with-them thing. It took me a long time to realize that."

MARIO BATALI

BABBO, ESCA, AND LUPA (NEW YORK)

food and wine—was magical," recalls Trotter. "That's when I realized that I wanted to try to put all the aspects together in a restaurant—ambiance, service, wine, cuisine—and really try to focus equal attention on all of them. Until then, I was certainly aware that those aspects

RICK BAYLESS OF FRONTERA GRILL
AND TOPOLOBAMPO ON

A Formula for Restaurant Success

DEANN [BAYLESS'S WIFE AND BUSINESS PARTNER] AND I ALWAYS TOOK our eating out very seriously. We would write critiques after a meal because we felt that if we didn't do that, all we could say is, "Well, we had a nice time, and the food was good."

So we kept a log. Since we knew we were headed toward opening our own restaurant, we always talked about the balance that has to be struck by any good restaurant. We looked at four things: the food, the ambiance, the service, and the value offered. Our thinking was that three out of the four had to be really strong. We would take notes and decide afterward what we thought about a restaurant from each one of those perspectives.

If you only have a little money to start your restaurant with, then you have to realize that if you can't invest in décor, you have to figure out cheap ways to decorate it that will catch people's attention, so that the ambiance is there. Or if you can't really do much for ambiance, then you're going to have to be very strong in food, service, and value.

On the other hand, if you've got great décor, great food, and great service, then value is a little less important. People don't have to go away saying, "Well, that was a good deal." You can charge a lot of money for it, which you usually have to do if you've got great ambiance.

Of course, if you can be strong in all four areas, then in most cases you're going to have a place that is really successful.

That was what we calculated to be behind Frontera Grill's success. We have also realized over time that as we put more money into our décor, our prices can go up. Or as we refine our service at Topolobampo, for instance, then we can charge more for it. From the value side of the equation, I always wanted to give people a little more than what they would expect to get. Of course, that is essentially the same philosophy behind the little *amuse-gueule* at the beginning of a meal and the free *petit fours* at the end of a meal in a French restaurant.

were important, but I was pretty much a cook, so it was all about food, food, food, food, food. It began to dawn on me that food actually tastes better when everything else is working well. After traveling around Europe and visiting Moulin de Mougins and Troisgros, I finally realized, 'This is the kind of thing I want to work on.' It was the combination of these experiences—each one made me a little more aware, a little more savvy."

Gale Gand of Tru and Brasserie T (Chicago) underscores that it's sometimes the quirky things that can make a dining experience great. "For example, the bathrooms at Anton Mossiman in England are so terrific—they have an antique phone, water to spritz on your face, and chilled Champagne with glasses. They also have a chaise longue, in case you're feeling faint," says Gand with a laugh.

"At Ducasse, they provide a tableside stool for your purse, so we decided to do that here at Tru," she says. "They also had a bread cart, which to me reflects a real dedication to bread—treating breads like jewels, as you would *petit fours*. Ducasse's *petit fours* service inspired me to do four courses of *petit fours* at Tru. They come in waves: first fruit, then nuts, then chocolate, and then we end with lollipops. I hate good-byes, and *petit fours* are like a good-bye kiss. We keep giving you kiss after kiss before you leave! We want our customers to feel well fed—aesthetically as well as literally."

Gain Inspiration For Your Own Creative Process

Eating food created by a professional chef often introduces a whole new range of flavor and texture combinations to a diner. Experiencing these new possibilities can be profoundly inspiring, and it is this inspiration which helps fuel the creative process.

However, inspiration must be followed by conception and execution— both highly evolved skills that take time to develop. Many aspiring chefs seem to forget this, thinking instead that whimsy is all that is necessary to create. Leading professional chefs complain about newly minted culinary graduates who believe their diplomas are proof that they've mastered all they need to know. Innovation can be achieved only after a chef has established a solid culinary foundation and has mastered an understanding of what has already been done.

Dining out is a key component of building this knowledge. By experiencing how professional chefs express themselves through their cooking, aspiring chefs can evaluate their own strengths and weaknesses and further develop their own creative responses.

THE CUTTING EDGE: EL BULLÍ

One of the newest Michelin three-star restaurants, El Bullí (outside Barcelona) is inspiring chefs around the globe through its innovative use of technique. Chef Ferrán Adrià may be best known for his use of "foams" of sauces or ingredients in his dishes. Chefs across America who have traveled to Spain to eat at El Bullí have been struck by how it is pushing the limits of restaurant cuisine.

Chef Ferrán Adrià

NORMAN VAN AKEN,
NORMAN'S
(CORAL GABLES, FL)

"When I ate at El Bullí I was sitting next to Todd English and Charlie Trotter, and I think it took Todd a while to warm up to it, certainly longer than it took me and Charlie. I can see why some people would not like it. It takes several hours to get there—up a mountain, down a mountain, and there's nothing else around. You have to be committed to make that journey, and I think that's partly why the restaurant works. It's not just that the chef thought these dishes up—it's that he put them at the end of the earth, and you have to go there to get to them. It's unique, and it shows an absolute commitment to his belief."

TODD ENGLISH,
OLIVES AND FIGS
(BOSTON AND LAS VEGAS)

"Eating at El Bullí is kind of a journey into the mind of Ferrán Adrià, and an exploration of his ideas about food; it's fascinating, but I think you have to be somewhat of an educated or experienced diner to go there. It would blow your mind if you weren't. For example, the vegetable plate consisted of nothing but purées, foams, and sorbets. Pretty wild! A little scoop of white sorbet was turnips. Beet root foam, almond sorbet, cauliflower sorbet, basil jelly, and golden beet ice were some of the other things on there. Each of the flavors was excellent and amazing—you really tasted the golden beet in the ice and the almond in the sorbet. But I was worried that at some point a waiter was going to bring out a plate of pills like Willy Wonka, saying, 'That little pill is the blueberry pill. . . .' Another dish that was pretty fascinating was a little cube of breaded and fried veal marrow, with a big dollop of caviar on top. Basically, you took one bite and this bubbling marrow shot down your throat, accented by the saltiness of the caviar. An inexperienced diner might have been shocked by that."

JACQUES TORRES,
FORMERLY OF LE CIRQUE 2000
(NEW YORK)

"In 1984 or '85, I was working with Jacques Maximin giving a demonstration in Cannes, and Ferrán Adrià was there. He asked Maximin, 'What is innovation?' Maximin replied, 'Innovation is when you don't copy anyone; you do your own food, taking nothing from anyone else.' Adrià went back to his restaurant and decided to change everything, and started innovating. Now he is considered the most innovative chef in Europe. Great restaurants share things in common—great service, atmosphere, and products. What separates them after that is technique. I recently ate at El Bullí, and I understood the techniques of only half the dishes I ate. When the chef came out, I told him, 'I have to ask you at least ten questions!' Chefs have a super experience when they learn, and for me, El Bullí was the ultimate learning experience. It showed me that you can go farther with food. You look at their food and think, 'Wow—I have no idea how they put that together! I have no idea how it is possible because to me, until now, it was impossible.' They covered chocolate ganache with hot caramel, which I couldn't figure out because when you dip ganache in hot caramel, it melts. They told me, 'That's an easy one!' They will take something that they know is impossible and find a way to get around it."

CRAIG SHELTON,
THE RYLAND INN
(WHITEHOUSE, NJ)

"I spent three days working at El Bullí, and on my last night I had the thirty-five-course dinner. It was as though time stood still. The dining room is unpretentious, warm, and friendly. It brings you great comfort and feels like a family setting. I thought it was a perfect showcase for the daring of his food. It doesn't cosset that idea of cuisine as supreme art form and deify the food. In the early days, you went to Girardet [in Switzerland] to have your eyes opened to the limitless possibilities of food. Then it was Ducasse, Robuchon, and Chapel. Those were meals you had to have to realize that there were no limits other than yourself. At El Bullí, I was astounded by Ferrán Adrià's creativity, daring, and risk taking. His brother Alberto is the pastry chef and stands as no second. I admire their courage, humility, and integrity, which has become a benchmark for me. There was a ten-year period where chefs, and certainly I among them, were looking to the limits of ingredients as the horizon. Then came the question, 'What hasn't been discovered with technique?' I don't see the value of criticizing the food at El Bullí. Someone once said, 'The only meaningful definition of artistic freedom is the freedom to fail as well.' So if you are not risking failure, you don't have the courage he does. If I am not risking failure every night, then I am not pushing myself."

NANCY SILVERTON,
CAMPANILE
(LOS ANGELES)

"Our experience at El Bullí was very educational, to say the least. I tend to judge a meal or a dish great if I wake up in the morning and the first thing I think is, 'I can't wait to taste that again!' I didn't have that experience with any of the food at El Bullí. I have a passion for natural flavors, and the food that I am attracted to is simply prepared. I'm not saying that he didn't work with flavors, because that was his whole thing—deconstructing flavors—but I am much less technical and don't have a bag of tricks. His food is all about a bag of tricks. I did appreciate what he was doing and how well he did it, but it wasn't something that I was remotely inspired by or that I wanted to copy in any way. Yet I absolutely could sit back and appreciate what this 'mad scientist' was doing. There are a few things he's come up with that I think are particularly interesting, including a way to layer temperatures and flavors, and making sauces and dishes with gelatin. He's using canisters to extrude foam sauces, and he's influencing chefs all over Spain and beyond. While you may go to Spain expecting to eat chorizo and drink sherry, you'll see that a lot of chefs are actually trying to mimic him. I am absolutely glad I went, because I got to see somebody expertly doing something that is completely different from what we are doing. It doesn't even go into the realm of like or dislike. It's more of an artistic encounter."

EL BULLÍ

Apartado 30,
17480 Rosas en Cala Montjoi,
Spain
Phone: (34) 972 15 04 57
Fax: (34) 972 15 07 17
E-mail: Bulli@grn.es
www.elbulli.com
Closed from October 15 to
March 15

With the help of José Andres of Jaleo (Washington, DC), who formerly cooked at El Bullí, we were able to pose questions to chef Ferrán Adrià about his approach:

Q: How would you describe your cuisine?

A: It is always difficult to describe something you are participating in, because you are only partially objective. But we could define it as a cuisine that searches for ways to trigger emotions through new techniques, concepts, and products. To me, cuisine is about the flavors, textures, visuals, and aromas that activate the senses when we eat—plus a sixth sense, which is the magic, the surprise, the culture. In terms of technique, it is the obligation of a chef to have good technique, and if you create new techniques or concepts, you will help cuisine evolve.

Q: Whom do you consider to have been most influential on your cuisine?

A: I never had teachers, nor was I influenced by a family atmosphere that was excessively gastronomic. That is why I always try to ask myself the "why" of things, and never to do things just because they have always been done that way. Otherwise, we would never evolve.

Q: What is your biggest source of inspiration, and what is your creative process?

A: We do the creation of new dishes in a very professional manner in our work studio in Barcelona. I participate with my brother, Albert Adrià, and Oriol Castro. First, we look for concepts, techniques, and new products, and then we finish the dishes. Yet when it comes to creativity, there is a word that I like to use: "magic." The magic involved is what is difficult to explain.

Q: Could you mention two or three dishes on your menu that you are especially proud of?

A: More than dishes, [I take pride in these] techniques and concepts: using gelatin as a sauce or soup, the use of hot gelatin, the treatment of shellfish, and the foams.

Q: How did you develop the idea to use the CO_2 canisters to create foams?

A: The foams are made with N_2O [nitrous oxide, more commonly known as laughing gas]. I got the idea through wishing to create new mousses that were lighter and more flavorful. Foams open up an [incredible new culinary frontier], because it is a new technique and concept, and there is a lot still to be developed in it.

Q: How can you cover chocolate ganache [a delicate filling] with hot caramel?

A: This is possible with a new technique of caramelization by using solid caramel instead of hot caramel and using the salamander [small broiler] as the heat element. With this technique, you can caramelize things that were previously not thought possible.

Q: How would you describe the service and ambiance at El Bullí?

A: Juli Soler and I have tried to create an ambiance as familiar as possible, with the maximum professionalism. We are by the sea, outside of the city, which gives the restaurant a very relaxed atmosphere. We have sixty-five people working for forty-five guests, and the satisfaction of our guests is the main objective of the restaurant.

Q: Your cuisine is influencing other chefs around the globe. Is imitation indeed the sincerest form of flattery?

A: I believe what we have achieved is to demonstrate that there are other ways, and other things, still to be created in cuisine. What really pleases us is that this is encouraging other chefs to look for new ways as well.

Q: What has been your experience dining out in America?

A: I am a lover of what is happening in the United States. There is a generation of chefs that is looking for new things, and who, in short, will be the world's avant-garde.

HOW TO TaSTe

PART II

TEN STEPS TO EDUCATING A PALATE—AND BECOMING A BETTER COOK

CITRONELLE (WASHINGTON, DC)

"You have to educate your own palate. If you want to be a great cook, it is very important that you do this first. If you don't know what food is supposed to taste like, if you don't have the references, you are cooking in the dark."

"Sometimes achieving the best flavor involves buying more expensive ingredients. I use more organics than I ever used to. I used to pooh-pooh the idea that organic products were superior, thinking they weren't worth the extra money—but they are."

CHRISTINE KEFF
FLYING FISH (SEATTLE)

WHILE LEADING CHEFS POINT TO DINING OUT as one of the most important ways in which one can develop a palate, the process doesn't start and stop there. Rather, it must start long before that point if it is to be successful.

Anne Rosenzweig of the Lobster Club (New York) says, "Cooks need to refine their knowledge of food as well as their critical faculties before they're able to learn much from dining out. I have heard young cooks say that they went to a restaurant and thought some gimmick or garnish was amazing—while I will be thinking, 'They don't get it at all!' The problem is that they don't always know enough about food to discern what is truly special and outstanding from what is merely gimmicky."

George Germon of Al Forno (Providence) agrees. "There are a lot of times when I'll go to a restaurant and I won't really think much of the experience, and then one of my cooks goes to the same restaurant and says he had a fabulous meal. It makes me really want to strangle him," he laments. "Too often, young people are impressed with the fluff, the presentation, the trends, and if they go to a restaurant that has these qualities, they're impressed."

"After doing this for twenty-plus years, my approach to food has gone through a lot of different stages," admits Christine Keff of Flying Fish (Seattle). "Unfortunately for the people who have eaten my food, it's not until the last four or five years that I've really considered flavor paramount. Before that, style and appearance were very important to me, as was what everybody else was doing and how my food compared

to that. I had to mature as a cook
before I realized that the most important thing is how the food tastes. Once
I realized that flavor is key, I was
encouraged and inspired to keep
pushing to find the most flavor I could
put on a plate."

So how is a palate developed? Step
by step.

1. Understand Ingredients and Their Essential Qualities

"Raw ingredients have to have a good
flavor when they come in," says
Christine Keff. "We've been working
a lot at encouraging everyone who
deals with products—from the person
who receives them in the morning to
the person who cooks them at night—
to make preserving those flavors
paramount."

"I have tried to research just about
everything I cook with—everything
down to the most basic ingredients,
including butter, salt, and water,"
says Paul Bertolli of Oliveto (Oakland,
CA). "In addition to that, I cure all our meat. I spend a lot of time in
Italy up in the hills above Parma and in the whole Po Valley area,
learning how to make fermented sausages and prosciutti, various
kinds of salami, and all those things."

To truly understand and appreciate ingredients, chefs must first understand their essential qualities, including:

· Taste/Texture
· Seasonality
· Freshness/Stages of Ripeness
· Variations

Each is described in detail in the following sections.

TASTE/TEXTURE

Two of the most basic qualities of food are two of the most important:
taste and texture. It is important to develop a keen awareness of how

something *actually* tastes and feels on your palate, as well as familiarity with how it *should* taste and feel.

"I find a lot of young cooks very limited in their palates," laments David Waltuck of Chanterelle (New York). "You can learn technique, but if you don't also have an understanding of what things should taste like, and when they don't taste the way they should, you can never be a very good cook."

Patrick O'Connell of the Inn at Little Washington (Washington, VA) tells this story: "When there was a dialogue to see who would be the next chef at the White House, Alice Waters put the pressure on for it to be an American. They asked, 'If you tried out, what would you cook for the president?' One of Alice's assistants said, 'Why don't you tell them about the perfect peach?' And Alice said, 'Well, yes, that's what I would do. I'd say, 'Tonight we'll have the peach, the perfect peach, and that's it.' And it was funny, but it was telling at the same time—she has an absolute passion for using only the very best ingredients, and serving them simply.

"The great deficiency I see with kids just out of culinary school is they can't yet tell a ripe peach from an unripe peach, a good tomato from a bad tomato. And to be a good cook, it's imperative to be able to identify quality in ingredients," O'Connell insists.

Chefs can develop a following based on their understanding of ingredients and the way they convey that knowledge on their menus. "I like Lydia's themes," says Mark Miller of Coyote Café (Las Vegas and Santa Fe), speaking of Lydia Shire of Biba (Boston). "She serves lamb kidneys, rack of lamb, and lamb sirloin, and understands that different parts of the animal have different consistencies and flavors. She is visceral and loves the primal element of the animal being transformed into the dish. Lydia feels a chef's job is to represent the animal."

seasonality

Developing sensitivity to growing seasons is critical. Not only does this determine how certain foods taste, but it also affects what might accompany them on the plate.

Anne Rosenzweig of the Lobster Club (New York) has taken staff members on field trips to the Union Square Greenmarket to see what ingredients are in season. "When you go to the farmers' market, you can see the synergy of why certain combinations of ingredients work," Rosenzweig explains. "At the Lobster Club, we serve a lobster salad with celery root and a Concord grape vinaigrette, which sounds wacky, but after going to the market in the fall and seeing Concord grapes alongside celery root, you understand that it's a dish that is very much a celebration of the season. So many young cooks have gone to restaurants where they have seen the same ingredients served year round that they never develop the sense that a particular ingredient will taste best in October, not in June, and all the properties it has in October will be missing in June."

"On my first trip to the Four Seasons in New York, I remember awakening to the concept of dining by the season," says Marcel Desaulniers of the Trellis (Williamsburg, VA), who takes a seasonal approach in his own cuisine. "Later on, in the 1970s, I pursued my interest in this by going to Chez Panisse, and to the River Café to eat Larry Forgione's food. Those places were so ahead of anyone else in terms of the quality of their ingredients—and not a small part of that was because they only used what was in season."

FRESHNESS/STAGES OF RIPENESS

"It's important for cooks to understand stages of ripeness, so that we can capture things when they are at their peak," says Paul Bertolli of Oliveto (Oakland, CA). He believes it is the job of the chef to preserve what is great about a particular ingredient. "If it's a perfect fruit or vegetable, such as a tomato, that you can simply put on a plate and let it speak for itself, then you do that," he say. "You get yourself out of the way."

VARIATIONS

Individual ingredients vary in flavor, and this affects how they should be cooked—with a little less added acid, perhaps, or a little more roasting time—so a chef needs to be attuned to these variations when shopping and cooking. Nancy Silverton is quoted in our second book, *Culinary Artistry*, as saying that she won't use strawberries picked just after it has rained because they will have absorbed too much water and their flavor will be diluted. In cooking, a salmon fillet from the middle of the fish cooks differently than a fillet from the tail, where the fish is thinner. If the salmon is freshwater salmon, the time of year it is caught will affect the fattiness of the fish and therefore its cooking time.

Because customers prize consistency, it's important for a chef to understand the variations that can thwart it. "The potato-wrapped sea bass is a signature dish at Daniel, and I'm obsessed with it every day. I

never get tired of it," insists Daniel Boulud of Restaurant Daniel (New York). "But sometimes people will come just for that dish, so it's very important to maintain it with the highest respect and the highest consistency. It's the most difficult dish to maintain, because the potatoes can vary so widely in taste and texture, yet people expect that dish to always taste the same."

Understanding variations will allow a restaurant to educate customers on those differences, adding depth and interest to the dining experience. "When you go the market, you can taste various cheeses and notice how they change throughout the year," observes Anne Rosenzweig. "I'll explain to customers that the cheeses' flavors depend on the seasons, which determine what the goats and cows have been eating, which in turn affects the flavors."

2. Understand the Effect of Various Techniques on Ingredients

"If you have an eggplant, you obviously can't just cut it up and put it on a plate—you've got to do something to it," says Paul Bertolli of Oliveto. "But what is it about the ingredient that you want to preserve? When you start asking questions like that, and you start observing what the quality of the fruit or vegetable is, it will tell you what to do: 'Peel me,' or 'Fry me,' or 'Salt me first, because I've got a lot of water.' One of the major differences between great cooking and derivative cooking is the cook's acuteness of observation and level of response to the ingredients."

"It takes a long time to really understand how something like garlic or an onion works," observes Anne Rosenzweig . "If you roast garlic, it has a certain flavor and texture. But if you put it through a press, it has a hotness to the flavor and a different texture. And if you slice and sauté it, it has still another. That all takes a long time to understand and can only be learned through experience."

The starting point is mastering the basics. "Aspiring cooks need to explore and absorb, and to try to understand as much as they can about classic preparations, what they are and why they have been established that way," points out Todd English of Figs and Olives (Charlestown, MA, and Las Vegas). "There is a basic way to make things, and without understanding that, you will never go beyond it and create something else."

3. Understand How to Season

"One problem, particularly with young cooks, is that they think of salt as a flavor," laments Elizabeth Terry of Elizabeth on 37th (Savannah). "They reach for it automatically, instead of fresh herbs or toasted spices.

Caramel coulis
with fleur de
sel* butter and
seven spices

Bringing the World Back to Your Restaurant

WE HAD A REALLY PIVOTAL MEAL IN THE YUCATAN. WE WERE ABOUT TO open another restaurant, but couldn't decide if we wanted to open a hamburger joint or a taco stand in our little City Café location on Melrose. After tossing it around for a while, we decided on tacos, partly because we've got all these guys in the kitchen who make such delicious salsas for the staff meal every day.

We went to Mexico to do research and were walking down the street in Mérida on a quest for tacos when we decided to ask a policeman—in very broken Spanish—where to get really delicious tacos. He sent us to a storefront that we would never have noticed otherwise. We stood in front of the glass window, looking at these plates heaped with all different things: crab, lobster, shredded venison. There was this big Mayan-looking man standing back there filling these fresh yellow and dark yellow corn masa tortillas, then squeezing bitter oranges—called *naranja agria*—over them, with a drizzle of olive oil. They looked delicious.

We literally stood there watching for fifteen minutes, taking notes on everything we saw. He made a couple of tacos, came out to the street, handed us each a taco and a little beer, and got us to come inside. We started talking about food and told him that we owned a restaurant. We spent the whole afternoon there, drinking little six-ounce beers and eating tacos. It was the best taco experience we have ever had. The owner was generous of spirit and would not let us pay. We exchanged all kinds of ideas and had a great afternoon.

When we went back a couple of years later the place was gone, but we eventually found the new location. We weren't hungry because we had stuffed ourselves all day and we were leaving the next afternoon, but he said, "Well, I am closed tomorrow, but why don't you come in around eleven and I'll make something special for you." He made a red bean stew for us, and we shared more ideas.

A lot of this stuff ended up on our menu. In fact, our fish station at Border Grill was totally inspired by that trip. We wanted guests to see people making tacos, because it had been such an incredible experience for us.

Mary Sue Milliken and Susan Feniger

If something tastes a little flat, they don't review the dish—they just add more salt. Salt is not a flavor; it is a flavor *enhancer*. Getting over the habit of adding salt to 'fix' things is, I think, something that happens as a cook eats more in the dining room."

If additional saltiness is called for in a dish, there are ways to achieve this other than by simply adding salt to it. In an Asian dish, one could add soy sauce. In an Italian dish, one might add a salty Parmesan cheese. In a Mediterranean dish, one could add anchovy paste. These "salt substitutes" are more complicated than mere salt, so a mature hand is needed to ensure that the right balance is struck in a particular dish.

Seeing the great importance to chefs of understanding which herbs, spices, and other flavorings allow them to bring out the best flavor in various ingredients—from meats to produce—led to our extensive research on this topic for our book *Culinary Artistry*. The book features an extensive guide to ingredients and the flavorings and complementary ingredients that best enhance their essential qualities in a dish, from classic flavor combinations (such as apples and cinnamon, asparagus and lemon, lobster and tarragon, sausages and mustard, tomatoes and basil, and so on) to more cutting-edge combinations employed by leading chefs across America.

4. Understand How Ingredients Combine with Other Ingredients

"One day I was by myself in Rome, and someone had suggested that I go to a wine bar called Il Simposio," recalls Joyce Goldstein, formerly of Square One (San Francisco). "I had a plate of six cheeses—ranging from soft, moist mozzarella that had been made twenty minutes before to an aged Parmesan—along with things like chestnut purée, sliced pear, green tomato conserve, and a slice of fig salami, which is compressed figs sliced paper thin. I sat and mixed and matched all the food with the wine, and it was an epiphany. I kept going back and forth saying things like, 'Oh, that chestnut purée was really incredible with the mascarpone—I've got to remember this.' Because I was by myself, I was able to really taste slowly and savor all the textures and flavors and understand what I liked."

Learning through experimentation which combinations are most pleasing to one's own palate is a useful exercise. In addition, it can be helpful to study classic ingredient combinations (such as liver and bacon or onions, pork and apples, prosciutto and melon, rhubarb and strawberries, salmon and lentils; see *Culinary Artistry* for additional examples) as a starting point before reinterpreting combinations in new ways.

5. Understand the Fundamentals of Various Cuisines

Before cooks start borrowing from various cuisines or creating dishes inspired by another culture, they should first seek out and sample authentic renditions of that cuisine or dish so that their cooking is rooted in an understanding of its fundamentals.

Patrick O'Connell of the Inn at Little Washington (Washington, VA) recalls the time a cook in his kitchen prepared a dish of Peking duck for him. "I asked him, 'Have you had this before?' The reply was, 'No, but I've always wanted to make it.' I observed, 'But you don't know what it's supposed to taste like, right?' And he answered, 'Well, no, but I'm going to do it a little bit different.' And I thought, 'I'm sure you are!'"

A good place to start one's research is in an ethnic neighborhood that represents the culture you are trying to understand. If you live in San Francisco, you might head to the Mission district to eat in taquerias and restaurants that specialize in the regional cooking of Mexico. In Chicago, the Maxwell Street Market would offer opportunities to taste some authentic Mexican preparations and flavors.

Traveling to other cities or countries offers additional opportunities to learn and to begin to master knowledge of a cuisine. "My landmark Chinese eating experiences have all been in Asia," admits Barbara Tropp, formerly of China Moon Café (San Francisco). "The exception is some of [the noted San Francisco dim sum restaurant] Ton Kiang's rice-dough-wrapped dumplings, which are finer than anything that I've had in my Asian travels, and several of which are benchmarks for me. But, on the whole, all of my informative Asian eating experiences have taken place in Asia. I think I'm probably not unlike Rick Bayless in needing travel to inform me about the cuisine that I'm most focused on. For me, Asian travel is a real must.

"However, if I were a young chef or student in this country without the money to go to Asia, I'd eat my way through every Chinese restaurant in the city, from A to Z," says Tropp. "I have lived in those cultures and still have frequent access to them, but if I didn't, I'd start going to restaurants and trusting my own palate."

Jim Becker of Rauxa (Somerville, MA) agrees. "Most young cooks don't have big dining budgets, so if they live in the bigger cities, they're fortunate, because there are so many inexpensive ethnic restaurants that can introduce them to new taste combinations," he points out. "Different cultures play up different tastes and textures, such as Asian cultures' love of bitterness."

"In order to develop your palate, it's important to ask yourself what you think, and to trust yourself when you cook and when you eat out," advises Chris Bianco of Pizzeria Bianco (Phoenix). "You should ask yourself, 'Do I really like this restaurant? I know it got a great review, but what do *I* think?' Similarly, you can say to yourself, 'I know that foie gras and Beluga caviar are supposed to be good, but they taste like liver and stinky fish to me.' It's okay if you don't like certain things. People get confused, though, about knowing whether something is not good or just not to their taste. If you don't like a particular restaurant, you can't just say, 'It wasn't good.' *Why* wasn't it good? Wasn't the food hot? Weren't the salad greens fresh and cold? Or did you not like the anchovies in a dish you were served? Ask yourself, and be specific."

Wherever the flavors are tasted, it's important to note what's going on in your mouth. "When you taste exotic cuisines, you can see how they put together salty and sweet, or savory and bitter. Those are good lessons, because you can start to understand how other cuisines put together flavors in a very elementary way," says Anne Rosenzweig of the Lobster Club (New York). "I find young cooks want to go from zero to a hundred overnight instead of taking the small, incremental steps necessary to really understand ingredients, the seasons, tastes, and what is satisfying about them.

"One of the exciting things about going out to eat, whether it is Pho Viet Huong [a modest Vietnamese restaurant in Manhattan's Chinatown] or [the four-star restaurant] Jean Georges, is encountering an unexpected configuration of tastes," says Rosenzweig. "When you see a chef combine X, Y, and Z ingredients into an astonishing taste, it can be a mind-expanding experience."

6. Develop Taste Benchmarks by Sampling the Best Versions of a Dish Possible

Once you have tasted the best possible preparations of a particular dish, you can refer to these taste memories when evaluating the same or a similar dish. Think of all the pasta you've eaten over the years, and ask yourself which dishes stand out in your memory as being among the best. Analyze why you prefer one rendition over another, and what factors contribute to your preferences. Define for yourself: What makes this dish work? What makes this version the best you ever had? In the case of pasta, was it a question of texture or doneness? Do you tend to prefer dried pasta over fresh pasta? Was it a matter of having just the right amount of sauce?

Andrew Carmellini of Café Boulud (New York) was researching spring rolls, and sampled them all over New York's Chinatown until he found the one he liked the best. "In trying to unlock the secret of what made it so good, I figured out that the best time to get them was at lunch, just after they had been made for the day, when they tasted fresher," he says.

Steven Chiappetti of Mossant Bistro (Chicago) believes that in different places you should seek out benchmarks for different dishes. "In France, for instance, you can order ratatouille in nearly any restaurant, and there is nothing particularly unique or creative about it. But what makes each restaurant's ratatouille unique is that the chef puts his own taste behind it. Some chefs might put more acid or tomato base in the ratatouille because it cuts through the fattiness of something like pork or lamb, while another chef might serve it cold, because it goes well with the mayonnaise that way. It's important that aspiring chefs understand the different tastes that are possible, and the reasons other chefs might want to do things a certain way."

"With all food, it's important to establish a reference point," says Patrick O'Connell of the Inn at Little Washington (Washington, VA). "Part of the intent of my journeys to Europe in the early days was to find the best versions of particular dishes in the whole world, whether cassoulet or *coq au vin* or sweetbreads. Between our visits to the three-star restaurants, we made lots of stops in smaller local restaurants to search out particular dishes. Some versions might make you wonder, 'What's all the fuss about?' or think, 'Geez, I could improve on this.' But that's how you learn what a dish is supposed to taste like, and you file that knowledge away."

O'Connell challenges himself to seek out and experience the best of everything. "All food, pizza, bagels, dim sum—whatever," he says. "Any time people comment that they've tasted something especially great, I try to check it out. I heard there was a pizza oven up in Princeton, New Jersey, where a guy has been making pizza for twenty years [Conte's], and I made sure to make a detour to check out that pizza."

Mark Miller of Coyote Café (Las Vegas and Santa Fe) agrees that culinary benchmarks can be established anywhere—from a four-star restaurant to a private home. "I had a great tortilla made by a Mexican woman in the middle of nowhere in Mexico, and I spent two days working with her, trying to learn the secret of her extraordinary tortillas," he remembers. "The intense flavor of that corn still lingers in my memory. For better or for worse, every single tortilla I've tasted since, not to mention every piece of corn and everything made with corn, has been compared to that benchmark."

7. Duplicate a Dish You Have Tasted Elsewhere

This exercise can help you develop an appreciation of the subtleties involved in reproducing a dish you like.

"I always try to really ingest a dish first and create an indelible imprint of it on my taste memory. Then I try to replicate it precisely, working and working until I've perfected it. Once I get to that point, I

"Eating out is one of the most important things a chef can do, because you discover what you like—your flavors and your style."

JEAN-GEORGES VONGERICHTEN

JEAN GEORGES (NEW YORK)

can say, 'Well, for my palate or for our clients' palates, I might soften this or change that. Some might call that Americanizing a dish, but I would never screw around with a dish until I had mastered it," says Patrick O'Connell.

"My inspiration was always this book written by Paula Peck, who was an amateur cook," he continues. "She basically taught herself to cook. Each Saturday, she would set aside time to make croissants, because her husband loved them so much. Every year they'd go to Paris, and every year she'd measure her croissant against the croissants they had in Paris. On one trip to Paris, she finally crossed the line: Her husband tasted a croissant and said, 'God, these are awful!' And from then on, he could only eat her croissants. It took her nine years, setting aside every Saturday, to perfect her croissants. I think it's important that people understand that learning to cook isn't instantaneous."

Tom Colicchio of Gramercy Tavern and Craft (New York) says he will never forget the first time he ate at Pierre Gagnaire, an innovative three-star restaurant in France. "It was the first time that I could not figure out what a chef was doing," admits Colicchio. "I knew the flavors, but I couldn't figure out the techniques being used. He is the only chef who has ever made me ask, 'How did he do that?' By comparison, if you eat the food of Alain Ducasse, it is incredible, but it is pretty straightforward. At Gagnaire, he served a dessert that was a crystal-clear lemon jelly. Lemon juice isn't clear when you reduce it, it's cloudy. Eventually, I figured it out: It finally occurred to me that he might have clarified the lemon juice the same way you would a consommé. I tried it, and it worked."

Jean-Georges Vongerichten of Jean Georges (New York) believes that once you know how to cook, you learn a lot from eating out. "Because you know how to put food together, you can figure out the technical part of the dish. You can also analyze what you like about it and get inspired this way, too."

Lydia Shire of Biba and Pignoli (Boston) used to drive five and a half hours to Montreal just to have lunch at Les Mas des Olivier. "This restaurant made the best *soupe de poisson*—the base for bouillabaisse—with an incredible *rouille* and grated Gruyère cheese. I would leave my house at seven A.M. just to have this soup for lunch! It was the next best thing to hopping on a plane to France.

"So for years I worked on that soup. I kept reading everything I could about fish soup, and I talked to the chef at Les Mas des Oliver, who told me he used all these different fish bones in the stock and flavored it with Pernod. It was the best soup I had ever tasted in my life, and there was just something about it that drove me crazy! I kept making it over and over and over until eventually mine was as good as theirs. I finally got it down.

"I think it's like that with anything: If you're persistent and just go after something, you'll eventually get it," says Shire. "However, I never did learn how to make a *rouille* as good as theirs, so I'll have to go back to the drawing board for that!"

8. Explore How Chefs Around the Country (and the World) Are Taking Cuisine in New Directions

This will help you to expand your knowledge of cuisine by looking at how other chefs experiment successfully with new ingredients, flavor combinations, and techniques.

"Once you have an understanding of how ingredients taste, and how other cultures and cuisines put ingredients together and why, then and only then can you begin to understand the complexity of what a great chef like Jean-Georges Vongerichten, who is known for his use of innovative flavor combinations and techniques, is doing," says Anne Rosenzweig of the Lobster Club (New York).

Barbara Tropp, formerly of China Moon Café (San Francisco), agrees. "If I'm in New York, as a cook of Chinese food, I will learn more by eating a meal cooked by Daniel Boulud [through his personal interpretation of French cuisine at his four-star Restaurant Daniel] than I will learn by going downtown to eat in Chinatown."

Mark Miller of Coyote Café (Las Vegas and Santa Fe) recalls, "At Biba in Boston, which is a challenging restaurant, I had a rendition of the classic Milanese dish of *vitello tonnato* [cooked veal with a tuna sauce]—only Lydia Shire reversed it, serving fresh tuna in a veal sauce. It was a matter of really understanding a classic theme, but then presenting it in a way that exemplifies what it is about. It was like turning a sculpture around and looking at it from the top: same sculpture, different perspective. That was a great dish."

9. Develop Your Own Taste and Style

Once you understand the nuances of a dish thoroughly—what makes it work and what any shortcomings might be—see if you can find a way to improve it and put your own stamp on it.

"If you want to stand out from everyone else, find a style that is yours," advises Tom Colicchio. "It doesn't have to be some crazy, outlandish thing. Find what you are natural working with. When you eat at Ducasse, Jean Georges, or the French Laundry, pay attention to what things strike a chord in you, cultivate those things, and then come up with your own style. If you are going to imitate dish by dish, you are never going to stand apart. If your food looks like [New York chef] Alfred Portale's, you are not doing anything new."

"I think people need to search out restaurants that really have a huge effect on their lives," advises Mark Miller of Coyote Café (Santa Fe and Las Vegas). "It's sort of like the difference between being madly in love with someone versus liking them. You need to have mad, passionate affairs with food! They might last a day, they might last a year, or they might last a lifetime, but you have to go out and find food that you are passionate about."

"I think that you end up eating what you like," says Chris Schlesinger of the East Coast Grill (Cambridge, MA). "I encourage cooks to try to find something that they're particularly interested in, and to pursue that. Choose restaurants that help you become more knowledgeable. Specialize in something that you are excited about—whether it's organics, heirloom vegetables, seafood, seaweed, or whatever—and then go eat at places that are doing exciting things with them.

"When I was trying to figure things out in the early 1980s, I was traveling and going to Thai, Chinese, and Salvadoran restaurants, while everybody else was eating nouvelle cuisine," remembers Schlesinger. "And that set me on my own unique path."

10. Treat the Ingredients and the Process with the Utmost Respect

Jimmy Schmidt of the Rattlesnake Club (Detroit) was struck by an experience he had at a European fish restaurant run by an entire family of fishermen. "Everything is right out of the ocean—they catch it, and they serve it. They are in love with being fishermen and in love with the fish they are serving. You are part of their family when you are there, and the fish that is served is a part of their family, too.

"Once when I was there, the owner served a *loup de mer* cooked in salt, and even the way he described the recipe for the dish clued me in to their level of dedication. He explained, 'You put it in the oven, bake it, then watch the head of the fish. If your wife comes by, tell her to leave you alone. If your mistress calls on the phone, tell her, 'Later.' You don't move until one tear comes from the fish's eye—then it is done. At that point, you take the fish out of the oven and thank the Lord, then you serve it with a little olive oil, lemon, and chopped parsley. Anything else is sacrilegious. And if anyone gets up from the table, they can't have any.'"

Michel Richard of Citrus (Los Angeles) and Citronelle (Washington, DC) once visited a farmer in California who was growing *haricots verts*. "I was so moved by the way he was doing it and all the love that he brought to growing them that I brought three fifty-pound bags of *haricots verts* back with me to Washington.

"It's as if the farmer says to the chef, 'These are my babies—I did everything I could to give a good life to these great *haricots verts*. Now I give them to you to take over from here.' As chefs, we don't want to break that chain of love, so we treat them with respect, too.

"When we serve them to our customers, and some of our customers don't eat them, we want to scream, 'Please eat these *haricots verts*! We brought them from France, we planted them in California, I brought them to this restaurant, and we have done all we can in this chain of love, just so you could eat them!' And it is a chain of love to bring an ingredient from the farm to the customer with as much respect as we do."

"To treat things with respect . . . we don't get many chances, really," concurs Patrick O'Connell, of the Inn at Little Washington (Washington, VA). "We've been in business twenty-two years, and we just finished the tomato season. I came to realize that that's only twenty-two incarnations of a tomato salad. It's not that many. When you think of a lifetime, it is just such a fleeting moment."

HOW TO DINE

PART III

EATING LIKE A CHEF: CULTIVATING DISCRIMINATION AND APPRECIATION

Terrance Brennan

CHARLIE TROTTER

CHARLIE TROTTER'S (CHICAGO)

"When I agree to do an event somewhere, first I'll very quickly make restaurant reservations, then I'll book my hotel, and last I'll book my flights. I had to go to Paris last weekend for a Tradition et Qualité conference, and the first thing I did was figure out where I could eat. The minute I got off the airplane, I went right to L'Ami Louis to have some roasted chicken and foie gras. That night, I went to a brasserie to have oysters and steamed Dover sole. And the next day, I went to Arpège for the meeting."

For professional chefs, dining out involves a delicate balance between education and enjoyment. When a musician attends a concert, he or she hears the music, but also the mistakes. To focus too much on the mistakes makes it difficult to enjoy the concert. Conversely, not to pay close enough attention to the music results in the loss of an opportunity to learn. It's important to strike the right balance in order to maximize both learning and pleasure.

Tempering Expectations

Having a set of expectations when dining in a renowned restaurant is unavoidable. If you have read the reviews or heard about the incredible signature dishes or service from colleagues who have previously eaten there, how can you *not* have expectations? But are diners' expectations fair to the restaurant? Some argue that overly high expectations can prevent diners from perceiving the experience for what it is, or cause them to be disappointed if their actual experience is not identical to what was expected.

Traci Des Jardins of Jardinière (San Francisco) points out that if you've read about a chef and have expectations about what the experience in his or her restaurant is supposed to be like, you might be let down. "It's easy to be misunderstood, and it may be the case that what has been written about them is not necessarily the way they want to be represented," she says. "So it's important to keep an open mind and to be open to what a restaurant is trying to achieve."

Eric Ripert of Le Bernardin (New York) says, "I think it's very important to dine out with a free spirit, with no opinion whatsoever. When I go to Carnegie Deli, my expectations are not the same as when I go to Daniel. I know what to expect from Carnegie Deli, and that's important. You cannot go to a little neighborhood restaurant and expect to have the experience of your lifetime, because that's not what the restaurant is trying to do."

Rocco DiSpirito of Union Pacific (New York) contends that the most important part of dining out is going with an open mind. He believes you must remove your preconceptions about dining, and even your ideas about the flavors that you prefer, if you are going to be able to experience what you're there to experience. "When I was younger, I found myself dining and criticizing concurrently: 'Oh, this could taste better, that could taste better,'" he admits. "But there's a lot to learn when dining out, and if you're using half your mental resources criticizing, you have only the other half left to observe and absorb everything there is to absorb. I suggest that you devote one hundred percent of your resources to absorbing the experience, and to taking what's valuable from it."

"I think the biggest problem with young chefs—and diners in general—is that they compare each meal to their last experience," says Chris Bianco of Pizzeria Bianco (Phoenix). "If you eat at John's Pizza in Manhattan, for example, and then come into Pizzeria Bianco looking for Frank Sinatra on the CD player, the big Sophia Loren poster on the wall, or other things that you associate with your memory of that experience, it is unfair to me. When I go out, I wipe away everything that I think I know about food and then try to understand what that restaurant is trying to achieve."

Raji Jallepalli of Restaurant Raji (Memphis) can recall having incredible meals at Daniel, Jean Georges, and Le Bernardin in New York. "The staffs rise to such levels and standards that you almost have to reset your expectations to go anywhere else," she points out. "However, you can't judge all restaurants by these standards, because every chef and restaurateur sets up their own template of who they want to be. As a chef-owner, I should be more open than anyone to what an experience will be like, but if you are in the business, you frequently have preconceived notions, which is not fair to that restaurant. How can you fault someone for not being Jean Georges or Daniel?"

"For cooks, going out to dinner is important—it's an investment in themselves. When they eat out, they need to watch everything with a critical eye. They're there to enjoy the experience, of course, but they should also do a little work and analyze it: try to figure out how the chef achieved a certain effect, for example, or observe the seasonality and the composition of the menu."

MICHAEL ROMANO
UNION SQUARE CAFE (NEW YORK)

Being a critical Diner

Keeping your expectations in check does not mean turning off your critical eye. The dining room is the center ring of the circus, where the whole restaurant comes together, and leading chefs agree that it's important to pay attention to everything that's happening throughout the course of a meal. Absorb as much of it as possible, because the more you can take away, the richer the experience will be, and the more you will have to draw from the next time you dine out.

"Many people do not see what a chef sees; they don't have our eye," says François Payard of Payard Pâtisserie and Bistro (New York). "You will see how someone runs a dining room by how fast the staff is moving and the way the staff speaks. Those details make such a big difference to the dining experience. In the best restaurants, no matter what is happening, the staff appears calm."

Because astute chefs notice so many details when dining out, it can be extremely helpful to dine out with another chef.

"Let's face it—the more you taste, the more you are [as a culinary professional]," says Joyce Goldstein, formerly of Square One (San Francisco). "It is important to eat out with other chefs because you can learn so much more that way. I eat out with [San Francisco chef] Alain Rondelli a lot. We discuss food and share our enthusiasm for it, and we enjoy the food even more because we have different perspectives on it. Even by eating out with other chefs who may not share the same palate, you can learn from those differences, so I strongly recommend doing so."

Gordon Hamersley of Hamersley's Bistro (Boston) agrees. "I went to a dinner at a Chinese restaurant that was hosted by Nina Simonds, where the guests included Jasper White, Lydia Shire, Julia Child, Anne Willan, and our spouses," recalls Hamersley. "My knowledge of Chinese food is not that good, and as the dishes came out of the kitchen, Nina, who has written a number of Chinese cookbooks, explained what each dish was all about. I felt like I was on a culinary adventure for the evening, with all these really dedicated food people, and it was both educational and enjoyable."

Others' reactions can provide a clue as to what to really pay attention to. Rocco DiSpirito recalls, "I was sitting with Gray Kunz [the former four-star chef of Lespinasse in New York] at Arun's, an upscale Thai restaurant in Chicago, and I remember his being completely awestruck. It was an amazing thing, watching his reaction to the food and seeing the delight on his face and his sense of amazement.

"To see Gray so excited made me realize that something very special was happening, and I kind of turned up my senses to take it all in," says DiSpirito. "His reaction just further emphasized that I'd better really focus and pay attention. I realized then that you can always be sur-

Diane Forley and Michael Otsuka

40　CHEF'S NIGHT OUT

prised; no matter how much you have eaten or seen, someone, some-day, is going to surprise you with something so new or so personal that you'll have to take notice of it!"

being a too-critical diner

As helpful as it can be to eat out with other culinary professionals who can help you make important distinctions, this can sometimes be taken too far. Have you ever been to a movie based on a book with someone who has read the book, while you haven't? They keep telling you how the movie

wining and dining

OFTENTIMES, WINE IS AN INTEGRAL PART OF THE DINING EXPERIENCE. Yet when cooks taste a dish in the kitchen, they probably have not been drinking a glass of wine with it. More likely, it was accompanied by water or that favorite beverage of cooks, coffee.

In a restaurant dining room, food and wine that complement each other can create a unique marriage of flavors that augments and trans-forms the best qualities of each. Conversely, ill-matched food and wine detract from each other. Learning about wine can seem daunting, but din-ing out provides the perfect opportunity to build a base of knowledge.

It is very common for restaurants that offer tasting menus also to of-fer matching wines. During a visit to Norman's in Florida, the sommelier broke the "rule" of always moving from white to red wines; the reds served were lighter and completely appropriate before the bigger white wines that followed. So, in addition to food that, in a sense, broke the rules by the choice of exotic ingredients, the experience was further heightened by a daring wine program.

"You need to pay attention to the reaction between wine and food, be-cause a great wine can be spoiled by a mismatched flavor," explains Traci Des Jardins of Jardinière (San Francisco). "Young cooks are often intimi-dated by wine and don't realize how easily they can learn by getting a glass of wine in front of them and seeing how different foods react to that wine." "When an order comes into our kitchen, we look to see what wine the din-ers are drinking with their dinner, and we talk about it," explains Craig Shelton of the Ryland Inn (Whitehouse, NJ). "A 1996 Montrachet will re-act to the food significantly differently than a 1986. So I teach our cooks that we may need to put a drop more acidity into the food paired with the young wine, and hold back slightly for the older wine. We learn ways to flatter the wines, depending on their structure and age."

"It's important that people realize that there's a great deal to be learned from negative lessons."

patrick o'connell
THE INN AT LITTLE WASHINGTON
(VIRGINIA)

and the book are different, talking the whole time, and ruin the movie-watching experience for you. That is what it can be like to dine with other chefs whose idea of discussing a meal is sustaining a running commentary on everything that is wrong with it.

Granted, there is a fine line between rigorously critiquing a meal and tearing it apart, but it is an important distinction to try to make. Once when we were dining with a nonrestaurant professional, we were commenting to each other about the room, the bread service, and other details when our guest asked if we wanted to leave and go to another restaurant! Although we believed at the time that we were just making distinctions for our own reference, our comments struck him as too critical, and he mistook this as displeasure. Now, unless it's just the two of us, we try to take everything silently in stride. But we found that we weren't alone in our tendency to criticize.

"When my husband, John, and I came out of school as young chefs, we were very critical of every place and everything we ate," admits Caprial Pence of Caprial's Bistro (Portland). "We spent so much time picking everything apart that we missed the overall experience. Now we tend to have a better time and learn more from our dining experiences because we are not so bent on criticizing everything. Even in the worst situation, you can still learn something—you just look for the shining light in that experience."

Raji Jallepalli of Restaurant Raji (Memphis) has observed the same phenomenon. "Too many chefs who go out are wearing a food critic's hat, and five minutes after they arrive, they are tearing the meal apart," she observes. "That's why I would usually prefer not to be in a chef's company when I dine out. As someone who works in a restaurant every night, I need to be fair to myself when I go out, and just have a good time. Being in the business makes me more forgiving, so if I see a struggling waiter or sense that the kitchen is having a bad night, I still try to have fun despite that."

Terrance Brennan of Picholine (New York) believes it's important to focus on the totality of the dining experience. "What I used to do was just concentrate on the food and pick it apart. That's easy to do," says Brennan. "But perfection is impossible, even at a great restaurant. When I ate at Alain Chapel, which is a Michelin three-star restaurant, I was served overcooked salmon. But even though my particular piece of salmon was overcooked, it's still a great restaurant.

"Too often, when young cooks go to the so-called grand restaurants—and even I was guilty of this at one time—they taste a dish and think, 'What's the big deal?' However, it takes a certain maturity level to appreciate dishes that don't blow you away, dishes that are simple yet perfect," Brennan observes. "That level of appreciation comes with time."

"I always feel that a restaurant experience is justified if you take away even one idea. It doesn't matter about what; it doesn't even have to be about food. But if a good idea costs you a couple of hundred dollars, it is worth it."

PATRICK O'CONNELL
THE INN AT LITTLE WASHINGTON
(VIRGINIA)

The Last Word

When dining out, it is also important to be humble. Be open to the experience and to what you can learn. Any great chef knows there is no perfect night, so don't put yourself in the position of calling the kettle black—it just might be *your* work under the microscope next time.

IT DOESN'T HAVE TO BE

A Four-Star Restaurant

MANY CHEFS MAY CHOOSE TO GO TO CERTAIN RESTAURANTS FOR A particular dish or atmosphere. They do not always seek over-the-top, four-star experiences. In fact, we have found that when most chefs eat out, they actually like to get away from the elaborate cooking they do in their own restaurants, and so they often go to offbeat places. They may go to a favorite sushi place where the chef makes great rolls, or to a Greek place for the best gyro, or to any number of places for special dishes and to satisfy cravings. The only common denominator among these places is quality: that whatever the restaurant does, it does well.

"The most important things to me are good ingredients, simplicity, good execution, and a sense of place in a restaurant," says Joyce Goldstein, formerly of Square One (San Francisco). "It doesn't have to be an expensive place, just a place where the energy level is nice and the staff is in harmony—where they look like they're having a good time, and are comfortable serving whatever they are serving."

"We really appreciate a deeper cultural experience than most high-end restaurants provide," comment Susan Feniger and Mary Sue Milliken of Border Grill and Ciudad (Los Angeles). "There is just something about those very down-to-earth, family-run restaurants where the families work together to bring you these meals that are not fancy, just cooked from their hearts. We really respond to that, and we'd encourage students who are on a budget not to worry if they can't eat at all the very expensive, highly publicized restaurants across the country. That's not necessarily what they need to do to experience incredible food."

"Between Lyon and the restaurant Georges Blanc, in Vonnas, there is a swamp called La Vallée de Dombre," says Daniel Boulud of Restaurant Daniel (New York). "It's the best region for frogs' legs in France—it's like the French bayou. I remember going to a little place there—not quite a truck stop, but a little local café—that had the best frogs' legs in the world. Tasting something perfect like that, where they have been cooking them for so long, can be an inspiration."

"You can learn something new anywhere—not only in well-known restaurants. You might go to Restaurant Daniel [in New York City] one day, and the next day somewhere simple—but you can learn something from both if you pay attention."

ANDRÉ SOLTNER

FORMERLY OF LUTÈCE

"Sometimes when I am in the kitchen and see a young cook cutting corners or just not executing a dish correctly, I will stop him in his tracks and ask, 'Would you pay ten dollars for that?'" says Hans Röckenwagner of Röck and Röckenwagner (Los Angeles). "You have to understand how price and quality are related, and you pick up on those things by going out to other restaurants."

RICK BAYLESS on

One of the Best Meals of His Life

I HAD A MEAL IN A SMALL ZAPOTEC INDIAN VILLAGE JUST OUTSIDE OF THE city of Oaxaca. The first time I went to the restaurant, which was opened by Abigail Mendoza and her family, I had an experience that was so exciting to me that I kept wanting to jump up out of my seat! It didn't have the luxuriousness of eating at Taillevent or the big-city shimmer of eating at the Four Seasons. But it was an experience so deeply rooted in the land, in that village, that I just couldn't believe what resonance I kept getting out of these dishes.

When I talked with her about how they made their dishes, I was told, "Well, we go out back where the oregano patch is, and we pick the oregano. That's that flavor you taste in that dish." And I'd hear, "The corn that thickens this beautiful soup is grown by my brother-in-law's family." Or "Of course we raise the chickens ourselves. And the chiles that we have in this dish are the ones that the Indians in the *sierra* bring down for market day every Sunday." She could tell me where every single ingredient that was in every dish, down to the salt, came from. And every dish was so elegantly balanced, prepared so beautifully and with such care, that I was stunned.

It was at that moment that I realized that all of the dining experiences that I had ever had in great restaurants had something very distinctive, very unique about them that I could pinpoint, but that I had never before had an experience of food that resonated so much with its environment. Most of the time, you think about great restaurant experiences as happening in cities, so that there is an automatic disconnect from the land. This was an experience where there was absolutely no disconnect from the land. Not only was there great skill in getting all those ingredients woven together in perfect balance, because the cooking is very complex down there, but there was also a perfect balance with nature. I just loved it. I was so in tune with that environment, and with those dishes, that it felt exhilarating to me.

ROCCO DISPIRITO
UNION PACIFIC (NEW YORK)

"I would encourage up-and-coming chefs to dine out as much as possible, to learn the sort of etiquette and protocol of dining as it relates to ordering in a restaurant and interacting with the waiters, owners, maître d's, and other guests. That's something that has not been focused on at all in culinary school. And that's a shame, because you have chefs out there who are phenomenal talents who don't always know the appropriate clothing to wear, or the appropriate protocol in terms of making or canceling a reservation, or writing thank-you notes, or all the kinds of things that I find important. I would advise young students to start paying attention to these things as early as possible."

Christopher Gross of Christopher's Fermier Brasserie (Phoenix) once got upset with one of his cooks who had come back from a restaurant complaining about a couple of the dishes. "I didn't say too much about it at the time," he recalls. "But then the next night, I had to stop him from serving three dishes because they were wrong, and I sort of lost it. I said, 'You have the nerve to criticize someone else, and you are not even taking the time to make this properly? You don't have any room to complain. Wait until you know a little more.'

"Sometimes young people who work in nice restaurants go out and try to be master chefs and critique everyone else. It's good for young cooks to take it all in, because if they see something wrong, it can be a wake-up call to themselves. To this day, when my wife—who is general manager of our wine program—and I go out and see something being done wrong, we just hope we aren't doing it, too," he admits.

Internalizing the importance of striving to get everything right—down to the last detail—can be an important side benefit of dining out. Pastry chef Emily Luchetti of Farallon (San Francisco) comments, "Excellence is in the details. It doesn't matter if you're talking about a fine-dining restaurant or a little café, because how things are handled down to the last detail is what will determine whether a customer comes back or not. And as a chef, you can't lose sight of that. It's so easy in the heat and the pressure of the day to let go of your standards for a minute, thinking, 'Well, it's just this one time…' But that's one time too many—it could be Julia Child who's being served the dish you knew wasn't perfect!"

As chefs and diners raise their mutual standards of excellence, the quality of the dining experience can continue to rise to untold heights.

Mario Batali of Babbo, Esca, and Lupa (New York) notes, "In the last twenty years, with the rise of the ZagatSurvey and the increased media coverage of restaurants, what we've seen is that going out to dinner has become the primary event for a lot of people. It used to be 'We're going to catch a movie and some dinner.' Now it's 'We're going to Le Bernardin!' Now people go out and talk about their meal for the entire time that they're there.

"This puts a whole lot more pressure on us as chefs to make sure we're sharp," Batali points out. "Instead of just making people's palates happy, now there's an intellectual component to putting together menus and wine lists. We have to show that we've taken the time to find ingredients that customers may not recognize, or that we're serving them in ways that haven't been done before."

Isn't that putting too much pressure on chefs to stay on top of the latest restaurant and dining trends, as customers as well as chefs?

"The whole creative process is intellectually stimulating," counters Batali. "And that makes it even more fun for chefs to do what we do."

where the chefs eat

PART IV

A GUIDE TO CHEFS' FAVORITE SPOTS—AND HOW YOU CAN ENJOY THEM, TOO

Pearl Oyster Bar (New York City)

"Whenever I am in another city, I want to suck up whatever it is that makes it tick."

americans have a vast array of choices when dining out, ranging from some of the finest four-star restaurants in the world to the humblest of ethnic restaurants. The chefs' favorites described in the pages that follow reflect this extensive range, depending on whether a chef is in the mood to check out a respected colleague's restaurant for cutting-edge cuisine—or is so exhausted that she barely has the energy to order a pizza for delivery from around the corner. In either case, you can bet that the quality level will be high!

We asked leading chefs to tell us about a few of their favorite restaurants, the places where they eat most often on their nights off. We also asked them for the best spots in their city for various popular items (such as hamburgers, oysters, and pizza) as well as regional specialties (for example, you'll read about their favorite pastrami sandwiches in Manhattan and celebrity-watching restaurants in L.A.); these are summarized in the city highlights sections. In several cases, particularly mobile chefs have recommended restaurants in cities other than their own.

Because of the growing popularity of seasonal and market menus that vary frequently (sometimes even daily), dishes that might be recommended today may no longer be on the menu tomorrow. Instead, chefs might mention particular ingredients or techniques with which the restaurant has a way.

We've also asked chefs to mention something about their own cuisines and/or restaurants, and what it is they are aiming to achieve. This can provide a useful context for diners, allowing them to understand in advance what they might expect during a visit to those restaurants. After all, the restaurants of the chefs interviewed for this book are arguably among the very best in America today—and should be a starting point for any discerning diner's culinary journey!

In addition to having an extraordinary dining guide to steer restaurant enthusiasts toward worthwhile culinary experiences, the reader will also learn about the recommending chef's cuisine through a better understanding of his or her influences and preferences. In our book *Culinary Artistry*, we chronicled leading chefs' ten favorite ingredients to cook with. Reading about their favorite restaurants is yet another way of coming to understand leading chefs' palates and "what they like."

*"I put in my pictures
everything I like."*

PABLO PICASSO

atlanta

barbecue, pulled pork

FAT MATT'S RIB SHACK

1811 Piedmont Avenue N.E., Atlanta (404) 607-1622

"*This is a great place for pulled pork sandwiches, ribs on white bread, and sweet iced tea. They blare blues music, and they also have live bands sometimes—in a place the size of a walk-in refrigerator!*"

—CLIFFORD HARRISON AND ANNE QUATRANO, BACCHANALIA

barbecue, ribs

THELMA'S RIB SHACK

302 Auburn Avenue N.E., Atlanta (404) 533-0081

"*They have great barbecued ribs.*"

—CLIFFORD HARRISON AND ANNE QUATRANO, BACCHANALIA

bread

ALON'S BAKERY

1394 N. Highland Avenue, Atlanta (404) 872-6000

"*Their breads are excellent, especially the sourdough farm bread.*"

—GUENTER SEEGER, SEEGER'S

CORNER BAKERY

3368 Peachtree Road N.E., Atlanta (404) 816-5100

"*Their bâtard [a type of baguette] is very simple and fresh.*"

—GUENTER SEEGER, SEEGER'S

chicken-fried steak

OK CAFÉ

1284 W. Paces Ferry Road, Atlanta (404) 233-2888

"*This is a classic meat-and-potatoes place—you choose your meat and then you choose your sides. They have elevated chicken-fried steak ever so slightly.*"

—CLIFFORD HARRISON AND ANNE QUATRANO, BACCHANALIA

steak

BONE'S

3130 Piedmont Road, Atlanta (404) 237-2663

"*We get rib-eye steak here. They also have lamb T-bones, and double-cut lamb chops served with a big old hunk of mint jelly.*"

—CLIFFORD HARRISON AND ANNE QUATRANO, BACCHANALIA

CHOPS

70 W. Paces Ferry Road (at Peachtree Road), Atlanta (404) 262-2675

"*Chops has the best steak in America! Nothing competes with it. I call Pano Karatassos, the owner, before I leave New York to make sure I can get a table. I like to get the porterhouse for two, because it's very thick. Then I'll share a little. Pano gets great-quality meat—but he won't tell me where he gets it from!*"

—ERIC RIPERT, LE BERNARDIN (NEW YORK)

vietnamese

BIEN THUY

5095-F Buford Highway, Doraville (404) 454-9046

"*We love to get their pho [beef noodle soup] and their salt-and-pepper shrimp, fried whole with their heads on. They're great!*"

—CLIFFORD HARRISON AND ANNE QUATRANO, BACCHANALIA

CLIFFORD HARRISON and ANNE QUATRANO are chef-owners of Bacchanalia and the Floataway Café, and have recently opened Star Provisions, a retail cook's market adjacent to Bacchanalia. Much of the organic local produce that they use in their restaurants comes from their own property, Summerland Farm, where they also keep Jersey cows for cheese and butter. In 1995, *Food & Wine* voted Harrison and Quatrano among the Ten Best New Chefs in the nation. Bacchanalia was voted number one in the 2000 Atlanta *ZagatSurvey,* and *Gourmet* rated it number one in Atlanta in 2000.

OUR FOOD At Bacchanalia, we want to provide our guests with a relaxed, comfortable setting where they can enjoy food that's been simply prepared with the freshest ingredients. We place a heavy emphasis on organic, seasonal produce that's locally grown.

The menu at Floataway Café specializes in country French and Italian cuisine. A lot of restaurants in Atlanta are midrange in price and food, not to mention quality; more emphasis is placed on atmosphere than food. At Floataway, we want to change that. We want to create an atmosphere for the people who will pay fourteen dollars for a chanterelle mushroom pizza. Some people will never appreciate what we're doing, but fortunately there are apparently enough who will, because we are quite busy. We get people who come in to eat twice a week and have been doing so for over a year.

CLIFFORD AND ANNE'S PICKS

FLOATAWAY CAFÉ
1123 Zonolite Road
(at Briarcliff Road), Atlanta
(404) 892-1414
For dining out on an everyday basis [i.e., Tuesday through Saturday, when the restaurant is open], it's Floataway. We have the cooks make us some gnocchi or pasta or something. We could eat there every day, not just because it's free, but because the food is to our taste. (See also p. 52.)

SEEGER'S
111 W. Paces Ferry Road, Atlanta
(404) 846-9779

THE DINING ROOM
3434 Peachtree Road
(in the Ritz-Carlton), Atlanta
(404) 237-2700

When we've got some dough to spend, we go to Seeger's, for its modern classic cuisine, or the Dining Room, for its French-Asian menu. They're always doing different things and striving for really high levels of quality. We measure ourselves against them, and they encourage us. In part, we go to reassure ourselves that we're doing the right thing, that we're working hard and making good food. (See also p. 52.)

SOTO
3330 Piedmont Road N.E., Atlanta
(404) 233-2005

The chef-owner of this Japanese restaurant, Sotohiro Kosugi, runs it at an extraordinarily high seventy percent food cost, which should say it all. If you can't appreciate that, go home. He's an incredible Japanese sushi chef; he likes to experiment. My favorite thing on his menu now is raw squid with black truffles. It's really incredible, and so is his *matsutake* custard. Also, we always like his spicy tuna tartare. We usually drink beer here, but he has a good selection of cold sake, too. (See also p. 52.)

ZOCALO MEXICAN TAQUERIA
187 10th Street (at Piedmont), Atlanta
(404) 249-7576
We love the *anchos rellenos* at Zocalo, which are *ancho* chiles stuffed with a meat-and-fruit filling and served in a walnut sauce. They're incredible. All their desserts are great—they make a custard called *cajeta* out of burnt goat's milk. They serve tequila upside-down in a glass of beer, and the owner has dozens of really cool tequilas and mescals that she brings back from Mexico.

Clifford Harrison and Anne Quatrano

BACCHANALIA
1198 Howell Mill Road
Atlanta, GA 30318
Phone: (404) 365-0410
Fax: (404) 365-8020

FLOATAWAY CAFÉ
1123 Zonolite Road
Atlanta, GA 30306
Phone: (404) 892-1414
Fax: (404) 892-8833

Guenter Seeger

SEEGER'S

111 W. Paces Ferry Road

Atlanta, GA 30305

Phone: (404) 846-9779

Fax: (404) 846-9217

www.seegers.com

GUENTER SEEGER is chef-owner of Seeger's. When he was growing up in Germany, his parents ran a wholesale fruit-and-vegetable business; he began his first culinary apprenticeship at age thirteen. He earned a Michelin star for a restaurant he opened in Germany before being lured to the United States, where he eventually landed at the Dining Room in the Atlanta Ritz-Carlton. Seeger's earned four stars from the *Atlanta Journal-Constitution* and was named *Esquire*'s 1998 Restaurant of the Year. In 1996, Seeger won the James Beard Award as Best Chef: Southeast. He was one of the founders of the Georgia Organic Growers Association.

MY FOOD I have been striving for simplicity in my work for years, and I continue to search for better and better products. Simplicity is really not that simple! We like to be very honest with everything at Seeger's, from food to décor. There is no hiding, and it's not a big show. We don't like to be more than what we are. We have tasting menus and a pretty big wine program, with over eight hundred bottles hand-picked by me and my sommelier. We write a new menu every day. That way, we stay challenged!

GUENTER'S PICKS

ANDALUZ BAR DE TAPAS

903 Peachtree Street, N.E., Atlanta

(404) 875-7013

This is the only restaurant in Atlanta serving authentic tapas [classic Spanish appetizers, such as prawns with garlic and parsley, Serrano ham with tomato slices, and paella]. They have a chef from Spain [José María "Pepe" Lindres of Barcelona, who was brought in by proprietor Gladys Parada, who formerly worked at Seeger's].

FLOATAWAY CAFÉ

1123 Zonolite Road, Atlanta

(404) 892-1414

I like to go to the Floataway Café for the simple, Italian-inspired food cooked by Anne Quatrano and Clifford Harrison. (See also p. 51.)

MAJOR MCGILL'S FISH HOUSE

5603 Main Street, Flowery Branch

(770) 967-6001

This is an unusual restaurant where I go when I'm in the mood for a weird restaurant experience. It's right out of the 1960s. They serve beautiful smoked trout, but I have to take the strawberry garnish off. I drink Dom Perignon along with it. That's it. I've had the fried smelt there, which is also pretty weird.

SOTO

3330 Piedmont Road N.E., Atlanta

(404) 233-2005

At this small, unpretentious Japanese restaurant, the chef, Sotohiro Ko-sugi, buys only the best-quality ingredients. He does a fantastic job with everything—from classics like sashimi and sushi to daily specials like sea bass carpaccio with black truffles. Go for the food, not the service or the décor. (See also p. 51.)

"When we've got some dough to spend, we go to Seeger's."

CLIFFORD HARRISON AND ANNE QUATRANO

BACCHANALIA AND FLOATAWAY CAFÉ

LOCAL HIGHLIGHTS

COFFEE

ONE WORLD CAFÉ

904 S. Charles Street (at E. Hamburg Street), Baltimore
(410) 234-0235

"It's a super-funky coffeehouse with an all-vegetarian menu and great coffee."

—JERRY PELLEGRINO, CORKS

CRAB CAKES

PIERPOINT

1822 Aliceanna Street, Baltimore
(410) 675-2080

"Chef-owner Nancy Longo's smoked crab cakes are out of this world!"

—JERRY PELLEGRINO, CORKS

PRIME RIB

1101 N. Calvert Street, Baltimore
(410) 539-1804

"Their crab cakes defy gravity, as they contain next to no filler."

—JERRY PELLEGRINO, CORKS

SCOTCH

BIRDS OF A FEATHER

1712 Aliceanna Street, Baltimore
(410) 675-8466

"This place [has a 'divey' atmosphere and] carries a nice selection of [dozens of] Scotches."

—JERRY PELLEGRINO, CORKS

SUSHI

MATSURI

1105 S. Charles Street, Baltimore
(410) 752-8561

NICHIBAN

1035 S. Charles Street, Baltimore
(410) 837-0818

"They serve some of the best sushi in the city."

—JERRY PELLEGRINO, CORKS

HAMBURGER

KOOPER'S TAVERN

1702 Thames Street, Baltimore
(410) 563-5423

"They have one of the best burgers in town."

—JERRY PELLEGRINO, CORKS

MOTHER'S FEDERAL HILL GRILLE

1113 S. Charles Street, Baltimore
(410) 244-8686

"This hangout for young professionals also serves a great hamburger."

—JERRY PELLEGRINO, CORKS

"Maryland crab is ubiquitous. We serve a lot of soft-shell crabs, which are sweet and rich. We like to serve them on salad greens with an Old Bay—seasoned mayonnaise. I like a Sauvignon Blanc with soft-shell crabs. There is a new one from Santa Barbara called Bander, which they call a natural. It is a big, full-blown, barrel-fermented Sauvignon but still maintains a grassy herbaciousness that is great with the soft-shells. Rockfish is the local indigenous fish, which runs in the spring and fall. I don't think you will find it much beyond Baltimore. It is a firm, white flaky fish that is a little rich and pairs well with beurre blanc or corn. It goes well with a big-mouth wine, like a Chardonnay."

JERRY PELLEGRINO   CORKS

Jerry Pellegrino

CORKS

1026 S. Charles Street
Baltimore, MD 21230
Phone: (410) 752-3810
Fax: (410) 752-0639
www.corksrestaurant.com

Jerry Pellegrino is the chef-partner, with Joel Shalowitz, of Corks in Baltimore. An alumnus of Johns Hopkins University, Pellegrino was previously a Ph.D. candidate before becoming chef of Corks, which *Baltimore* magazine has cited as one of the city's best restaurants since its opening in 1997. *Baltimore* magazine also gave Corks its Best Wine List award for 1999.

MY FOOD Everything I like to do revolves around wine. When we put the menu together, the dish usually starts out with a bottle of wine. If I wanted to drink a bottle of Pinot Noir, what would I eat with it? Each entrée is paired with a suggested wine. As we put together a plate of food, we try to put all the flavors that are going to be in the wine on the plate. Since we are very wine-sensitive, we use very few foods that are high in acid. We use verjus instead of vinegar. We did a wine dinner with David Lett of Eyrie Vineyards, and he came up afterward and thanked us for not doing a salad course. He said, "I spend most of my life trying not to make vinegar!"

JERRY'S PICKS

CHARLESTON

1000 Lancaster Street
(at Central Street), Baltimore
(410) 332-7373

Chef Cindy Wolf, who co-owns Charleston with her husband, Tony Foreman, describes her cuisine as "low-country cooking"—with dishes like shrimp with creamy grits, and a benne-seed-encrusted buttermilk chicken. Other dishes on their menu are more classic, like rack of lamb and bacon-wrapped filet mignon. They are one of the only restaurants with a cheese cart, which Tony does a great job with, and they have a great wine list. (See also p. 55.)

MARIA D'S

1022 Light Street, Baltimore
(410) 727-5430

They have the best gyro platter in the city, which they serve with a great yogurt dressing and the best fries, made from scratch. They also make a really good pizza.

OBELISK

2029 P Street N.W., Washington, DC
(202) 872-1180

Baltimore is less than an hour from Washington, DC. Obelisk serves upper-end Italian cuisine and its fixed-price, four-course menu, with typically three options per course, is worth the drive. Everything here is made in-house, including the breads and the pastas. (See also p. 287.)

TEN-O-SIX

1006 Light Street, Baltimore
(410) 528-2146

They serve a Thai-American menu. I stick to the Thai offerings, which are so much better. Their Thai duck with basil sauce is to die for! The breast is crispy, and the leg is like a confit. They also have a great lobster spring roll, served with a sweet-and-sour sauce. I usually drink a local Clipper City Pilsner when I'm here.

VESPA

1117-21 S. Charles Street, Baltimore
(410) 385-0355

Vespa, an informal Italian restaurant and wine bar, is just up the street from us, and has the best antipasto plate: fresh mozzarella, prosciutto, roasted garlic cloves, and frittata, served with bread. I like it with a Monsanto Chianti.

CINDY WOLF is executive chef and owner of Charleston, which has won a *Wine Spectator* Award of Excellence and is one of Baltimore's most critically acclaimed restaurants. *Baltimore* magazine gave the restaurant its Best Service award in 1999. Cindy is a 1987 graduate of the Culinary Institute of America.

Cindy Wolf

CHARLESTON

1000 Lancaster Street
Baltimore, MD 21202
Phone: (410) 332-7373
www.charlestonrestaurant.com

MY FOOD My food is American—based on classical French cuisine but inspired by the traditional and modern foods of the American Southeast. We do spins on classic or local dishes from the South, such as shrimp and grits. It's a breakfast dish in the South, but we serve it at night. I feel we update southern dishes. We make our own corn bread, biscuits, and baguettes. We do a baguette because I hate not having bread to mop up my sauce! We get products, including fish, from down south, and I get squab, pheasant, and quail from South Carolina. Our daily menu changes constantly except for the few dishes we can't take off.

CINDY'S PICKS

BANJARA

1017 S. Charles Street, Baltimore
(410) 962 1554

I love Indian food. Banjara is a pretty restaurant, and it's decorated with things from India. I like the chicken *tikka masala* and the mulligatawny soup. They have a sampler appetizer plate that is always fun if you are bringing someone new to the restaurant. I have even taken my cooks there for a fun meal! It is a relatively inexpensive restaurant, and very different from what I do.

B.O.P.

800 S. Broadway, Baltimore
(410) 563-1600

For pizza, I like to go to B.O.P., which stands for "brick oven pizza." They do a pizza with several different types of cheese, and another with gorgonzola and fresh tomatoes. You can also bring your own wine here.

CORKS

1026 S. Charles Street, Baltimore
(410) 752 3810

I like the way Jerry Pellegrino experiments with food. You can tell that he is having fun in his kitchen! I know there will always be something interesting on the menu at Corks. (See also p. 54.)

JIMMY'S

801 S. Broadway (at Lancaster Street), Baltimore
(410) 327-3273

Julia Child ate here when she was in Baltimore recently. While the diner serves its breakfast, lunch, and dinner menu all day, having breakfast here is a casual Baltimore tradition. Two eggs, two hotcakes, coffee, and a choice of breakfast meat will set you back only about four dollars!

TAMBER'S NIFTY FIFTIES DINER

3327 St. Paul Street, Baltimore
(410) 243-0383

It's a real American diner where you can get a great malted and a burger. And, believe it or not, they also serve Indian food.

BOSTON

"If you come to New England, you should not miss the seafood: the Wellfleet oysters, littleneck clams, and lobster."

PAUL O'CONNELL

CHEZ HENRI

CHEESE

FORMAGGIO KITCHEN

244 Huron Avenue, Cambridge
(617) 354-4750

"I don't crave sweets; I crave cheese. This is one of the best cheese stores in America. The owner finds all kinds of people making [hundreds of] cheeses outside the United States, like this woman who lives at the top of a hill in some village who's ninety years old and has been making cheese for about the last eighty of those."

—TODD ENGLISH, FIGS AND OLIVES

COFFEE

1369 COFFEE HOUSE

1369 Cambridge Street (at Inman Street), Cambridge
(617) 576-1369

"One of the best spots in town for coffee. They also serve soups, salads, and sandwiches at lunch, and have outdoor tables during the summer."

—CHRIS SCHLESINGER, EAST COAST GRILL

CHINATOWN

SHANGHAI CAFÉ

232 Tremont Street, Boston
(617) 338-8686

"I always like the dry-fried chow fun noodles and the pea pod tendrils with garlic."

—SUSAN REGIS, BIBA

PEACH FARM

4 Tyler Street, Boston
(617) 482-3332

"I like to go here for Singapore curry noodles. I also love pork chops marinated in a spicy dry rub, then wok-fried and mixed with spicy squid and lots of scallions. That dish is to die for! It is killer. Lydia Shire introduced me to it."

—SUSAN REGIS, BIBA

CLAM CHOWDER

LEGAL SEA FOODS

Multiple locations, including:
26 Park Plaza, Boston
(617) 426-4444

"Their clam chowder is most consistently the best."

—TODD ENGLISH, FIGS AND OLIVES, AND PAUL O'CONNELL, CHEZ HENRI

BARBECUE

JAKE'S BOSS BARBECUE

3492 Washington Street, Jamaica Plain
(617) 983-3701

"His beef brisket is the best I've ever had."

—CHRIS SCHLESINGER, EAST COAST GRILL

BREAKFAST

CHARLIE'S SANDWICH SHOPPE

429 Columbus Avenue
(at Holyoke Street), Boston
(617) 536-7669
Open for breakfast and lunch only.

"For the pancakes and omelets."

—TODD ENGLISH, FIGS AND OLIVES

Fried clam plate at Woodman's

DIM SUM

CHINA PEARL RESTAURANT

9 Tyler Street, Boston (Chinatown)
(617) 426-4338

"The best dim sum in Boston."

—LYDIA SHIRE, BIBA AND PIGNOLI

"I like going here for dim sum on Sundays. I also crave spicy-hot Chinese food, and this is where I go to find it. China Pearl is like a big Hong Kong–style restaurant."

—CHRIS SCHLESINGER, EAST COAST GRILL

FRIED CLAMS

WOODMAN'S

121 Main Street (Route 133), Essex
(978) 768-6451 or (800) 649-1773

"I usually go every year— it's a great New England experience."

—TODD ENGLISH, FIGS AND OLIVES

"Their fried clams are unbelievable!"

—GEORGE GERMON AND JOHANNE KILLEEN, AL FORNO

"This is where they invented fried clams. It has picnic tables and is great after the beach. To me it is a real American restaurant. The clams are caught in the next town over and are super fresh. They also have the best fish and chips."

—PAUL O'CONNELL, CHEZ HENRI

"They have the most amazing fried clams."

—CHRIS SCHLESINGER, EAST COAST GRILL

HAMBURGER

CHARLIE'S SANDWICH SHOPPE

429 Columbus Avenue
(at Holyoke Street), Boston
(617) 536-7669

"A good, greasy burger."

—TODD ENGLISH, FIGS AND OLIVES

"Charlie's has a good hamburger. I like mine extra rare with bacon—no cheese— and lots of Worcestershire."

—LYDIA SHIRE, BIBA AND PIGNOLI

MR. BARTLEY'S BURGER COTTAGE

1246 Massachusetts Avenue, Cambridge
(617) 354-6559

"This place is a classic! It has all this political stuff on the walls. Get a burger, and fries or onion rings. I like bacon and cheddar cheese on my burger."

—SUSAN REGIS, BIBA

HOT DOGS

BOSTON SPEED'S

A stand in Newmarket Square (Boston's wholesale food district); located parallel to Massachusetts Avenue, right below Theodore Glynn Way, Roxbury. There's no telephone number, and no way to know for certain whether it's open—you gotta take your chances.

"They're legendary, they're good, and they're huge—possibly the world's biggest hot dogs."

—CHRIS SCHLESINGER, EAST COAST GRILL

ICE CREAM

CHRISTINA'S ICE CREAM

1255 Cambridge Street, Cambridge (617) 492-7021

"I especially like their mint chocolate chip ice cream."

—CHRIS SCHLESINGER, EAST COAST GRILL

ITALIAN

TERRAMIA RISTORANTE

98 Salem Street, Boston (North End) (617) 523-3112

"They have great antipasti, pastas, and gnocchi. Sometimes the chef, Mario, will do salt cod fritters, or homemade gnocchi baked in a crock with tomato sauce or gorgonzola cream with walnuts. He also makes a great veal chop with fresh porcini mushrooms."

—PAUL O'CONNELL, CHEZ HENRI

LOBSTER

THE BARKING CRAB RESTAURANT

88 Sleeper Street, Boston (617) 426-2722

"When you visit Boston, you should have lobster. In the summer, go to the Barking Crab and sit near the water."

—SUSAN REGIS, BIBA

ANTHONY'S PIER 4 RESTAURANT

140 Northern Avenue, Boston (617) 423-6363

"Anthony Athanas, the owner, is in his eighties, and he's still there seven days a week. When you go in, he knows you right away. I go with my husband, Uriel, and my nine-year-old son, Alex, who loves their popovers. I order a male lobster, because I like a lot of tomalley [lobster liver]. Some people prefer females because they say the meat is more tender, but I eat lobster as much for the tomalley as the meat. They also have one of the best wine lists in Boston. It's comfortable, it's easy, and it's great."

—LYDIA SHIRE, BIBA AND PIGNOLI

"[Boston chef] Jody Adams had her birthday party here this year, and we had a great meal. The owner, Anthony Athanas, has been in the restaurant business a long time, and he's at the door every night. It's inspiring to see dedication and professionalism like that. And the lobster was really good, too!"

—CHRIS SCHLESINGER, EAST COAST GRILL

POPOVERS

ANTHONY'S PIER 4 RESTAURANT

140 Northern Avenue, Boston (617) 423-6363

"Anthony's serves great popovers—the waitresses in the frilly aprons keep coming around with fresh batches of them. I love it."

—TODD ENGLISH, FIGS AND OLIVES

LUNCH

LOCKE-OBER

3 Winter Place, Boston (617) 542-1340
Opened in 1875 and still serving a menu of classics ranging from Oysters Rockefeller to Baked Alaska, this weekday-only power lunch spot didn't admit women until 1970.

"For lunch, never for dinner. It's the most beautiful as well as one of the oldest restaurants in Boston. I always order lobster stew, and I always have a martini."

—LYDIA SHIRE, BIBA AND PIGNOLI

PIZZA

EMMA'S PIZZA

40 Hampshire Street, Cambridge
(617) 864-8534

"I love the pizza here—it's a thin-crust pizza offering a choice of sauces, cheeses, and vegetable toppings. But you've got to get one before they close at eight P.M."

—SUSAN REGIS, BIBA

PIZZERIA REGINA

Multiple locations, including:
11 Thatcher Street, Boston
(the original)
(617) 227-0765

"The original Regina's still serves really good thin-crust pizza."

—TODD ENGLISH, FIGS AND OLIVES

"I still think their pizza is the best. I like it because it's oily. Some people order it with extra oil."

—LYDIA SHIRE, BIBA AND PIGNOLI

RAW BAR

LEGAL SEA FOODS

Multiple locations, including:
33 Columbus Avenue
(Park Plaza), Boston
(617) 426-4444

"*They have a great raw bar.*"
—GEORGE GERMON AND JOHANNE KILLEEN, AL
FORNO (PROVIDENCE)

"*I like going to Legal for the oysters!*"
—CHRIS SCHLESINGER, EAST COAST GRILL

RICE BALLS

UMBERTO GALLERIA

289 Hanover Street, Boston
(North End)
(617) 227-5709

"*Rice balls—with ground meat, tomatoes, and peas in the middle—when done right, are a thing of beauty. These are crispy on the outside, with the soft rice oozing mozzarella and the well-flavored meat in the middle. Afterward, go across the street for an espresso at Café Della Sport.*"
—PAUL O'CONNELL, CHEZ HENRI

SANDWICH

UMBERTO GALLERIA

289 Hanover Street, Boston
(North End) (617) 227-5709

"*They have great sandwiches, and the arancine [rice balls] are amazing.*"
—TODD ENGLISH, FIGS AND OLIVES

SAUSAGES

SANTARPIO'S

111 Chelsea Street, Boston (near the airport) (617) 567-9871

"*I like to get the grilled sausages and a Budweiser. And, if you want, I am sure you can bet on a dog or a horse race while you are here.*"
—PAUL O'CONNELL, CHEZ HENRI

"*They say the pizza is great, but I always get the lamb skewer and pork sausage combo with extra peppers. They grill over coals. It's hilarious—they don't serve vegetables, and there's a bunch of old men waiting tables.*"
—CHRIS SCHLESINGER, EAST COAST GRILL

STEAK

GRILL 23 AND BAR

161 Berkeley Street, Boston
(617) 542-2255

CAPITAL GRILLE

359 Newbury Street, Boston
(617) 262-8900

"*Grill 23 and Capital Grille serve my two favorite steaks in Boston. Ordering a sirloin is the only way to go. I drink whatever big red wine my wallet allows—and I especially like an American Pinot Noir, like Jed Steel's.*"
—SUSAN REGIS, BIBA

SUSHI

GINZA

16 Hudson Street (at Kneeland Street),
Boston (Chinatown)
(617) 338-2261

"The best sushi in Boston."

—TODD ENGLISH, FIGS AND OLIVES; LYDIA
SHIRE, BIBA AND PIGNOLI

*"I like the eel, which is a
little sweet. I'll also have
the yellowtail and salmon
skin rolls. I like to have a
a Sapporo beer with my
sushi here."*

—SUSAN REGIS, BIBA

SWEETS

NEW PARIS BAKERY

10 Cypress Street, Brookline
(617) 566-0929

*"The coffee éclair here is
great."*

—LYDIA SHIRE, BIBA AND PIGNOLI

TURKISH

SULTAN'S KITCHEN

72 Broad Street (at Milk Street),
Boston
(617) 338-7819

*"This casual, lunch-only
cafeteria-style restaurant,
with tables downstairs and
upstairs, is one of the places
we miss most since we
moved from Boston to New
York. Chef-owner and
cookbook author Ozcan
Ozan cooks some of the
finest Turkish cuisine we've
ever tasted. His soups are
amazing."*

—AUTHORS ANDREW DORNENBURG AND
KAREN PAGE

Jim Becker

RAUXA CAVA BAR AND RESTAURANT
70 Union Square
Somerville, MA 02143
Phone: (617) 623-9939
Fax: (617) 623-4699

JIM BECKER is chef-owner of Rauxa. Becker spent many years studying Chinese language and culture before pursuing a culinary career. His culinary training included three years with Lydia Shire at Biba. Rauxa has been recognized as one of the Top Five Hot Restaurants in Massachusetts by the Phantom Gourmet.

MY FOOD Diners should understand that this restaurant is not a tapas bar. I'm cooking from a really specific region in Spain—Catalonia—and someone who's thinking Spain is probably going to be disappointed. Catalans don't eat tapas. There are tapas bars in Barcelona, but they're sort of an exotic experience for natives of Barcelona—mostly they are for tourists.

I'm trying to educate the public about Spanish food—it's very regional, as much so as Italian food, although there are common threads among the regions. There are always authentic Catalan dishes on the menu, as well as dishes that we create but have been inspired by Catalan ingredients and techniques. My food probably has more in common with southern France than with the rest of Spain. People will have a better experience if they order an appetizer and an entrée than if they approach the meal as tapas and try to order several appetizers.

JIM'S PICKS

B-SIDE LOUNGE
92 Hampshire Street, Cambridge
(617) 354-0766
B-Side Lounge is basically where all the chefs go to eat when they get off work. You run into people there, and it's a nice place to eat and drink beer. It's crowded and noisy, like an upscale dive. They have incredible oyster po' boys. They change the menu regularly and have some great dishes, but since I always get the po' boy, I usually ignore the rest of the menu.

CASABLANCA
40 Brattle Street, Cambridge
(617) 876-0999
I like going to Casablanca. Ana Sortun, the chef, is a friend of mine, and I love her food. I think we have similar styles of presentation and cooking—rustic and Mediterranean. Ana's gone off in a direction that's a Middle Eastern—Turkish—Moroccan sort of angle, and she changes the menu frequently. I love her short ribs, which she flavors with star anise, and her really great scallop pizza. I eat here a lot.

Jim Becker and Ana Sortun at Casablanca

CHINA PEARL RESTAURANT

9 Tyler Street, Boston (Chinatown)
(617) 426-4338

I go to China Pearl for dim sum whenever I can. It's got that sleazy seventies look to it—I always feel like John Travolta when I walk in there. As the carts go by, I pull the waiters over and ask them to open each steamer so I can see what's inside. For someone who has never had dim sum before, the safest things are the dumplings, because 99 percent of them are a combination of pork—or pork fat—and seafood. A lot of vegetarians don't realize that pork fat is frequently used as a binder in the seafood dumplings—it gives them a nice flavor. There are very few really vegetarian foods when it comes to dim sum. If someone hasn't eaten dim sum before, I would stay away from the chicken feet; they're an acquired taste. Usually in dim sum places there are stations where you can go up and get things like clams in black bean sauce, or more exotic things like coagulated duck blood, which I don't dislike, but I wouldn't go out of my way to order either. I recommend that people simply look closely at things, because the language barrier makes it difficult to get most of your questions answered.

JP SEAFOOD CAFÉ

730 Centre Street, Jamaica Plain
(a few miles southwest of Boston)
(617) 983-5177

When I eat out, I like to satisfy cravings that I can't satisfy at Rauxa. When I crave sushi, I usually go to JP Seafood, because their sushi is incredible. I order à la carte off the sushi list—spicy tuna, crispy salmon skin *maki*, soft-shell crab *maki*. I always order the flying fish roe and sea urchin.

KING FUNG GARDEN

74 Kneeland Street, Boston
(Chinatown) (617) 357-5262

King Fung Garden is run by a guy from Shanghai who makes homemade Shanghai-style noodles. It's a very rustic, square-cut noodle that he stir-fries with pork and cabbage, and it's delicious. They also have great hot-and-sour soup, and great Peking ravioli. You can have a feast for four or five dollars per person. In the winter, he does a really great Mongolian hot pot, which is a pot of hot broth in which you cook your own food, so it's a place to go with a group of people. I think this is the restaurant where Lydia Shire, of Biba, learned how to make scallion pancakes, so, as you can imagine, they're great.

LUMIERE

1293 Washington Street, West Newton
(617) 244-9199

I like to check out all the new restaurants. One place that I really like right now is Lumiere. It has an upscale bistro feel to it. I find chef Michael Levitan's food really simple, focused, and delicious. He does a great halibut—right now he does it with wild mushrooms and parsley oil—and everything is perfectly cooked.

TABERNA DE HARO

999 Beacon Street, Brookline
(617) 277-8272

This is a little tapas place where the food is very traditional and authentic. They have lamb kebab with Moorish spices; a Catalan *coca*, which is like a pizza with caramelized onions and olives; and a wood-grilled chicken served over homemade potato chips. They also have plates of fresh and canned anchovies. They have a really nice wine and sherry list. I drink *fino* sherry when I'm here. He's from Spain, and she's American—they actually did American food in Spain, and now they're doing Spanish food in Boston!

TODD ENGLISH is executive chef of the Olives Group, whose restaurants include the original Olives and Figs, both in Charlestown, as well as multiple Olives and Figs restaurants around the country. He also owns Miramar at the Inn in Westport, Connecticut, and King Fish Hall in Boston. English was the first recipient of the Robert Mondavi Award for Culinary Excellence. In 1991, he won the James Beard Award as Rising Star Chef of the Year, and in 1994, he won the James Beard Award as Best Chef: Northeast. He is the author of two cookbooks: *The Figs Table* and *The Olives Table*.

Todd English

MY FOOD Somebody might come here with the expectations of a three-star dining experience, when really it is much different. When I go out to dinner, I don't want to put a jacket and tie on. I want to go in my jeans, sit down in a fun environment, hang out, and have a really great food experience without the stuffiness. That's what we do here. We don't have tablecloths or take reservations, and yet we strive for three-star Mediterranean country-style food. That's always been my philosophy.

FIGS

Multiple locations, including the original at: 67 Main Street Charlestown, MA 02129 Phone: (617) 242-2229 Fax: (617) 242-1333

OLIVES

Multiple locations, including the original at: 10 City Square Charlestown, MA 02129 Phone: (617) 242-1999

TODD'S PICKS

BIBA

272 Boylston Street, Boston
(617) 426-7878

Lydia Shire, the chef-owner, has got one of the greater imaginations that I know. I always see something interesting at Biba. Her lobster pizza is always available, but other than that, the menu is hardly ever the same. No matter—anything you order is likely to be great. (See also pp. 69, 71.)

DALI RESTAURANT AND TAPAS BAR

415 Washington Street, Somerville
(617) 661-3254

Dali is a great, festive place to go in Boston. It's a very cool place for tapas—they offer more than forty varieties, as well as signature dishes such as salt-baked whole fish. They serve sangria, and also have an extensive Spanish wine list. (See also p. 69.)

EAST OCEAN CITY

25-29 Beach Street, Boston (Chinatown)
(617) 542-2504

East Ocean City is one of those places where I don't order off the menu—I order whatever they want me to have. They do one of the most inspired, amazing dishes I've ever had, which they make with geoduck clams—those really big and ugly honkers. They look like steamer clams, but they're about thirty times bigger. They have them in the tanks there. They slice them paper-thin and cook them in hot sesame oil and ginger. It's insane. I always have a good time here.

GINZA

16 Hudson Street, Boston
(617) 338-2261

I think Ginza has the most inspired sushi around. It's owned by Koreans, and they do a Korean-influenced tartare that is awesome. I tend to go for the spicy stuff, and they do this thing with chopped salmon that is nice and spicy. All my kids love sushi, big time, and they love the tuna *maki* here. (See also p. 60.)

INDIAN SAMRAAT RESTAURANT

51 Massachusetts Avenue, Boston
(617) 247-0718

They make this great red curry chicken that is basically a tandoori chicken. Even my kids will ask, "Dad, can we order that red chicken?" They also serve a stew of curried spinach, chickpeas, and potatoes that is also great. And I love their stuffed *naan*—last night, we had an onion and fenugreek *naan*. We often do a big spread there on Sundays.

"I think Todd is an over-the-top kind of guy who is a great cook and deserves all credit he gets."

LYDIA SHIRE

BIBA AND PIGNOLI (BOSTON)

HAMERSLEY'S BISTRO

553 Tremont Street
Boston, MA 02116
Phone: (617) 423-2700
Fax: (617) 423-7710
www.hamersleysbistro.com

Gordon Hamersley

GORDON HAMERSLEY is chef-owner of Hamersley's Bistro in Boston. Hamersley's has been voted to *Boston* magazine's Hall of Fame by the magazine's readers and is continually cited as one of Boston's top three restaurants in both the *ZagatSurvey* and the *Gourmet* Reader's Poll. In 1988, Gordon Hamersley was voted one of *Food & Wine*'s Ten Best New Chefs. He won the 1995 James Beard Award as Best Chef: Northeast.

MY FOOD We have evolved over time, and will hopefully continue to evolve, but we haven't really changed our original plan: to present people with simple, well-cooked food inspired by the bistros of France and the trattorias of Italy. If you let us do what we do well, then you'll have a great time. Let the waiter be your guide, because that waiter has eaten everything that we cook and tasted every wine on the list. His or her job is to help you experience the restaurant the way it was intended. The food is simple, elegant, well cooked, and fun. It's relatively down to earth, and it's just simple and it's good.

We always have a small tasting menu available, and we can make a more elaborate one if that's what you want. Specials are a good way to go—they give us an opportunity to showcase something new, or bring back something that people have loved. Recently we did a beef special with a simple mashed potato cake, and a wild mushroom and red wine sauce. Fiona [Hamersley, Gordon's wife and the restaurant's co-owner] works very hard to make sure that we have some great wines. For instance, if you were going to have that beef special, you could have a good barnyard-y Bandol to go with it. We do those things well.

Sometimes I think to myself, "The Cape scallops are coming in—they will be little nuggets of gold, that's what we want to sell, let's take those and use them when they're fresh and perfect and at their best." I don't want to fool around with things too much. In this day and age when you can get anything, any way you want it, I think that we should celebrate the things that are still seasonal and only last for a few fleeting moments. Just finding those things that you can only get once a year—morels in the spring, chanterelles in the fall—roots the restaurant to the rest of nature.

"We recently had a wonderful meal at Hamersley's—and Gordon Hamersley wasn't even there! It was a great compliment to Gordon that his staff did such a fabulous job. Everything was done beautifully. There was a liveliness to the food that was just dynamite. It was an extraordinary meal."

JOHANNE KILLEEN
AND GEORGE GERMON
AL FORNO (PROVIDENCE)

GORDON'S PICKS

BIBA

272 Boylston Street, Boston
(617) 426-7878

I like Biba a lot. From a culinary point of view, Lydia Shire and Susan Regis walk the line every night, and I have such great respect for that. I go to Biba when I want to have interesting food that I know is going to be well prepared. I had arguably the best meal I've eaten in America at Biba. We were there one night with Nancy and Jasper White, with whom Lydia used to cook. We sat in the corner, overlooking the Public Garden, and it was snowing—and everything clicked! (See also pp. 69, 71.)

CHARLIE'S SANDWICH SHOPPE

429 Columbus Avenue, Boston
(617) 536-7669

This is more than a diner; it's a community meeting place. Arthur Manjourides, who runs it, is a great guy. I always have good meals here, whether I order the meat loaf, the hot turkey sandwich, or two eggs with toast. I like to sit at the counter and watch the way they work, because I always learn something. (See also pp. 56, 57, and photo on p. 66.)

GORDON HAMERSLEY ON
One of the Best Meals of His Life

I MOVED TO FRANCE IN 1983 AND HAD A TRANSFORMATIVE MEAL AT Alain Chapel's [eponymous Michelin three-star] restaurant. Clearly the food was spectacular, but the thing that was amazing to me as a budding chef was the balance of the meal, and the balance of everything going on. You know how sometimes you go into a restaurant and the food is great, but the place looks old and dingy, or the other way around: The place is spectacular, but the food is out of balance somehow? At this restaurant, everything was perfect. It defined for me what I wanted to aspire to when I became a chef.

It was a meal that appeared to have almost happened without trying. Even though you knew that there was a ton of work that went into providing this meal and this service for us, as well as the one hundred and forty other guests there that night, it just seemed so effortless. There was something about it. Everything seemed so natural. It was almost like a Zen experience, in that there were wildflowers on the table, perfect damask linens . . . Everything was clean and it was beautiful, and almost as if they did it without trying. To me, that about defines the perfect meal.

The service was like that as well. People were there when we needed them, and weren't there when we didn't. We sat outside, and usually French gardens are all pretty well manicured, but this one . . . There were herbs in the garden, there were wildflowers, it just seemed so perfect to me. I said to myself, "This is what I want my cooking to be like!" One can never aspire to perfection, but this was about as close as it came for me.

The other word that comes to mind is *graceful*. It had so much grace and dignity about it and it almost took on a personality of its own. I asked our waiter at a certain point, because I was totally in awe of Alain Chapel and his artistry, whether Monsieur Chapel was in the restaurant, and he looked at me and said, "He stepped out of the kitchen for a moment . . ." Of course, that was his way of saying that Monsieur Chapel had the night off, but what a great way of saying it!

EAST COAST GRILL AND RAW BAR

1271 Cambridge Street,
Cambridge (Inman Square)
(617) 491-6568

I really love East Coast Grill. It's always had a warm place in my heart, not just because Chris Schlesinger, the chef, is great, but also because I have so many fond memories of eating there—so many great ribs and oysters. My daughter Sophie's first restaurant experience was there, when she was about three months old. Chris walked up, patted her on the back, and said, "My dear, it's never too soon to get into pork products." If you asked her today what her favorite restaurant is, it would probably be a toss-up between East Coast Grill and New Shanghai—but that's because Chris gives her presents, like twizzle sticks. People come to our restaurant and order the chicken and I get frustrated, thinking, "Can't you order something else?" but I go to East Coast Grill and always order the ribs. I love the way Chris combines simple grilled foods—like big hunks of tuna—with simple salsas, and his raw bar is great. I love his sense of humor. We had our Christmas party there last year, in the Lava Room—it has a gigantic mural of a volcano that explodes every seventeen seconds. There's [Michelin three-star French chef] Alain Chapel and then there's Chris Schlesinger, and there's a lot in between, but they're both great chefs. (See also pp. 58, 69, 70.)

FRANKLIN CAFÉ

278 Shawmut Avenue, Boston
(617) 350-0010

This place is owned by David Dubois and Mo MacLaughlin; Dave is from New York and Mo, the bartender, is from Lowell. They took over an old tavern and turned it into this kind of cool, dark bar, with food. The food is fabulous, and everything is under twelve dollars. When you go there, have the meat loaf. He does great chicken livers, too. It's the kind of place that makes me wish I still drank beer. It's filled with an eclectic array of South Enders, and it's a great place. They play good solid rock-and-roll, and they serve until one A.M., so all the cooks go there when they finish work.

NEW SHANGHAI RESTAURANT

21 Hudson Street, Boston (Chinatown)
(617) 338-6688

We recently went to New Shanghai for my daughter Sophie's birthday. She loves the turnip cake, which is a pastry stuffed with flaked turnip. I think the chef here [C. K. Sau] is probably, by about a thousand times, the most underrated, undiscovered chef in Boston. Nobody really writes about him. We've eaten here with Lydia Shire, Jasper White, Julia Child, and once even with Jacques Pepin.

WOODMAN'S

121 Main Street, Essex
(978) 768-6451

When I want a quintessential New England meal, I'll go to Woodman's in Essex. It's a very simple clam shack. I'll order fried clams, steamed lobster, and cole slaw. (See also p. 57.)

Arthur Manjourides and Gordon Hamersley at Charlie's Sandwich Shoppe

Paul O'Connell

PAUL O'CONNELL is chef-owner of Chez Henri in Cambridge. After studying culinary arts at Johnson and Wales, he landed his first job with Lydia Shire in 1985 before going on to cook with Jasper White, Chris Schlesinger, and Todd English. He opened Providence in Brookline in 1993 (which he closed in 1999) and Chez Henri in Cambridge in 1995. Restaurant critic John Mariani wrote of it in *Esquire*, "Prepare to be dazzled."

CHEZ HENRI
1 Sheppard Street
Cambridge, MA 02138
Phone: (617) 354-8980
Fax: (617) 441-8784

MY FOOD I am trying to run Chez Henri as a place where you can be blown away either by some great dish or by a simple roast chicken. The bar is pretty fun and funky, yet it has some surprises—like a Cuban sandwich, and great wines by the glass. The dining room is a place to come with friends and have a great dinner. I get a kick out of surprising people—we just look like a simple storefront place, but I have high standards, and that comes through.

PAUL'S PICKS

BLUE FIN

1815 Massachusetts Avenue, Cambridge
(617) 497-8022

I eat a lot of Asian food, to try to get the hot flavors that I crave. In Porter Square in Cambridge, there is a little mall and food court with all these tiny Asian restaurants, and these are some of my favorite places there. One shop does soba, one does ramen, and so on. At the ramen noodle place, the dish with ground pork, tons of vegetables, and miso broth is great. It's about six dollars and could feed a family of four! Each restaurant has about twenty seats. There are other types of stores selling everything from perfume to sushi. Blue Fin is the only full-service restaurant in the mall where you can get a beer. I start with kimchi salad, then get fire beef over rice. They also have excellent, and inexpensive, sushi.

CAFÉ MAMI

1815 Massachusetts Avenue, Cambridge
(617) 547-9130

Café Mami is just a counter, but this little Japanese place serves great *katsu* pork and *katsu* chicken with fried eggs on top. It is awesome. They like to brag that they cook their gravy for forty-eight hours. (See also p. 71.)

BLUE ROOM

1 Kendall Square, Cambridge
(617) 494-9034

When I am with Lisa, my wife, I like to go to restaurants whose owners I know—places where there's not a big scene. I like to go to the Blue Room for Sunday brunch. While the food at Blue Room is influenced by cuisines from around the world, chef-owner Steve Johnson uses local ingredients and works with local farmers. It is good, fresh food simply prepared and served in a casual atmosphere. Sometimes when you go out you get experimented on, but Steve's food is tried and true—including roast chicken with rosemary and garlic mashed potatoes, or pork tenderloin with honey and chipotle peppers. You can also get great wines with proper stemware and wine service. And the staff is mature. (See also p. 69, 70.)

EAST COAST GRILL AND RAW BAR

1271 Cambridge Street, Cambridge
(617) 491-6568

I like to go here with the kids because it is loud and I can get good food. I think Chris Schlesinger, the chef-owner, has fun with food. If I get out of work early, I like to sit at the bar here with my bartender and eat oysters. I really like the raw bar, and they also have really good barbecue. (See also pp. 69, 70.)

FLORA

190 Massachusetts Avenue, Arlington
(781) 641-1664

Chef Bob Sargent is an American-food guy, and Flora is one of Lisa's and my favorites for great American food and wines. I was at Flora during August and had a great tomato salad with blue cheese dressing, followed by a roasted *poussin* [baby chicken] done under a brick, whacked into four pieces, and served with some beautiful summer squashes.

SEOUL FOOD

1759 Massachusetts Avenue (between Harvard and Porter Squares), Cambridge
(617) 864-6299

This is a small place with about six Formica tables. It used to be a grocery store called Korean Deli, but I told them to forget about the groceries—which weren't moving anyway—and to just serve their food, which was great! So they did. Now it's called Seoul Food, and they have a little sign taped to the door: "No More Groceries"! I like to have the pork and kimchi soup, and the short ribs. They also have a really interesting fried dumpling stuffed with tofu and vegetables.

**Clara Byun and Paul O'Connell
at Seoul Food**

Susan Regis

susan regis is the executive chef of Biba in Boston. She won the 1998 James Beard Award as Best Chef: Northeast. She was also twice named Best Chef in Boston by the *Improper Bostonian*. She previously cooked at the Beverly Hills Four Seasons Hotel and at Seasons in The Bostonian Hotel.

BIBA
272 Boylston Street
Boston, MA 02116
Phone: (617) 426-7878
Fax: (617) 426-9253

MY FOOD We don't want people to be challenged or scared by our food, but we want to pique their curiosities. The white pumpkin and oyster stew is a good example of a dish that is interesting but not too challenging. It is half oyster stew and half pumpkin soup, and on the side we serve Oysters Casino with crispy garlic, leeks, and bacon. A dish on the other end of the spectrum would be gooseneck sausage with huckleberries served on a rosti parsnip potato—now that's a challenge!

susan's PICKS

BLUE ROOM

1 Kendall Square, Cambridge
(617) 494-9034

It is fun, smart food that is real, yet modern. I had great baby back ribs with hominy the last time that I was here. Chef-owner Steve Johnson also does great work over the fire. (See also pp. 67, 70.)

DALI RESTAURANT AND TAPAS BAR

415 Washington Street, Somerville
(617) 661-3254

Go to this Spanish restaurant for great tapas, such as the baby eels with garlic and the goat cheese with sherry. It is unpretentious and authentically delicious. The vibe there is always buzzing. (See also p. 63.)

EAST COAST GRILL AND RAW BAR

1271 Cambridge Street, Cambridge
(617) 491-6568

East Coast Grill is fun and light-hearted. It doesn't take itself too seriously, yet the food is consistently delicious. I love the oyster bar, which has some of the best oysters in Boston. At the East Coast Grill, you can have great food—anything from seafood to barbecue—and a great time, and not have to analyze everything. And there is something wonderful about that! (See also p. 70.)

EMMA'S PIZZA

40 Hampshire Street, Cambridge
(617) 864-8534

You have to call at four in the afternoon to find out when you can pick up your pizza. It is a thin, Roman-style pizza with meager, delicious toppings, which include caramelized onions, goat cheese, and rosemary sauce. They only do take-out.

OLGA'S CUP AND SAUCER

261 W. Main Road, Little Compton, RI
(401) 635-8650 or (401) 831-6666
Open late June through Labor Day;
then weekends only through
October 31.

Olga's is across the street from Sakonnet Vineyards. It is super funky. Two women run it; they have a bakery and also do pizzas and burritos. One of the women is an artist who does wire sculptures for the cakes. There is a farm right next door, so it is farm-to-oven-to-person in a beautiful, humble, and simple setting. (See also p. 230.)

TRUC

560 Tremont Street, Boston
(617) 338-8070

It has Hayward Wakefield furniture and a great design. The place is cozy and stylish without trying. Chef Amanda Lydon [one of *Food & Wine* magazine's Ten Best New Chefs of 2000] serves basic, classic French bistro food done really well. They have a great hanger steak and *frites*. I also had excellent pork rillettes here.

Chris Schlesinger

**EAST COAST GRILL
AND RAW BAR**

1271 Cambridge Street
(Inman Square)
Cambridge, MA 02139
Phone: (617) 491-6568
Fax: (617) 868-4278

BACK EDDY

1 Bridge Street
Westport, MA 02790
Phone: (508) 636-6500

CHRIS SCHLESINGER is chef-owner of East Coast Grill and Raw Bar in Cambridge and Back Eddy in Westport, MA (see p. 298). His cookbooks include *The Thrill of the Grill* (winner of the 1990 James Beard Cookbook Award); *Salsas, Sambals, Chutneys and Chowchows*; *Big Flavors of the Hot Sun*; *Lettuce in Your Kitchen*; and *License to Grill*. He co-authors a monthly article in the *New York Times* and is a contributing editor to *Saveur*. He also helped found Chefs Collaborative 2000. In 1996, he won the James Beard Award as Best Chef: Northeast.

MY FOOD At East Coast Grill, we do bright, interesting, casual food, with an emphasis on fresh, local ingredients. The atmosphere is fun and lively. Barbecue is one of the things I love and am interested in.

At Back Eddy, we feature local seafood. Bristol County, where we're located, is the largest farming community in Massachusetts, so we serve all fresh, local ingredients. We have boats pull up to our dock and bring us fish, and we feature a couple of local wineries—it's all about local ingredients and products.

CHRIS'S PICKS

FRANK'S STEAK HOUSE

2310 Massachusetts Avenue,
Cambridge
(617) 661-0666
They've got keno—which is like gambling on bingo—and TVs. I like to go down there and order a "sizzling platter": the $13.95 sirloin special with baked potato and salad. It's a straight-up neighborhood place.

BLUE ROOM

1 Kendall Square, Cambridge
(617) 494-9034
Steve Johnson, the chef-owner, goes shopping every day in Chinatown to get his Asian ingredients, and he does a lot of different Asian dishes, such as steamed halibut with spicy black bean sauce. Steve's one of the driving forces

CHRIS'S PICKS

behind the local Chefs Collaborative 2000 chapter, so he has long-standing relationships with a lot of the farmers. He always has super-fresh vegetables, and makes different dishes depending on what's in season. I like his skirt steak. He changes the preparation, but there's always one on the menu. We like to sit at the bar and talk to Reggie, the bartender. (See also pp. 67, 69.)

HANA SUSHI

2372 Massachusetts Avenue, Cambridge
(617) 868-2121
At Hana, they make a special roll for me with toasted salmon skin and cucumbers. The chef knows me, and when I come in, he just makes up a plate of three or four of the freshest things. When striped bass is in season, I like to order that, as well as *toro*, which is the fatty tuna belly. The chef gets some different fish in here—from fluke to a lot of local fish that you don't really see in other sushi restaurants. With my sushi, I generally have beer—whatever's cold, no particular brand.

TUSCAN GRILL

361 Moody Street, Waltham
(617) 891-5486
It's really good, clean Italian food. Jimmy Burke, the chef-owner, travels to Italy a lot. His pastas, such as ricotta ravioli served with a sage-parsley sauce, are great, and he does a lot of roasted meats in addition to dishes like homemade venison sausage and lamb osso buco. Also, he grows a lot of his own produce. I'll go and just order whatever his specials are. If I have friends in town, this is where I bring them.

ALL THE NOODLE SHOPS

at 1815 Massachusetts Avenue (Porter Exchange), Cambridge
In this mall, there are six or seven Asian restaurants—including Café Mami, Ittyo, Masao's, Sapporo Ramen, and Tanpopo—that have a few communal tables. Eating here is a casual lunch situation—you just have a bowl of noodles. I especially like the noodles with fish and vegetables, and the *soba* noodles with toppings. (See also p. 67.)

LYDIA SHIRE is executive chef-owner of Biba and Pignoli. Shire was executive chef at Seasons in Boston and at the Four Seasons in Beverly Hills before returning to Boston to open her own restaurants, where she is known for her innovative and eclectic combinations of flavors. She won the 1992 James Beard Award as Best Chef: Northeast.

Lydia Shire

BIBA

272 Boylston Street
Boston, MA 02116
Phone: (617) 426-7878
Fax: (617) 426-9253

PIGNOLI

79 Park Plaza
Boston, MA 02116
Phone: (617) 338-7500
Fax: (617) 338-7691

MY FOOD My food has been described as "vivid, sensuous, full-flavored food that is exhilarating to eat" as well as "not for the faint of heart" in this day of conservatism. Why? Because I love salt and I love fat—and I could never imagine cooking without them.

"Lydia Shire's food is so weird. For a town that doesn't have stuff that's out there, it's out there. I love it, and I would recommend anything she does."

MARIO BATALI   BABBO, ESCA, AND LUPA (NEW YORK)

CAPITAL GRILLE

Multiple locations, including:
250 Boylston Street, Chestnut Hill
(617) 928-1400

GRILL 23

161 Berkeley Street (Stuart Street),
Boston
(617) 542-2255

I would call myself a carnivore. I love great steaks. At the end of the day, it's probably what makes me happiest! I can't say I ever go out and crave a piece of monkfish, but I do crave a good steak. For that, I'll go to Grill 23 or Capital Grille, which have two of the best. Capital Grille also has this funny salad that I love: a wedge of iceberg lettuce with blue cheese dressing and crumbled bacon. (See also p. 59.)

HAMERSLEY'S BISTRO

553 Tremont Street, Boston
(617) 423-2700

Gordon Hamersley is a true craftsman and a very good cook. I never liked beets until I met Gordon, and

"Lydia's food gets me thinking! I love her lobster pizza, which is made with a lot of lobster and fresh garlic."

BOBBY FLAY

BOLO AND MESA GRILL (NEW YORK)

"The food at Biba is always challenging."

MARK MILLER

COYOTE CAFÉ
(LAS VEGAS AND SANTA FE)

"I crave Lydia Shire's food—her combinations are great. I love that she's got everything on her menu from marrow to foie gras. She's unique."

CHRIS SCHLESINGER

EAST COAST GRILL

now, because of him, I've come to love beets. He likes vinegar. He'll put a little vinegared or pickled thing with another thing, and it's a great balance. Gordon and I find we like a lot of the same things, like salt cod, so we have similar tastes, even though the food we cook is very different. (See also p. 64.)

OLIVES

10 City Square, Charlestown
(617) 242-1999

I think Todd English, the chef, is such a good cook. Talk about over the top! His menu is so big, I'm always amazed—it's almost like a Chinese restaurant, where they have about a hundred dishes on the menu. Some of his classics are great, like his Parmesan custard with pea sauce. There's an excitement to his menus. Todd will put a plate of food down on the table and it will turn Uriel [Lydia's husband] off—he just doesn't like seeing that much food on one plate. I chuckle, because I'm sure there are people out there who would say, "Todd, calm down, you don't have to put so much food on the plate!" But that's his personality—Todd's very generous, and I love that about him. That's what makes Todd Todd. (See also p. 63.)

PEACH FARM

4 Tyler Street (near Beach Street),
Boston (Chinatown)
(617) 482-1116

Peter is the English name of the chef at Peach Farm. He does a dish that is so incredible: little pieces of bone-in pork chops fried with salt-and-pepper squid. I would absolutely kill to get the recipe. It's just delicious, and you have to order it as the salt-and-pepper-squid-with-pork-chop combination. I tend to have a Chardonnay with it. They also have braised pork belly that's delicious, served with preserved vegetables. It's like eating bacon that's been braised—it's very dark and really good.

TORCH

26 Charles Street, Boston (Beacon Hill)
(617) 723-5939

Torch is a pretty new bistro-style restaurant. The chef, Evan [Deluty], is doing a really nice job, and the food is really, really good. It's a little tiny place; the kitchen is the size of a closet, and he doesn't even have a walk-in refrigerator. We had a great foie gras dish there—I love foie gras—and a corn soup with chanterelles and bacon. It was fabulous.

Bar

FRONTERA GRILL AND TOPOLOBAMPO

445 N. Clark Street, Chicago (312) 661-1434

"For the shaken margaritas made with fresh lime juice."

—MARK MILLER, COYOTE CAFÉ (LAS VEGAS AND SANTA FE)

Barbecue

N.N. SMOKEHOUSE

1465 W. Irving Park Road, Chicago
(773) 868-4700

"Larry Tucker does great barbecue. His wife is Filipino, and you can taste that influence in his food, which is interesting. This guy's a real character, a larger-than-life sort of figure. Sometimes for a staff meal, we'll order enough for fifty people and have it delivered."

—CHARLIE TROTTER, CHARLIE TROTTER'S

Brasserie

BRASSERIE JO

59 W. Hubbard Street, Chicago
(312) 595-0800

"The best reasons to go? It's a nice brasserie, and to see [chef] Jean Joho."

—JEAN-GEORGES VONGERICHTEN,
JEAN GEORGES, JO JO, AND VONG (NEW YORK)

Cajun-Creole

HEAVEN ON SEVEN

Multiple locations, including:
The Garland Building, 111 N. Wabash Avenue, 7th floor, Chicago (312) 263-6443
600 N. Michigan Avenue (at Rush Street), 2nd floor, Chicago (312) 280-7774

"Sometimes when we have chefs visiting from out of town, we go to Heaven on Seven. It's something they would never see anywhere else—it's so unique. The original is located on the seventh floor of the Garland Building and looks like a coffee shop but serves Cajun-Creole specialties, such as gumbo and jambalaya."

—CHARLIE TROTTER, CHARLIE TROTTER'S

Cakes

BITTERSWEET

1114 W. Belmont Avenue, Chicago
(773) 929-1100

"Judy Contino is the former pastry chef of Ambria, and creates very refined cakes."

—RICK BAYLESS, FRONTERA GRILL AND TOPOLOBAMPO

Caramel Corn

GARRETT'S POPCORN SHOP

Multiple locations, including:
670 N. Michigan Avenue (between Erie and Huron), Chicago
(312) 944-2630
1-888-4-POPCORN (for deliveries across the United States)
www.garrettpopcorn.com

"You shouldn't leave Chicago without having the caramel popcorn from Garrett's! We send tins of it to friends in other cities."

—RICK BAYLESS, FRONTERA GRILL AND TOPOLOBAMPO

PHOENIX RESTAURANT

2131 S. Archer Avenue (at Wentworth Avenue), Chicago (Chinatown) (312) 328-0848

"The best dim sum in the city."

—RICK BAYLESS, FRONTERA GRILL AND TOPOLOBAMPO

GYRO

GYROS ON THE SPIT

3138 N. Broadway Street (at Briar Street), Chicago (773) 472-1537

"Owner George Sakus works every single day the place is open. He makes his own gyro with lamb and pork, which he marinates, seasons, and grinds. It is not Spam-on-a-spit—this is real gyro. It is the best you will eat in your life, bar none. Billy Joel eats at Spiaggia, and once when I was heading over to his show, I called him to see if he wanted anything. He said, 'Don't be offended, but could you pick up a couple of those gyros?' Whenever I turn someone on to this place, they are hooked! The other thing you should know is that you have to also have fries and an RC Cola. No Coke, no Pepsi: RC. That's what brings the whole experience together."

—PAUL BARTOLOTTA, FORMERLY OF SPIAGGIA

HAMBURGER

JOHNNY ROCKETS

Multiple locations, including: 901 N. Rush Street, Chicago (312) 337-3900

"Since our daughter, Lanie, has come around, we'll go out for hamburgers. I have never been much of a hamburger fan, but I've actually gotten into it lately because my family likes it. Johnny Rockets is this fifties-ish diner chain that Lanie really likes."

—RICK BAYLESS, FRONTERA GRILL AND TOPOLOBAMPO

WILDFIRE

159 W. Erie Street, Chicago (312) 787-9000

"I also like Wildfire. They cook everything either in a wood-burning oven, or on a rotisserie over a wood-burning fire. Their hamburgers are really delicious."

—RICK BAYLESS, FRONTERA GRILL AND TOPOLOBAMPO

HOT DOG

JIM'S HOT DOG STAND

1320 S. Halsted Street (at Maxwell), Chicago
(312) 666-0533

"It's been there since the 1930s, and is open twenty-four hours."

—RICK BAYLESS, FRONTERA GRILL AND TOPOLOBAMPO

HOT FUDGE SUNDAE

MARGIE'S CANDIES

1960 North Western Avenue (near Armitage Avenue), Chicago
(773) 384-1035

"It hasn't changed since the 1920s—it's the funkiest place in the whole world, and they make homemade hot fudge for their sundaes, which are a great special-occasion treat."

—RICK BAYLESS, FRONTERA GRILL AND TOPOLOBAMPO

ITALIAN

DAVE'S ITALIAN KITCHEN

1635 Chicago Avenue (between Church and Davis Streets)
(847) 864-6000
www.davesik.com

"We still love eating at Dave's Italian Kitchen, where Karen waitressed during college and the motto is 'real, healthful homemade food at reasonable prices for over 28 years.' Don't miss Dave Glatt's wonderful spinach-ricotta cheese pie, stuffed zucchini, pastas, and pizzas—or the great bargains on the ever-changing wine list, like a 1992 Ridge Mataro for twenty-nine dollars!"

—AUTHORS ANDREW DORNENBURG AND KAREN PAGE

MEXICAN

MAXWELL STREET MARKET

Canal Street and Roosevelt Road, Chicago

"Go on Sundays, when more than four hundred vendors sell a variety of merchandise year round."

—RICK BAYLESS, FRONTERA GRILL AND TOPOLOBAMPO

"You can eat very typical Mexican street food at the Maxwell Street Market, and it is a lot of fun."

—PAUL BARTOLOTTA, FORMERLY OF SPIAGGIA

ITALIAN BEEF

AL'S NUMBER 1 ITALIAN BEEF

1079 W. Taylor Street (at Eberdon Street), Chicago (312) 226-4017

"You've got to go downtown to the original Al's, founded in 1938, for an Italian beef sandwich—it's similar to a French dip—and afterward go right across the street for lemon ice at Mario's, which is open only during the summer. This is a Chicago must!"

—STEVE CHIAPPETTI, MOSSANT

MR. BEEF

666 N. Orleans Street, Chicago (312) 337-8500

"Mr. Beef is an amazing Italian beef place, and kind of legendary. You have to see it. They have one thing on the menu: Italian beef. If you hesitate for a second about how you want it, they'll crush you. You want to have it 'hot and wet,' which means with peppers and a little jus."

—CHARLIE TROTTER, CHARLIE TROTTER'S

PORTILLO'S HOT DOGS

Multiple locations, including: 100 W. Ontario Street, Chicago (312) 587-8910

"The best Italian beef."

—GALE GAND AND RICK TRAMONTO, BRASSERIE T AND TRU

KOREAN

CHICAGO KALBI KOREAN RESTAURANT

3752 W. Lawrence Avenue (at Hanling Street), Chicago (773) 604-8183

"They bring out the charcoal and have you grill your own beef at the table. They also have beef marinated in egg yolk and sesame oil. It's similar to a tartare, and it's unbelievable."

—PAUL BARTOLOTTA, FORMERLY OF SPIAGGIA

KOREAN RESTAURANT

2659 W. Lawrence Avenue (at Washpenaw Avenue), Chicago (773) 878-2095

"It is great late at night after work. The chap chae [stir-fried vegetables and noodles] is especially good."

—PAUL BARTOLOTTA, FORMERLY OF SPIAGGIA

CHICAGO LOCAL HIGHLIGHTS

PIZZA

GINO'S

Multiple locations, including:
Gino's East of Chicago
2801 N. Lincoln Avenue, Chicago
(773) 327-3737

"*For deep-dish pizza, I used to go to Pizzeria Uno and Pizzeria Due, but they were sold and I don't know how good they are anymore. But Gino's is good.*"

—CHARLIE TROTTER, CHARLIE TROTTER'S

PIZZERIA DUE

619 N. Wabash Avenue, Chicago
(312) 943-2400

"*For the pepperoni and spinach deep-dish pizza. It's a thick, thick pie—we're talking about pizza that is two and a half inches thick. It's like eating a whole loaf of cheese! That's Chicago.*"

—STEVE CHIAPPETTI, MOSSANT

SEAFOOD

BOB CHINN'S CRAB HOUSE

393 S. Milwaukee Avenue, Wheeling
(847) 520-3633

"*When we have people visiting from England, we always take them here. It's enormous! It seats about eight hundred people. The waitresses wear headsets. They have tanks in their kitchen for the lobsters and fish. They post their invoices for the fish every day, so you know how fresh it is and how much they paid for it. It is a simple restaurant, but they have great crab, especially the steamed Dungeness crab. They are also famous for their mai tais—but you need to be careful or you will get ripped on them.*"

—GALE GAND AND RICK TRAMONTO, BRASSERIE T AND TRU

QUICK MEAL

BIG BOWL

Multiple locations, including:
159½ W. Erie Street, Chicago
(312) 787-8297

"*This is a great place to stop for a bite when you're short on time—try one of their Asian specialty noodle dishes.*"

—BRADLEY OGDEN, THE LARK CREEK INN AND ONE MARKET (SAN FRANCISCO)

RIBS

ROBINSON'S NO. 1 RIBS

Multiple locations, including:
655 W. Armitage Avenue, Chicago
(312) 337-1399

"*Robinson's ribs are pretty good, and it's close to our restaurant.*"

—CHARLIE TROTTER, CHARLIE TROTTER'S

PAUL BARTOLOTTA

On Italian Cuisine

If you look at the evolution of Italian food in the United States, there are four pretty distinct waves.

The First Wave

The first wave of Italian immigrants were my grandparents' generation, and most of them were from central-southern Italy. They were leaving hardship in Italy, and after landing in the United States, they created little Italian enclaves. They didn't want to be part of America's melting pot—they wanted to maintain their own traditions. So, we got Little Italys in the big cities. Then they found that the best way to enter society was to open restaurants. The food they made was reminiscent of the old country, but unfortunately they had none of the ingredients or professionalism to do it authentically.

The Second Wave

The second wave was after World War II. That is when people like [New York restaurateurs] Tony May [of San Domenico], Sirio Maccioni [of Le Cirque], and Lidia Bastianich [of Felidia] were landing in America, saying, "This isn't Italian food." They were right; it was Italian-American food.

Many of them were from central or northern Italy and they started opening restaurants. Many had worked on cruise ships and had a high level of professionalism and training. As a result, the restaurants were more sophisticated. The right kinds of products were also beginning to be available. We started thinking of these restaurants as northern Italian and the others as southern. "Cream sauce is north, red sauce is south" was the gross generalization.

The Third Wave

The next wave was the cookbook era. This was when Italian cookbook authors Marcella Hazan and Giuliano Bugialli started to write about Italian cuisine. For the first time, we started hearing about Italian food and regionality. By showing authentic regionality and sparking more interest, we in turn started to be able to get even better products.

The Fourth Wave

The French Revolution created professional restaurateurs, because the chefs who cooked for the rich and nobility had to find work on their own in the 1730s. In Italy that never occurred, so the food remained local and regional, which is what trattoria cooking is all about. As a result, we didn't see the development of professional Italian kitchens until recently. The new wave of Italian kitchens is the wave of the professionally trained chef.

The future will involve applying modern techniques to classic recipes and current products so that the flavors and spirit are never lost.

Paul Bartolotta

FORMERLY OF **SPIAGGIA**

980 N. Michigan Avenue,
2nd floor
Chicago, IL 60611
Phone: (312) 280-2750
Fax: (312) 943-8560

PAUL BARTOLOTTA is the former chef of Spiaggia (whose kitchen is now headed by Tony Mantuano). Bartolotta left in 2000 in order to open his own restaurant. He won the 1994 James Beard Award as Best Chef: Midwest.

MY FOOD I had worked in some of the best restaurants in Italy and then worked in about thirteen trattorias, from Sicily all the way up to the Alps. They did very typical local foods, and they taught me about flavor, food combinations, ingredients, history, and food culture.

During this time, I also worked at three-star restaurants in France: Roger Vergé's restaurant Le Moulin de Mougins, Bocuse, Troisgros, and Taillevent. I also spent time studying pastry at Lenôtre. Then I went back and continued to work in the trattorias.

This led me to realize that the future of Italian cuisine was a more professional kitchen that uses traditional, local food as inspiration—recipes that are brought to a more sophisticated level, without taking away from their spirit.

The food of Spiaggia begins with recipes that are regional, traditional, and as authentic as they could possibly be outside of their native country. I also do some dishes that are regionally inspired.

My mission as a chef is to demonstrate that Italian food can rival what is, without question, the benchmark in cooking—French food. When you eat my food, you taste the same professionalism that is in a French kitchen, only you have flavors and food combinations that are identifiably Italian.

PAUL'S PICKS

ARUN'S

4156 N. Kedzie Avenue (near Berteau Avenue), Chicago
(773) 539-1909

I love to go to Arun's, which only serves tasting menus—they have up to eighteen different courses. I think it is the most unbelievable Thai food in America. It is definitely the best Thai food I have ever had. (See also p. 85.)

CHARLIE TROTTER'S

816 W. Armitage Avenue, Chicago
(773) 248-6228

His restaurant is the most complete restaurant in Chicago, with attention paid to the tiniest details. I don't go there for a specific dish. I go there because every once in a while I am ready for the "Charlie experience." It is the antithesis of what I do from a culinary standpoint. I have never had a bad meal there. (See also p. 84.)

THE DINING ROOM

160 E. Pearson Street (in the Ritz-Carlton), Chicago
(312) 266-1000

I have eaten the French-inspired cuisine here many times and have found that Sarah Stegner, the chef, does wonderful things with foie gras. Last time I was here, she made a foie gras dish with melted caramel, ginger, and tangerine. The foie gras was just a dream. It was perfect. It was a little bitter from the zest and sweet from the caramel, and a little acidic. It was one of the greatest foie gras dishes I have ever eaten in my life.

EVEREST

440 S. LaSalle Street, Chicago
(312) 663-8920

First and foremost, chef Jean Joho always has some unbelievable Alsatian wine I have never heard of. Plus, I love his food, which favors foods from Joho's native Alsace. He is very respectful of the fact that he is cooking with American products, and he does wonderful things. Last time I was here, he did a lobster with Riesling sauce that was great. (See also pp. 83, 85.)

PAUL'S PICKS

SEASONS

120 E. Delaware Place
(in the Four Seasons Hotel), Chicago
(312) 649-2349

Chef Mark Baker is a guy who loves beef, which is served a lot here. It's a progressive American restaurant with New England and Asian influences. He once made me a seared rib-eye in a really rich Cabernet sauce, and I will never forget how perfectly cooked it was. It was unbelievable—the dish was a total bull's-eye! (See also p. 85.)

TOPOLOBAMPO

445 N. Clark Street, Chicago
(312) 661-1434

I had a group of Italian journalists in town and I wanted them to have some unusual and exciting food, so I took them here for the best Mexican cuisine they had ever eaten. They were absolutely blown away, because Rick Bayless struggles the way I do, in that a lot of people don't understand the food he is doing. When you sit in the restaurant and eat his food, it is a cultural experience as well as a gastronomic one.

Rick Bayless

RICK BAYLESS is chef-owner of Frontera Grill and Topolobampo, and author of *Authentic Mexican*, *Rick Bayless's Mexican Kitchen*, and *Mexico One Plate at at Time*, which is also the title of the PBS television series he hosts. In 1991 he won the James Beard Award as Best Chef: Midwest. In 1995, he won both the James Beard Award as Outstanding Chef of the Year and the International Association of Culinary Professional's Chef of the Year Award. Bayless's cookbook *Mexican Kitchen* won an IACP Julia Child Cookbook Award as Best Cookbook of the Year in 1996, and also won this honor from the *Chicago Tribune*. In 1998, Bayless won the James Beard Award as Humanitarian of the Year.

MY FOOD We knew that when we opened Frontera Grill [Bayless's first restaurant], we had to have credibility that we knew what we were doing, that this wasn't just "made-up" Mexican food. We didn't like what other people were doing and calling "Mexican." I think our biggest success was the fact that our first cookbook—*Authentic Mexican*—was published right before the restaurant opened, so we came with instant credibility, if you will.

If young chefs are going to save their money and come to Topolobampo, I wouldn't want them to come in not knowing anything about the real cuisine of Mexico. I would recommend that they get some cookbooks—either ours or others of very traditional Mexican food—and read through them so that they will be at least conversant with the preparations and ingredients before they get here. Otherwise, I don't think they're going to have the ability to really take away the full experience.

FRONTERA GRILL AND TOPOLOBAMPO

445 N. Clark Street
Chicago, IL 60610
Phone: (312) 661-1434
Fax: (312) 661-1830
www.fronterakitchens.com

"For Mexican food I go to Chicago—to Frontera Grill."

JOYCE GOLDSTEIN
FORMERLY OF SQUARE ONE
(SAN FRANCISCO)

"Whenever I'm in Chicago, I always, always eat here."

MARK MILLER
COYOTE CAFÉ
(LAS VEGAS AND SANTA FE)

MATSUYA

3469 N. Clark Street (at Sheffield Avenue), Chicago (773) 248-2677

Matsuya has very well prepared Japanese food that is not at all trendy. It's just consistently good quality. You wouldn't necessarily go out of your way to eat here, but we happened to live two blocks away for years, so we got to know it. It's bizarre in that all the sushi chefs are Mexican. They love to make what they call "Mexican *makis*," with a piece of yellowtail, hot sauce, avocado, and cilantro. It's wonderful what they create. We love the whole cross-cultural experience of sitting at the sushi bar and chatting in Spanish with the sushi chefs!

PS BANGKOK

3345 N. Clark Street (between Roscoe Street and Buckingham Place), Chicago (773) 871-7777

I am a real fan of green curry with Thai eggplant. That's one of my very favorite things. I also like red, or what they call Panang, curry, which is sweeter and more coconut-milky. But the green curry is very aromatic. It's made with green chile, and it's more pungent. The flavors are just so bright, and I really like that. They also have great dumplings here.

SAI CAFÉ

2010 N. Sheffield Avenue (at Armitage Avenue), Chicago (773) 472-8080

This Japanese restaurant, which is known primarily for its sushi but also offers noodles and other entrées, is closer to where we live now. The quality of the food is excellent here, and you get a greater sense of freshness. I like to eat a good variety of sushi, and I find that after a really busy week, the serenity and purity of Japanese food is

RICK BAYLESS on

Thailand, the "Mexico of Asia"

I HAD THE WONDERFUL OPPORTUNITY TO GO TO THAILAND TWO YEARS AGO It was astonishing for me because I discovered the other country in the world that could captivate my heart. I call Thailand the "Mexico of Asia," in that Thai food is as complex as Mexican food in its seasonings.

If I could be very blunt about the way that I would differentiate the two, I would say that the flavors that are typical in the Thai kitchen are very compatible with white wines, and the flavors that are typical of the Mexican kitchen are very compatible with red wines. Otherwise, they are very similar cuisines in the way that they approach cooking. They are very much about people celebrating food, so you'll find lots of street food. I didn't think there was a place that could have more street food than Mexico, until I got to Thailand. It has twice as much street food. You can't take ten steps without coming upon a street vendor!

We ate everywhere. It is the only place that I have ever been in the world where I didn't have a bad meal, or even a mediocre meal. We ate in every kind of restaurant you could imagine, from street vendors all the way up to really beautiful places. In fact, the only meals that might have been lacking were in the really fancy restaurants, and that often happens when people become too self-conscious and are no longer cooking from their heart.

Thai food is really it. We have started having a Thai woman who's an excellent cook come to our house to cook with us every couple of months. We are learning how to make some of the stuff, but we are also tasting really delicious, freshly prepared versions of it all.

just the tonic I need. I'm not a real big sake fan, so I usually just drink beer—a Kirin or a Sapporo—when I'm here. (See also p. 85.)

SPAGO

520 N. Dearborn Street (at Grand Avenue), Chicago (312) 527-3700

Beside Spiaggia, Lanie's very favorite restaurant in town is probably Spago. It's just a block away from us, and she's the restaurant kid in the neighborhood, so she knows everyone. François Kwakn-Dongo, the chef here, will take Lanie back in the kitchen and let her make pizza for herself. She loves to do that! But she also likes going here because they have great pasta and pizza.

SPIAGGIA

980 N. Michigan Avenue (at Oak Street), 2nd floor, Chicago (312) 280-2750

The fine dining restaurant where we eat the most is Spiaggia. It works really well for us as a family because Italian food is very kid-friendly and the food is delicious and excellently prepared here. We know the wine steward, and he's always bringing us things that really enhance the experience. Our daughter, Lanie, loves to go to fine-dining restaurants. We use it as family time, and we play games. We might pull out question-and-answer game cards, or ask the waiter for a piece of paper so we can play hangman.

STEVEN CHIAPPETTI is the executive chef of Mossant at the Hotel Monaco in Chicago. He was formerly chef-owner of Mango, Rhapsody, and Grapes, and has previously been nominated for the James Beard Award as Rising Star Chef of the Year.

Steven Chiappetti

MOSSANT

Hotel Monaco
225 N. Wabash Avenue
Chicago, IL 60601
Phone: (312) 236-9300
Fax: (312) 236-3230
www.kimptongroup.com

MY FOOD My food is very simple. Cooking shouldn't be complex. It doesn't take a rocket scientist to cook—it just takes a lot of passion. At Mango, the idea was to keep everything simple and understated. Then all of a sudden, you might find something unique like the creative sconces on the wall. It's the subtleties of everything. That's part of my creative side, going out there and finding things for the restaurant. I'm always looking for something unique or creative.

STEVEN'S PICKS

FRONTERA GRILL
445 N. Clark Street, Chicago
(312) 661-1434
I always like the appetizer plate here—which changes, but has featured ceviche, quesadillos, shrimp, and taquitos—but the best thing is one of their desserts, the *tres leche* cake, which is like a pudding made with three different types of milk. It's a very classic Mexican dessert. That and his Mexican coffee are not to be missed. I also love the margaritas that they shake tableside. They're made with fresh lime juice, and you can really taste the difference. (See also p. 79.)

HOUSTON'S RESTAURANT
612 N. Rush Street, Chicago
(312) 649-1121
I think prime rib is the best cut of beef, period. I think it has the most amount of flavor—fat flavor. I get it with a loaded baked potato. They also have a spinach dip and a tortilla soup that are both great. For dessert, don't miss the five-nut brownie with maple ice cream.

LULU'S
626 Davis Street, Evanston
(just north of Chicago)
(847) 869-4343
The chef used to be the chef at Mikado, which was a three-star restaurant in Chicago. He is Asian-French, and Lulu's is pan-Asian. It's very good. The cold sesame spinach with rice wine vinegar is really nice, but the best dishes are the spicy noodles with peanut sauce and the potato croquettes.

MON AMI GABI
2300 N. Lincoln Park West, Chicago
(773) 348-8886
This is Gabino Sotelino's place, next to Ambria. I can tell you what I eat when I go here, because it's the same thing every time: his wonderful chicken liver pâté, followed by lamb paillard with pommes frites and rosemary aioli, and then profiteroles for dessert. I love it, every time.

NANIWA
607 N. Wells Street (at Ohio), Chicago
(312) 255-8555
They make a unique spicy tuna maki. It is a spicy tartare, more or less, and they mix scallions in it and roll it into sushi. I like to have it with sake.

TRU

676 N. St. Clair Street
Chicago, IL 60611
Phone: (312) 202-0001
ChefTramonto@aol.com

BRASSERIE T

305 S. Happ Road
Northfield, IL 60093
Phone: (847) 446-0444
Fax: (847) 446-0454
BrasserieT@aol.com

GALE GAND and RICK TRAMONTO are the pastry chef and chef, respectively, of Tru, which received four stars from *Chicago* magazine and the *Chicago Tribune*, and Brasserie T. Among their many honors are being included on *Food & Wine*'s list of the Top Ten Best New Chefs in 1994. That same year, Gand won the Robert Mondavi Culinary Excellence Award. In 1995, Tramonto was selected by Robert Mondavi as America's Rising Star Chef. They are the authors of *American Brasserie* and *Butter Sugar Flour Eggs*.

OUR FOOD We wanted to re-create fine dining with a sense of humor. We have been eating together for fifteen years, and we found that the more money we paid for a meal, the less fun we had. That didn't seem right to us. We decided that, as the next generation of chefs in America, it was our mission to redefine dining. Our food is whimsical [with dishes like venison in Valrhona and cherry sauce], and our menu changes all the time—our guests have fun, the place is alive. We don't want people to feel intimidated by not knowing which fork to use. If a customer ever got nervous about something like that, the waiter would joke that he didn't know which fork to use, either. You don't have to go to finishing school to eat here or enjoy the fruits of the earth in the finest, unadulterated way. The French chef Pierre Gagnaire has probably had the biggest influence on Tru's food. He is brave enough to do chocolate and foie gras together, or sweetbreads cooked in bladder. His presentations have inspired meal after meal here. Also, his sauces are amazing. Rick's sauce work echoes his, and he inspired Rick to think out of the box. If we come up with something brilliant, we credit it to the spirit of Pierre Gagnaire.

GALE AND RICK'S PICKS

BLACKBIRD

619 W. Randolph, Chicago
(312) 715-0708
Paul Kahan (formerly sous chef to Rick Bayless at Topolobampo) is a chef's chef, and this is a place you'll find a lot of Chicago chefs eating. It's a great Continental restaurant in the West Loop serving delicious food that's simple and clean [ranging from seared arctic char to grilled guinea hen].

FRONTERA GRILL

445 N. Clark Street, Chicago
(312) 661-1434
This is a great Mexican place—tasty, earthy, and fun. Rick Bayless, the chef, is a great guy, and that makes the experience low-stress. You can walk in there and be brain-dead and say, 'Feed me,' and whatever you're served will be wonderful. (See also p. 79.)

PORTILLO'S HOT DOGS

100 W. Ontario Street, Chicago
(312) 587-8910
We like to go here for black cows [root-beer floats] and a killer Italian beef. That is a great night. You have

them together; it is the classic combination of salt and sweet. We have eaten every Italian beef in the city, and we think this is the best one. They have great bread, the sandwiches are not too heavily dipped, and they're served with good *jus*.

SUSHI WABI

842 W. Randolph Street, Chicago
(312) 563-1224
This is a small, relaxing place in a funky neighborhood where you can graze for hours. It is cutting-edge stuff. He will do a dragon roll with sweetbreads, tuna, and hot Japanese mustard. He also does interesting tempura, like uni and smoked eel. It is wild, wacky stuff. We like to drink

sake or beer with this food, and he has a big selection of both.

TONY'S SUBMARINE SANDWICH

1480 Waukegan Road, Deerfield
(847) 940-7352
Gale: I cannot live without this place! It is the best sub in America. What makes them so good is that they put on olive oil and dry oregano. My favorite is ham and provolone. He also has a good root beer float. Rick: I am a tuna nut, and the tuna is served here on black olive bread with tomatoes, roasted red peppers, and extra-virgin olive oil. It's yummy.

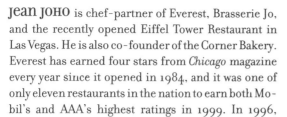

Jean Joho

Jean JOHO is chef-partner of Everest, Brasserie Jo, and the recently opened Eiffel Tower Restaurant in Las Vegas. He is also co-founder of the Corner Bakery. Everest has earned four stars from *Chicago* magazine every year since it opened in 1984, and it was one of only eleven restaurants in the nation to earn both Mobil's and AAA's highest ratings in 1999. In 1996, Brasserie Jo won the James Beard Award for Best New Restaurant, and Joho won the 1995 James Beard Award as Best Chef: Midwest.

MY FOOD I like to blend noble ingredients like caviar and foie gras with simple ingredients like potatoes and turnips. The union of simple and noble makes for unique flavor combinations. The best way to experience our food at Everest is to order a multi-course dégustation meal. This will give you an opportunity to see how truly creative we can be.

EVEREST
440 S. LaSalle Street
Chicago, IL 60605
Phone: (312) 663-8920
Fax: (312) 663-8802

BRASSERIE JO
59 W. Hubbard Street
Chicago, IL 60610
Phone: (312) 595-0800
Fax: (312) 595-0808
www.brasseriejo.com

Jean's PICKS

BRASSERIE JO

59 W. Hubbard Street, Chicago
(312) 595-0800
This is the only restaurant of mine where I sit down to eat. I like to come in around ten P.M. Why *not* eat your own food? Steak tartare and steak *frites* are wonderful things!

FRONTERA GRILL

445 N. Clark Street, Chicago
(312) 661-1434
Rick Bayless, the chef-owner, has great food. It is always a surprise—they will always make something I have never had before. I like to start with a margarita and finish with beer, unless I decide to have a good Alsatian wine. (See also p. 79.)

GIBSONS BAR AND STEAKHOUSE

1028 N. Rush Street, Chicago
(312) 266-8999
At Gibsons I order the New York steak, medium rare. Their side dishes change a lot, and I like almost everything. With steak I'll order red wine, and I love to find a new red wine on the list that I have never tasted before. If you come to Chicago, you should go to a steakhouse. It's so Chicago to have a steak—and this steak is my favorite. We have many good steakhouses in Chicago, but Gibsons is the best in the entire Midwest!

PAPAGUS

620 N. State Street, Chicago
(312) 642-8450

CAFÉ BA-BA REEBA!

2024 N. Halsted, Chicago
(773) 935-5000
I like the lively atmosphere at both of these places. At Papagus, it's Greek. At Café Ba-Ba Reeba!, it's Spanish—the food as well as the flamenco music!

SPIAGGIA

980 N. Michigan Avenue, Chicago
(312) 280-2750
I spent eight years cooking in Italy, and I think the kitchen at Spiaggia is doing pretty authentic Italian cooking. I always enjoy whatever I eat there. (See also p. 78.)

CHARLIE TROTTER'S

816 W. Armitage Avenue

Chicago, IL 60614

Phone: (773) 248-6228

Fax: (773) 248-6088

www.charlietrotters.com

CHARLIE TROTTER is chef-owner of Charlie Trotter's, which won the 2000 James Beard Award for Outstanding Restaurant and was named Best Restaurant in the World for Wine and Food by *Wine Spectator* in 1998. In 1993, Charlie Trotter's won the James Beard Award for Outstanding Wine Service. Among his many honors are the 1992 James Beard Award as Best Chef: Midwest, and the 1999 James Beard Award as Outstanding Chef of the Year. His four cookbooks include *Charlie Trotter's; Charlie Trotter's Vegetables; Charlie Trotter's Seafood;* and *Charlie Trotter's Desserts;* he is also the subject of *Lessons in Excellence.* In addition, he has created the television series *The Kitchen Sessions with Charlie Trotter* for public television.

"I love this place!"

JEAN-GEORGES VONGERICHTEN

JEAN GEORGES, JO JO, AND VONG (NEW YORK)

MY FOOD In my cooking, I stress the use of pristine seasonal ingredients and naturally raised foodstuffs, and small independent farmers from around the country supply me with most of my ingredients. Free-range and organic products taste the best, and it's good to know that you're eating unadulterated food and supporting growers who are directly connected to the land. I combine the highest-quality ingredients with European techniques and Asian minimalism in order to create dishes that are light and elegant. Unlike sauces that use a lot of butter or cream, our approach doesn't mute or block the basic flavors of the ingredients they are meant to support.

It's important to me that diners enjoy a perfect balance. I don't want guests walking out of the restaurant feeling overindulged because they are challenged by excessive cream, butter, and alcohol. I want them to feel stimulated and alert. Food doesn't have to be rich to taste good.

We try to customize the dining experience for pretty much every table. The entire staff is very sincere and honest—they take it personally if something goes awry with a table. We've never had a perfect day, and that's part of the motivation for continuing to push and bump things up. If someone has a problem with something, our team will be bothered by that. If ninety-five of our one hundred customers had a wonderful time and five didn't, then that day wasn't successful. That's how we approach it. The idea is, every day, "How do we elevate this? How do we refine this?"

"Visitors to Chicago should really experience his restaurant. The table and wine service are just so polished. It is a wonderful inspiration to try to keep up with him; we are fortunate that he is in Chicago."

GALE GAND AND RICK TRAMONTO

BRASSERIE T AND TRU

CHARLIE'S PICKS

ARUN'S

4156 N. Kedzie Avenue, Chicago
(773) 539-1909

My eight-year-old doesn't really like food. Arun Sampanthavivat, the chef-owner of this upscale Thai restaurant, will customize the experience for us, so my son can just have noodles and plain chicken. I know Arun very well—he's a dear friend—and being able to visit with him certainly enhances our experience here. Arun uses high-quality ingredients. He's a Renaissance man in a lot of ways: He painted some of the things that are hanging on the walls, he's done the woodworking on a lot of different things, and he speaks five or six different languages. He was working on his Ph.D. at the University of Chicago when he began to cook, and he just kept with it. (See also p. 78.)

EVEREST

440 S. LaSalle Street, 40th floor, Chicago
(312) 663-8920

I've known chef Jean Joho over the years and been friendly with him. Everest is a romantic place. I don't really order there—he just usually makes the menu. Jean has that whole brilliant Alsatian influence: He juxtaposes simple things and luxury items, like cabbage and skate with truffles, or salsify and truffles. He's also very good with game birds. (See also pp. 78, 83.)

FRONTERA GRILL

445 N. Clark Street, Chicago
(312) 661-1434

Frontera Grill has a style of food that's really different from ours. I like hot food and I like chiles, but we don't really use a lot of that in our repertoire. I like Rick Bayless's sensibility, and his support of farmers and natural products. His food is pure and clean. I don't think I've ever had a bad dish there; everything is just great. It's a great place to take chefs from out of town, or out of the country. When we had Marc Veyrat in from France to cook at the restaurant for a couple of days, we took him to Arun's and Frontera Grill. It's a way to show chefs some of the unique food being served in Chicago that they're not going to find at home. (See also pp. 79, 81, 82.)

LE FRANÇAIS

269 S. Milwaukee Avenue, Wheeling
(45 minutes west of Chicago)
(847) 541-7470

Roland and Mary Beth Liccioni came in after founding chef Jean Banchet went to Atlanta, and they ran it for ten years [before Banchet returned]. During their run, we went here about a half dozen times. They're all professional friends, and I like what they do. Le Français's food is more French than ours, so it's been nice to eat here sometimes.

SAI CAFÉ

2010 N. Sheffield Avenue
(at Armitage Avenue), Chicago
(773) 472-8080

We know the chef at Sai Café very well, and my wife will give him ideas based on things that she's had at other sushi places. He's able to either invent, craft, or customize things. He's one of these guys who is always at his restaurant, so he's not out looking at the world and letting that influence his food. Still, he's very open to hearing about new things and trying new things. He learns from his customers as opposed to having to see things on his own. I just let him do whatever he wants to do for me—which is mainly sashimi and rolls. (See also p. 80.)

SEASONS

120 E. Delaware Place
(in the Four Seasons Hotel), Chicago
(312) 649-2349

Seasons is a sentimental choice: My wife and I got married here, and we try to come back every so often. The general manager sends his kids to the same grade school I went to. And we know chef Mark Baker very well—he's a nice guy. (See also p. 79.)

> *"When my wife and I went to Charlie Trotter's for dinner, time truly stood still. It was the synchronization of the entire staff, the level of sincerity, the respect for the product. The entire composition of the meal was like a symphonic structure."*
>
> CRAIG SHELTON   THE RYLAND INN (NEW JERSEY)

Creating a Memorable Dining Experience

WHAT WE'RE STRIVING FOR IS TO HAVE A LEVEL OF TRUST WITH OUR GUESTS so that they just let us do anything we want. Whether that's trust based on the fact that people have heard about the restaurant over the years, or trust based on their being repeat customers, we want people to be willing to say, "Here's a place where we don't even have to bother with the menu, because we know it's going to be special."

We give away a lot of extra portions of food; almost every table gets one or more extra portions. I know what it's been like for me to be a diner and to receive something I didn't order, and how special that is. So whether it's a foie gras course with the appropriate wine, or a fish course, or an extra dessert, it's easy enough for the restaurant to do and it makes a big impression.

We convert a lot of menus and change the menu. Somebody might sit down and order a bottle of Opus One and not want to go with our program of wines matched to each course, even though that might be a little more ideal for the menu. So what are we going to do, serve the next three courses that are raw or marinated fish with Opus? Well, we could, or we'll ask the guest, "Would you like us just to group this menu into something that might be a little more suitable for this wine?" We'll start with a quail dish and move from there, as opposed to what we were going to do.

It's always a matter of putting yourself in the customer's place and trying to imagine what they want. It's simultaneously taking over the situation and doing things that are above and beyond, and doing things that the customer doesn't have the chance to ask for, gaining their trust so that you can control things, give them what they want, and ultimately blow their mind. Ultimately, we hope, they will be willing to give up more and more control of the experience. The better they know you, the more they trust you. The more control we have, the greater the likelihood that we can completely blow somebody away. The more they try to keep control, the less chance that can happen. So our job is to get them to give up control of the experience. All that the-customer's-always-right stuff couldn't be further from the truth. That is why you must seize control of the circumstance and dominate the evening, to make sure your guests have an awesome time.

The Golden Rule

For me, it goes back to being a diner. I always think, "What if that happened to me? What would I like to see happen?" That's one of the reasons we, very early on in the restaurant's life, were very eager to say to any excited diner, "Would you like to see our kitchen before you depart?" They'd say, "Oh, you mean we can?" We'd say, "Of course—come right this way!" Then we'd bring them back and one of us would give them anywhere from a two-minute to a twenty-minute guided tour of the kitchen.

We started doing that for several reasons. One was because, as a young diner, I often inquired to see the kitchen at a lot of restaurants, and was told no—"It is not a good time," or "The chef never allows that," or "It's not possible." I thought that should never be the case; the kitchen should always be pristine and accessible. So we made a point of going to the other extreme and having a situation where people could be in our kitchen at any time, even at the height of service, so the kitchen needed to be as meticulous as the dining room. Once we instilled this sort of mindset, that this is important, it's not that difficult to maintain.

We give a lot of tours to guests of our kitchen, our wine cellars, our studio kitchen. I think people are curious. Yes, they can sit in a dining room where they know of the chef and have an experience that might be amazing. But if they can go in the back and see the faces and see the activity, even if it's just a one-minute glimpse, it can enhance the evening so much. It takes so little to push the experience over the top.

A Memento

I've been to many places and had many, many great meals and said, "I wish I could get a menu." Then you find out that the chef is doing something spontaneous, and there isn't really a menu available of that. So we make sure that everybody who leaves our restaurant, if they want it, can have a document of the experience, whether it gets handwritten that night or typed out at the end of service and mailed to them. This is very tricky at our restaurant, because many diners do have customized or spontaneous menus.

So, creating a memorable experience is wrapped up in a lot of little touches—a lot of little touches done with sincerity.

DALLAS

Barbecue

SONNY BRYAN'S SMOKEHOUSE
Multiple locations, including:
2202 Inwood Road, Dallas (original location)
(214) 357-7120
302 N. Market Street, Dallas
(214) 744-1610

"Their pork spare ribs are great!"

—KENT RATHBUN, ABACUS

"You have to go to the original Sonny Bryan's. There is something about the atmosphere and the way they chop the meat at the place. I order the BBQ beef sandwich. Of course, you also have to get the beans and cole slaw."

—DAVID HOLBEN, SEVENTEEN SEVENTEEN

"The original Sonny Bryan's is a big deal down here. It's interesting, because it's been the same for years and years. And why shouldn't it be? It's based on long-smoked meat and just a very basic, simple barbecue sauce. I still have visions from years ago of walking through the door and seeing him there, chopping the barbecue. The beef brisket sandwich is good, and the pork sausage is really good, but the ribs are my favorite. The atmosphere is great, too—you sit either on the roof of your car out in the parking lot, or inside at one of the four school desks. The other Sonny Bryan's locations are more touristy, atmosphere-wise, but the food is pretty good."

—STEPHAN PYLES, AQUAKNOX

"The building's a shack, and the food is good stuff. I like the ribs, the beef brisket, and the pork."

—TOM COLICCHIO, GRAMERCY TAVERN (NEW YORK)

BLTs

THE FAIRMONT HOTEL
1717 N. Akard Street, Dallas
(214) 720-2020

ADAM'S MARK HOTEL
400 N. Olive Street (at Pearl and Live Oak Streets), Dallas (214) 922-8000

"We have a hobby, which is studying BLTs wherever we go. We study who has the best or most expensive. It's what we use to rate a hotel. The best was on the Queen Elizabeth II. We were part of a guest chef series, and we got to the point where we had one waiting for us every night in our room. The toast was still warm when they spread the mayonnaise on—that is the secret! Plus, since it was English, the crusts were cut off. In the United States, we think the best BLTs are in Dallas at the Mark or the Fairmont. The Fairmont's is awesome: It has smoky bacon, perfect lettuce and tomato, whole-wheat bread, a perfect pickle, and good big chips like Lay's."

—GALE GAND AND RICK TRAMONTO, TRU (CHICAGO)

DREAM CAFÉ

2800 Routh Street, Dallas (214) 954-0486

"They're known for big, beautiful breakfasts."

—KENT RATHBUN, ABACUS

MOTHER'S

3719 Spring Avenue, Dallas (214) 426-2495

"Mother's is everything it sounds like—a diner where seventy-year-old waitresses make sure the biscuits, gravy, and sausages flow freely!"

—KENT RATHBUN, ABACUS

KEL'S

5337 Forest Lane, Dallas (972) 458-7221

"This used to be a Pizza Hut. At night it does all-you-can-eat, from catfish to country-fried chicken. For breakfast they do grits, waffles, and any type of eggs, just like a good diner. It is simple and good, with sixty-year-old waitresses running around. I like to get corned beef hash, pancakes, and two eggs over easy on top of the pancakes. That holds me all the way through my gardening on a Sunday!"

—DAVID HOLBEN, SEVENTEEN SEVENTEEN

DALLAS FARMERS' MARKET

1010 S. Pearl Expressway, Dallas (214) 670-5879

"We have a very good one. They have everything, including cooking demonstrations. Little farmers from down south bring in everything, from black-eyed peas to beautiful tomatoes. You can't believe how many types of chiles are there. Just when you think you've seen them all, you'll go there and find one more you've never seen."

—DAVID HOLBEN, SEVENTEEN SEVENTEEN

DALLAS LOCAL HIGHLIGHTS

GOOD EATS

Multiple locations, including:
14905 Midway Road, Dallas (972) 392-3287

"They claim they serve the biggest chicken-fried steak in Dallas, but I think it's also the best. It's hand-breaded, and served with mashed potatoes on the side."

—KENT RATHBUN, ABACUS

MAMA'S DAUGHTER'S DINER

Multiple locations, including:
2014 Irving Boulevard, Dallas (214) 954-0486

"Chicken-fried steak is a big deal around here; everybody has what they perceive to be the best. Good chicken-fried steak has to be pan-fried, and so many places, especially the chains, deep-fry it because it's quicker. It's like fried chicken—the really good places fry it in a pan, where there's only so much oil. That's what they do at this place, and it's great."

—STEPHAN PYLES, AQUAKNOX

FRIED CHICKEN

BUBBA'S CHICKEN

6617 Hillcrest (Snyder Plaza), Dallas
(214) 373-6527

"They serve the best fried chicken and also have great biscuits."

—KENT RATHBUN, ABACUS

HamBurger

BALLS HAMBURGERS

3404 Rankin Street (Snyder Plaza), Dallas
(214) 373-1717

"Really good burgers and deep-fried onion rings [plus a video arcade room with a baseball theme]."

—KENT RATHBUN, ABACUS

SNUFFER'S

3526 Greenville Avenue, Dallas
(214) 826-6850

"They have old-fashioned, medium-rare, pile-it-on fried burgers that are really good."

—STEPHAN PYLES, AQUAKNOX

Mexican

JAVIER'S

4912 Cole Avenue, Dallas
(214) 521-4211

"This is one of the original-style restaurants doing the food of Mexico City. You'll find interesting Mexican dishes here, like moles and traditional Mexican food."

—DAVID HOLBEN, SEVENTEEN SEVENTEEN

CANTINA LAREDO

Multiple locations, including:
6025 Royal Lane (Site 250),1 Dallas
(214) 265-1610
8121 Walnut Hill Lane, Dallas
(214) 987-9192

"This is more Tex-Mex food. They have great cabrito [goat], which they do two different ways—with rice and beans, or as a soft taco with caramelized sweet onions. Both are delicious."

—DAVID HOLBEN, SEVENTEEN SEVENTEEN

PIZZa

BROTHERS PIZZA

13317 Montfort Drive, Dallas
(972) 458-1375

"The owner, Eli, and his wife bake great New York–style pizza at this hole in the wall. You order your pizza from Eli, have a Budweiser, and talk with him about what's going on, and then take your pizza home. I like mine with pepperoni, black olives, and jalapeños. Yeah, we are in Texas!"

—DAVID HOLBEN, SEVENTEEN SEVENTEEN

"Tex-Mex is what a lot of Americans think Mexican food is. They think it is tacos, cheese dip, enchiladas, chimichangas, buracho beans, and guacamole, but it is more simplistic than Mexican food."

DaVID HOLBeN   SEVENTEEN SEVENTEEN

southwestern

STAR CANYON

3102 Oak Lawn Avenue, Dallas
(214) 520-7827

THE MANSION ON TURTLE CREEK

2821 Turtle Creek Boulevard, Dallas
(214) 559-2100

"Visitors should definitely have southwestern cuisine while they are here. Both Stephan Pyles's Star Canyon and Dean Fearing's Mansion on Turtle Creek do it very well, yet their food is very different from each other's." (See also p. 94.)

—DAVID HOLBEN, SEVENTEEN SEVENTEEN

steak

CAPITAL GRILLE

500 Crescent Court, Dallas
(214) 303-0500

"They do a nice job with steak here—even though they're not Texan."

—KENT RATHBUN, ABACUS

PAPPAS BROTHERS STEAKHOUSE

10477 Lombardy Lane, Dallas
(214) 366-2000

"The Pappas Brothers have a chain of very successful restaurants, and they just recently opened their second high-end steak restaurant, which is something to see. They use all prime meats and fifteen-hundred-degree broilers. I always have a rib-eye—I love the fat, and the meat is so moist!"

—KENT RATHBUN, ABACUS

thai

THAI NIPA RESTAURANT

4315 Lemmon Avenue, Dallas
(214) 526-6179

"Their soups are fantastic. And the red curry is full of flavor!"

—DAVID HOLBEN, SEVENTEEN SEVENTEEN

vietnamese

GREEN PAPAYA

3211 Oak Lawn Avenue, Dallas
(214) 521-4811

"It's really good—basic, but pretty authentic Vietnamese cuisine. And it's in my neighborhood."

—STEPHAN PYLES, AQUAKNOX

taqueria

VICTOR'S TAQUERIA

4447 Maple Avenue, Dallas
(214) 521-0121

"For everything from menudo [tripe stew] to tacos de lingua [tacos made with tongue]."

—KENT RATHBUN, ABACUS

tex-mex

PRIMO'S BAR AND GRILL

3309 McKinney, Dallas
(214) 220-0510

"This place does great Tex-Mex. The quesadillas are delicious, and grilled on mesquite. It's been a chefs' hangout for over ten years. On Friday and Saturday nights there will be at least fifteen chefs and cooks there. After service, it's like, 'What did you eat during work?' 'Nothing, let's go get some late-night food and beers at Primo's.'"

—DAVID HOLBEN, SEVENTEEN SEVENTEEN

"It's a chefs' hangout, so on Friday and Saturday nights around ten or eleven P.M., you'll find chefs from around town ordering margaritas here. I love the pork picante, which is a big Mexican pork stew served with tortillas."

—KENT RATHBUN, ABACUS

David Holben

BISTRAL

2900 McKinney Avenue
(at Allen Street)
Dallas, TX 75204
Phone: (214) 220-1202
Fax: (214) 220-1197

SEVENTEEN SEVENTEEN

in the Dallas Museum of Art
1717 N. Harwood Street
(at Ross Avenue)
Dallas, TX 75201
Phone: (214) 922-1260
Fax: (214) 351-3344
www.wynnwood.com

DAVID HOLBEN is vice president of culinary operations for Wynnwood, a Dallas-based restaurant management, catering, and special-events company. Its properties include Bistral and Seventeen Seventeen, whose chefs are Dan Landsberg and Raoul Orosa, respectively. After graduating with honors from The Culinary Institute of America, Holben won a scholarship to study in France with such notable chefs as Roger Vergé and Paul Bocuse. In 1990, *Food & Wine* named him one of America's Top Ten Chefs. Prior to joining Wynnwood, he opened and ran several acclaimed restaurants, including the Riviera, where he earned a 29 (out of 30) food rating from the Dallas *ZagatSurvey*.

MY FOOD My overriding philosophy is to let the flavors speak for themselves. A chef's challenge is to enhance the flavor of food, not mask it. They also need to keep it interesting and unusual at the same time, but that doesn't mean it has to be something that you've never seen before. I still like to go back to classic dishes and bring in new flavors in order to give them a little twist—it helps give the dish a newness without making the customer insecure. I want to educate the customer, but not overwhelm them with a list of ingredients they have not heard of.

Bistral features new American cuisine with French and Italian influences in a comfortable yet refined atmosphere. The restaurant also offers a reasonably priced wine list of over four hundred selections. Seventeen Seventeen is located in the Dallas Museum of Art, and features French-influenced Asian cuisine in a fine-dining atmosphere.

DAVID'S PICKS

AMICI SIGNATURE ITALIAN

1022 S. Broadway Road, Carrollton
(a few miles northwest of Dallas)
(972) 245-3191
This is a small place. He has a classic Italian menu, but his specials are unbelievable—they are three times as good as his regular menu. And his venison is fantastic! He is trying to appeal to both crowds—those who want old-style Italian cuisine, and those people who want a place to bring in a special bottle of wine. It is BYOB, so it's an opportunity to bring in a great bottle of wine you want to enjoy.

CHAMBERLAIN'S

5330 Belt Line Road, Addison
(immediately north of Dallas)
(972) 934-2467
In Dallas, you have to have a good steak restaurant. Chamberlain's does a great steak, but they will also do fresh clams with a mango relish. So it is more interesting than just steak and vegetables. I like the sirloin, and I am sorry, but I like Worcestershire sauce on it! My wife is a vegetarian, so she'll order pasta. I also really like the service at this restaurant, because you always feel taken care of.

LEFTY'S LOBSTER AND CHOWDER HOUSE

4021 Belt Line Road, Addison
(immediately north of Dallas)
(972) 774-9518
Lefty's has good, fresh seafood, and they know you by name. It is very casual, a little loud, and somewhat family-oriented, so we can bring the kids in. My daughter, who is three, loves the lobster bisque, and the lobster fra diablo is to die for.

DAVID'S PICKS

THE RIVIERA

7709 Inwood Road, Dallas
(214) 351-0094

The Riviera [which earned a 29 out of 30 food rating in the *ZagatSurvey* when Holben was its chef] is still the best restaurant in town! The current chef, Mike Marshall, is doing a great job. [Overseen by the owner, Franco Bertolasi], the restaurant experience represents a complete package, from the valet greeting the customer by name, all the way through the meal, which might feature classic dishes such as Dover sole or veal saltimbocca. Everything just flows.

YAMAGUCHI

7713 Inwood Road, Dallas
(214) 350-8660

I started going to Yamaguchi when I worked at the Riviera because it is next door. We used to trade food: I would bring them a dessert or a special, and they would give me a platter of sushi. It came to be known as a "David's platter." The chef here does everything extremely well. My kids love *udon* noodles because they get to have fun slurping them. I like to get eel, *toro*, sea urchin—all the low-fat items that are good for you! (See also p. 95.)

Stephan Pyles

STEPHAN PYLES is chef-owner of AquaKnox and Fishbowl, a pan-Asian restaurant adjacent to Aqua-Knox, as well as executive consulting chef of Star Canyon restaurants in Dallas and Las Vegas. *Food & Wine* voted AquaKnox Dallas's Best New Restaurant in 1998. A fifth-generation Texan, Pyles has been recognized as one of the founders of southwestern cuisine. His cookbooks include *The New Texas Cuisine*, *Tamales*, and *New Tastes from Texas*, which is the companion volume to his PBS cooking series of the same name. He won the 1991 James Beard Award as Best Chef: Southwest, and was a founding board member of Share Our Strength.

AQUAKNOX

3214 Knox Street
Dallas, TX 75205
Phone: (214) 219-2782
Fax: (214) 219-0022

FISHBOWL

3214 Knox Street
Dallas, TX 75205
Phone: (214) 219-2695

MY FOOD First of all, I think it's important to maintain the integrity—and, to a degree, the authenticity—of the food of your region. What is authenticity in America? It's such a fusion of so many kinds of food, from European to Mexican to Native American. Even though I can't quite get my hands around it, I know it when I see it, as they say. I know what Texas cooking is about, and the cooking of the Southwest, and certainly the cooking of Mexico, so I want people to realize that that's where I'm coming from. I'm trying to bring it up a level, though, making it a little more sophisticated, a little more creative, and a little healthier for today's palate. Just because you don't find foie gras in tamales in Mexico doesn't mean that it doesn't work and that you can't fuse those flavors.

It took me a while to realize what I was doing, but I've taken the ingredients and recipes inherent in the many cultures and historical eras of Texas and created original dishes. If someone sort of forced me to describe my food in only one sentence, I'd say that it's a cross between French and Mexican.

"I had one of my best meals of the last five years [when Stephan Pyles was] at Star Canyon."

NORMAN VAN AKEN
NORMAN'S (CORAL GABLES, FL)

CUQUITA'S

2326 N. Henderson Avenue, Dallas
(214) 823-1859

Cuquita's is more of a taqueria, but it's an expanded version. It has mariachi music, and it's a great experience. I take a lot of visiting chefs there late at night because it's happening, and it gives you a real feel for the Hispanic side of Dallas. Order the *pozole* [a hominy stew] here—it's really authentic. It's got a lot of pork and green chile in it, and it tastes the way *pozole* should. Drink Mexican beer or a margarita. In typical Mexican taqueria fashion, they've also got great *agua frescas*—the tamarind and the hibiscus flavors are especially good.

THE GREEN ROOM

2715 Elm Street, Dallas
(214) 748-7666

It's a weird combination of things that makes the Green Room great. It's unique in that it's in Deep Ellum, which is the oldest part of town. In Dallas, we're known for tearing down buildings that are fifteen years old, but Deep Ellum has kept the integrity of its nineteenth-century buildings. It's a young crowd, and retro hip, and the food is pretty creative and delicious, with influences spanning the Southwest, Asia, and the Mediterranean. The menu features dishes such as horseradish-crusted sea bass with bok choy, and escolare with coconut risotto. (See also p. 95.)

LIBERTY

5631 Alta Avenue, Dallas
(214) 887-8795

Liberty is an Asian noodle bar, and chef-owner Annie Wong is Thai. My favorite dishes are the *udon* noodles and the "people's noodles," which are *chow fun* noodles with beef and chicken curry. She does rice noodles with bell peppers and egg strips, and she does a green Thai curry vermicelli that's fantastic. Liberty is a good example of what Thai food and the whole Asian concept of restaurants is: The food is authentic, it's happening, and it's unique to Dallas.

THE MANSION
ON TURTLE CREEK

2821 Turtle Creek Boulevard, Dallas
(214) 559-2100

Mansion is a classic Dallas experience. Chef Dean Fearing's food is incredible and features such specialties as tortilla soup, lobster tacos, and crème brûlée with raspberry sauce. Dean is one of the founders of southwestern cooking, and he has a style all his own. The setting is what a lot of people perceive Dallas to be after watching the TV series *Dallas*—it's very plush, and you can just imagine J. R. Ewing in the Mansion, with all its attention to detail. It's very expensive, so when you want to splurge and pamper yourself, you go to the Mansion for an incredible experience of glamour and indulgence.

MIA'S TEX MEX

4322 Lemmon Avenue, Dallas
(214) 526-1020

Mia's is run by a Mexican family of about thirteen people who all work in the restaurant, which is run by Mama Mia. There's a neon sign that says, "If Mama ain't happy, ain't nobody happy." They have different combination plates—beef enchiladas, tacos, pork tamales, *pico de gallo*—and all sorts of different salsas, including *habanero* and *chipotle* tomato. They serve tamales with sunset sauce, which is kind of a red and orange salsa.

"In 1983, I had just gotten out of The Culinary Institute of America and still didn't know where I wanted to go in the restaurant field. Then I had an unbelievable dinner at Stephan Pyles's Routh Street Café, where everything was done to perfection. Stephan was setting a path with Texas cuisine, and bringing sophistication to it. The overall package was elaborate and creative and it all came together—that was incredibly inspiring to me."

JIM COLEMAN

TREETOPS AT THE RITTENHOUSE HOTEL (PHILADELPHIA)

KENT RATHBUN is chef-proprietor of Abacus. His résumé includes stints as sous chef of the American Restaurant in Kansas City, and the Mansion on Turtle Creek in Dallas. Previously, he was executive chef of the Landmark Restaurant in the Dallas Melrose Hotel, and he also developed and ran dani Special Events, a catering company. The *Dallas Morning News* named Abacus the Best New Restaurant of 1999, and *D* magazine recognized it as one of the top six restaurants in Dallas.

Kent Rathbun

ABACUS
4511 McKinney Avenue
Dallas, TX 75205
Phone: (214) 559-3111
Fax: (214) 559-3113
www.abacus-restaurant.com

MY FOOD We are about making the food tasty and well cooked, and using the best possible product. People can expect a good range of global cuisine when they come here. I have worked around the Midwest and Louisiana and Texas, and I have also spent time in Asia. That all gets reflected on the menu, so we don't have any limitations. The food here is very eclectic.

KENT'S PICKS

ARC-EN-CIEL

3555 W. Walnut Street, Garland
(about 15 miles northeast of Dallas)
(972) 272-2188
They have a gigantic menu, but they do a wonderful job. I get a few things every time, like the spring rolls. They are so good I had them teach me how to make them! They also have a Vietnamese salad with an awesome vinaigrette, topped with sliced spring rolls and charcoal-grilled pork.

DADDY JACK'S LOBSTER AND CHOWDER HOUSE

Multiple locations, including:
1916 Greenville Avenue, Dallas
(214) 826-4910
This is a fish house. I order surf and turf, which sounds so boring for a chef, but it's great here because they know what they are doing. It is cooked properly, and has plenty of lemon and butter. This is comfort food. You feel good even on the way there, be-cause you know you are going to have such a good meal. Then you feel great again when you are done!

DUCK INN

503 Main Street, Lake Dallas
(940) 497-2412
This is a hole-in-the-wall that's been around for thirty or thirty-five years, which you go to for one reason and one reason only: the catfish. My grandparents were fishermen, and I grew up on this kind of food. Once every couple of months, I'll go for the all-you-can-eat catfish fillets, which I eat with just a little squeeze of lemon. Given their specialty, I don't know why they call it Duck Inn.

THE GREEN ROOM

2715 Elm Street, Dallas
(214) 748-7666
The chef is Mark Castle, and his food is eclectic, like mine. Eating his food is sort of like researching my competition in Dallas. He is a very good chef, and I like to see what he is coming up with. Last time I was there, he did a lamb loin on couscous that was cooked perfectly. (See also p. 94.)

YAMAGUCHI

7713 Inwood Road, Dallas
(214) 350-8660
The technique behind this sushi bar is about as flawless as I have ever seen. One of the chefs is the owner, and the other is a woman who came to our restaurant to help us with sushi. They do some great rolls, and I think their steak *tataki* is outrageous. It is sirloin, marinated with a variety of chiles, and grilled fast at high heat so that it's raw in the center. They slice it and serve it on pickled onions with lime vinaigrette. It is so fresh-tasting. The tempuras are also great. (See also p. 93.)

LOCAL HIGHLIGHTS

BREAD

DENVER BREAD COMPANY

3200 Irving Street, Denver
(303) 455-7194

"They serve what is without question the best bread in Denver. DBC is a bread shop, and that's it. A trip in the morning inside the steamy square building and you know the owner, Greg Bortz, and company are serious about bread. They make a rustic boule that we serve in our restaurant, and their brioche and scones are first-rate as well."

—SEAN KELLY, AUBERGINE CAFÉ

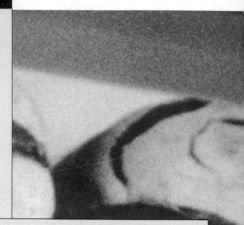

GELATO

GELATO D'ITALIA

250 Detroit Street, Denver
(303) 316-9154

"I especially like the gianduja, which is a chocolate-hazelnut-flavored gelato. In addition to great gelato, they have really good biscotti and a good cappuccino, too."

—SEAN KELLY, AUBERGINE CAFÉ

MEXICAN

EL TACO DE MEXICO

714 Santa Fe Drive, Denver
(303) 623-3926

"People line up for their menudo [tripe stew] on Sundays."

—SEAN KELLY, AUBERGINE CAFÉ

LA PASADITA INN

1959 Park Avenue, Denver
(303) 832-1785

"The owner's wife makes the tamales. For five dollars, you can get rice and beans, and a shredded pork tamale covered with a wonderful green chile salsa. When I find myself with a free half hour, I'll spend it here eating a tamale and reading the New York Times's food section."

—SEAN KELLY, AUBERGINE CAFÉ

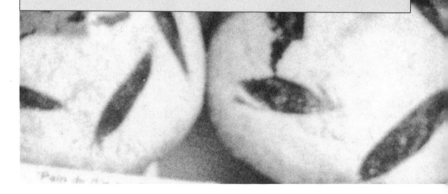

Sean Kelly

sean KELLY is chef-owner of Aubergine Café, which has been cited as one of Colorado's top twenty restaurants by *Gourmet* and one of Denver's top ten restaurants by local critic Bill St. John. He has recently opened the Biscuit, a European coffee bar serving breakfast and lunch, also located in Denver. Kelly was voted Best Chef in Denver by the readers of *5280: Denver's Mile-High Magazine,* and Aubergine Café has been on the magazine's top ten list for several years as well.

MY FOOD I opened Aubergine Café, which has forty-five seats, very inexpensively by doing a lot of the work myself. We've re-created the feeling of a bistro in the south of France, and I serve Mediterranean-inspired food. Our menu changes daily to accommodate produce purchased directly from local farms during the Colorado growing season. While the press we've received has resulted in some people pulling up to our restaurant in their limousines, we have the word café in our name, and my intention is to create a place where people can come for dinner and a glass of wine and enjoy good cooking at approachable prices. And I'm proud that our service is at or above the level of any other restaurant in Denver.

AUBERGINE CAFÉ
225 E. 7th Avenue
Denver, CO 80203
Phone: (303) 832-4778
Fax: (303) 832-3532

BISCUIT
719 E. 17th Avenue
Denver, CO 80203
Phone: (303) 831-1297

"I feel like I'm responsible for hosting a party five nights a week."

sean KELLY
AUBERGINE CAFÉ

sean's PICKS

ANNIE'S CAFÉ AND BAKERY
20 Lakeview Drive (at State Highway 119), Nederland
(303) 258-3600
I go here for good, homemade food. While they serve both breakfast and lunch, I especially like their breakfast. I'll often have homemade corned beef hash, scrambled eggs, and home fries, covered with hot sauce. Their pancakes and French toast are good, too.

ENZO'S END PIZZERIA
3424 E. Colfax Avenue (at Madison), Denver
(303) 355-4700
They make a great pizza. It starts with an excellent thin, very chewy crust and just the right amount of cheese. High-quality and sometimes hard-to-find toppings are used, like prosciutto, calamata olives, and roasted eggplant. I usually order white pizza with fresh tomatoes, hot peppers, and red onions.

JAX FISH HOUSE
1539 17th Street (at Wazee), Denver
(303) 292-5767
It's the best fish house in Denver, featuring a great raw bar with a wide variety of oysters. The bar scene is happening—loud, typically three deep, and you always see people you know. The kitchen turns out first-rate fish in many guises, most with a little N'awlins influence.

NEW SAIGON RESTAURANT
630 S. Federal Boulevard, Denver
(303) 936-4954
On my night off, I crave flavors that are completely different from those in my own food, and this Vietnamese restaurant is one of my favorite places to go. It's got vinyl booths and zero atmosphere, but I love the curried shrimp and potatoes over rice noodles, the duck salad, and, in the summer, the soft-shell crab salad.

POTAGER
1109 Ogden Street (at 11th Avenue), Denver
(303) 832-5788
This place is one of my favorites in Denver. Potager serves consistently good, solid, bistro-style cooking in a very relaxed and funky atmosphere surrounding an always-bustling open kitchen and wine bar. Chef-owner Teri Rippeto supports local farmers, grows her own herbs, and cooks in a straightforward manner that I truly appreciate. Order anything from the wood-fired oven, including one of their great pizzas.

LOCAL HIGHLIGHTS

APPLE CIDER

FRANKLIN CIDER MILL

7450 Franklin Road, Bloomfield Hills (248) 626-2968
Open September through November.

"This is a really good cider mill—the cider is made on the premises. And their homemade doughnuts taste great when they're fresh!"
—TAKASHI YAGIHASHI, TRIBUTE

YATES CIDER MILL

1990 E. Avon Road, Rochester (248) 651-8300

"This is the cider mill our family used to visit regularly when I was growing up in the suburbs of Detroit. Open since 1863, it's been recognized as one of the oldest businesses in Michigan. On recent visits, the flavors stand up to the delicious memories!"
—KAREN PAGE, AUTHOR

"Cider mills are all over the place. A lot of orchards grow heirloom apples, which are listed in the local agricultural books. You ask for Romas or Snows and they juice them right there to make your cider. They might even have a little fryer hooked up for fresh doughnuts. Buy some pumpkins, and you're all set. I write for the Detroit Free Press and spent three years trying to track all the cider mills down, and I finally gave up. I would be out there every Saturday and Sunday driving like crazy, trying to rate them all. It was nuts!"
—JIMMY SCHMIDT, THE RATTLESNAKE CLUB

BREAD

STONE HOUSE BREAD

407 S. Main Street, Leland (231) 256-2577 or (800) 252-3218

"Their sourdough and semolina breads are especially good."
—TAKASHI YAGIHASHI, TRIBUTE

"A great time to visit Detroit is during apple cider season, September through November. There are perhaps more cider mills in Michigan than in any other state."

JIMMY SCHMIDT   THE RATTLESNAKE CLUB

DOUGHNUTS

DUNKIN' DONUTS

Multiple locations

"I crave their powder-sugared Bavarian Kreme doughnuts when they're fresh."
—TAKASHI YAGIHASHI, TRIBUTE

FISH

CHUCK MUER RESTAURANTS

Multiple locations, including:
Chuck Muer's Seafood Tavern
5656 West Maple Road, West Bloomfield
(248) 851-2251
www.muer.com

"This chain of restaurants is good. They probably do the best commercial job in the marketplace. The original was the oldest fish restaurant in the city—it goes back four or five generations. Chuck Muer made a lot of money by moving out to the suburbs and developing the concept into a chain. When Hurricane Andrew came through, though, he was lost at sea while sailing—he went to live with the fishes. So, in the end, the fish got him back."
—JIMMY SCHMIDT, THE RATTLESNAKE CLUB

HOT DOG

LAFAYETTE CONEY ISLAND

118 W. Lafayette Boulevard, Detroit
(313) 964-8198

"A Detroit classic, the hot dogs are topped with chili, mustard, and onions."
—JIMMY SCHMIDT, THE RATTLESNAKE CLUB

Jimmy Schmidt

JIMMY SCHMIDT is chef-owner of the Rattlesnake Club, which was named Restaurant of the Year in 1995 by the *Detroit Monthly* and was included in *Gourmet*'s list of America's Top Tables in 2000. Schmidt writes a weekly column for the *Detroit Free Press*/Knight Ridder News Service and is a contributor to *Food Arts* magazine. His cookbooks include *Cooking for All Seasons*, *Jimmy Schmidt's Cooking Class*, and *Heart Healthy Cooking for All Seasons* (co-authored with Alice Waters and Larry Forgione). He serves on the boards of Chefs Collaborative 2000 and Share Our Strength. In 1993, he won the James Beard Award as Best Chef: Midwest.

THE RATTLESNAKE CLUB
300 River Place Drive
Detroit, MI 48207
Phone: (313) 567-4400
Fax: (313) 567-2063
www.rattlesnakeclub.com

MY FOOD At the Rattlesnake Club, we try to collide contrasting flavors and ingredients that will enhance the food, but we don't want to put so many things on a plate that you lose the beauty of what you ordered. If you order salmon, everything on the plate is going to be a supporting ingredient to the salmon. We try not to overhandle the food. We put a lot of work into the sauces so as not to have to make the dishes overly complicated.

JIMMY'S PICKS

ANNAM
22053 Michigan Avenue, Dearborn
(313) 565-8744
This is a great new Vietnamese restaurant. The spicy catfish is my favorite.

THE MINI RESTAURANT
475 University Avenue West, Windsor (Ontario, Canada, which is right across the Detroit River from Detroit)
(519) 258-5707
Before it expanded, this Vietnamese restaurant originally only had eight tables—hence the name. I like the spicy noodle dishes, which are flavored with homemade chili paste. They also do exotic fruit-slushy type drinks, with things like jackfruit and durian; it is crazy stuff, and I like it!

MON JIN LAU
1515 E. Maple Road, Troy
(248) 689-2332
Mon Jin Lau is a family-owned Chinese restaurant. As the third-generation owner, Marshall Chin is breaking out of the family barriers and starting to do food with a pan-Asian twist, such as eggplant glazed with ginger-garlic sauce and stuffed with Vietnamese rice noodles, and Chilean sea bass cooked in a banana leaf. They have great duck and a crossover tuna tartare. (See also p. 101.)

TAPAWINGO
9502 Lake Street, Ellsworth (about five hours north of Detroit)
(231) 588-7971
I always go to Tapawingo when I am on vacation in northern Michigan. Chef-owner Harlan "Pete" Peterson does a great job. It is modern American food, stylish and elegant in presentation, but featuring great local ingredients and solid flavors. The dinner menu changes daily [and features dishes such as roasted apple and parsnip soup, and duck prosciutto salad], but the food is always very satisfying.

TRIBUTE
31425 W. 12Mile Read, Farmington Hills
(248) 848-9393
Chef Takashi Yagihashi and host Mickey Bask deliver fabulous food and service for an impressive night out. They serve great risotto with white truffles and venison with parsnips.

A COUPLE OF PLACES WHERE I GO WITH MY KIDS:

MAMA ROSA'S
15134 Mack Avenue, Detroit
(313) 822-3046
They make a good neighborhood pizza pie. We like the pepperoni.

VILLAGE GRILLE
16930 Kercheval, Grosse Point
(313) 882-4555
They've got great hamburgers and patty melts, which my kids and I enjoy.

JIMMY SCHMIDT on
Visiting Michigan

IF YOU ARE GOING TO SAMPLE LOCAL INGREDIENTS IN DETROIT, MAKE sure you have some of the local fish. Lake perch, pickerel—also called yellow wall-eye—and whitefish are three indigenous fish that are popular, and you won't see them in other parts of the country. They are sweet and tender white fish. That's what the Great Lakes are all about. If you go thirty-five miles out of the city, you are in orchards and farmland. Certain areas are particularly good for seasonal produce:

- FRANKENMOUTH is in the middle of the state, and is good for potatoes.

- HOLLAND is known for bulbs, like tulips.

- KALAMAZOO is where you'll find celery and mint. This area supplies all the mint for Wrigley's spearmint gum.

- LEAMINGTON is where they have huge asparagus and blueberry production.

- PORT HURON, on the east side of the state near the waterfront, is where a lot of apple orchards are.

- TRAVERSE CITY is where you'll find cherries galore.

TAKASHI YAGIHASHI is executive chef of Tribute. He was formerly the chef under Gabino Sotelino at the four-star restaurant Ambria in Chicago. He earned Tribute a four-star rating from the *Detroit Free Press*, which named Tribute Restaurant of the Year in 2000. The *New York Times* has hailed Tribute as "the best restaurant in Detroit." In 1999, Yagihashi was nominated for the James Beard Award as Best Chef: Midwest, and in 2000 he was named one of America's Best New Chefs by *Food & Wine* magazine.

Takashi Yagihashi

TRIBUTE
31425 W. 12 Mile Road
Farmington Hills, MI 48334
Phone: (248) 848-9393
Fax: (248) 848-1919
www.tribute-restaurant.com

MY FOOD I believe you have to start with the best ingredients, and then you can approach cooking two ways: keeping it very simple with pure ingredients, or make it more complex. A ratatouille is many flavors, combined to make one. I am working at a style that combines both approaches. I do contemporary French food with Asian influences, in a not too intimidating atmosphere. You don't have to concentrate and be uptight to eat here. This is an informal atmosphere with serious food.

TAKASHI'S PICKS

ANNAM RESTAURANT
VIETNAMESE

22053 Michigan Avenue, Dearborn
(313) 565-8744
I love this simple but elegant small Vietnamese restaurant, where the food is very eclectic. At lunch I like to order *pho ha noi*, a Hanoi-style noodle soup with beef, which is a great dish!

CHERRY BLOSSOM
JAPANESE RESTAURANT

43588 W. Oaks Drive, Novi
(248) 380-9160
I go to this Japanese restaurant a lot, and luckily my kids like it, too. They are open until ten-thirty P.M., so sometimes I sneak in after work. I like to order a lot of Japanese appetizers. They do homey stuff, like steamed soybeans and sushi. My wife likes the tuna with fermented soybeans.

EMILY'S RESTAURANT

505 N. Center Street, Northville
(248) 349-0505
Emily's is a small, sixty-seat American bistro. I like to go here with just my wife. It is similar to a small, cozy inn, and they have wonderful food. I often order the veal chop—which is from a local farm, Sommerfield—or a light pizza. The wine list is very good here, too, with lots of Californian wines.

FORTE

201 S. Old Woodward Avenue, Birmingham
(248) 594-7300
Forte is close to my house, so sometimes after work I will sit at the bar and have an appetizer with a nice glass of wine. It is fine dining in a lively atmosphere, with great wine and good seafood. They make Mediterranean-influenced food, like pizza and pasta, and they have a wood-burning oven. I usually get a pizza with broccoli and anchovies, or a California-type pizza with salmon. They also do a beautiful rack of lamb.

MON JIN LAU

1515 E. Maple Road, Troy
(248) 689-2332
This is another place that's open late. It is modern American-Chinese, with a sushi bar. I like to get the spicy stir-fried calamari with chiles. They have a good wine list, too. I usually get a wine from Alsace, like Pinot Alsace or Gewürztraminer. I think Chinese food works well with Alsatian wines. (See also p. 99.)

Roy Yamaguchi

ROY'S

6600 Kalanaianaole Highway
Honolulu, HI 96825
Phone: (808) 396-7697
Fax: (808) 396-8706
www.roysrestaurant.com

ROY YAMAGUCHI is executive chef-owner of Roy's Restaurants, which has multiple locations, including the original flagship restaurant in Honolulu. After graduating from The Culinary Institute of America, Yamaguchi cooked in several southern California kitchens, including L'Escoffier, L'Ermitage, and Michael's, before opening his own restaurant. In 1988 he opened Roy's, which has been voted Most Popular Restaurant in the Hawaii *ZagatSurvey*. Yamaguchi has played a primary role in the development of Hawaiian regional cuisine. He won the 1993 James Beard Award as Best Chef: Northwest and Hawaii, and is the author of *Roy's Feasts from Hawaii* and the host of the PBS series *Hawaii Cooks with Roy Yamaguchi*.

MY FOOD I think of my approach to food as a way to preserve my personal creativity, and I call my cooking style contemporary Euro-Asian. I like strong, assertive flavors and unusual combinations, and I insist on using absolutely fresh produce, meat, and fish, all preferably from local sources. When I opened the original Roy's, my goal was to serve exciting, innovative, fun food of the highest quality in an elegant yet casual atmosphere, and at affordable prices. I also wanted to emphasize service and provide our customers with as much as possible—I call this the "aloha spirit." Luckily, the combination of these things struck a chord.

Now when we open a new Roy's, we bring certain things from the original menu, but we also encourage the chef to develop his own ideas. I say, "Okay, listen. This is a Roy's, so we have certain goals, flavors, and philosophies and a certain boldness that we want in our food, but you can go ahead and create. Just create within our realm." I make the standard menu, then I work with the chef to incorporate local tastes and ingredients.

Recently, a number of chefs in Hawaii have banded together to form the Hawaii regional cuisine movement. One of our aims is to encourage local food growers and suppliers to work in partnership with restaurants. It has been exciting to witness the growth of high-quality Hawaiian-grown products.

Hawaii is very beautiful, with the mountains and the ocean, but the dining is very limited. I usually don't go out for dinner until very late, so there are even fewer places to choose from. Hawaiian and Japanese restaurants are about your only choices after nine-thirty P.M.

ROY'S PICKS

ALAN WONG'S

1857 S. King Street, 5th floor, Honolulu
(808) 949-2526

The only place I go that's on the upscale side is Alan Wong's. The food is
very artistic and very tasty. He uses
different-colored plates, a lot of
height, and a lot of symmetry. When
he decorates a plate, you can tell
without knowing who created it. You
can see that he is strongly influenced
by Asia. He has a tomato shooter
made from green and yellow juices
that's served in a long, thin, almost
fluted glass, and served really cold
with a Kalua pig and foie gras sandwich. It's the greatest thing on earth!
What's great is that the soup is so cold
and creamy and that the sandwich is
almost like a buttered, well-grilled
cheese sandwich. It's one of the
greatest things you can put in your
mouth. He also makes a really neat
amuse-gueule—it's like a really tiny
hamburger, about the size of a quarter, but instead of using meat he uses
tuna. (See also p. 297.)

DYNASTY

1778 Alamoana Boulevard, Honolulu
(808) 947-3771

Dynasty is open until four A.M. I like to
order *congee* [Chinese rice porridge]
here, and I also like the Chinese soup
with the preserved egg that looks
translucent on the outside. They
make a good stew with cod, tofu, and
shiitake mushrooms that's served in a
really rich, sweet and spicy sauce—almost like an oyster sauce. They also
have a really nice dish with Chinese
broccoli and dried flounder. They
dice the dried flounder like bacon and
actually flavor their vegetable with
this dried fish and fish sauce. It
smells a little bit, but it's great.

IMANAS
IZAKAYA NOMBEI

3108 Olu Street, Honolulu
(808) 734-5574

Imanas is a good place for late-night
food. In Japanese, a restaurant like
Imanas is called an *izakaya*—they are
places for drinking, socializing, and
eating. At Imanas, you can have
sushi as well as different types of
cooked Japanese food. I like *donburi*,
which is served in a large soup bowl
with a cover—inside you have cooked
rice, a pork cutlet with sautéed
onions on top, and an over-easy egg
with some sweet soy sauce on it.
They also have plain deep-fried
shrimp. It's like a restaurant that has
Japanese comfort foods.

LEUNG'S CAFÉ

2343 N. King Street, Honolulu
(808) 845-0301

At Leung's Café, they specialize in
Hawaiian food. They serve everything from *poi* [taro root that has
been peeled, cooked, and then
pounded into a smooth paste] to
poke, which is tuna mixed with salt or
seaweed and soy sauce. They have
different soups also. Luau soup is
made with taro leaves, and you can
have it with squid. I like to go here
with one or two other people, because the portions are so large.

SIDE STREET INN

1225 Hopaka Street, Honolulu
(808) 591-0253

A lot of people come here to drink,
but they also have great food, and
they are open until two A.M. They are
known for their fried pork chops,
and they use local pork for them.
They cut the chops about an inch
thick, and flour, spice, and fry them,
and then they slice them open and
serve them with ketchup. They make
their own *poke*, and they have a
sliced twelve-ounce Spencer steak.
The food is plain, but it's really
good. They also serve some noodles,
like plain Chinese chow mein noodles. I usually have a cold beer, or
Absolut on the rocks. It's a great
place. I used to go with Alan Wong
all the time.

Barbecue

GOODE COMPANY BARBEQUE

8911 Katy Freeway, Houston
(713) 464-1901
5109 Kirby Drive, Houston
(713) 522-2530

" Their ribs are Texas-style with dry seasoning and mesquite-smoked, which gives them some sweetness. The sauce is not ketchupy or sweet—it's more like pan drippings with a little bit of tomato in it. They probably use molasses, but it's not shiny and it's not a glaze. We always have some chicken and brisket. You've got to eat brisket—it's one of the great variations of barbecue. I always like the potato salad, cole slaw, and beans. "

—ROBERT DEL GRANDE, CAFÉ ANNIE

OTTO'S BARBECUE AND HAMBURGERS

5502 Memorial Drive, Houston
(713) 864-2573

" A good barbecue place. It was founded in 1950 and serves more than twelve hundred pounds of barbecue daily. A lot of people like Otto's, maybe even President Bush—in whose honor Otto's named a combo plate on its menu. "

—ROBERT DEL GRANDE, CAFÉ ANNIE

Hamburger

BECK'S PRIME HAMBURGER PLACE

Multiple locations, including:
2615 Augusta Drive, Houston (713) 266-9901

" They have charcoal-grilled burgers, and the best part about it is that they have outdoor seating under this enormous oak tree that must be a hundred and fifty years old, which they built the restaurant around. The biggest thing for me about a burger is to be able to order it rare, and to have it served rare or even medium-rare without signing a waiver or something. Every once in a while I like to have a chili burger, but I have to lie down afterward, so I save that for Sundays. "

—ROBERT DEL GRANDE, CAFÉ ANNIE

CAFÉ EXPRESS

Multiple locations, including:
3200 Kirby Drive, Houston (713) 522-3994

" They make really good burgers. "

—ROBERT DEL GRANDE, CAFÉ ANNIE

RIO RANCH

9999 Westheimer Road, Houston
(713) 952-5000

" They have a great cowboy-type burger out at the Rio Ranch, for which I consult. They have a wood fire, which they roast Anaheim or poblano chiles on, and they make real authentic ranch-style Mexican beans. It's kind of a knife-and-fork burger, but it's pretty incredible. "

—ROBERT DEL GRANDE, CAFÉ ANNIE

ROBERT DEL GRANDE on

What to Drink with Barbecue

WHAT SHOULD YOU DRINK WITH BARBECUE? BEER IS ALWAYS GOOD, but Alsatian Gewürztraminer is a particularly great match because it picks the smoke up well, and it's good with pork. There are actually a lot of strong German influences in Texas. Syrah works pretty well, too—something that's kind of country-style and fresh. And we always chill them down to about sixty degrees or so, and serve them a bit cool.

PIZZA

FUZZY'S PIZZAS

Multiple locations, including:
613 S. Mason Road, Katy
(281) 579-0100

"*Even former president George Bush still goes there, and you can tell because probably every time he goes in, they try to take his photograph to put on the wall. It's a loaded-up pizza, usually with sausage, pepperoni, and artichoke. It's not really thick-crust, nor cracker-thin; it's more focaccia-like.*"

—ROBERT DEL GRANDE, CAFÉ ANNIE

STEAK

PALM

6100 Westheimer Road, Houston
(713) 977-2544

"*There are certainly enough Texas steakhouses, but for some reason, we always go to the Palm, which originated in New York. The beef is pretty good. I only order one thing there, and that's the New York strip. It's the one prime steak that's actually prime there. It's pretty casual, so I'll take my daughter, who likes their fried calamari.*"

—ROBERT DEL GRANDE, CAFÉ ANNIE

TEX-MEX

NINFA'S

Multiple locations, including:
2704 Navigation Boulevard, Houston
(713) 228-1175
Founder Ninfa Laurenzo is credited as the creator of *fajitas,* and the restaurant is also known for its avocado hot sauce.

"*What do you do when people come in from out of town? One option is to go have barbecue, and the other is to go to a Tex-Mex restaurant, just because it has the word Texas in the name of the cuisine itself. It's a funny cuisine, because on the one hand, it certainly doesn't have the great depth and complexity of Mexican cooking, but on the other, it's sort of a wacky, fun thing. Everyone goes to Ninfa's on Navigation, which is the original location downtown, because it maintains a certain religious quality that you can never quite define, and it hasn't been diluted.*"

—ROBERT DEL GRANDE, CAFÉ ANNIE

Robert Del Grande

CAFÉ ANNIE
1728 Post Oak Boulevard
Houston, TX 77056
Phone: (713) 840-1111
Fax: (713) 840-1558
www.cafe-express.com

ROBERT DEL GRANDE is chef-partner of Café Annie, the Café Express restaurant concept, Rio Ranch, and Taco Milagro. After receiving a Ph.D. in biochemistry, Del Grande accepted a kitchen position at Café Annie, which turned into a long-term apprenticeship and eventual partnership. He has been a primary figure in the evolution of southwestern cuisine. Café Annie was included in *Gourmet*'s 1997 and 1998 America's Top Tables lists, and the magazine cited Café Annie for Top Food and Top Wine List in Houston in 1999. It ranked number one in popularity in the 1999 Houston *ZagatSurvey*. Among Del Grande's honors is the 1992 James Beard Award as Best Chef: Southwest.

MY FOOD Our goal was to build local restaurants that made you feel like you were in Texas—not because of shtick, but to give you a feel of what the local tastes are. We try to use as many local products as possible in dishes such as fresh corn tamales with wood-grilled shrimp and *crema fresca*, and venison sausage with red chile barbecue sauce and white grits. Our intent is for everything to feel personal to us. What we want is an authentic effort, so we don't imitate anyone else.

ROBERT'S PICKS

CAFÉ EXPRESS

Multiple locations, including:
3200 Kirby Drive, Houston
(713) 522-3994

We go to our own casual, self-service place, Café Express, because it's quick, fast, and good food. The menu includes salads, including a Caesar salad with grilled chicken, hamburgers, roasted chicken, pastas, and desserts, including chocolate-pecan brownies. It's funny—when you visit your own restaurant, you have to decide whether you are going to eat or going to work!

MAI'S RESTAURANT

3403 Milam Street, Houston
(713) 520-7684

Mai's is a Vietnamese restaurant downtown. It's run by Mai Thi Nguyen's parents, who opened Houston's first Vietnamese restaurant in 1975. It's open late, until three A.M., and its authentically spicy food [which includes specialties such as spring rolls, garlic chicken, and Alaskan king crab legs] is very good.

NIT NOI THAI RESTAURANT

2426 Bolsover Street, Houston (Rice Village)
(713) 524-8114
6395 Woodway Drive, Houston
(713) 789-1711

This family-run Thai restaurant—one of Houston's first—is really good, and close to us. You have to order by the number. Getting my kid set at a restaurant is a major thing, but my daughter really likes the *pad thai* here. We usually get a coconut soup, and then Thai eggplant and Tiger Cried, which is a really spicy beef dish. Their noodle dishes are good, too.

OTILIA'S MEXICAN RESTAURANT

7710 Long Point Road (at Wirt Road), Houston
(713) 681-7203

For Mexican food, I like Otilia's. It's a taqueria, but they also have a full menu of Mexican food. Their *mole* is really good, and I especially like the chicken *mole*. The enchiladas are good, too. This is not just typical straight-up Tex-Mex stuff; they also have dishes like *gorditas*, *pozole* [hominy stew], and banana-roasted pork. It's very casual, like a drive-through.

TACO MILAGRO HANDMADE FOOD AND TEQUILA BAR

2555 Kirby Drive, Houston
(713) 522-1999

When eating out, I try to balance going to other places with visiting our own to make sure we're competitive. Taco Milagro is our own Mexican restaurant, which blends Mexico's European and Indian past into a celebration of food and décor. The menu features dishes such as pork enchiladas and skirt steak tacos, as well as a salsa bar and a tequila bar featuring more than forty artisanal tequilas and mezcals, as well as specialty margaritas.

ROBERT DEL GRANDE on

Tequila

When I'm not drinking Maker's Mark or Knob Creek bourbon, I'm drinking tequila. Here's my honest take on that: I love tequila and margaritas. There are two types: "residential" margaritas and "commercial" margaritas. Most commercial margaritas you find in restaurants are crummy; they're just loaded with junk. At Taco Milagro, we actually try to take a stand on this. We have a tequila bar with all the one-hundred-percent-agave, smaller-boutique tequilas, and we make the margaritas with just Cointreau and fresh lime juice. My first choice is Heradera tequila, which is a good value and extremely well made. I think Chinako is really good, and El Tesoro is good, too.

"I love to eat at Café Annie when I'm in Houston."

STEPHAN PYLES

AQUAKNOX (DALLAS)

MONICA POPE is the chef-owner of Boulevard Bistrot. In 1996, she was named one of the ten best new chefs by *Food & Wine* magazine. Boulevard Bistrot has been described by Houston restaurant critic Alison Cook as "the closest thing Houston has to Chez Panisse." Pope is a charter member of the Chefs Collaborative 2000, and her restaurant earmarks a percentage of its Wednesday sales for various Houston charities.

Monica Pope

BOULEVARD BISTROT
4319 Montrose Boulevard
Houston, TX 77006
Phone: (713) 524-6922
Fax: (713) 524-9728

MY FOOD My bent on food is a mix of different cultures and spices and herbs. I hesitate to put a label on it, but it is just American food. We start with great ingredients, then try to take them a step further. We try to combine flavors that people remember. When people tell me six months later what they had, I know I'm succeeding. If they come in and say they had great service and loved the atmosphere but can't remember the food, I know we missed that one.

I am not doing authentic ethnic cuisine; I am just doing food that reflects all the influences I have had. I have never wanted to pigeonhole myself or to have to do one type of food. My food has been described as eclectic, patchwork, melting-pot cuisine, but I would just like it to be thought of as American food. Our main focus at the bistro is that we want people to eat here every day. The food is not so unusual or rich that it's possible to do that. It works; some customers joke that this place is their living room! And we keep our prices at a level so that it can happen.

ASHIANA

12610 Briar Forest, Houston
(281) 679-5555

Ashiana is run by a woman who came in here about a year or two ago. Houston is laid out in a kind of loop system, and Ashiana is way outside the loop. But when I finally got out there, I was just blown away. It was wonderful! We went on a Sunday night, and when we walked in, there were a hundred and fifty Indian people there celebrating. I just thought, "This is the place!" They have a tandoori chef and a curry chef, and we had a tandoori snapper, on the bone, that was really nice. She does a really nice lentil dish that's just so rich it's unbelievable. There are also a lot of different kinds of bread that are all really wonderful.

EL MESON

2425 University Boulevard (between Morningside and Kirby), Houston
(713) 522-9306

One place I go on a pretty regular basis is El Meson, which is a very casual restaurant serving a hybrid of Cuban-Mexican food. We'll typically order the *ropa vieja* [shredded beef brisket, stewed Cuban style]. They also have good paella, plantains, and things like that.

FUSION CAFÉ

3722 Main Street, Houston
(713) 874-1116

At the Fusion Café, they're fusing southern food with West Indian food. I always appreciate when I can get chicken that's been braised on the bone, or stews and curries or a simple rice dish. They also have funky things, like fried chicken on waffles and cream gravy, and they have really good carrot cake and ginger beer. About once a month, it's fun to go here.

LA VISTA PIZZERIA AND ITALIAN CUISINE

1936 Fountain View Drive, Houston
(713) 787-9899

La Vista is a little Italian café in a strip center run by Gregory Gordon, who used to work at Daily Review Cafe. One of his signature dishes is a really good fig pizza with caramelized walnuts, served on really good bread. And he's got great, simple bowls of pasta. It's a little hole in the wall, but that's what I tend to like.

PAULIE'S

1834 Westheimer Road, Houston
(713) 807-7271

I'll go to another place, Paulie's, right down the street, just to get a PB-and-J or spaghetti and meatballs. They always laugh and ask, "Who's this for?" but the truth is we never cook at home. Kathy and Bernard Petronella, the owners—the restaurant is named after son Paulie—cook like home cooks in a professional setting. The food is not cutting-edge—the menu features salads, sandwiches, pastas, and desserts—but it's refreshing to go there and just have a counter-style lunch or early dinner [as the restaurant closes at 9 P.M.].

BarBecue

LC'S BAR-B-QUE

5800 Blue Parkway, Kansas City (816) 923-4484

"A hole in the wall known for its baby back ribs."
—MICHAEL SMITH AND DEBBIE GOLD, THE AMERICAN RESTAURANT

JACK'S STACK BARBECUE OF MARTIN CITY

13441 Holmes Road (at 135th Street), Kansas City (816) 942-9141

"For barbecued beef, chicken, and pork."
—MICHAEL SMITH AND DEBBIE GOLD, THE AMERICAN RESTAURANT

Beer

BOULEVARD BREWING COMPANY

2501 Southwest Boulevard, Kansas City (816) 474-7095

"The best beer in Kansas City. They're obsessed with using only the highest-quality ingredients and make a lager, pale ale, wheat beer, porter, stout, and others. Don't miss it when you're in town."
—MICHAEL SMITH AND DEBBIE GOLD, THE AMERICAN RESTAURANT

Fried CHICKen

STROUD'S

1015 E. 85th Street, Kansas City (816) 333-2132

"I'm from Kansas City, and whether I go back for two weeks or two days, I always make time to go to Stroud's. It's a home-style restaurant that serves fried chicken family-style. You can order any kind of chicken part you want, whether it is livers, gizzards, or white or dark meat. I always order the chicken gizzards, which come in an outrageously huge portion. All their sides are great—mashed potatoes and gravy, green beans, soup. Just like Grandma made. It's the sort of place you go just to see good cooking. I was happy to see them recognized by the James Beard Awards." (See also p. 111.)
—KENT RATHBUN, ABACUS (DALLAS)

Pizza/Deli

D'BRONX

3904 Bell Street, Kansas City (816) 531-0550

"Good food in a mom-and-pop atmosphere."
—MICHAEL SMITH AND DEBBIE GOLD, THE AMERICAN RESTAURANT

Michael Smith and Debbie Gold

THE AMERICAN RESTAURANT

200 E. 25th Street
Kansas City, MO 64108
Phone: (816) 426-1133
Fax: (816) 426-1190

MICHAEL SMITH and DEBBIE GOLD are the chefs of the American Restaurant. They were named Chefs to Watch in 1997 by *Esquire* magazine, and have consistently been awarded four-star Mobil and four-diamond AAA ratings. In 1999, they won the James Beard Award as Best Chefs: Midwest.

OUR FOOD The American Restaurant is a twenty-year-old fine-dining legend in Kansas City. From thirty-foot ceiling-to-floor windows on two sides of the dining room, guests can view the spectacular Crown Center and downtown skyline. The food is an elegant representation of modern American cuisine. We feature an abundance of locally grown, organic agriculture. Chicken, lamb, duck, and eggs come from Campo Lindo Farms, and countless varieties of fresh produce arrive daily from Susan's Herb Garden.

MICHAEL AND DEBBIE'S PICKS

LAMAR'S DONUTS

Multiple locations, including:
240 E. Linwood, Kansas City
(the original)
(816) 931-5166
315 N.E. Vivion Road, Kansas City
(816) 455-7888
or call (800) 533-7489 to have "the donut of your dreams" delivered
The original LaMar's is a converted gas station that fries [in lard, just as they have since 1960] the best doughnuts in the country. The owner, Ray LaMar, who's probably eighty-five years old, is there every morning when LaMar's opens, at six A.M. It's located in a rough part of Kansas City, and you usually stand in a long line that swings out the door. LaMar's glazed doughnuts are the best. It's rumored that each LaMar's location sells more than eleven thousand doughnuts daily.

ORTEGA'S MINI MARKET AND RESTAURANTE

2646 Belleview Avenue, Kansas City
(816) 531-5415
This Mexican hole in the wall serves up fresh tacos, *gorditas*—which are described on the menu as Mexican corn pita bread sandwiches—and *nopale* cactus salads daily. Ortega's is a Mexican grocery with a six-table restaurant in back. It's a familiar place for business or a local neighborhood hangout—whichever you're in the mood for.

THE PEANUT

5000 Main Street, Kansas City
(816) 753-9499
This is the oldest continually operating bar in Kansas City. The place is an absolute dive but serves an outstanding BLT. It seems unusual, but many of our guests can be seen enjoying Sunday brunch at the Peanut. They also serve good burgers.

SAIGON 39

1806½ W. 39th Street, Kansas City
(816) 531-4447
Saigon 39 is a small Vietnamese café serving wonderful soups and noodle salads. We get cravings for their simple house salad with fish sauce dressing. We want our daughters to experience as many flavors as possible at a young age, and this casual, family-owned restaurant allows them to do exactly that.

STROUD'S

1015 E. 85th Street, Kansas City
(816) 333-2132
This restaurant won a James Beard Award in 1998 for great American regional cooking. They do killer fried chicken, gizzards, mashed potatoes, and green beans. There is always an hour wait. We usually down a few Boulevard Pale Ales while we anticipate the large platters of fried chicken. Their slogan is "We choke our own chickens!"

Bertolli Olive Oil America's Regional Classics recognize "restaurants of timeless appeal, loved in their region for quality food that reflects the character and history of their communities."

2000

Camp Washington Chili
3005 Colerain Avenue
Cincinnati, OH
(513) 541-0061

Helena's Hawaiian Foods
1364 North King Street
Honolulu, HI
(808) 845-8044

Mario's
2342 Arthur Avenue
Bronx, NY
(718) 584-1188

Moosewood
215 North Cayuga Street
Dewitt Mall
Ithaca, NY
(607) 273-9610

Mrs. Wilkes Dining Room
107 West Jones Street
Savannah, GA
(912) 233-8970

**The Original
Sonny Bryan's**
2202 Inwood Road
Dallas, TX
(214) 357-7120

Swan Oyster Depot
1517 Polk Street
San Francisco, CA
(415) 673-1101

White House Sub Shop
2301 Architect Avenue
Atlantic City, NJ
(609) 345-1564

1999

The Berghoff
17 W. Adams Street
Chicago, IL
(312) 427-3170

Café Pasqual's
121 Dawn Gaspar Avenue
Santa Fe, NM
(505) 983-9340

**Doumar's Cones and
Barbecue**
20th and Monticello Avenue
Norfolk, VA
(757) 627-4163

**Frank Pepe Pizzeria
Napoletana**
157 Wooster Street
New Haven, CT
(203) 865-5762

Mosca's
Highway 90 West, four miles beyond
the Huey P. Long Bridge
Avondale, LA
(504) 436-9942

Original Pancake House
8601 S.W. 24th Avenue
Portland, OR
(503) 246-1049

The Oyster Bar
Grand Central Terminal, lower level
New York, NY
(212) 490-6650

Philippe's—The Original
1001 N. Alameda Street
Los Angeles, CA
(213) 628-3781

1998

**Doris and Ed's Seafood
Restaurant**
348 Shore Drive
Highlands, NJ
(732) 872-1565
www.dorisandeds.com

Durgin Park
340 Faneuil Hall Marketplace
Boston, MA
(617) 227-2038

**Emmett Watson's
Oyster Bar**
Pike Place Market
1916 Pike Place
Seattle, WA
(206) 448-7721

**Joe T. Garcia's Mexican Food
Restaurant**
2201 N. Commerce Street
Fort Worth, TX
(817) 626-8571

Joe's Stone Crab
11 Washington Avenue
Miami Beach, FL
(305) 673-0365

Second Avenue Deli
156 Second Avenue
New York, NY
(212) 677-0606

Stroud's
1015 F. 85th Street
Kansas City, MO
(816) 333-2132

Tadich Grill
240 California Street
San Francisco, CA
(415) 391-1849

LOCAL HIGHLIGHTS

ALL-DAY

ORIGINAL PANTRY

877 S. Figueroa Street, Los Angeles (213) 972-9279

"It's open twenty-four hours, and is right across from the L.A. produce market. You can get anything from fried eggs to sandwiches. It's owned by L.A. mayor Richard Riordan now, and it's always packed."

—CARRIE NAHABEDIAN, RESTAURANT NAHA (CHICAGO)

BAKERY

LA BREA BAKERY

624 S. La Brea Avenue (between Wilshire Boulevard and 6th Street), Los Angeles (323) 938-1447 www.labreabakery.com

"I love Nancy Silverton's croissants, and she also makes these little lemon muffins that are awesome."

—CHRIS BIANCO, PIZZERIA BIANCO (PHOENIX)

"I go here for Nancy Silverton's olive bread."

—MARK MILLER, COYOTE CAFÉ (LAS VEGAS AND SANTA FE)

"I love their breakfast stuff—croissants, muffins, pastries. It's inspiring to see such small things so carefully made."

—AMY SCHERBER, AMY'S BREAD (NEW YORK)

CHINESE

HARBOR SEAFOOD

545 W. Valley Boulevard, San Gabriel (626) 282-3032

VIP HARBOR SEAFOOD

11701 Wilshire Boulevard, West Los Angeles (310) 979-3377

"They are unsurpassed for the authenticity of their Chinese food, and offer such traditional dishes as shark's fin soup. They have adopted the idea that they are not going to bow to anything from the outside, but rather are sticking strictly to their heritage, and that is who they are cooking for. They don't change things for American tastes."

—HANS RÖCKENWAGNER, RÖCKENWAGNER AND RÖCK

BEACH

THE BEACH HOUSE

100 W. Channel Road (at the Pacific Coast Highway), Santa Monica (310) 454-8299

"They serve very consistent California cuisine, right on the beach!"

—CARRIE NAHABEDIAN, RESTAURANT NAHA (CHICAGO)

CELEBRITY SCENE

MORTONS

8764 Melrose Avenue, West Hollywood
(310) 276-5205

"There are certain restaurants that have a buzz that is not based on their cuisine or service or setting. These are places that have created an aura. The best example would be Mortons on a Monday night, when you will see all the movers and shakers convene. You'll see actors and directors there, and you can watch deals being made between tables."

—HANS RÖCKENWAGNER,
RÖCKENWAGNER AND RÖCK

SPAGO BEVERLY HILLS

176 N. Canon Drive, Beverly Hills
(310) 385-0880

"There's nothing like it anywhere else."

—MARK PEEL AND NANCY SILVERTON,
CAMPANILE

"Go here for the food and the whole experience, which are just over the top."

—SUZANNE GOIN, LUCQUES

"There is such an excitement about this place! And chef Lee Hefter's food is incredible."

—LYDIA SHIRE, BIBA AND PIGNOLI (BOSTON)

BREAKFAST

DU-PAR'S

6333 W. 3rd Street (at Fairfax Avenue), Los Angeles (323) 933-8446

"Du-par's is an old, classic place near the farmers' market where I go to get pancakes and rare bacon. The pancakes are perfect—not too fluffy, not too flat. They have a perfectly textured pancake, which is really hard to find. They are about a half inch thick, with butter poured all over them, and so satisfying! They are also famous for their blackberry syrup, which I accidentally used once and was so disappointed. So be careful!"

—SUZANNE GOIN, LUCQUES

"Du-par's is a taste of the style of old Hollywood. They have the best pancakes in all of Los Angeles—and California, for that matter. They're hot and fluffy, never heavy. I'm a purist: I love the regular buttermilk pancakes with maple syrup. My parents were eating here when David Letterman approached them to spend a day with him for his TV show!"

—CARRIE NAHABEDIAN, RESTAURANT NAHA (CHICAGO)

JOHN O'GROATS

10516 W. Pico Boulevard (near Beverly Glen Boulevard), West Los Angeles
(310) 204-0692

"It's just really delicious American food: really good granola, great eggs, and a good cappuccino. We can order our favorite thing that Susan [Feniger] turned me on to about twenty-five years ago: tomatoes and cottage cheese with olive oil, and a bagel, for breakfast."

—MARY SUE MILLIKEN, BORDER GRILL AND CIUDAD

ROSCOE'S HOUSE OF CHICKEN 'N' WAFFLES

Multiple locations, including:
5006 W. Pico Boulevard (at La Brea), Los Angeles (323) 934-4405

"I go to Roscoe's for breakfast for fried chicken and grits. I put Tabasco and salt and pepper on my grits. After not having had any salt or fat in eight hours, you need some!"

—SUSAN FENIGER, BORDER GRILL AND CIUDAD

"Roscoe's is a great place. I like the chicken and waffles. Sometimes a little syrup sneaks across the plate and does get on the edge of the fried chicken, and that's kind of nice."

—MARY SUE MILLIKEN, BORDER GRILL AND CIUDAD

"Thomas Keller, of the French Laundry in Napa Valley, took me there for chicken and waffles when he was cooking at Checkers in Los Angeles. I'm not sure I 'get' it, but it is good!"

—TOM COLICCHIO, GRAMERCY TAVERN (NEW YORK)

DELI

BAY CITIES ITALIAN DELI

1517 Lincoln Boulevard, Santa Monica
(310) 395-8279

"*This is the best deli—there is always a line. They have a huge case with all their cold cuts and salamis, which are of great quality, and they have great imported ingredients, like Parma ham, provolone cheese, and Sicilian olives. While many others take shortcuts on quality, they don't. Of course, they charge for that, but it is worth it. The place is only a five-minute drive or a fifteen-minute walk from the beach, so you can walk there and have a great L.A. eating experience.*"

—HANS RÖCKENWAGNER, RÖCKENWAGNER AND RÖCK

FALAFEL

EAT-A-PITA

465 N. Fairfax Avenue (between Melrose and Beverly), Los Angeles
(323) 651-0188

"*This place has the best falafel.*"

—SUSAN FENIGER AND MARY SUE MILLIKEN, BORDER GRILL AND CIUDAD

FRENCH DIP

PHILIPPE'S—THE ORIGINAL

1001 N. Alameda Street, Los Angeles
(213) 628-3781

"*They created the French dip sandwich here.*"

—CARRIE NAHABEDIAN, RESTAURANT NAHA
(CHICAGO)

ITALIAN

LOCONDA VENETA

8638 W. 3rd Street, West Hollywood
(310) 274-1893

"*This little Italian place is the closest thing you'll find to a New York restaurant in Los Angeles, where you enter the room and can see everything: some tables to one side, and an exposed kitchen to the other, all in one square room. They make beautiful handmade pastas and gnocchi. It's always jam-packed and full of energy.*"

—CARRIE NAHABEDIAN, RESTAURANT NAHA
(CHICAGO)

GREEK

C&K IMPORTING/ PAPA CRISTOS

2771 W. Pico Boulevard, Los Angeles
(323) 737-2970

"*C&K is a great grocery store, and next door, at Papa Cristos restaurant, they sell wonderful lamb kabobs and all kinds of Greek food. When you don't feel like cooking, you can pick food up to bring home. They are really good at catering, and even offer whole roasted lambs.*"

—MARY SUE MILLIKEN,
BORDER GRILL AND CIUDAD

TAVERNA TONY

23410 Civic Center Way, Malibu
(310) 317-9667

"*It's across from the ocean, in a shopping center, and you can eat outside. They have great Greek food— including souvlaki and mezze platters. They even have belly dancers!*"

—CARRIE NAHABEDIAN, RESTAURANT NAHA
(CHICAGO)

CITRUS

6703 Melrose Avenue
(at Highland Avenue), Los Angeles
(323) 857-0034

"We always have great meals there. Chef Michel Richard's cooking is flawless. It is a cool place for lunch because of the daylight and the open kitchen. The food is always inspirational. He is also one of the few great chefs who can do desserts as well as they do savory items. Many chefs don't do pastry well at all. He is one of the few who hve crossed over and are able to have fun."

—GALE GAND AND RICK TRAMONTO,
BRASSERIE T AND TRU (CHICAGO)

THE IVY

113 N. Robertson, West Hollywood
(310) 274-8303

"I love eating outside, and lunch at the Ivy is perfect for those days that you're feeling great— or not feeling great, because you'll be uplifted! It's all about overindulgence and chintz. In the summertime, the soft-shell crabs are great, and I love ordering their chopped vegetable salad with grilled chicken. It's the only place where chipped china is fashionable."

—CARRIE NAHABEDIAN, RESTAURANT NAHA
(CHICAGO)

APPLE PAN

10801 W. Pico Boulevard (at Westwood Boulevard), West Los Angeles
(310) 475-3585

"There is a little battle in L.A. between Jay's Jayburgers and Apple Pan. Apple Pan is the West Side's burger place and Jay's is the East Side's. I admit that Apple Pan is good, but I have to stick up for the East Side! Apple Pan has been around since the early 1900s. There is a horseshoe of stools—the kind that don't move— around the bar. When you get a Coke, it comes in a paper cone that sits in a plastic holder. There are two back-to-back griddles and fryers with one guy on each, and these guys are pretty intense. While they offer two kinds of burgers, you should only order the hickory. They have really good fries and pies—which Jay's doesn't—and the banana cream pie is especially good."

—SUZANNE GOIN, LUCQUES

JAY'S JAYBURGERS

4481 Santa Monica Boulevard, Silverlake
(323) 666-5204

"This is a little stand with maybe ten stools, and always has the same two guys running it. The burgers are grilled. I like mine with chili and cheese on them. Everything looks wrong, so when you go there, you will think, 'What the hell was she talking about?' Then you'll taste their hamburger, and you will see that it is super-satisfying."

—SUZANNE GOIN, LUCQUES

MO BETTER MEATTY MEAT BURGERS

5855 W. Pico Boulevard, Los Angeles
(323) 938-6558

"I've had really good burgers here."

—SUSAN FENIGER, BORDER GRILL AND CIUDAD

GRAND CENTRAL MARKET

Broadway and 3rd Street, Los Angeles
For fresh produce and meats at low prices

Susan Feniger: "I love the place that makes pupusas, those Salvadoran corn tortillas stuffed with meat, beans, or cheese, topped with tomato sauce and a pickled cabbage relish." Mary Sue Milliken: "I like the place around the corner, the one that makes gorditas—thick tortillas filled with anything from fish hash to shredded cheese."

—SUSAN FENIGER AND MARY SUE MILLIKEN, BORDER GRILL AND CIUDAD

Japanese

ITACHO

7311 Beverly Boulevard, Los Angeles
(323) 938-9009

"It is the best place to take people from out of town because of the setting: it is between a porno video store and a liquor store. It is a hip, bohemian-slash-Hollywoody-slash-arty place, and it's always packed. They serve lots of little dishes, like miso, eggplant, and spinach. They also have great yellowtail collar, which is the jaw of the fish, that is tender and falling apart, and seasoned with a little miso."

—SUZANNE GOIN, LUCQUES

"Itacho has fabulous, really impeccably fresh sashimi, and lots and lots of vegetables. I usually order things like lotus root, gobo, peppers, and soybeans. I love the yams and the gingko nuts—I order everything. It's really good and they always have the best sashimi. It's different all the time, but they might have giant clam, toro, or monkfish liver."

—SUSAN FENIGER AND MARY SUE MILLIKEN, BORDER GRILL AND CIUDAD

TOMBO

2601 Artesia Boulevard, Torrance (310) 324-5190

"We go there a lot. It's a Japanese restaurant that mostly serves okono miyaki, those pancakes that you make yourself on a griddle in front of you. They are really fantastic. You order the kind you want, and they bring you the stuff to mix up and fry for yourself. They even teach you how to do it. It's really great. We have them with cod roe or with fermented soybeans, or you can just get them with simple things, like shrimp or squid or pork. It's great, adventurous eating, and it's a great place for kids. When you walk in the door, all of the ten or twelve tables will be completely full, with about fifty people total—yet it's silent. Everybody is sitting there, each reading a different Japanese comic book. It's hysterical!"

—SUSAN FENIGER AND MARY SUE MILLIKEN, BORDER GRILL AND CIUDAD

Korean

MANPUKU

2125 Sawtelle, West Los Angeles
(310) 473-0580

"This Korean-Japanese barbecue place has fabulous raw beef."

—SUSAN FENIGER AND MARY SUE MILLIKEN, BORDER GRILL AND CIUDAD

SOOT BULL JEEP

3136 W. 8th Street, Los Angeles
(213) 387-3865

"This is a Korean barbecue restaurant whose name means something like 'ash fire house.' It is kind of grungy, in a not-so-great neighborhood. Each table has a little grill with ventilation that doesn't work very well. But they have the best marinated meats. You sit down and get all these little bowls of side dishes—from assortments of kimchi to scallion salad—and grill the meats yourself. It is a fun way to eat."

—HANS RÖCKENWAGNER, RÖCKENWAGNER AND RÖCK

Farmers' Market

To find the farmers' market closest to you in southern California, call the Southland Farmers' Market Association at (213) 244-9190.

HOLLYWOOD FARMERS' MARKET

Ivar Avenue at Selma, Hollywood
(323) 463-3171
Sundays from 8:30 A.M. to 1:00 P.M.

LOS ANGELES FARMERS' MARKET

6333 W. 3rd Street (at Fairfax Avenue), Santa Monica
(323) 933-9211

"No one should miss this! The Los Angeles Farmers' Market is huge, and you'll find something different there year round. It is also in Santa Monica, so you can hook in a stop at the beach."

—SUZANNE GOIN, LUCQUES

SANTA MONICA FARMERS' MARKET

Arizona Avenue (between 2nd and 3rd Streets), Santa Monica
(310) 458-8712

"One of our favorites."

—SUSAN FENIGER AND MARY SUE MILLIKEN, BORDER GRILL AND CIUDAD

martini

MUSSO AND FRANK'S GRILL

6667 Hollywood Boulevard, Hollywood
(323) 467-7788

"It's the oldest restaurant in Hollywood, and they have great martinis."

—SUSAN GOIN, LUCQUES

Mexican

BORDER GRILL

1445 4th Street, Santa Monica (310) 451-1655

"If you're looking for some great, spicy Mexican-style food, Border Grill is always fun."

—NANCY SILVERTON, CAMPANILE

EL CHOLO MEXICAN RESTAURANT

Multiple locations, including:
1121 S. Western Avenue, Los Angeles (323) 734-2773
1025 Wilshire Boulevard, Santa Monica (310) 899-1106

"Go for the atmosphere and the food, which is authentic Mexican, and go with a group for the chiles rellenos and the fresh-made tamales."

—CARRIE NAHABEDIAN, RESTAURANT NAHA (CHICAGO)

EL TAURINO

1104 S. Hoover Street, Los Angeles (213) 738-9197

"For the brain tacos and tongue tacos."

—NANCY SILVERTON AND MARK PEEL, CAMPANILE

LA SERANATA GARIBALDI

1842 E. 1st Street, Los Angeles (323) 265-2887

"For a little more elaborate Mexican food, this restaurant is known for more complex sauces and dishes, like Mexican sea bass with huitlacoche [corn fungus]."

—NANCY SILVERTON, CAMPANILE

LA SUPER-RICA TAQUERIA

622 N. Milipas Street, Santa Barbara (805) 963-4940

"Another good spot for tacos. This is a tiny place where you stand in line to order their soft tacos and frijoles—beans with bacon, sausage, and chiles."

—NANCY SILVERTON, CAMPANILE

"They have amazing soft tacos, served on fresh tortillas. They also do a mushroom burrito with hongos, which are like oyster mushrooms, and huitlacoche [corn fungus] that is out of control."

—MARIO BATALI, BABBO, ESCA, AND LUPA (NEW YORK)

Mexican cont.

TACO DELTA

3806 W. Sunset Boulevard (off Lucile), Los Angeles (near Silverlake) (323) 664-2848

"There is something honest about this place. It's just a little shack. Out behind it, they have picnic tables, and it is built sort of into a hill where someone has terraced it with coffeepots filled with flowers and potted plants. It is a family working there, so you can always see the people doing the cooking. The food is simple, and the tortillas are fresh and warm. They cook your meat to order unless it is braised. They always have a sharp, fresh garnish on everything. They also have those pickled carrots with jalapeños, and horchata, the rice-cinnamon drink."

—SUZANNE GOIN, LUCQUES

TACOS MEXICO

Multiple locations, including:
5120 E. Olympic Boulevard, Los Angeles (323) 266-0482

"It's just a little place in downtown Los Angeles, but it's delicious. And it's open twenty-four hours."

—NANCY SILVERTON, CAMPANILE

TLAPAZOLA GRILL

11676 Gateway Boulevard, West Los Angeles (310) 477-1577

"This is a little place run by a couple of guys from Oaxaca [a region of southern Mexico] who worked for me for a long time. They turn out very authentic Oaxacan specialties, and make fantastic mole dishes."

—HANS RÖCKENWAGNER, RÖCKENWAGNER AND RÖCK

MIDDLE Eastern

MAROUCH

4905 Santa Monica Boulevard, Los Angeles (323) 662-9325

"This place is like a Middle Eastern diner, but has fabulous food. I love the mouhamara [a spicy paste of chopped walnuts] that is served with pita bread. And their roasted salty chicken is great!"

—MARY SUE MILLIKEN, BORDER GRILL AND CIUDAD

Pizza

CALIFORNIA PIZZA KITCHEN

Multiple locations; for a complete list, visit www.cpk.com

"There are banners around town that L.A. is the home of the barbecue chicken, smoked Gouda, and red onion pizza served here. It's great! And you don't want to miss the amazing chopped vegetable salad with roasted corn and tortillas, which is served with limes to squeeze on top, as well as both ranch dressing and barbecue sauce."

—CARRIE NAHABEDIAN, RESTAURANT NAHA (CHICAGO)

PALERMO

1858 N. Vermont Avenue, Los Angeles (323) 663-1178

"Palermo's is a classic pizza and was the kind of pizza I grew up eating as a kid. The crust is not too thick, and it has just the right amount of cheese."

—SUZANNE GOIN, LUCQUES

PIZZA BUONO

2100 W. Sunset Boulevard, Los Angeles (213) 413-0800

"This is my favorite pizza. It's in kind of a scary neighborhood, but I love the marinated tomato pizza. I also like their antipasto, which has iceberg lettuce and garbanzo beans and stuff like that."

—SUZANNE GOIN, LUCQUES

salads

MUSSO AND FRANK'S GRILL

6667 Hollywood Boulevard, Hollywood
(323) 467-7788

"I like the salad of iceberg lettuce with anchovy dressing. I think it's supposed to be romaine, but I request iceberg. The anchovy vinaigrette has more anchovy than oil; it is almost not a dressing. I always try to get a double order, and the waiter won't let me, insisting, 'It is too big already—if you eat one then I will let you have another.' He is always right. The other food is not so great. But I love this salad."

—SUZANNE GOIN, LUCQUES

sandwiches

IZZY'S DELI

1433 Wilshire Boulevard, Santa Monica
(310) 394-1131

"It's great for corned beef and pastrami sandwiches, and matzoh ball soup. Plus it's open late at night."

—SUSAN FENIGER, BORDER GRILL AND CIUDAD

steak

MUSSO AND FRANK'S GRILL

6667 Hollywood Boulevard, Hollywood
(323) 467-7788

"It's the original Hollywood steak house. They serve great meats, and everything on the side—so whether you want creamed spinach or hash browns, you have to order it. And their drinks are huge—after just two, the average guy will have to take a taxi home!"

—CARRIE NAHABEDIAN, RESTAURANT NAHA (CHICAGO)

THE PALM

9001 Santa Monica Boulevard, West Hollywood
(310) 550-8811

"I love ordering a porterhouse, charred on the outside, rare on the inside. And I could never get sick of their tomato and onion salad, when the tomatoes are good."

—NANCY SILVERTON, CAMPANILE

sunday

HOLLYWOOD HILLS COFFEE SHOP

6145 Franklin Avenue, Los Angeles
(323) 467-7678

"This place is in a Best Western, and it is kind of a groovester hangout, which can be good or annoying, depending on your point of view. It's the embodiment of L.A. in that you'll see all sorts of different types of people here. The food is coffee shop plus some Mexican. It is a great place to go on a Sunday and watch the world go by."

—SUZANNE GOIN, LUCQUES

SUSHI

MATSUHISA

129 N. La Cienega Boulevard, Beverly Hills
(310) 659-9639

"For specialty sushi, like the black sea bass sashimi with hot oil poured on at tableside, and other dishes that incorporate luxury ingredients like black truffles and caviar."

—NANCY SILVERTON AND MARK PEEL, CAMPANILE

SUSHI GEN

422 E. 2nd Street, Los Angeles
(213) 617-0552

"Sushi Gen is downtown in a little mini-mall near Little Tokyo. L.A., by the way, is the master of mini-mall restaurants! Here they serve basic sushi. They have good monkfish liver, and they are also good at guiding you through the menu."

—SUZANNE GOIN, LUCQUES

SUSHI SASABUNE

11300 Nebraska Street, West Los Angeles
(310) 268-8380

"I am somewhat of a connoisseur of sushi. I don't go religiously twice a week, but I do go a couple of times a month and sit at the counter. This place is awesome—it is the most authentic sushi I have come across. It has no hype. There are a couple of other sushi restaurants that have reputations for being 'sushi Nazis,' where they dictate what you eat. This place is not like that—you can still choose what you eat. I get the crab hand roll, which is to die for!"

—HANS RÖCKENWAGNER, RÖCKENWAGNER AND RÖCK

Nobu Matsuhisa

THAI

CHAN DARA

310 N. Larchmont Boulevard,
Los Angeles
(323) 467-1052

CHAN DARA—HOLLYWOOD

1511 N. Cahuenga Boulevard,
Los Angeles
(323) 464-8585

"Whenever I used to bring up the idea of Thai food, I found that every man wanted to go here, where the waitresses all look like Thai models. In fact, Los Angeles magazine featured a photo spread of them, each more stunning than the next! And the food is wonderful, too. I love anything Thai—from pad thai to Thai iced tea to chicken soup with lemongrass and coconut to any kind of curry, especially yellow curry. Chan Dara does all of them well."

—CARRIE NAHABEDIAN, RESTAURANT NAHA
(CHICAGO)

SWEETS

DIDIO'S ITALIAN ICE

1305 Montana Avenue, Santa Monica
(310) 393-2788

"I have a big sweet tooth that I am trying to wean myself of, but this is the exception. They have Italian ices that are very tasty."

—HANS RÖCKENWAGNER, RÖCKENWAGNER
AND RÖCK

TAMALES

AUTHENTIC CAFÉ

7605 Beverly Boulevard (between Fairfax and La Brea Avenues),
Los Angeles
(323) 939-4626

"Their tamales are great. I got some for a staff event once, and everyone went bananas!"

—CARRIE NAHABEDIAN, RESTAURANT NAHA
(CHICAGO)

THAI HOUSE

8657 W. Pico Boulevard (at Bedford
Street), West Los Angeles
(310) 274-5492
1049 Gayley Avenue, Westwood
(310) 208-2676

*"This place has a very
industrial design, but great
Thai food."*

—CARRIE NAHABEDIAN, RESTAURANT NAHA
(CHICAGO)

BARNEY GREENGRASS

9570 Wilshire Boulevard (at Camden
Drive, in Barneys New York, fifth
floor), Beverly Hills
(310) 777-5877

*"The best view in Los Ange-
les—you can see all of Beverly Hills. I love the salads
and breads here, and it's
great for breakfast or lunch.
You can shop and eat in
beautiful surroundings!"*

—CARRIE NAHABEDIAN, RESTAURANT NAHA
(CHICAGO)

A Taste of L.A. History

Michael's
1147 3rd Street, Santa Monica
(310) 451-0843

GEORGE GERMON AND JOHANNE KILLEEN, AL FORNO (PROVIDENCE)

"In 1981, we drove to L.A. from San Francisco." ("Which was my idea," admits Killeen, "because I didn't realize how big California was!") "After a grueling drive, we had our first meal at Michael's, which was at lunch, because that was the only time we could get in. We were blown away, and begged to come back for dinner that night. We got to meet the owner, Michael McCarty, and saw the kitchen, where Jonathan Waxman was the chef. To this day, we still think about the food that we had there, and in New York at Jams, where Waxman also cooked. We think Jonathan is a total genius with food. Everything was very elegant without being stuffy, and Michael's really laid the groundwork for a new type of restaurant. This California approach to restaurants was refreshing, and had a huge impact on the rest of the country."

ROBERT DEL GRANDE, CAFÉ ANNIE (HOUSTON)

"A meal I had at Michael's in Los Angeles in 1980 is still crystal clear in my mind. I realized while I was there that it was a touchstone for me as to how tremendous a restaurant experience can be. This wasn't your grandparents' restaurant—it was different and removed from anything you would consider continental cooking. It had a beautiful garden in back, beautiful china, and it seemed so fresh and new. There was also seating out in the garden, which seemed like the right place to be. I remember the chicken with morels and my wife's scallops with watercress sauce. Everything was so delicious and not just a bunch of food piled on a plate, which was so drastically different from what everyone else was doing. While there was plenty of French technique, the restaurant was also very American. It seemed like a brand-new thing."

BORDER GRILL
SANTA MONICA

1445 4th Street
Santa Monica, CA 90941
Phone: (310) 451-1655
Fax: (310) 394-2049
www.millikenandfeniger.com

CIUDAD

445 S. Figueroa Street
Los Angeles, CA 90071
Phone: (213) 486-5171

BORDER GRILL
LAS VEGAS

Mandalay Bay Resort & Casino
3950 Las Vegas Boulevard South
Las Vegas, NV 89119
Phone: (702) 632-7403

SUSAN FENIGER and MARY SUE MILLIKEN are chef-partners in Border Grill restaurants and Ciudad. They are the authors of five cookbooks, including *Cantina*, *City Cuisine*, *Mesa Mexicana*, *Cooking with Too Hot Tamales*, and *Mexican Cooking for Dummies*. They are hosts of television's *Too Hot Tamales* and radio's *Hot Dish* and *Talk of the Table*. In 1993, they were invited to cook with Julia Child on her PBS series *Cooking with Master Chefs*. *Gourmet* hailed Border Grill as "one of America's best restaurants," and the *Los Angeles Times* wrote that Ciudad gives "the downtown dining scene a much-needed infusion of exuberance."

OUR FOOD We believe that dining should be a very full experience. For us, it's about making the food that we're passionate about. We try to explore a cuisine to give people an experience that maybe they haven't had before. At Border Grill, we serve food from all over Mexico, not any particular region. Ciudad serves food from all over the Latin world except Mexico.

Our goal with the restaurants is to serve great food at not too high a price. And to really keep it within a price range that we both feel makes someone want to go out two or three times a week, to make our restaurants their hangouts, their places.

Our food is all about flavor. First and foremost, our dishes have to be really delicious. That's how we decide whether a dish works or not—whether we think it's really fantastic. Texturally, everything on the plate has to have lots of contrast, so that you don't get bored with only one texture. We think of the whole plate working together; the entrée isn't really a complete dish without the starch and vegetable and sauce.

SUSAN AND MARY SUE'S PICKS

BOB BURNS

Multiple locations, including:
202 Wilshire Boulevard
(at 2nd Street), Santa Monica
(310) 393-6777

Susan Feniger: I still eat at Bob Burns in the bar a fair amount. I'll usually order pasta there, especially the penne with feta, garlic, broccoli, and flaked pepper. Mary Sue Milliken: I don't eat there as often as I used to, but I am eating there tonight. At Bob Burns, they have staff that have each been there over eighteen years! There is something about the way they must run it that these people have stayed. I think it's really important to try to make every experience a learning experience, so I ask myself, what has made them stay so long?

You really just need to look carefully at each restaurant experience and see what it is you can take from it.

GINZA SUSHI-KO

218 N. Rodeo Drive
(at Wilshire Boulevard), Beverly Hills
(310) 247-8939

Mary Sue Milliken: On very, very special occasions, I'll go to Ginza Sushi-Ko, which is probably the most expensive sushi bar in the world. What do I like about it? Everything! I usually only go about once a year on my birthday; we are considering going for our anniversary this year. They have *fugu* [considered the most delicious fish in Japan, its improper preparation may cause fatal poisoning] in every form you could eat it, which I really adore.

susan and mary sue's picks

RENU NAKORN

13041 Rosecrans Avenue, Norwalk
(562) 921-2124

We crave the Thai food at Renu Nakorn. It is so delicious. Because we eat so much Latin food in the restaurants, we almost always go out for Asian. We like their salads. We love the crispy rice salad and the papaya salad, and they have a wonderful catfish salad, too. They also do really interesting dishes that you don't find in any other Thai restaurants. It's great Thai food; when we were in Thailand, we didn't eat food that was quite as delicious.

YABU

11820 W. Pico Boulevard, Los Angeles
(310) 473-9757

Susan Feniger: The food at Yabu is pretty delicious; they even make their own *soba*. Mary Sue Milliken: It's not the best Japanese restaurant in town, but it has a really great feel. I just went there the other night with my son, who goes to Japanese immersion school. At the restaurant there was a sixty-year-old woman eating her dinner next to him and they got to talking in Japanese, because she didn't speak English. They exchanged addresses and decided that she would come over and babysit sometime. After we left, he said to me, "You know, she could be like my Japanese grandma." It was so sweet.

Suzanne Goin

suzanne goin is chef-partner of Lucques. Her résumé includes stints at Arpège, Chez Panisse, Al Forno, L'Orangerie, and Olives. In 1994, she was named Best Creative Chef by *Boston* magazine. Before opening Lucques, she was executive chef at Campanile in Los Angeles. *Los Angeles* magazine has called Lucques "a mecca for foodies." In 1999, she was named to *Food & Wine*'s list of the country's ten Best New Chefs.

LUCQUES

8474 Melrose Avenue
West Hollywood, CA 90069
Phone: (323) 655-6277
Fax: (323) 655-3925

my food Chez Panisse and Al Forno were big influences on me. Our food starts with whatever is available from our local farmers. I'll find out what is out there or what is coming in next. Then we apply whatever flavors or elements we feel like playing with that day. It really gets down to serving food I want to eat. Our food is not flashy. It should look edible, natural, and delicious, as opposed to causing people to ask, "How did they make that stand up like that?" We are excited to cook with the first ingredients of the season. When it is gone, we move on to the next.

CAMPANILE

624 S. La Brea Avenue (at 6th Street),
Los Angeles
(323) 938-1447

Eating at Campanile is like going home, after having worked there for two years. I love Mark Peel's food, and I love Nancy Silverton's desserts. The restaurant is comfortable and it is what I want food to be: It all tastes great and has such integrity. There is always something a little different going on, yet nothing is ever scary or forced. I like to go on Mondays, when they do a Monday night family dinner. Sometimes it will be a theme, like cassoulet, bouillabaisse, or even fried chicken. (See also page 125.)

FRED'S 62

1850 North Vermont Avenue, Los Angeles
(323) 667-0062

This grooved-out diner in Los Feliz is open twenty-four hours—it's always happening, and there are always a million people there. It's a fun, very L.A. place to go. Owner Fred Eric is the punk-rock chef of L.A. and serves everything from Thai noodles to hamburgers to apple pancakes. [Breakfast is served all day.]

MAKO

225 South Beverly Drive, Beverly Hills
(310) 288-8338

This is my favorite new place. The chef-owner is Mako Tanaka, who was the chef at Chinois on Main for years. The place is sweet—it's a storefront with a small, open kitchen, and his wife runs the front of the house. The food is really delicious and perfectly balanced Asian-fusion cuisine [featuring dishes such as marinated New Zealand roast lamb with plum wine and black olive sauce].

PANE E VINO

1482 E. Valley Road, Santa Barbara
(805) 969-9274

I try to get away sometimes to Santa Barbara on Sunday night and come back on Tuesday morning. This little Italian place is not the world's greatest restaurant, but it has been there a long time and it has that "it"—whatever that "it" is—that makes you want to be there. It is basic Italian food, but really well done. For a few years I was so sick of pasta I couldn't eat it. But the pasta is authentic here and not over-sauced. For me, it is perfect.

SOOT BULL JEEP

3136 W. 8th Street, Los Angeles
(213) 387-3865

I love Korean food. When you sit down at this Korean place they bring you all these little side plates of salads and pickles. Then they bring you the short ribs and throw them on the grill. Then a little lady comes around and cuts them with scissors. It's total escapism! They also do great spicy noodles, barbecued eel, and tofu soup. The experience makes me appreciate the contrast of foods.

MARK PEEL and NANCY SILVERTON are chef-owners of Campanile and La Brea Bakery. They were named to *Food & Wine*'s 1989 list of Best New Chefs and are the co-authors of two cookbooks: *The Food of Campanile* and *Mark Peel and Nancy Silverton at Home: Two Chefs Cook for Family and Friends.* Nancy Silverton's additional cookbooks are *Nancy Silverton's Breads from the La Brea Bakery, Desserts,* and *Nancy Silverton's Pastries from the La Brea Bakery.* Mark Peel's résumé includes apprenticeships at the Michelin three-star restaurants Le Tour d'Argent and Moulin de Mougins, and he was formerly sous chef at Michael's and head chef of Spago. He has been nominated several times for the James Beard Award for Best Chef: California. Silverton's training included time at the Ecole Lenôtre in France, and she was formerly head pastry chef at Spago. Among her many honors is being the first recipient of the James Beard Award for Outstanding Pastry Chef, in 1991.

OUR FOOD

Nancy Silverton: The food that we make here is very familiar food, not show-off food. We take our inspiration from local ingredients and familiar flavors. When you read our menu, it is very easy to visualize what you're going to be eating. We don't sit on the phone seeking out how to get the most obscure products and spices. As of the last few years, chefs have really been using the farmers' markets and keeping their food seasonal. When we were cooking like that at Campanile ten years ago, the approach was much less common.

Mark Peel: In a way, that's even more of a high-wire act. When a very good restaurant serves a simple roast chicken, there's no hiding it if the chicken isn't cooked right. There is no foie gras slathered all over it. There is no pool of butter sauce. There are no architecturally constructed deep-fried layers of gelatin. What is on the plate is either good, or it's not. That's how I think about our food: We have to do it right, or it's painfully obvious.

Mark Peel and Nancy Silverton

CAMPANILE AND LA BREA BAKERY
624 S. La Brea Avenue
Los Angeles, CA 90036
Phone: (323) 938-1447
Fax: (323) 938-5840
www.campanilerestaurant.com

"The first thing I do when I get off the plane in L.A. is go to Campanile."

CHRIS BIANCO
PIZZERIA BIANCO (PHOENIX)

"Campanile is a great restaurant. They've got a very interesting wine list, and I like their aesthetics."

CHRIS SCHLESINGER
EAST COAST GRILL (BOSTON)

ANGELI CAFFÈ

7274 Melrose Avenue, Los Angeles
(323) 936-9086

This is one of our favorite restaurants. The chef, [cookbook author] Evan Kleiman, is a friend of ours, and her food is always good—very simple and delicious. It's the perfect restaurant for kids. Our son Ben can always find a pasta, and our daughter can always find a salad. They let Oliver, our five-year-old, make his own pizza. We get something simple [such as the lemon-and-garlic-roasted chicken] and drink Chianti by the glass.

CHARMING GARDEN

111 N. Atlantic Boulevard,
Monterey Park
(626) 458-4508

We had steamed whole fish here, and it was great. [The restaurant's specialty is smoked pomfret, which is flown in from Taiwan and magnificently displayed.] Charming Garden is rather formal, with linen tablecloths, and is considered perhaps the best Hunan restaurant in Los Angeles.

MEILONG VILLAGE

301 W. Valley Boulevard, San Gabriel
(626) 284-4769

This is a great Chinese restaurant. They have delicious soup dumplings, which are dumplings filled with hot broth. I crave Chinese food, but often it will be too salty, too oily, or too sweet. They strike a wonderful balance with their flavors at Meilong Village.

SO KONG DONG

2716 W. Olympic Boulevard, #104 (at New Hampshire), Los Angeles
(213) 380-3737

This Korean restaurant serves big, boiling cauldrons of tofu in broth. You take a bowl of it, crack an egg into it, and stir in all sorts of different ingredients like beef, pork, seafood, or a combination of all three. That soup and *kimchi* [pickled cabbage] are all they have. We love it. We like going here with a big group of eight or ten people. You know you're in a real Korean place when you walk in and the waitress looks at you like, "What are *you* doing here?"

For sushi, we'll go to one of these three of our favorites:

IKE SUSHI

6051 Hollywood Boulevard, Los Angeles
(323) 856-9972

It's just a little counter with four tables, but we love the incredibly fresh sushi here, and go all the time. He is a master: His dexterity, the way he slices the fish and makes his rolls, is beautiful to watch.

ITACHO

7311 Beverly Boulevard, West Hollywood
(323) 938-9009

It's really delicious. We'll usually have a bit of sashimi, and more cooked food.

MATSUHISA

129 N. La Cienega Boulevard, Beverly Hills
(310) 659-9639

For specialty sushi, like the black sea bass sashimi with hot oil poured on at tableside, and other dishes that incorporate luxury ingredients like black truffles and caviar.

Hans Röckenwagner

Hans röckenwagner is the chef-owner of Röck, Röckenwagner, and the Röckenwagner Bakery. He completed his apprenticeship and three years of schooling in the Black Forest (Germany) and continued on to Zum Adler, a Michelin two-star restaurant near Basel, where he learned the fine points of classical French and nouvelle cuisine, incorporating elegant presentation. He achieved a great knowledge of technique, presentation, and the use of flavors while cooking and traveling in France and Switzerland. Hans came to the United States after being recruited by Jovan Trboyevic of Le Perroquet Restaurant in Chicago. He moved to Los Angeles in 1984 to open Röckenwagner, which gains renown year after year as one of the top restaurants in southern California. He is the author of *Röckenwagner*.

RÖCK
13455 Maxella Avenue
Marina del Rey, CA 90292
Phone: (310) 822-8979

RÖCKENWAGNER AND RÖCKENWAGNER BAKERY
2435 Main Street
Santa Monica, CA 90405
Phone: (310) 399-6504
Fax: (310) 399-7984
www.rockenwagner.com

MY FOOD My cuisine at Röckenwagner is ever-evolving. I was brought up on French techniques, both classic and nouvelle. After I came to the United States and saw more cuisines, I incorporated them into my food little by little. My food here is mostly influenced by European techniques, but with an accent of Asian influence.

For the longest time, I had put aside the food I grew up with as not "hip" or "cutting-edge." Yet some years ago, I went back to Germany during the white asparagus festival. Every spring for about eight weeks, all the menus change and everything is made with white asparagus—everything from soup to veal. During that visit, I realized that it was what made certain areas so special, and I thought it was fantastic. So I drew on that when I started the ritual of paying homage to my heritage by initiating a white asparagus festival at Röckenwagner.

The menu at Röck could be considered fusion, but the food is not. I cook dishes from places where I have lived and traveled, but the dishes remain true to their origins. I don't mess around on a single plate with multiple cultures. We have a Tuesday night "Stammtisch," which is a community table. It is based on a German tradition of regular customers gathering around a common table to eat and talk. It's an antidote to L.A. car culture—I wanted to get people out of their cars and talking to one another. Röck is family- and community-oriented. It's a place where someone can come for a glass of wine and some conversation.

Röckenwagner Bakery's ideology is to make available freshly baked European breads using only the best ingredients. Our full-scale bakery is now headed by German master baker and certified confectioner Norbert Heeren, who has joined us to create a more diversified line of baked products and sweets.

JODY MARONI SAUSAGE KINGDOM

Multiple locations, including:
2011 Ocean Front Walk, Venice
(310) 822-5639

This is a little stand located right on the beach. He offers what he calls "gourmet hot dogs." He serves a spicy duck sausage with sweet peppers, and he has a fennel-scented grilled Italian sausage that he serves with roasted onions and peppers on a soft bun. There are about a dozen different kinds available, which range from the familiar, such as knockwurst, to the inventive, like Mexican jalapeño sausage. It's a great culinary treat!

MILLIE'S

3524 W. Sunset Boulevard, Silverlake
(323) 664-0404

We go here for a great breakfast after going to the fish market at about six A.M. It is a small, slightly grungy place [and artists' hangout] that serves breakfast and lunch. There are sidewalk tables, but we always eat at the counter. They have good muffins, and the pancakes are fantastic. I've had fresh berry pancakes here that were awesome.

NAWAB OF INDIA

1621 Wilshire Boulevard
(at 17th Street), Santa Monica
(310) 829-1106

This place serves authentic Indian cuisine. They have really nice lamb in spinach sauce, tandoori chicken in spicy tomato sauce, and vegetarian cauliflower in a light curry. They also have especially good Indian breads. I love the different flavors of Indian cuisine because they are so different from the flavors I grew up with.

SPAGO BEVERLY HILLS

176 N. Canon Drive, Beverly Hills
(310) 385-0880

If we want to splurge a little and have a nice experience, we'll go to Spago, which is one of the top restaurants in Los Angeles. We might take someone from out of town for the ambiance, while my wife and I focus on the cuisine only. They feature dishes that incorporate hard-to-get ingredients and unusual presentations. (See also page 113.)

VINCENTI RISTORANTE

11930 San Vincente Boulevard,
Los Angeles
(310) 207-0127

If I want to go out for a very high-end, refined Italian dinner, this is where I go. Maureen Vincenti is the owner and maître d', and the chef is Gino Angeline. The menu features both authentic dishes [such as lasagna and tripe] as well as more progressive dishes, and they use the highest-quality ingredients that can be found. I like everything I eat here, whether it is a pasta or something from the wood-burning oven.

BAKERY

LA BAGUETTE FRENCH BREAD SHOP

3088 Poplar Avenue, Memphis
(901) 458-0900

"It's a French bistro that I like to go to for muffins and coffee in the morning, and they have great pastries. But if I'm going to do an eighteen-hour day, I like to get a latte at Starbucks, to power me through my day."

—RAJI JALLEPALLI, RESTAURANT RAJI

CITY BREAD

575 S. Mendenhall Road, Memphis
(901) 682-3500

"They supply the bread for Restaurant Raji, but they also have really nice chicken salad for ladies who lunch, and nice focaccia sandwiches."

—RAJI JALLEPALLI, RESTAURANT RAJI

BARBECUE

CORKY'S B-B-Q RESTAURANT

Multiple locations, including:
5259 Poplar Avenue, Memphis
(901) 685-9744
Phone orders: (800) 9-CORKYS

PAYNE'S BBQ

1762 Lamar Avenue, Memphis
(901) 272-1523
1393 Elvis Presley Boulevard, Memphis
(901) 942-7433

"Both Corky's and Payne's have similar menus and similar side dishes. For me, one is close to work and the other is close to home. I recommend the pulled pork and ribs at both. And get lots of napkins, because it's really messy—but that's okay, because that's what barbecue is all about! At either place, I like to drink a beer, preferably Sam Adams."

—RAJI JALLEPALLI, RESTAURANT RAJI

BREAKFAST

CAFÉ ESPRESSO AT THE RIDGEWAY INN

5679 Poplar Avenue, Memphis
(901) 763-3888

"It's a nice place for a long breakfast. My husband and I like to eat there."

—RAJI JALLEPALLI, RESTAURANT RAJI

PIZZA

BOSCO'S PIZZA KITCHEN AND BREWERY

7615 Farmington Boulevard, Germantown
(901) 756-7310

LE CHARDONNAY

2105 Overton Square, Memphis
(901) 725-1375

"They both do creative pizzas with good vegetable toppings."

—RAJI JALLEPALLI, RESTAURANT RAJI

RESTAURANT RAJI

712 Brookhaven Circle
Memphis, TN 38117
Phone: (901) 685-8723
Fax: (901) 767-2226
E-mail: raji1@aol.com

raji jallepalli is chef-owner of Restaurant Raji in Memphis. She is the author of *Raji Cuisine: Indian Flavors, French Passion*.

MY FOOD Obviously, fresh products are important to me, as well as flavors that are assertive yet delicate. Texture and creating layers of flavors are also very important. I stay away from excessive butter and cream. We are not trendy, and we try not to create too many bouquets. These are my beliefs in creating food. As you get older, you get to a level of comfort and confidence that you know what your cooking is about.

RAJI'S PICKS

AUBERGINE

5007 Black Road, Memphis
(901) 767-7840

Aubergine is considered one of the best restaurants in Memphis. Chef Jean Christophe Blanc is very talented, and worked with many culinary luminaries in France. His cuisine shows depth in classical French cuisine. When I want to celebrate, this is usually the place I go for dinner.

HOUSE OF INDIA

2617 Poplar Avenue, Memphis
(901) 452-5090

I like to get vegetable *biryani* [an elaborate Indian rice dish] here. They have a version that I think is one of the best I've ever enjoyed. [The restaurant also offers dishes such as tandoori chicken and lamb.] It always transports me back to my teenage years in India.

INDIA PALACE

1720 Poplar Avenue, Memphis
(901) 278-1199

This is the place I like to go for northern Indian food. I really like the tandoori specialties. The restaurant also offers vegetarian dishes, as well as a popular lunch buffet. He also does a beautiful job with the breads here, especially the naan and paratha.

SAIGON LE

51 N. Cleveland Street, Memphis
(901) 276-5326

It's fantastic! This is a casual Vietnamese and Chinese restaurant, which I love because I can show up in my blue jeans and Birkenstocks. The women who work here always choose my food, so I never see a menu. But they have great hot pots—the specialty dish of hot broth, in which guests cook their own food at the table—noodles, and vegetarian dishes. I'll always have spring rolls, no matter what, because they're fantastic here, and their egg rolls are great, too.

TSUNAMI

928 S. Cooper, Memphis
(901) 274-2556

Tsunami's chef is Ben Smith, who used to work with me. He's an incredibly passionate chef cooking pan-Pacific food. While he changes the menu frequently, often reworking and refining dishes, he is known for his red curry mussels, and his sea bass on black Thai rice with soy beurre blanc.

café con leche

LATIN AMERICAN CAFETERIA

Multiple locations, including:
875 N.W. 42nd Avenue, Miami (305) 642-4700
2727 S. Dixie Highway, Miami (305) 445-9339
9606 S.W. 72nd Street, Miami (305) 279-4353
2940 Coral Way, Miami (305) 448-7331

"This chain of places makes great Cuban sandwiches and café con leche."

—ALLEN SUSSER, CHEF ALLEN'S

caribbean

L.C.'S

19505 N.W. 2nd Avenue, North Miami
(305) 651-8924

"This place is run by a woman from Trinidad who makes wonderful fresh roti—thin bread filled with dry yellow split peas. She makes the dough fresh, and also makes really rustic lamb and chicken curries."

—ALLEN SUSSER, CHEF ALLEN'S

cuban

PUERTO SAGUA

700 Collins Avenue, South Beach
(305) 673-1115

"This is an old restaurant that serves the classics—like roasted chicken with lime and onions, and Cuban sandwiches."

—ALLEN SUSSER, CHEF ALLEN'S

ice cream

JAXON'S ICE CREAM

128 S. Federal Highway, Dania
(954) 923-4445

"Jaxon's is a funky ice cream parlor that makes nice and creamy ice creams. My favorite flavors are butter pecan and pistachio."

—ALLEN SUSSER, CHEF ALLEN'S

market

NORMAN BROTHERS PRODUCE

7621 S.W. 87th Avenue, Miami
(305) 274-9363

"No relation, of course! This is a retail market that's a great place to buy local Florida vegetables. It's run by guys who both grow their own produce and buy it from elsewhere."

—NORMAN VAN AKEN, NORMAN'S

key lime pie

JOE'S STONE CRAB

227 Biscayne Street, Miami Beach
(305) 673-0365

"A good Key lime pie is one of the hardest things to find these days. I would refer seekers to Joe's version."

—ALLEN SUSSER, CHEF ALLEN'S

oysters

BALEEN

4 Grove Isle Drive (in the Grove Isle Hotel), Coconut Grove
(305) 857-5007

"Robbin Haas, the chef, is always bringing in great fresh oysters [to this upscale restaurant with a relaxed, casual atmosphere]."

—ALLEN SUSSER, CHEF ALLEN'S

stone crabs

JOE'S STONE CRAB

227 Biscayne Street, Miami Beach
(305) 673-0365

"Joe's serves great stone crabs, and it's also a good value. Just being in the hub-bub of the place is fun!"

—ALLEN SUSSER, CHEF ALLEN'S

sandwiches

DELI DEN

2889 Stirling Road, Fort Lauderdale
(954) 961-4070

"For a good corned beef sandwich."

—ALLEN SUSSER, CHEF ALLEN'S

PANINI OTECA

801 Lincoln Road, Miami
(305) 538-0058

"They make beautiful little panini. Get the number three with the truffle oil!"

—JONATHAN EISMANN, PACIFIC TIME

RASCAL HOUSE

17190 Collins Avenue, Miami Beach
(305) 947-4581

"For turkey pastrami."

—ALLEN SUSSER, CHEF ALLEN'S

view

GARCIA'S SEAFOOD GRILL AND FISH MARKET

398 N.W. North River Drive, Miami
(305) 375-0765

"Garcia's is on the Miami River, and they serve what-ever fish they caught that day. Go by boat if you can. Rent a boat at Club Nautico and cruise up the river to Garcia's—then you'll have lived in Miami!"

—JONATHAN EISMANN, PACIFIC TIME

NEWS CAFÉ

800 Ocean Drive (at 8th),
Miami Beach
(305) 538-6397

"Sit outside at the News Café and watch the show! You may see Linda Evangelista, or somebody wearing watermelons as shoes. That is South Beach!"

—JONATHAN EISMANN, PACIFIC TIME

jonathan eismann is chef-owner of Pacific Time. Pacific Time earned four stars from the *Miami Herald* and was the first restaurant in Miami Beach to win a four-star Mobil rating.

PACIFIC TIME
915 Lincoln Road
Miami Beach, FL 33139
Phone: (305) 534-5979
Fax: (305) 534-1607

Jonathan Eismann

MY FOOD We are not pretentious—we don't fawn over bottled water. Because we are in a tourist area, we want you to have an experience that is more than what you might expect as a tourist. As for food, I am not a "Fed Ex chef"—I don't fly in berries and other ingredients from all over. I concentrate on local ingredients. I want you to know what you are eating. If you have a Szechuan sauce in my restaurant, you will taste the chile, ginger, garlic, and citrus.

The style of food, although certainly Asian-Pacific, migrates constantly, with strong influences from Indonesia, Vietnam, and India. It's our intention to provide a culinary experience that's unique, light, refreshing, and healthful. Flavors and textural combinations are bold, and our balance of aromatics and acidity is a major component in our cooking.

JONATHAN'S PICKS

CAFÉ ABBRACCI

318 Aragon Avenue, Coral Gables
(305) 441-0700
This elegant northern Italian restaurant, run by owner Nino Pernetti and chef Mauro Bazzanini, serves both lunch and dinner. They have *costoletta tricolore*, a pounded, grilled veal chop topped with tomatoes, radicchio, and arugula. It's so big it hangs off the plate—it's great. Their penne is really good, too. Plus, the service here is fast and not at all fussy.

LINCOLN ROAD CAFÉ

941 Lincoln Road, Miami Beach
(305) 538-8066
I will eat at any Cuban hole in the wall, but this is one of my favorites. Get the *vaca frita*, which means literally "fried cow." The pork chops, rice and beans, and plantains are also very good.

MARK'S LAS OLAS

1032 E. Las Olas Boulevard,
Fort Lauderdale
(954) 463-1000
This upscale restaurant serving new American Florida-style cuisine at lunch and dinner is excellent, and Mark [Militello, the chef-owner] is a very fine cook. The menu is well balanced, well seasoned, and well presented, and features signature dishes such as Maine lobster *brûlée* and grilled spiny lobster with a sauce of applewood-smoked bacon and conch, sweet plantain mash, and conch fritters. It is down-to-earth cooking.

ROD AND GUN CLUB

200 Riverside Drive, Everglades City
(about ninety miles west of Miami)
(941) 695-2101
During stone crab season, we go to Everglades City, where the crabs are two hours closer to the water. I have a pilot's license, so we fly there. It's about ninety miles away, so it only takes twenty minutes. While the Rod and Gun Club serves breakfast, lunch, and dinner, the thing to have here is the stone crabs with lemon and mustard sauce—and plenty of both.

S&S DINER

1757 N.E. 2nd Avenue, Miami
(305) 373-4291
S&S has been around since 1938, and it is probably my wife's and my favorite restaurant at the moment. The food is simple—just things like pot roast and broiled fish. We'll go there for both dinner and breakfast. For breakfast, I like the S&S special of chopped ham and eggs, served by Yolanda, our favorite waitress.

Allen Susser

CHEF ALLEN'S

19088 N.E. 29th Avenue
Aventura, FL 33180
Phone: (305) 935-2900
Fax: (305) 935-9062
www.chefallen.com

ALLEN SUSSER is chef-owner of Chef Allen's, which earned four stars from the *Miami Herald*. He is the author of *The Great Citrus Book* and *Allen Susser's New World Cuisine and Cookery*. Susser was named one of *Food & Wine*'s Chefs of the Year in 1991, and won the 1994 James Beard Award as Best Chef: Southeast. Chef Allen's was chosen as *Gourmet*'s Top Table for south Florida in 2000, and was ranked number one for food and popularity in the 1999 Miami *ZagatSurvey*. Susser has also created the New World Foods line of gourmet condiments, spices, and products.

MY FOOD I focus on exciting flavors and local fish. I love it when people taste the fish that we are able to offer. Even if another restaurant does have access to the same types of fish, do they know the fishermen we do? No. The fish we get are right off the dock and in the back door. We capture the freshness, and you can taste it. Our restaurant has a relaxed but professional atmosphere where everything is well orchestrated. My philosophy about cooking and my food are inseparable: simple, direct, and powerful flavors!

When I eat out, I usually like to go for Japanese food or some simple grilled food. Other times, I'll go see some of my chef friends and let them cook for me. I also have kids, so that's another factor in trying to sort out where to eat!

ALLEN'S PICKS

BALEEN

4 Grove Isle Drive
(in the Grove Isle Hotel),
Coconut Grove
(305) 857-5007
Chef Robbin Haas serves some very nice fresh seafood with straightforward flavors at Baleen. I love to get grouper or snapper there, however he's offering it—they keep changing the preparation to keep it interesting. (See also p. 132.)

DARREL AND OLIVER'S CAFÉ MAXX

2601 E. Atlantic Boulevard,
Pompano Beach
(954) 782-0606
Oliver [Saucy, the chef, who runs Café Maxx, and partner of Darrel Broek] is always doing some very interesting flavor combinations on his regional Floridian menu. He likes to work with wild game and foie gras. It's not overly serious, though—just some really great flavors.

NEMO

100 Collins Avenue, Miami Beach
(305) 532-4550
Nemo is probably more California cuisine than anything else, in a sense—although they'll probably shoot me for saying that! The flavors are very earthy. He does some really good seafood stews with mussels, a terrific red curry stew, and great homemade polenta fries with homemade ketchup.

ALLEN'S PICKS

PACIFIC TIME

915 Lincoln Road, Miami Beach
(305) 534-5979
Jonathan Eismann does some nice
pan-Asian flavors at Pacific Time.
He makes a giant-squid salad that is
great, and also a whole roasted yellowtail that is really nice. (See also
p. 133.)

TAKEYAMA

6920 Cypress Road, Plantation
(about 20 miles north of Miami)
(954) 792-0350
I like this Japanese restaurant, which
is very hidden away in Plantation.
The chef-owner is named Kenji, and
he is a very talented, creative sushi
chef. He is always coming up with
great combinations and concoctions,
as well as simple, straightforward
sushi and sashimi. Some of my favorite dishes are the stone crab hand
roll and the spicy tuna and seaweed
salad. He also serves Kobe beef. It's
almost raw—he very quickly sears and
slices it, and then sears and salts the
fat, and serves it with a dipping sauce.
It's tremendous!

NORMAN'S

21 Almeria Avenue
Coral Gables, FL 33134
Phone: (305) 446-6767
Fax: (305) 446-7909
www.normans.com

norman van aken is chef-owner of Norman's in Coral Gables, and is responsible for coining the term "New World cuisine." Among his many awards are the 1997 James Beard Award as Best Chef: Southeast, the 1996 Robert Mondavi Culinary Award of Excellence, and the 1999 *Food Arts* Silver Spoon Award. Norman's has been honored numerous times with *Wine Specta-tor*'s Award of Excellence, and by inclusion in *Gourmet*'s America's Top Tables. Van Aken's cookbooks include *Norman's New World Cuisine, A Feast of Sunlight*, and *Norman's New World Latin American*.

MY FOOD I'm trying to put south Florida on a plate. Not the south Florida of history, but the cosmopolitan city leading us into the next millennium. I have a new cook from Venezuela who asked me, "Do you have Latin blood or something? Why do you cook so many Latin things?" She's looking at me, a white person from the Midwest who speaks in a flat Chicago accent, and she can't figure out how I know about all these Latin ingredients or why I care about them. The answer is very simple: It's flavor. Flavors are what get my allegiance. Once you taste these flavors, there's no going back.

Many restaurants in North America have the same "menu-speak." They share a common list of ingredients that are northern European or North American in origin, and they are appropriate to those places. When you come here, though, you are moving toward the equator, into the tropics, and that is something I want people to taste when they taste my food. I want them to know that they are in Miami, and that the ocean is footsteps away.

NORMAN'S PICKS

CAPTAIN'S TAVERN

9621 S. Dixie Highway, Miami
(305) 666-5979
We eat here more often than any other place. It is not chic, but they have some of the best domestic wines to be found in Miami, and absolutely pristine fish. It's kind of retro. But it is "a clean, well-lighted place," to quote another "man of the sea"!

HY VONG

3458 S.W. 8th Street, Miami
(305) 446-3674
This is a Vietnamese restaurant where I like to order whatever specials they're offering that day. They have great beef noodle soup, spring rolls, and whole steamed fish.

ISLAMORADA FISH COMPANY

81532 Overseas Highway, Islamorada
(305) 664-9271
This restaurant is a great place to taste seafood fresh off the boat, including great Key West shrimp, stone crabs, conch, and yellowtail snapper.

NENA'S KITCHEN

3791 Bird Road, Miami
(305) 446-4881
Nena's Kitchen is a Cuban restaurant that has good *media noche*, or "midnight," sandwiches, which are pressed ham and cheese sandwiches served with olives and mustard. It's a very lusty sandwich.

EL PALACIO DE LOS JUGOS

5721 West Flagler Street, Miami
(305) 262-0070
In English, its name is Palace of Juices, and it's the first place I take people from out of town. It's a market that's open year round, and while most people are there to shop for great fruits and vegetables for home,

"I think Norman's is a restaurant that reaches new heights—he's so into fusion, and great bold flavors!"

STEPHAN PYLES

AQUAKNOX (DALLAS)

there's also a funky-looking kitchen corner where you can pick up food to eat at one of their picnic tables. There might be chickens walking around right next to you, or a guy whacking open coconuts. The specialties are roast pork and roast chicken—you might see fifty chickens roasting on a rotisserie at any given time. It's terrific. They have black beans and rice, and *yuca con mojo*—very rustic Cuban fare.

TAP-TAP HAITIAN RESTAURANT

819 5th Street, Miami Beach (South Beach)
(305) 672-2898
At Tap-Tap, [chef Jean Luckens Chery, a Johnson and Wales alum] is trying to elevate Haitian cuisine, in the spirit of what Rick Bayless [of Chicago's Frontera Grill and Topolobampo] has done so well with Mexican cuisine. It's one of the only places where I'll order goat, which they offer about four different ways, including as goat-and-eggplant skewers. The restaurant also features the work of many Haitian artists.

"Norman's is a great restaurant, and I think it's very professionally run. He's a little over the top, which I love."

LYDIA SHIRE
BIBA AND PIGNOLI (BOSTON)

NORMAN VAN AKEN ON
Cooking in Miami

THE CUBAN REVOLUTION IN 1959–60 CREATED AN IMMIGRATION WAVE THAT changed Miami into a cosmopolitan border city. With each passing generation, the culinary scene in Miami has moved forward a light-year. There's a lot of Haitian food here now, and Argentinian and Brazilian food are starting to come along. As the city was settled by one group and then another, there were a lot of difficulties, but the places where people stopped having those difficulties were always at the little food counters, the bodegas, and the food-pickup windows.

That's one of the great things about being a chef: You can disagree about politics, baseball, or whatever, but if somebody makes a really dynamite soup and you get a spoonful of it in your mouth, you figure that the person who made it couldn't possibly be all that bad.

Cooks paying their first visit to Miami should spend most of their time familiarizing themselves with the local products that are not available elsewhere. They should go to places where they can get cooked *yuca*, a root with a rough, woody skin and firm white flesh, or *mamey sapote,* a tropical fruit with a pink or reddish flesh that is sweet and slightly almondy, served in a simple form. Or they should come to us and hang out for a day in our kitchen at Norman's. But I think the most important thing for an aspiring chef to do is taste food. They should taste the fish and the tubers in the simplest ways first, then have them in their traditional preparations—for instance, a caramelized plantain in a Cuban café. But taste them and think about them, and even make notes. The thing is to taste the food, and to be like Adam and Eve in the garden for the first time. It's not a great idea to just go to the six most written-about restaurants, unless they have a lot of time.

If I leave Miami to go on a trip, the things I miss most are plantains. I love them! I can go weeks and weeks without having them, but the minute they're not around, it's unbearable.

A caramelized plantain with just a tiny bit of salt and lime juice is amazing. When I was living in Key West and I had barely two quarters to rub together, the places I'd go to eat were places like El Cacique, which had a big Indian head neon sign on the outside of it, where you could inexpensively get a plate of pork *asado*—pork that is grilled, often after being marinated—and black beans and rice, and pickled onions, and a pile of caramelized plantains. When you come from the Midwest, like I do, and somebody serves you bananas for dinner, you ask yourself, "What's going on?" But then you take a taste of them, and you push the pork to the side for a minute!

LOCAL HIGHLIGHTS

Bakery (Italian)

PETER SCIORTINO'S BAKERY

1101 E. Brady Street, Milwaukee
(414) 272-4623

"They make a really good sfingonie, which is a pizza with a thick crust that is almost like bread dough. They cook it in a sheet pan with a lot of olive oil on the bottom and top it with onions, olives, and some tomato. Their Italian cookies are also good."

—SANFORD D'AMATO, SANFORD

Beer

LAKE FRONT BREWERY

1872 N. Commerce Street, Milwaukee
(414) 372-8800

"You've got to try some beer when visiting Milwaukee, and the beers at this microbrewery are my favorites. Their pilsner—called Klish—is great, and they make a French ale for us. I also particularly like the East Side Dark."

—SANFORD D'AMATO, SANFORD

Cookies

SENTRY FOOD STORE

Multiple locations, including:
2938 N. Oakland Avenue (at Locust), Milwaukee
(414) 964-1340

"Their glazed butter cookies are kind of a Milwaukee tradition. They are cut out into different shapes depending on the season, but they are always the same cookie with royal icing on them. You can pound twelve of them really easily!"

—SANFORD D'AMATO, SANFORD

Frozen Custard

LEON'S FROZEN CUSTARD

3131 S. 27th Street, Milwaukee
(414) 383-1784
www.foodspot.com/leons/index.html

"Leon's makes real, egg-rich, soft-serve custard. Both the chocolate and vanilla are good. They are always busy, even in the middle of winter. The place was the prototype for Al's in Happy Days, and it looks like it should still have car hops."

—SANFORD D'AMATO, SANFORD

"Sanford's not kidding—he took a group of visiting chefs to Leon's, and we all thought it was incredible!"

—TAKASHI YAGIHASHI, TRIBUTE (DETROIT)

FISH FRY

JACK PANDL'S ORIGINAL WHITE FISH BAY INN

1319 E. Henry Clay Street, Milwaukee
(414) 964-3800

"You have to go to Jack Pandl's for a Friday night fish fry. They do a perch fry with potato pancakes and a great slaw. It is pretty much what everyone does in Milwaukee—it has traditionally been a very Germanic-Catholic city."

—SANFORD D'AMATO, SANFORD

sausages

DENTICE BROTHERS ITALIAN

1600 N. Jackson Street, Milwaukee
(414) 276-1314

"This is one of the oldest Italian sausage-making places in the city, and their sausages are phenomenal."

—SANFORD D'AMATO, SANFORD

USINGER'S

1030 N. Old World 3rd Street, Milwaukee
(414) 276-9100
www.usingers.com

"I would definitely recommend the sausages at Usinger's. When we ate there recently I bought a Usinger's sweatshirt, saying, 'Yeah, I'm going back to New York,' and the lady behind the counter said 'Well, be careful if you wear that sweatshirt on the street, because someone might think you've got sausages and jump you.' She wasn't joking either, she was serious!"

—MARIO BATALI, BABBO, ESCA, AND LUPA (NEW YORK)

German

JOHN ERNST

600 E. Ogden Avenue, Milwaukee
(414) 273-1878

"This is the oldest restaurant in the city—it's been around since the early 1800s. They have a good liver dumpling soup that is a light consommé with the liver dumpling floating in it. They also have good smoked pork chops."

—SANFORD D'AMATO, SANFORD

HOT DOGS

USINGER'S

1030 N. Old World 3rd Street, Milwaukee
(414) 276-9100

"Usinger's sausage company makes the best hot dogs. Chefs Rocco DiSpirito and Mario Batali were here recently from New York, and they gave me a hard time, saying I had never tasted hot dogs from Gray's Papaya in New York. I laughed and said, 'I lived in New York for eight years on Gray's Papaya dogs, and these are better!'"

—SANFORD D'AMATO, SANFORD

OUTDOOR DINING

THE HILTON

4700 N. Port Washington Road, Milwaukee
(414) 962-6040

"The Hilton has the most beautiful setting on the Milwaukee River. You just want to sit out there all night. They have a patio, and the ducks come wandering up from the river. It is very peaceful."

—SANFORD D'AMATO, SANFORD

milwaukee
LOCAL HIGHLIGHTS

SANFORD

1547 N. Jackson Street
Milwaukee, WI 53202
Phone: (414) 276-9608
Fax: (414) 278-8509
www.foodspot.com/sanford

COQUETTE CAFÉ

316 N. Milwaukee Street
Milwaukee, WI 53202
Phone: (414) 291-2655

SANDY D'AMATO is chef-partner of Sanford and Coquette Café. His many honors include being named one of America's Hot New Chefs by *Food & Wine* magazine in 1985, and being one of only twelve chefs in the nation chosen to cook for Julia Child on her eightieth birthday. He won the 1996 James Beard Award as Best Chef: Midwest. Sanford's was chosen as one of the Best New Restaurants of 1990 by *Esquire* and has received *Wine Spectator*'s Award of Excellence multiple times.

MY FOOD I don't think you can really explain what you are doing at a restaurant, or that customers are necessarily going to understand it if you do. Nor should they have to. Great food should be great by itself, with no explanation necessary. When people come into our place, they often try things they've never had before. What we do is contemporary ethnic food, which to me encompasses what new American food is. Yet we don't cross-culturalize. I think there is a reason certain products go with other products, which has to do with the soil and climate they're both a product of, and is why figs and pomegranates go together, for example. But that philosophy still gives you incredible latitude.

Probably the best restaurants here in Milwaukee are ethnic. It is a little more Middle European than other cities, with the Polish and Serbian influences here. And there have always been German restaurants!

"As Milwaukee is less traveled than other cities featured in this book, we'd like to attest that Sanford is absolutely worth the two-hour drive from Chicago!"

ANDREW DORNENBURG AND KAREN PAGE

SANDY'S PICKS

BEANS AND BARLEY MARKET AND CAFÉ

1901 E. North Avenue, Milwaukee
(414) 278-7878

This is one of the first health food stores, which has been around for about twenty-five years. It is not strictly health food, but it always has great ingredients. It has the best egg salad sandwich in the city, which is made with a little bit of sunflower seed in it so it is a little crispy, on good whole-wheat bread with a touch of celery salt. The salads are simple but very good, with tasty dressings. It also has the best iced tea, and really good desserts. They have good cakes, and great blueberry pie in season.

POLENEZ

2316 S. 6th Street, Milwaukee
(414) 384-8766

Polenez is a local Polish place that has great borscht, wonderful pierogi—which I like sautéed, not boiled—and pork chops with sauerkraut. They also have good Polish beer. The food is very straightforward, and they are just the sweetest people in the world. After eating there, we added a squab borscht with root vegetable pierogi to our own menu.

SANDY'S PICKS

SHAHRAZAD

2847 N. Oakland Avenue, Milwaukee
(414) 964-5475

Shahrazad is right near the University of Wisconsin—Milwaukee. The food is always good and tasty. They serve the best tahini I've ever had, and the lamb *kofta* is also delicious. Two other things we order regularly are the yellow lentil soup and the falafel. It is about five dollars for lunch, which includes a salad with feta cheese.

SPEED QUEEN BAR-B-Q

1130 W. Walnut Street, Milwaukee
(414) 265-2900

This is a drive-through rib place that used to be a laundromat with Speed Queen washers and dryers. Order the outside shoulder, which is all the crisp parts. And get half regular, half hot sauce. The taste is close to Kansas City barbecue. The rib tips are also good, and they're served with Wonder bread for slopping up the sauce.

ZAFFIRO'S PIZZA AND BAR

1724 N. Farwell Avenue, Milwaukee
(414) 289-8776

Their pizzas have a thin crust and are really crispy. I love this type of pizza, especially topped with pepperoni and onions, with a beer on the side. As for atmosphere at Zaffiro's, there is none. Half of it is a bar, and the other half a dining room with red velvet banquettes and red vinyl chairs.

"*I was just out in Milwaukee last week. Sandy D'Amato does a good job, and he's a really nice guy. We went to a tailgate party together where we had these amazing Italian sausages and bratwursts. It was a goose-bump experience, it was so good! Then Sandy took us to this frozen custard place, Leon's, where we had a blast. Then we had dinner at his place, which was out-of-control perfect. When I looked around, I saw he's really the only thing going on out there. One guy against the world. And his restaurant's beautiful ...*"

MARIO BATALI   BABBO, ESCA, AND LUPA (NEW YORK)

BREAKFAST

CAMELIA GRILL

626 S. Carrollton Avenue, New Orleans
(504) 866-9573

"While the Camelia Grill serves breakfast, lunch, and dinner, I think it's an especially great place for breakfast. I recommend the omelets, which are huge."

—JAMIE SHANNON, COMMANDER'S PALACE

DUNBAR'S

4927 Feret Street, New Orleans
(504) 899-0734

"Go to Dunbar's for grits that are topped with all kinds of different things, from liver to eggs."

—CINDY PAWLCYN, BUCKEYE ROADHOUSE, FOG
CITY DINER, AND MUSTARDS GRILL
(SAN FRANCISCO)

TAKE-OUT

FOODIES KITCHEN

720 Veterans Boulevard, Metairie
(504) 837-9695

"Foodies Kitchen—owned by the Brennans—is a place we really needed. Probably nobody needs home-meal replacements more than chefs! My wife will go here on a Tuesday and bring home three days' worth of meals for when I get home late at night. They also sell a hundred types of homemade breads and individual desserts."

—FRANK BRIGTSEN, BRIGTSEN'S

CAFETERIA

MOTHER'S

401 Poydrus Street, New Orleans
(504) 523-9656

"This restaurant, which has been serving breakfast and lunch, including such items as biscuits, corn bread, crawfish étouffée, grits, ham po' boys, omelets, and red beans and rice, since 1938, is an experience."

—NORMAN VAN AKEN, NORMAN'S (CORAL GABLES, FL)

COFFEE

COMMUNITY COFFEE WITH CHICORY

Multiple locations, including:
900 Jefferson Avenue (at Magazine Street), New Orleans
(504) 891-4969

P&J'S

634 Frenchman Street, New Orleans
(504) 949-2292

"I am a coffee junkie; I drink it day and night. Coffee with chicory is so much a part of our culture in New Orleans. Sometimes I remember to bring it with me when I travel, but when I don't— boy, do I miss it! New Orleans coffee is full-flavored, and has a dark, roasted richness to it that I have not seen anywhere else. The chicory gives it a bitter flavor, but in a pleasant way. Community Coffee is the brand I drink, which has a bunch of cafés called CC's. Another place is P&J's. Both are at the top of my list."

—FRANK BRIGTSEN, BRIGTSEN'S

ZEA

1655 Hickory Avenue, Harahan
(504) 738-0799

"They have a fantastic rotisserie chicken, and the spinach salad with a pepper jelly vinaigrette. It's a very unusual salad, with raisins, currants, blue cheese, and sun-dried tomatoes in it. I never get tired of it!"

—FRANK BRIGTSEN, BRIGTSEN'S

GUMBO

GUMBO SHOP

630 St. Peter Street, New Orleans
(French Quarter)
(504) 525-1486

"In New Orleans, we all know that everyone's own mother makes the best gumbo, but the gumbo at this place is definitely good. They don't skimp on the sausage or the fish."

—JAMIE SHANNON, COMMANDER'S PALACE

HAMBURGER

CAMELIA GRILL

626 S. Carrollton Avenue,
New Orleans
(504) 866-9573

" Order the 'fully dressed'
hamburger, which comes
with fried onions and both
cheddar and American
cheese."

—CINDY PAWLCYN, BUCKEYE ROADHOUSE, FOG
CITY DINER, AND MUSTARDS GRILL
(SAN FRANCISCO)

" Camelia Grill makes a good
burger, and it's a cool place."

—SUSAN SPICER, BAYONA

PORT OF CALL

838 Esplanade Avenue, New Orleans
(504) 523-0120

" The burgers are really good
at this restaurant. It's also
known for its steaks."

—SUSAN SPICER, BAYONA

BEIGNETS

CAFÉ DU MONDE

1039 Decatur Street, New Orleans
(504) 587-0835

" For beignets [fritters] and
coffee, twenty-four hours
a day. I love to take my
son here—it's so fun to get
powdered sugar all over
the place!"

—JAMIE SHANNON, COMMANDER'S PALACE

ITALIAN CREOLE

MOSCA'S

4137 U.S. Highway 90 West, Avondale
(45 minutes from New Orleans)
(504) 436-9942

" This was supposedly an old
Mafia hangout. It's about
forty-five minutes out of the
city, but it's worth the trip.
The style of food is Italian-
Creole. Everything is super-
garlicky! It is good to go
with friends, because then
you can all smell like garlic
together! The shrimp is
good, and so is the chicken
grande."

—JAMIE SHANNON, COMMANDER'S PALACE

INSTITUTIONS

K-PAUL'S

416 Chartres Street, New Orleans
(504) 524-7394

" The best food—from appetizers to entrées to desserts—in New
Orleans."

—CINDY PAWLCYN, BUCKEYE ROADHOUSE, FOG CITY DINER, AND MUSTARDS GRILL (SAN FRANCISCO)

UGLESICH RESTAURANT AND BAR

1238 Baronne Street, New Orleans
(504) 523-8571
Lunch only.

" For a fried oyster po' boy, or the muddy water trout."

—TODD ENGLISH, FIGS AND OLIVES (BOSTON)

" Whatever they have, order it. Then order more."

—ANNE ROSENZWEIG, THE LOBSTER CLUB (NEW YORK)

" It's fantastic."

—CHARLIE TROTTER, CHARLIE TROTTER'S (CHICAGO)

" They post their specials on construction paper, which I haven't
seen since second grade. Everything is terrific."

—NORMAN VAN AKEN, NORMAN'S (CORAL GABLES, FL)

PO' BOYS

UGLESICH RESTAURANT AND BAR

1238 Baronne Street, New Orleans
(504) 523-8571
Lunch only.

" Especially the shrimp,
oyster or crab po' boys."

—SUSAN SPICER, BAYONA

" This place is a chefs' hangout and only serves lunch.
The soft-shell po' boy is
great. The fried oysters are
shucked to order and then
cooked in a black cast-iron
skillet, just like your mama
would do."

—JAMIE SHANNON, COMMANDER'S PALACE

new orleans
LOCAL HIGHLIGHTS

ACME OYSTER AND SEAFOOD HOUSE

724 Iberville Street (off Bourbon Street), New Orleans
(504) 522-5973
Acme opened in 1910, and has its own oyster beds, with oysters selected by Nick Bezmalinovic.

"This place is just fun. They have local oysters from different bayous. I do have areas that I favor for oysters: I like Grand Isle, which is in the Barataria Bay system, and also oysters from a town called Empire. Bayou Cook and Bay Adams are two of my other favorites. Generally, I like my oysters to come from west of the Mississippi. The river flows out to the east, so there is more fresh water being put into that part of the Gulf. The water, and the oysters, are slightly saltier to the west. And I love them all with an ice-cold Dixie beer."

—JAMIE SHANNON,
COMMANDER'S PALACE

JAMIE SHANNON on

The Difference Between Creole and Cajun Cooking

I COULD GO ON AND ON ABOUT THE DIFFERENCES FOR HOURS, BUT HERE IS the short version:

Creole is old New Orleans food. It is what put the old New Orleans restaurants like Antoine's and Arnaud's on the map. Think of Trout Almondine and all those other old, great dishes your parents might have eaten. Creole food involves a lot more technique than Cajun, and includes more desserts; they will do custards and flans that they learned from Europe. It is also city food. New Orleans is a port city, and people came here from around the world, so it has incorporated many ethnic influences, including French, Spanish, Italian, African, American Indian, and Caribbean. The food is more refined.

Cajun, on the other hand, was influenced by the Nova Scotians, who came down the river from Canada as far as they could go and settled in southwest Louisiana. It incorporates great charcuterie and more country-style, one-pot cooking. They would use cayenne instead of peppercorns because they couldn't get peppercorns.

CASAMENTO'S RESTAURANT

4330 Magazine Street, New Orleans
(504) 895-9761

"But only during oyster season—that's typically September through April." [Authors' note: Anthony Uglesich would argue that that's not always the case, and that sometimes the oysters are even better in June and July than they are in September; it depends on a number of factors, such as the weather and the water.]

—SUSAN SPICER, BAYONA

FELIX'S RESTAURANT AND OYSTER BAR

739 Iberville Street, New Orleans
(504) 522-4440

"Felix's, plus Uglesich and Acme, is one of the big oyster specialists. They source good oysters, and that is what you should find at all three of these places. I wouldn't go to a steakhouse to order oysters. These are oyster restaurants, so you know you are going to get the best quality."

—FRANK BRIGTSEN, BRIGTSEN'S

Frank Brigtsen is chef-owner of Brigtsen's in New Orleans. In 1988, Brigtsen was named one of *Food & Wine*'s Top Ten New Chefs, and readers voted Brigtsen's Top Cajun Restaurant in the 2000 *ZagatSurvey*. Brigtsen won the 1998 James Beard Award as Best Chef: Southeast.

Frank Brigtsen

BRIGTSEN'S
723 Dante Street
New Orleans, LA 70118
Phone: (504) 861-7610
Fax: (504) 866-7397

MY FOOD To me, being a chef in New Orleans is like being a football player in Green Bay: There is a tremendous history and tradition that you are a part of. The history of Louisiana cooking is over two hundred years old. While I need to understand what that means in a contemporary context, I am a New Orleans boy, and we are a Louisiana restaurant, and I have a tremendous love and respect for the tradition of Louisiana cuisine. I make gumbo and jambalaya—and it may not be so cutting-edge, but I don't care. If I, as a chef in New Orleans, don't make a good gumbo, who will? I feel honored and blessed to be part of the continuum that is Louisiana cuisine. And I share the philosophy of Chez Panisse's Alice Waters when it comes to sourcing foods. Too many people have lost contact with the origins of food. Today, chefs—including myself—are encouraging local farmers to bring their products to the restaurants. My philosophy is that if they grow it, I will cook it and sell it.

FRANK'S PICKS

CRESCENT CITY STEAK HOUSE

1001 N. Broad, New Orleans
(504) 821-3271
This is a great old-style steakhouse. You walk in and feel like you're in the 1950s—nothing's changed. They do their steaks New Orleans—style, which means broiled at an extremely high temperature and served with a butter sauce. The place has white-tile floors, and against one wall you'll find booths with curtains, which is where we usually sit. I get a T-bone or a porterhouse, and garlic bread.

DRAGO'S

3232 N. Arnoult Road, New Orleans
(504) 888-9254
The families that own Drago's and Uglesich's are both Croatian, and the oyster industry in Louisiana is run mostly by Croatians. Drago's has its own truck, and they go down to the Empire area, where they have contacts with other Croatians and get great oysters. Their specialty dish is charbroiled oysters, which are shucked, basted with garlic butter and Parmesan, and broiled. They are unbelievable! All the seafood is very good here in general.

UGLESICH RESTAURANT AND BAR

1238 Baronne Street, New Orleans
(504) 523-8571
This restaurant has been here a long time, and is only open for lunch. I think Mr. Anthony and Gail are the second- or third-generation owners. They are some of my heroes in this business. They put their heart and soul into the place. It is a dive, but it is a magic place to me. They specialize in Louisiana seafood, and oysters in particular, which is my favorite food in the whole world. They also serve soft-shell crabs and great po' boys. (See also p. 143.)

COMMANDER'S PALACE

1403 Washington Avenue,
New Orleans
(504) 899-8221

We like to go to Commander's Palace for special occasions. They offer everything: a wide variety of great [haute Creole] food, a great wine list, great service, and a great environment—the site has been a restaurant since 1880. They do sort of what I do: They offer new dishes, but they also have a handle on the history and tradition of New Orleans. That is something that I admire. The Brennans, who have owned the restaurant since 1974, are my heroes in this business; what they have done for New Orleans cuisine is an ongoing phenomenon. (See also p. 147.)

KIM SON

349 Whitney Avenue, New Orleans
(504) 366-2489

This restaurant is Vietnamese, which is a cuisine that is different from what I normally eat and is so refreshing. It's a fun place. Things that sound so simple on the menu are unbelievably good, like steamed fish with black bean sauce. We have a good-sized Vietnamese population here, and a lot of them are fishermen or gardeners. I also like to get a side of stir-fried Chinese broccoli with garlic, because I know it will be incredible.

FRANK BRIGTSEN ON

Eating Oysters in New Orleans

OYSTERS ARE MY FAVORITE FOOD IN THE WORLD. WHEN I WAS A KID, MY DAD was a great oyster fan, but I could never stand them. Then, when I was about twenty-one, I fell in love with them. Now I just can't get enough of them.

My absolute favorite way to eat them is raw, on the half shell, with nothing on them. I think oysters have a great subtlety of flavor, depending on the time of year, and depending on which bay, bayou, or lake they are from. There are certain qualities of sweetness, saltiness, and minerals that I really enjoy.

We buy oysters from a company that sells just oysters. The same family has owned it for three generations, so they have the contacts needed to get the very best. An oyster is unique in that it is a seafood that doesn't swim around, so it is influenced by its environment more than other seafoods. An oyster will filter fifty gallons of water a day, and water quality has a tremendous impact on flavor.

One place I like oysters from is Chinaman's Bayou. There is a guy there who will harvest his oysters in the bay, and then move them to marshes where the current is stronger. He'll let them sit a few days, then harvest them a second time before bringing them to market. That purifies them and brings up the salt level. Now that is someone who cares! He is doing double work, but, then again, no one works harder than oyster men! That's a fact.

I will eat oysters year round, but my favorite time is February or March, when they are their fattest and their best. We'll go to Drago's and Uglesich's almost every week until my wife gets tired of it. She knows how much I love them.

I have been known to eat a meal of only oysters—I mean, three courses of oysters! I will start with a dozen on the half shell and then have a dozen charbroiled. Depending on my mood, I'll follow that with either oyster pasta or fried oysters, and sometimes both. And I have been known to have more oysters for dessert. No kidding!

"The first thing that anyone visiting New Orleans should taste is our seafood. When we describe our seasons, we don't use 'spring, summer, fall, and winter'—we use 'crawfish, shrimp, crab, and oyster'! The backyard crawfish boil in Louisiana is one of the greatest eating and social pleasures we have. There are plenty of restaurants where you can get boiled crawfish; it is the epitome of Louisiana."

FRANK BRIGTSEN   BRIGTSEN'S

Jamie Shannon is chef of Commander's Palace. Since 1984, he has worked his way up the restaurant's ladder—from garde-manger to executive chef. Commander's Palace won the James Beard Award for Outstanding Service in 1993 and the James Beard Award for Outstanding Restaurant in 1996. *Food & Wine* rated it the number one restaurant in America in 1995. In 1999, Shannon won the James Beard Award as Best Chef: Southeast, and was named the *Robb Report*'s number two chef in the world.

Jamie Shannon

COMMANDER'S PALACE

1403 Washington Avenue
(at Coliseum Street)
New Orleans, LA 70130
Phone: (504) 899-8221
Fax: (504) 891-3242

MY FOOD We do local food at its best, with all local products—it is seasonal New Orleans food. We have a regular à la carte menu, daily specials, and a tasting menu of eight courses. The tasting menu always includes foie gras, and might also include caviar, truffles, and handmade cheese. We have some great local cheese. I like the Chicory Farm cheeses, and the St. John, which is a hard cheese—it's good on Creole tomatoes or grated on things. That's what you want to do when you come to Commander's Palace: taste what is in our backyard!

JAMIE'S PICKS

BAYONA
430 Rue Dauphine, New Orleans
(504) 522-0588
I like Susan Spicer's eclectic, contemporary cuisine because it is light and elegant with Mediterranean, Asian, Indian, and southwestern twists. I always take friends here to see what she's cooking, since she is always doing new things. (See also p. 148.)

BRIGTSEN'S
723 Dante Street, New Orleans
(504) 861-7610
For special occasions or when I'm in the mood, I love Frank Brigtsen's restaurant because I know that when I go in, Frank will be cooking my dinner. He does a lot of southwest Louisiana and New Orleans food, as well as both contemporary Creole and Cajun dishes, using local food products. (See also p. 145.)

CENTRAL GROCERY
923 Decatur Street, New Orleans
(504) 523-1620
This old-style Italian grocery and deli, with a few counter stools, is the place to go for a muffuletta—a sandwich made with a variety of Italian lunch meats, cheeses, and a vinegar-based olive salad. It is sort of a New Orleans hoagie.

EMERIL'S
800 Tchoupitoulas Street, New Orleans
(504) 528-9393
I worked with Emeril Lagasse, the chef-owner, for five years, so I know everybody at this "new New Orleans" restaurant, which uses traditional Creole ingredients as starting points. It is fun to visit. The service is great, and the food is really phenomenal.

FOODIES KITCHEN
720 Veterans Boulevard, New Orleans
(504) 837-9695
I'm in the kitchen five days a week, so it is great to know that I can go to Foodies Kitchen and get restaurant-quality meals to take home to my family. Better yet, if I'm entertaining, I can pick up all the food for the party at Foodies Kitchen [which also has seating on the premises].

FRANKY AND JOHNNY'S
321 Arabella Street, New Orleans
(504) 899-9146
This neighborhood joint is the place to go for a crawfish boil in season. The other thing to order is onion rings, which are the best ever and not at all greasy. They also have crawfish pies and red beans.

MR. B'S BISTRO
201 Royal Street (at Iberville Street), New Orleans (French Quarter)
(504) 523-2078
I like to go to this regional Creole restaurant—it's owned by the Brennan family, who buys from local farms and makes its own sausage, pickles, and chutneys, and smokes its own meats—for barbecued shrimp, which are not really barbecued at all, but done in a pan with beer and seafood seasoning. It is a great Creole dish. You cook the shrimp with the head on, because it has fat and gives the shrimp great flavor. They also have great gumbo ya ya, which is made with chicken and andouille sausage.

Susan Spicer

BAYONA

430 Rue Dauphine
New Orleans, LA 70112
Phone: (504) 522-0588
Fax: (504) 522-0589

HERBSAINT

701 St. Charles Avenue
New Orleans, LA 70130
Phone: (504) 524-4114
Fax: (504) 522-1679

SUSAN SPICER is chef-owner of Bayona and Herbsaint. The daughter of an American naval officer and a Danish mother, Spicer's childhood travels influenced her global approach to food. *Food & Wine* named Spicer to its list of Ten Best New Chefs for 1989, and in 1993, she won the James Beard Award as Best Chef: Southeast.

MY FOOD As the restaurant has gotten older, my style has evolved. I trained with French chefs, and my goal has always been to stay focused. I will borrow from other cuisines and cultures, but I will not do anything hodgepodge. I am very proud of our service because it provides continuity. We have a smallish menu with a few dishes we can't take off, like our duck breast with pepper jelly. We have also had sweetbreads on our menu forever—it's my mother's favorite dish. We also have a courtyard, which I think is one of the best things about New Orleans and the French Quarter—all the beautiful courtyards that are hidden. It's part of the beauty and mystery that is here; you enter them and you are in a secret world. To have a little bit of that element in Bayona is important to me.

SUSAN'S PICKS

CLANCY'S

6100 Annunciation Street,
New Orleans
(504) 895-1111

This is a restaurant with local flavor and a great wine list. It's a classic New Orleans restaurant that shows great respect for the food. They've got wonderful crabmeat dishes, veal, fried eggplant, and a signature dish of smoked, then fried, soft-shell crabs.

MONA'S CAFÉ

3901 Banks Street, New Orleans
(504) 482-0661

On my nights off I like to go to Mona's, which is a Middle Eastern restaurant. I love their falafel, which is crisp and not at all greasy. They also have great hummus and baba ganouj.

SAMURAI SUSHI

239 Decatur Street, New Orleans
(French Quarter)
(504) 525-9595

When I'm in the mood for sushi, I go here. I'm a total avocado nut, and they make a "caterpillar roll," which is wrapped in thin slices of avocado—it is really pretty. They also have good mussels in a wasabi cream sauce, and a terrific octopus salad.

TAQUERIA CORONA

5932 Magazine, New Orleans
(504) 897-3974

This is the one decent taqueria we have in the city. I love the spicy chorizo, tongue, and fried fish tacos, and the spicy sauce they serve with them. Their margaritas are good, too.

BAGEL

H&H

Multiple locations, including:
2239 Broadway, Manhattan (original location)
(212) 595-8003
1551 Second Avenue, Manhattan
(212) 734-7441
639 W. 46th Street, Manhattan
(212) 595-8000

"H&H bagels are really good, especially the everything bagel. They put a lot of everything on it: salt, sesame, poppy, onion, garlic. I think my taste buds are getting pretty jaded, so I need the big spice fix!"

—REBECCA CHARLES, PEARL OYSTER BAR

"I love bagels. I like them nice and crisp the way H&H makes them, not big and doughy the way others do. The only thing I don't like about H&H is that I have to wait in line!"

—FRANÇOIS PAYARD, PAYARD PÂTISSERIE AND BISTRO

"H&H has the best bagels in New York."

—ERIC RIPERT, LE BERNARDIN

"After running on Sundays, I will stop at H&H for a bagel. I like to get a cinnamon-raisin, onion, or an everything. They are especially good when they are still warm from the oven."

—JACQUES TORRES, formerly of LE CIRQUE 2000

ESS-A-BAGEL

Multiple locations, including:
831 Third Avenue (between 50th and 51st Streets), Manhattan
(212) 980-1010
359 First Avenue (at 21st Street), Manhattan
(212) 260-2252

"I like a salt bagel with a little cream cheese and salmon."

—TOM COLICCHIO, GRAMERCY TAVERN

PICK-A-BAGEL

Multiple locations, including.
1101 Lexington Avenue (at 77th Street), Manhattan
(212) 517-6590

"I like to get the everything bialy. Why? It has onions!"

—LAURENT TOURONDEL, CELLO

Jacques Torres (*right*) and Kris Kruid enjoy H&H bagels after a Sunday run

BAGUETTE

PAYARD PÂTISSERIE AND BISTRO

1032 Lexington Avenue (between 73rd and 74th Streets), Manhattan
(212) 717-5252

"I just love a good baguette. We make a Swiss baguette now that's twisted like a breadstick. How can you tell a good baguette? Once you start eating one, you can't stop! In France, you'll see ladies on the street, eating their fresh baguettes. When they get home, it's three-quarters gone!"

—FRANÇOIS PAYARD,
PAYARD PÂTISSERIE AND BISTRO

Bar

BLUE RIBBON

97 Sullivan Street (between Prince and Spring Streets), Manhattan
(212) 274-0404

FOUR SEASONS

99 E. 52nd Street (between Lexington and Park Avenues), Manhattan
(212) 754-9494

THE KING COLE BAR

2 E. 55th Street (in the St. Regis Hotel, between Fifth and Madison Avenues),
Manhattan
(212) 339-6721

"These are three great places to go for a drink in Manhattan."

—MARK MILLER, COYOTE CAFÉ (LAS VEGAS AND SANTA FE)

Barbecue

LEXINGTON RIB CO.

1364 Lexington Avenue (between 90th
and 91st Streets), Manhattan
(212) 410-5600

*"It's just a storefront with
tables, but they have really
good ribs. There's an old-
fashioned water pump, and
you pump water to wash
your hands over a barrel
when you're through."*

—ANNE ROSENZWEIG, THE LOBSTER CLUB

Blintz

RATNER'S

138 Delancey Street (between Norfolk
and Suffolk Streets), Manhattan
(212) 677-5588

*"Ratner's is a dairy restaurant
that also serves smoked fish,
potato soup, and cheesecake.
They have the greatest
blintzes. The plain farmer's
cheese or the blueberry and
cheese are the best."*

—FRANKLIN BECKER, LOCAL

Bread

AMY'S BREAD

672 Ninth Avenue (between 46th and 47th Streets), Manhattan
(212) 977-2670
75 Ninth Avenue (in Chelsea Market, between 15th and 16th Streets), Manhattan
(212) 462-4338

"I love Amy's fennel raisin sticks."

—TOM COLICCHIO, GRAMERCY TAVERN

"I really like Amy's breads."

—JACQUES TORRES, formerly of LE CIRQUE 2000

BALTHAZAR

80 Spring Street (between Broadway and Lafayette Street), Manhattan
(212) 965-1414

*"I love the chocolate breakfast bread and the cranberry bread at
Balthazar."*

—TOM COLICCHIO, GRAMERCY TAVERN

"Paula Oland, Balthazar's baker, does a really good job."

—AMY SCHERBER, AMY'S BREAD

*"I have been all around France, and I think Balthazar's bread
compares to any being made in France. It is the same bread I ate
when I was young. I brought my parents here, and my father
thought it was unbelievable—he couldn't believe we weren't in
France! They also have an excellent sticky bun."*

—LAURENT TOURONDEL, CELLO

Bread cont.

ECCE PANIS

Multiple locations, including:
1120 Third Avenue, Manhattan
(212) 535-2099

"Their fruit focaccia is really good, and the olive oil fougasse is, too."

—DIANE FORLEY, VERBENA

LE PAIN QUOTIDIEN

1131 Madison Avenue (between 84th and 85th Streets), Manhattan
(212) 327-4900
100 Grand Street (at Mercer Street), Manhattan
(212) 625-9009

"Their bread is the best."

—JEAN-GEORGES VONGERICHTEN, JEAN GEORGES, JO JO, AND VONG

SULLIVAN STREET BAKERY

73 Sullivan Street, Manhattan
(212) 334-9435

"The ciabattas [flat, oval Italian breads] are crusty, floury, and chewy."

—DIANE FORLEY, VERBENA

"Their pizza bread is wonderful."

—ANNE ROSENZWEIG, THE LOBSTER CLUB

"Their bread is really good."

—AMY SCHERBER, AMY'S BREAD

Breakfast

BALTHAZAR

80 Spring Street (between Broadway and Crosby Street), Manhattan
(212) 965-1785

"I love their sticky buns."

—JEAN-GEORGES VONGERICHTEN, JEAN GEORGES, JO JO, AND VONG

LE PAIN QUOTIDIEN

Multiple locations, including:
1131 Madison Avenue (at 84th Street), Manhattan
(212) 327-4900
833 Lexington Avenue (at 64th Street), Manhattan
(212) 755-5810
100 Grand Street (at Mercer Street), Manhattan
(212) 625-9009
www.painquotidien.com

"Le Pain Quotidien is a great place that serves breakfast and lunch. It's very European, and we buy bread from them. There is a communal table in each location, set with with jam and butter. They also have hazelnut butter that you spread on your baguette—mmm . . . I go there every Saturday and Sunday and have a big bowl of café au lait, like the one I grew up with. They also have nice sandwiches—pâté de campagne and things like that."

—JEAN-GEORGES VONGERICHTEN, JEAN GEORGES, JO JO, AND VONG

"This is a great place to stop and have a bowl of latte."

—ANNE ROSENZWEIG, THE LOBSTER CLUB

GRAMERCY TAVERN

42 E. 20th Street (between Broadway and Park Avenue South), Manhattan
(212) 477-0777

"At Gramercy, I like sitting in the tavern, eating an appetizer, and having a plate of cheese. Add a glass of red wine, and that's the whole lunch."

—MARIO BATALI, BABBO, ESCA, AND LUPA

PICHOLINE

35 W. 64th Street (between Broadway and Central Park West), Manhattan
(212) 724-8585

"I love the variety of cheeses at Picholine [which features more than fifty]."

—MARIO BATALI, BABBO, ESCA, AND LUPA

LA MAISON DU CHOCOLAT

1018 Madison Avenue (between 78th and 79th Streets), Manhattan (212) 744-7117
At Bergdorf Goodman, 254 Fifth Avenue, 7th floor, Manhattan (212) 753-7300, ext. 8069

"For the truffles."

—ROCCO DISPIRITO, UNION PACIFIC

"For the chocolate-covered almonds."

—EMILY LUCHETTI, FARALLON (SAN FRANCISCO)

"For their dark chocolate bark, made with pistachios, hazelnuts, almonds, and orange zest. They make a killer hot chocolate—it's amazing! They offer two or three different kinds of hot chocolate, and they're all so rich that they're served with a side of hot cream so you can make it a little less rich!"

—ANNE ROSENZWEIG, THE LOBSTER CLUB

"I love the brownness of this place—it's like walking into a big piece of chocolate! Their flavors are subtle, and I especially like their coffee-flavored chocolates and their chocolate-covered nuts."

—AMY SCHERBER, AMY'S BREAD

RICHART DESIGN ET CHOCOLAT

7 E. 55th Street, Manhattan (212) 371-9369

"They have very challenging flavors, such as seven spices with fleur de sel."

—MARK MILLER, COYOTE CAFÉ (LAS VEGAS AND SANTA FE)

NEW YORK NOODLE TOWN

28½ Bowery (at Bayard Street),
Manhattan
(212) 349-0923

"For salt-baked soft-shell crabs."

—MICHAEL ROMANO, UNION SQUARE CAFE

"The roast pork is great—it's got the crispy skin that cracks. All the roasted meats are perfect. They do a dish called sea bass chunks with flowering chives. It is one of the great dishes of all time. It's on the special menu, always. The fish is unbelievable—it's unctuous, not crispy, except the skin. There's not much sauce, and there's a big old handful of flowering chives."

—MARIO BATALI, BABBO, ESCA, AND LUPA

Caramel coulis with fleur de sel* butter and seven spices

CHOCOLATE CONT.

VARSANO'S CHOCOLATES

179 W. 4th Street (between Avenue of the Americas and Seventh Avenue), Manhattan
(212) 352-1171 (800) 414-4718

"Our favorite uptown chocolatier is La Maison du Chocolat. But this is our favorite downtown chocolatier, without question! You can often watch owner Marc Varsano hand-dipping chocolates right behind the counter. We never liked chocolate-covered pretzels until we tasted Varsano's dark chocolate-covered version!"

—AUTHORS ANDREW DORNENBURG AND KAREN PAGE

clams

AN AMERICAN PLACE (AT THE BAR)

565 Lexington Avenue (in the Benjamin Hotel), Manhattan
(212) 888-5650

"Their fried clams are perfect! And the tartar sauce is homemade."

—MARK MILLER, COYOTE CAFÉ (LAS VEGAS AND SANTA FE)

croissant

BALTHAZAR

80 Spring Street (between Broadway and Lafayette Street), Manhattan (212) 965-1414

"They make a good croissant."

—LAURENT TOURONDEL, CELLO

CHEZ LAURENCE

245 Madison Avenue (at 38th Street), Manhattan (212) 683-0284

"None of the chefs we'd asked about the best croissant in New York had tasted one from Chez Laurence. When they're fresh out of the oven at seven A.M., they're hard to beat! We ran into their baker on the street one day and asked him about the secret of his croissants. 'Love,' Adolf replied with a wink and a smile—convincing us further that he is definitely our kind of chef! The croissants are best enjoyed with fruit confitures that are made on the premises; our favorites are the cherry and peach flavors."

—AUTHORS ANDREW DORNENBURG AND KAREN PAGE

LE PAIN QUOTIDIEN

Multiple locations, including:
1131 Madison Avenue (at 84th Street), Manhattan (212) 327-4900
100 Grand Street (at Mercer Street), Manhattan (212) 625-9009

"They make a fantastic croissant."

—JEAN-GEORGES VONGERICHTEN, JEAN GEORGES, JOJO, AND VONG

PAYARD PÂTISSERIE AND BISTRO

1032 Lexington Avenue (between 73rd and 74th Streets), Manhattan (212) 717-5252

"The croissant and the pain au chocolat are both incredible, yet very different."

—EMILY LUCHETTI, FARALLON (SAN FRANCISCO)

SARABETH'S

Multiple locations, including:
75 Ninth Avenue, Manhattan (in Chelsea Market) (212) 989-2424

"My staff and I did a tasting of the croissants reputed to be the best in New York, and we thought Payard's and Sarabeth's were definitely the best. They're both carefully made and really delicious."

—AMY SCHERBER, AMY'S BREAD

DELI

ADELMAN'S

1906 Kings Highway, Brooklyn
(718) 336-4915

"They have the best corned beef sandwich. It is huge. With a hot corned beef sandwich on rye, Gulden's spicy mustard, french fries, and a Dr. Brown's black cherry soda, I am in heaven!"

—FRANKLIN BECKER, LOCAL

CARNEGIE DELI

854 Seventh Avenue (at 55th Street), Manhattan
(212) 757-2245

"For the pastrami sandwich."

—ERIC RIPERT, LE BERNARDIN

"Delis are pretty special; they're so different from anything in France. When you ask for a sandwich in France, you get one thin slice of ham on a baguette. Here you get five, ten, or more slices! I love both pastrami and corned beef, but it's special; I wouldn't eat it every day. One time I took [Michelin three-star chefs] Paul Bocuse, Georges Blanc, Michel Guérard, and Roger Vergé to Carnegie Deli. They loved it! They ordered two sandwiches, and it was enough for four people."

—JEAN-GEORGES VONGERICHTEN, JEAN GEORGES, JO JO, AND VONG

Rocco DiSpirito at Katz's, having a "quintessential New York experience."

KATZ'S

205 E. Houston Street
(at Ludlow Street), Manhattan
(212) 254-2246

"*Having a pastrami sandwich at Katz's is a quintessential New York experience.*"

—ROCCO DISPIRITO, UNION PACIFIC

SECOND AVENUE DELI

156 Second Avenue (at 10th Street), Manhattan
(212) 677-9696

"*If you don't have a Jewish grandmother, this is the place to go! The matzoh ball soup here is the best of any New York restaurant. Order it 'with everything.' If you don't say 'with everything,' all you get is a matzoh ball and the soup. If you say 'with everything,' you get the tiny square noodles that you only see in Jewish food, and chopped fresh dill and carrots. Their pastrami, chopped liver, and corned beef are also great. I used to be a corned beef person, but now I'm becoming a pastrami person—it's a little more of a taste sensation.*"

—REBECCA CHARLES, PEARL OYSTER BAR

"*When I'm not feeling well, I call them and order two quarts of matzoh ball soup without noodles, a turkey sandwich with a lot of Russian dressing on it, and some chopped liver, to go. The soup is the remedy, and the rest is just comforting.*"

—BOBBY FLAY, BOLO AND MESA GRILL

"*Second Avenue is my favorite deli.*"

—DIANE FORLEY, VERBENA

"*I have a customer who goes downtown once every three weeks and brings me a pastrami sandwich from Second Avenue Deli. I love it now, but when I first saw all that pastrami on two small slices of bread, it looked inedible!*"

—FRANÇOIS PAYARD, PAYARD PÂTISSERIE AND BISTRO

"*I think Second Avenue still remains the most authentic.*"

—MICHAEL ROMANO, UNION SQUARE CAFE

"*I love to go here when I'm in Manhattan.*"

—ALLEN SUSSER, CHEF ALLEN'S (MIAMI)

NEW SILVER PALACE RESTAURANT

52 Bowery (at Canal Street), Manhattan
(212) 964-1204

"*The restaurant has tables that each seat about fourteen people. When I first came to New York, I remember being shocked to see the little pushcarts [that roam the dining room and from which the little dishes are served]. Every time you want something, they give you a little punch on your card. When you can't eat any more, you get up and pay, based on the number of punches on your card. Two cooks just visited from France last week, and I sent them here and they were shocked. They told me, 'We ate as much as we wanted, and it was only fifteen dollars!'*"

—FRANÇOIS PAYARD, PAYARD PÂTISSERIE AND BISTRO

TRIPLE EIGHT PALACE

88 E. Broadway, Manhattan
(212) 941-8886

"*They have really good spinach-and-leek dumplings.*"

—DIANE FORLEY, VERBENA

FINE DINING

DANIEL

60 E. 65th Street (between Madison and Park Avenues), Manhattan
(212) 288-0033

"If you're visiting from out of town, you should definitely hit one or two of the big New York institutions—like Daniel. It is something you can't experience anywhere else."

—ROCCO DISPIRITO, UNION PACIFIC

GOTHAM BAR AND GRILL

12 W. 12th Street (between Fifth Avenue and University Place), Manhattan
(212) 620-4020

"We worked here together when the restaurant got its first three-star review. Alfred Portale's food is delicious. He has great raviolis and soups. His garde-manger work is stellar. He is one of the few chefs whose main courses are as good as his appetizers."

—GALE GAND AND RICK TRAMONTO, BRASSERIE T AND TRU (CHICAGO)

JEAN GEORGES

1 Central Park West (in Trump International Tower, between 60th and 61st Streets), Manhattan
(212) 299-3900

"It's the sexiest four-star restaurant in America—and the only four-star restaurant with action at the bar!"

—BOBBY FLAY, BOLO AND MESA GRILL

LE CIRQUE 2000

455 Madison Avenue (in the New York Palace Hotel, between 50th and 51st Streets), Manhattan
(212) 303-7788

"Le Cirque is a New York experience, and it is a particular experience worth having."

—DAVID WALTUCK, CHANTERELLE

"Don't focus on any small things that might go wrong, and don't look for reasons to justify what you're spending. When you go to a place like Le Cirque, it's an experience that can't be duplicated."

—ROCCO DISPIRITO, UNION PACIFIC

FARMERS' MARKET

UNION SQUARE GREENMARKET

17th Street at Broadway, Manhattan
(212) 788-7900 (for more information on this and other New York City markets)
Open Mondays, Wednesdays, Fridays, and Saturdays

"Strolling through the Union Square Greenmarket to shop for everything from organic produce to baked goods to cheeses to flowers is a not-to-be-missed New York experience!"

—AUTHORS ANDREW DORNENBURG AND KAREN PAGE

FISH SANDWICH

PEARL OYSTER BAR

18 Cornelia Street (between Bleecker and W. 4th Streets), Manhattan
(212) 691-8211

"Their fried fish sandwich is the best! Sometimes it's cod, sometimes it's grouper, but it's always served on a crisp roll with an unbelievable homemade tartar sauce."

—MARIO BATALI, BABBO, ESCA, AND LUPA

FRENCH FRIES

BALTHAZAR

80 Spring Street (between Broadway and Crosby Street), Manhattan
(212) 965-1414

"Fries are a lot of work to do perfectly, and Balthazar has really good fries. They are made correctly and come out crispy."

—TERRANCE BRENNAN, PICHOLINE

German

ROLF'S

281 Third Avenue (at 22nd Street),
Manhattan
(212) 473-8718

*"It's a fun place, with a lot of
ambiance. They keep their
Christmas lights up year
round. Their sausages are
really good, and at happy
hour you can taste great
beers and complimentary
sandwiches."*

—DIANE FORLEY, VERBENA

Ice cream

CUSTARD BEACH

Multiple locations, including:
Grand Central Station (Dining
Concourse), Manhattan
(212) 983-4707

*"I love Custard Beach. My
favorite flavor is vanilla,
and it's so good that it never
occurred to me that they
had any other flavors."*

—MARIO BATALI, BABBO, ESCA, AND LUPA

Hamburger

BIG NICK'S BURGER JOINT

2173 Broadway (between 76th and 77th Streets), Manhattan
(212) 362-9238

"I like their burgers with bacon and cheddar."

—ANDREW CARMELLINI, CAFÉ BOULUD

*"They grill their burgers on what I swear is no bigger than a two-
foot grill, right in the front window. It's a really tiny place, and
their burgers are just delicious. They use very good meat, and
their pickles are really good, too. You sit in the back in tiny
wooden booths. They also frost their mugs, so you get icy cold
beer."*

—REBECCA CHARLES, PEARL OYSTER BAR

BLUE RIBBON

97 Sullivan Street (between Prince and Spring Streets), Manhattan
(212) 274-0404

"For a great turkey burger."

—MARIO BATALI, BABBO, ESCA, AND LUPA

CORNER BISTRO

331 W. 4th Street (at Jane Street), Manhattan
(212) 242-9502

*"It's a real burger. For the most part, I just have it with ketchup, or
occasionally a piece of Swiss. The only reason you eat burgers
and fries is for ketchup!"*

—TOM COLICCHIO, GRAMERCY TAVERN

"They have really good burgers."

—DIANE FORLEY, VERBENA

J.G. MELON

1291 Third Avenue (at 74th Street), Manhattan
(212) 744-0585

"The best cheeseburger ever!"

—BOBBY FLAY, BOLO AND MESA GRILL

LEXINGTON RIB CO.

1364 Lexington Avenue (between 90th and 91st Streets), Manhattan
(212) 410-5600

"It's a great burger!"

—ANNE ROSENZWEIG, THE LOBSTER CLUB

new york
LOCAL HIGHLIGHTS

INDIAN

PONGAL

110 Lexington Avenue (at 27th Street), Manhattan (212) 696-9458

"When I'm in New York, I'll have dinner at Daniel and lunch at Pongal, which is the best south Indian restaurant in the city. I especially love their dosai *[spicy and crispy Indian crêpes]. It might even be the one of the* world's best south Indian restaurants."

—RAJI JALLEPALLI, RESTAURANT RAJI (MEMPHIS)

ITALIAN

BAMONTE'S

32 Withers Street (between Lorimer Street and Union Avenue), Brooklyn (Williamsburg) (718) 384-8831

"It is old-style food, and the place has the best mobster-movie feel. The waiters wear tuxedos, and you can imagine that many a hit man has been here. It has great nostalgia. Their baked clams and pastas are wonderful."

—FRANKLIN BECKER, LOCAL

JEWISH

SAMMY'S ROUMANIAN

157 Chrystie Street (at Delancey Street), Manhattan (212) 673-0330

"It is a dive. Order the Roumanian tenderloin, which is the best thing here. They also have great kasha varnishkas *and meatfilled pierogis. Finish with an egg cream—they bring the seltzer bottle to your table. It is a bit of a show. If you are not Jewish, they insult the hell out of you, and if you are Jewish, you survive."*

—FRANKLIN BECKER, LOCAL

KNISH

CARNEGIE DELI

854 Seventh Avenue (at 55th Street), Manhattan
(212) 757-2245

"They have an amazing knish that's unlike anything else I've ever seen in New York. It's more like a pie than a square knish—it has more of a pastry crust than a traditional knish crust, and the potato is spiced."

—REBECCA CHARLES, PEARL OYSTER BAR

KNISH NOSH

101–02 Queens Boulevard (near 67th Road), Queens (Forest Hills)
(718) 897-5554

"Knish Nosh has New York's first-runner-up knish."

—FRANKLIN BECKER, LOCAL

MRS. STAHL'S KNISHES

1001 Brighton Beach Avenue, Brooklyn (Brighton Beach)
(718) 648-0210

"They are the best knishes, hands down. A good knish has nice density but is not leaden—the dough should be light and almost break apart from the potatoes and onions inside. The best way to eat one is with Gulden's spicy brown mustard. Anything other than potatoes and onions in a knish is blasphemy."

—FRANKLIN BECKER, LOCAL

KNISH CONT.

YONAH SCHIMMELL'S KNISHES

137 Houston Street (between First and Second Avenues), Manhattan (212) 477-2858

"New York's second-runner-up knish."

—FRANKLIN BECKER, LOCAL

korean

DAILY CHOW

325 Bowery (at 2nd Street), Manhattan (212) 254-7887

"It's a restaurant with a fun feeling to it, and I really like their bibimbap [a traditional Korean rice dish]."

—AMY SCHERBER, AMY'S BREAD

HANGAWI

12 E. 32nd Street (between Fifth and Madison Avenues), Manhattan (212) 213-0077

"I love this place, because the serenity of the dining room takes you so far from New York. It's a completely transporting experience. I love not knowing what I'm eating, so I'll order the tasting menu of ten different courses, which covers the whole flavor spectrum." [Authors' note: Be prepared to remove your shoes before being seated at one of the restaurant's sunken tables.]

—AMY SCHERBER, AMY'S BREAD

LATE NIGHT

BALTHAZAR

80 Spring Street (between Broadway and Crosby Street), Manhattan (212) 965-1414

"A great place for late at night."

—FRANÇOIS PAYARD, PAYARD PÂTISSERIE AND BISTRO

"Balthazar has a great hamburger that they serve from midnight until three A.M. It's also a great place for steak frites."

—JEAN-GEORGES VONGERICHTEN, JEAN GEORGES, JO JO, AND VONG

BLUE RIBBON

97 Sullivan Street (between Prince and Spring Streets), Manhattan (212) 274-0404

"It's a great place to hang out."

—MARK MILLER, COYOTE CAFÉ (LAS VEGAS AND SANTA FE)

"Another great place to go late at night."

—FRANÇOIS PAYARD, PAYARD PÂTISSERIE AND BISTRO

"Great for late-night dining."

—MICHAEL ROMANO, UNION SQUARE CAFE

BLUE RIBBON SUSHI

119 Sullivan Street (between Prince and Spring Streets), Manhattan (212) 343-0404

"Great for late-night sushi."

—JEAN-GEORGES VONGERICHTEN, JEAN GEORGES, JO JO, AND VONG

NOODLES

HONMURA-AN

170 Mercer Street (between Houston and Prince Streets), Manhattan (212) 334-5253

"For the ultimate soba noodle."

—MARK MILLER, COYOTE CAFÉ (LAS VEGAS AND SANTA FE)

"Honmura-An has the most amazing noodles."

—ANNE ROSENZWEIG, THE LOBSTER CLUB

NEW YORK NOODLE TOWN

28½ Bowery (at Bayard Street), Manhattan (212) 349-0923

"For pan-fried noodles."

—MARK MILLER, COYOTE CAFÉ (LAS VEGAS AND SANTA FE)

REPUBLIC

37 Union Square W. (between 16th and 17th Streets), Manhattan (212) 627-7172

"For a simple, fast bowl of noodles in broth. I like to order udon with a coconut milk, mint, and basil sauce, which comes out this weird green color. But I love it. It's so refreshing and delicious."

—DIANE FORLEY, VERBENA

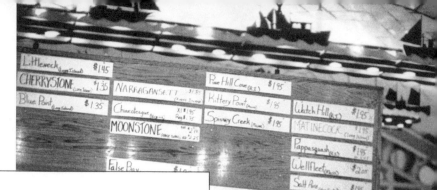

AQUAGRILL

210 Spring Street (at Avenue of the Americas), Manhattan (212) 274-0505

"They get really good oysters."

—FRANKLIN BECKER, LOCAL

BALTHAZAR

80 Spring Street (between Broadway and Crosby Street), Manhattan (212) 965-1414

"I love their oysters—I can eat two or three dozen for dinner."

—FRANÇOIS PAYARD, PAYARD PÂTISSERIE AND BISTRO

"They've got great oysters."

—TOM COLICCHIO, GRAMERCY TAVERN

BLUE RIBBON

97 Sullivan Street (between Prince and Spring Streets), Manhattan (212) 274-0404

OYSTER BAR

42nd Street at Park Avenue (in Grand Central Station, lower level), Manhattan
(212) 490-6650

"For oysters I go to Blue Ribbon or Balthazar. That's just because they're open at the time when I want oysters, though. I would love to go to the Oyster Bar at Grand Central and sit down at a real classic oyster bar, but they typically close at nine-thirty P.M. The Oyster Bar has oysters that are as big as your stereo! Giant. I had Hood Canal oysters that were almost as big as my sock! I was like, 'Whoa, that's almost too much, guys—why don't you throw those in my pan roast?'"

—MARIO BATALI, BABBO, ESCA, AND LUPA

"The Oyster Bar has a great oyster pan roast."

—MARK MILLER, COYOTE CAFÉ (LAS VEGAS AND SANTA FE)

CITY HALL

131 Duane Street (between Church Street and W. Broadway), Manhattan
(212) 227-7777

"For an oyster pan roast, I like City Hall."

—FRANKLIN BECKER, LOCAL

The Oyster Bar at Grand Central

Peruvian

PIO PIO

84-13 Northern Boulevard (between 84th and 85th Streets), Queens (718) 426-1010

"Every year I take my daughter Lily to the track, because you can teach math at the track. One year it was rainy and terrible, but I said, 'Come on, come on, it's going to be great.' We won a dollar—and how many people leave the racetrack ahead? Then we went to Pio Pio, which is an unbelievable Peruvian chicken place. Crowds gather in the street to wait for tables. All they serve is chicken, but it's tremendous chicken. They have sides like rice and beans, french fries, and sweet and green plantains. To drink, they serve wine, beer, and pisco sours, which are Peruvian margaritas. And it's really cheap—seven of us had dinner there for less than a hundred dollars."

—ANNE ROSENZWEIG, THE LOBSTER CLUB

Pizza

JOHN'S PIZZERIA

Multiple locations, including:
48 W. 65th Street (between Columbus Avenue and Central Park West), Manhattan (212) 721-7001
408 E. 64th Street (between First and York Avenues), Manhattan (212) 935-2895
278 Bleecker Street (between Avenue of the Americas and Seventh Avenue), Manhattan (212) 243-1680

"Sometimes I'll order one to the restaurant, or I'll go over and have one at the bar."

—TERRANCE BRENNAN, PICHOLINE

"I really like it because it doesn't have too much dough, like too many other pizzas do."

—FRANÇOIS PAYARD, PAYARD PÂTISSERIE AND BISTRO

"I like the crust, and the ratio of crust to topping. Other places tend to put on too much cheese and sauce, so you end up with a gloppy mess. It should be restrained, I think."

—MICHAEL ROMANO, UNION SQUARE CAFE

L&B SPUMONI GARDENS

2725 86th Street (near Avenue U), Brooklyn (718) 372-8400

"They have been around for eighty years. It's a massive pizzeria where you can sit outside during the summer. They sell two hundred or three hundred Sicilian pies a day. They put the cheese on before the sauce, then sprinkle Parmesan on top of the sauce, and use a lot of olive oil. The pizza comes out with a crusty outside and a soft, melting cheese texture inside. They are also known for their spumoni."

—FRANKLIN BECKER, LOCAL

LOCAL HIGHLIGHTS
new york

LOMBARDI'S

32 Spring Street (between Mott and Mulberry Streets), Manhattan (212) 941-7994

"Lombardi's has the best pizza in Manhattan."

—ROCCO DISPIRITO, UNION PACIFIC

"For the white clam pizza."

—BOBBY FLAY, BOLO AND MESA GRILL

"Any of Lombardi's pizzas are great. I always sit in the kitchen, where they have two booths. You can watch TV with the guys who make the pizza and help answer the phones for the to-go orders, like when Smith Barney calls for thirty pies."

—ANNE ROSENZWEIG, THE LOBSTER CLUB

"It's got a great, bubbly crust that's a bit charred on the edges. I love the taste!"

—AMY SCHERBER, AMY'S BREAD

MEZZALUNA

1295 Third Ave (between 74th and 75th Streets), Manhattan (212) 535-9600

"They have really good pizza."

—BOBBY FLAY, BOLO AND MESA GRILL

PATSY'S PIZZA

Multiple locations, including:
509 Third Avenue (between 34th and 35th Streets), Manhattan (212) 689-7500

"I love Patsy's pizza."

—TOM COLICCHIO, GRAMERCY TAVERN

"I crave it."

—BOBBY FLAY, BOLO AND MESA GRILL

SCOPA

27 E. 28th Street (between Madison Avenue and Park Avenue South), Manhattan (212) 686-8787

"Vinnie Scotto's grilled pizzas kill."

—MARIO BATALI, BABBO, ESCA, AND LUPA

TABLA

11 Madison Avenue (at 25th Street), Manhattan (212) 889-0667

"I had an Indian-inspired pizza here made with sheep's-milk cheese, paneer, and fresh cilantro that provided fascinating layerings of flavor."

—MARK MILLER, COYOTE CAFÉ (LAS VEGAS AND SANTA FE)

Owner John Brescio of Lombardi's, which has been serving pizza since 1905

PIZZa CONT.

TOTONNO PIZZERIA NAPOLITANO

Multiple locations, including: 1524 Neptune Avenue (between 15th and 16th Streets), Brooklyn (Coney Island), (718) 372-8606
The original, open since 1924.

"This is the best pizza, hands down. It's made in a brick oven, and they do a great basil, tomato, and fresh mozzarella version. They close the doors when they sell out. You have to buy it by the pie, not the slice, and you have to be very nice. If it's busy and taking a long time, you can't ask, 'Where is my pie?' or they will throw you out!"

—FRANKLIN BECKER, LOCAL

ReTaIL

BALDUCCI'S

424 Avenue of the Americas (between 9th and 10th Streets), Manhattan
(212) 673-2600

DEAN AND DELUCA

560 Broadway (at Prince Street), Manhattan
(212) 221-7714

"I like to walk through for inspiration."

—LAURENT TOURONDEL, CELLO

sandwiches

LE PAIN QUOTIDIEN

1131 Madison Avenue (between 84th and 85th Streets), Manhattan
(212) 327-4900
100 Grand Street (at Mercer Street), Manhattan
(212) 625-9009

"Le Pain Quotidien is kind of European, and their sandwiches are really nice. If you order a roast beef sandwich, it's served open-faced, with salad. It's very simple and nicely done, and unlike anything else I've ever seen."

—ANNE ROSENZWEIG, THE LOBSTER CLUB

VIA QUADRONNO

25 E. 73rd Street (between Madison and Fifth Avenues), Manhattan
(212) 650-9880

"The owners of St. Ambroeus opened this little place. They just do pressed sandwiches and really good espresso. It's very European in feeling."

—ANNE ROSENZWEIG, THE LOBSTER CLUB

seafood

LE BERNARDIN

155 W. 51st Street (between Avenue of the Americas and Seventh Avenue), Manhattan (212) 489-1515

CELLO

53 E. 77th Street (between Madison and Park Avenues), Manhattan
(212) 517-1200

"These are two of the best restaurants serving seafood in Manhattan."

—FRANÇOIS PAYARD, PAYARD PÂTISSERIE AND BISTRO

SHELLFISH

BALTHAZAR

80 Spring Street (between Broadway and Crosby Street), Manhattan
(212) 965-1414

"I love going for plateau [a multi-tiered presentation of fresh seafood on ice]."

—ROCCO DISPIRITO, UNION PACIFIC

"I always have the seafood platter here."

—FRANÇOIS PAYARD, PAYARD PÂTISSERIE AND BISTRO

SHORT RIBS

BALTHAZAR

80 Spring Street (between Broadway and Crosby Street), Manhattan
(212) 965-1414

"Their short ribs are superb. The sauce is so concentrated and reduced that it's practically black! And the meat is always perfectly braised. They have great meat, great steaks, and great fries."

—REBECCA CHARLES, PEARL OYSTER BAR

new york
LOCAL HIGHLIGHTS

SOUP

SOUP KITCHEN INTERNATIONAL

259 W. 55th Street, Manhattan
(212) 757-7730
The take-out place that inspired the "Soup Nazi" character on *Seinfeld* is open for lunch only, Monday through Friday. Closed all summer.

"I think he's pretty amazing. His lobster chowder—wow! The menu changes all the time, but whatever he has is always great. This guy knows how to make soups."

—JEAN-GEORGES VONGERICHTEN, JEAN GEORGES, JO JO, AND VONG

BALTHAZAR

80 Spring Street (between Broadway and Crosby Street), Manhattan (212) 965-1414

"Their steak au poivre is the best in New York."

—LAURENT TOURONDEL, CELLO

CITY HALL

131 Duane Street (between Church Street and West Broadway), Manhattan (212) 227-7777

"City Hall's steaks are great. They age all their own meat, which is impressive. He's got all the right accompaniments: onion rings, creamed spinach—all that stuff. He does prime rib, too, which nobody does anymore, and I love that."

—REBECCA CHARLES, PEARL OYSTER BAR

GAGE AND TOLLNER

372 Fulton Street (at Jay Street), Brooklyn (718) 875-5181

"They have a steak that is like butter. Years ago, I never craved steak, but now I really look forward to a good prime, dry-aged sirloin steak, charred on the outside, rare inside, with a good bottle of red wine. That's something I crave!"

—TERRANCE BRENNAN, PICHOLINE

LES HALLES

411 Park Avenue South (between 28th and 29th Streets), Manhattan (212) 679-4111

"At Les Halles, I always order the same thing: the côte de boeuf for two, which I strong-arm whomever I'm with into getting with me. The place is fun, and I like the fact that they have a butcher shop in the front."

—REBECCA CHARLES, PEARL OYSTER BAR

PETER LUGER

Original location:
178 Broadway (at Driggs Avenue), Brooklyn (718) 387-7400
255 Northern Boulevard, Long Island (Great Neck) (516) 487-8800

"The best steak in New York."

—FRANÇOIS PAYARD, PAYARD PÂTISSERIE AND BISTRO

"If you want to get into Peter Luger without a reservation, you go to the location in Great Neck. That's the secret."

—FRANKLIN BECKER, LOCAL

STEAK CONT.

RUTH'S CHRIS STEAK HOUSE

148 W. 51st Street (between Avenue of the Americas and Seventh Avenue), Manhattan
(212) 295-9600

"It's right across the street from us, and their steaks are consistently good."

—ERIC RIPERT, LE BERNARDIN

SPARKS STEAK HOUSE

210 E. 46th Street (between Second and Third Avenues), Manhattan
(212) 687-4855

"They have a great wine list, and I love the shell or strip steaks."

—MICHAEL ROMANO, UNION SQUARE CAFE

SUSHI

BLUE RIBBON SUSHI

119 Sullivan Street (between Prince and Spring Streets), Manhattan
(212) 343-0404

"I love their sushi—I'll let them make me whatever they want."

—MARIO BATALI, BABBO, ESCA, AND LUPA

"I spent nine months in Japan, and I think Blue Ribbon's sushi is the best!"

—CINDY PAWLCYN, BUCKEYE ROADHOUSE, FOG CITY DINER, AND MUSTARDS GRILL (SAN FRANCISCO)

KURUMA ZUSHI

7 E. 47th Street (between Fifth and Madison Avenues), 2nd floor, Manhattan
(212) 317-2802

"I don't have a favorite sushi restaurant. Instead, I kind of categorize my sushi experiences. When I want to approach it from the purist point of view, Kuruma Zushi is the place."

—ROCCO DISPIRITO, UNION PACIFIC

NEXT DOOR NOBU

105 Hudson Street (at Franklin Street), Manhattan
(212) 334-4445

"For the best, highly sophisticated sushi."

—AMY SCHERBER, AMY'S BREAD

NOBU

105 Hudson Street (at Franklin Street), Manhattan
(212) 219-0500

"Nobu is great for an expanded Japanese experience."

—ROCCO DISPIRITO, UNION PACIFIC

SACHI

1350 Madison Avenue (between 94th and 95th Streets), Manhattan
(212) 534-5600

"They do some incredible rolls here, like eel wrapped with slices of avocado."

—ANNE ROSENZWEIG, THE LOBSTER CLUB

SUSHIHATSU

1143 First Avenue (between 62nd and 63rd Streets), Manhattan
(212) 371-0238

"I like the old guy behind the counter at night. But he is very moody. They make you sweat for your sushi! He won't sell it to you if he thinks you won't appreciate it. And if he's low on, say, sea urchin, he won't want to give you an extra order of it, so you have to fight for it."

—ERIC RIPERT, LE BERNARDIN

"I don't know if I should tell you about this place, because then it won't be mine anymore. . . . There's an amazing guy here who's been doing sushi for forty-eight years. He has the best sushi in town, and all the sushi chefs in the city go there to see him. You have to let him make whatever he wants, and you have to sit at the sushi bar and be very focused. Don't go with too many people—four, maximum. It's perfect for late at night, because he is only there from nine P.M. to three A.M., so I go around eleven or twelve at night. I always have sake, something dry."

—JEAN-GEORGES VONGERICHTEN, JEAN GEORGES, JO JO, AND VONG

SUSHISAY

38 E. 51st Street (between Madison and Park Avenues), Manhattan
(212) 755-1780

"I like to go to Sushisay for lunch. It's very traditional, with the chefs wearing white coats and black ties. I will let them make whatever they want for me. Once, they sent me a brochette of broiled calamari mouth. At first I said, 'No way!' But I tried it, and it was excellent."

—ERIC RIPERT, LE BERNARDIN

TAKA

61 Grove Street (between Bleecker Street and Seventh Avenue), Manhattan
(212) 242-3699

"When I want sushi that's interesting and fun, I'll go to Taka in the West Village, a little twelve-seat restaurant. The owner makes her own pottery, and makes every dish herself. She also interacts with customers a lot."

—ROCCO DISPIRITO, UNION PACIFIC

BALTHAZAR

80 Spring Street (between Broadway and Crosby Street), Manhattan
(212) 965-1414

"The cannlets [a custardlike cake infused with vanilla and rum] are made in copper molds and are the best in New York."

—LAURENT TOURONDEL, CELLO

DA SILVANO

260 Avenue of the Americas (between Bleecker and Houston Streets), Manhattan (212) 982-2343

"Have the panna cotta [eggless custard, served chilled], covered with chocolate sauce [at this Italian restaurant]."

—JEAN-GEORGES VONGERICHTEN, JEAN GEORGES, JO JO, MERCER KITCHEN, AND VONG

PAYARD PÂTISSERIE AND BISTRO

1032 Lexington Avenue (between 73rd and 74th Streets), Manhattan
(212) 717-5252

"I love François Payard's cookies, which have great flavor and technique. They remind me of the shops from my childhood in France."

—ERIC RIPERT, LE BERNARDIN

SERENDIPITY 3

225 E. 60th Street (between Second and Third Avenues), Manhattan
(212) 838-3531

"My first job was making the [famous] 'frozen hot chocolate' here. It's great: cold, frosty, and chocolatey."

—MICHAEL ROMANO, UNION SQUARE CAFÉ

THAI

JAI YA THAI

81-11 Broadway (between 81st and 82nd Streets), Queens
(718) 651-1330

"They have fantastic Thai food."

—FRANKLIN BECKER, LOCAL

WONDEE SIAM

792 Ninth Avenue (between 52nd and 53rd Streets), Manhattan
(212) 459-9057

"I order take-out from here a lot. My favorites are the soup made with coconut milk and lime, and the green curry with either vegetables or chicken and jasmine rice."

—AMY SCHERBER, AMY'S BREAD

VIETNAMESE

CYCLO

203 First Avenue (between 12th and 13th Streets), Manhattan (212) 673-3975

"This restaurant has a nicer atmosphere and more creative dishes than many of the Vietnamese restaurants in Chinatown. One of their specialties is sugar-cane shrimp. They also have great spring rolls that you wrap in lettuce leaves."

—AMY SCHERBER, AMY'S BREAD

PHO BANG

Multiple locations, including:
157 Mott Street (between Broome and Grand Streets), Manhattan
(212) 966-3797
3 Pike Street (between Canal and Division Streets), Manhattan
(212) 233-3947

"My favorite Vietnamese place—I love seasoning the pho *[beef noodle soup] with the condiments on the table."*

—JEAN-GEORGES VONGERICHTEN, JEAN GEORGES, JO JO, AND VONG

PHO VIET HUONG

73 Mulberry Street (between Bayard and Canal Streets), Manhattan
(212) 233-8988

"In the back there's a very cool little shrine to Buddha, with the incense and the fake banana trees. In addition to the pho *[noodle soup], they have the best green papaya and grilled beef salad. They also own a restaurant on the Upper East Side called Miss Saigon."*

—ANNE ROSENZWEIG, THE LOBSTER CLUB

A bowl of *pho* with accompaniments at Pho Bang

BABBO

110 Waverly Place
New York, NY 10011
Phone: (212) 777-0303
Fax: (212) 777-3365

ESCA

402 W. 43rd Street
New York, NY 10036
Phone: (212) 564-7272

LUPA

170 Thompson Street
New York, NY 10012
Phone: (212) 982-5089

MARIO BATALI is chef-partner of Babbo, Esca, and Lupa, all Italian-influenced restaurants in Manhattan. He studied Spanish theater at Rutgers University before devoting himself to the culinary arts. After an apprenticeship in London with Marco Pierre White, he spent three years cooking and learning in a northern Italian village. Batali hosts the popular show *Molto Mario* on the Food Network, and has written two cookbooks, *Mario Batali Simple Italian Food: Recipes from My Two Villages* and *Mario Batali Holiday Food.* He is also a partner of Italian Wine Merchants in Manhattan. In 1998, Babbo won the James Beard Award for Best New Restaurant.

MY FOOD The food at Babbo is New York–centric, more specifically about the Hudson Valley region. The dishes are both simple and whimsical.

Lupa is chef de cuisine Mark Ladner's and my interpretation of Roman cooking at its very simplest, and Esca is a southern Italian seafood trattoria headed by chef de cuisine David Pasternack.

"I've never had a single thing at Babbo that wasn't delicious."

ANDREW CARMELLINI
CAFÉ BOULUD (NEW YORK)

MARIO'S PICKS

BLUE RIBBON

97 Sullivan Street (between Prince and Spring Streets), Manhattan
(212) 274-0404
This is probably where I eat most often, just because it's open late. One of my favorite dishes from the restaurant's eclectic new American menu is the marrow bones with oxtail marmalade. I always order the calamari, which is garlicky and perfectly cooked. My very favorite dish is the turkey burger with cheese. I usually drink a very nice bottle of Burgundy with it. Everyone orders all this fancy stuff here, and I always order the turkey burger. I end up giving half of it away to others at the table who want to try it because it's just perfect. It goes so well with good red wine. I had an extern from The Culinary Institute of America who was a wine geek, and since I wasn't paying him a salary, every Sunday we'd go out for turkey burgers and Cabernet, and I'd allow him to choose the wine. On his last day, we had turkey burgers with a seven-hundred-dollar magnum of '85 Lafite. It was perfect.

DA CIRO

229 Lexington Avenue (at 33rd Street), Manhattan
(212) 532-1636
I go to this Italian restaurant for two dishes. The first is the *bucatini alla amatriciana*, which is bucatini with a spicy tomato sauce, a little pancetta, and pecorino cheese. I like bucatini; it's a very "me" noodle. The other is the white pizza with robiola cheese and truffle oil. Their pizza is the best in town.

GRAY'S PAPAYA

402 Avenue of the Americas (at 8th
Street), Manhattan
(212) 260-3532
2090 Broadway (at 72nd Street),
Manhattan
(212) 799-0243

While we were building Babbo, I
probably ate more at Gray's Papaya
than anywhere else in the city. If you
order the dogs well done, they have
that "caviar crunch." If they're un-
dercooked, they're wrong, because
there's no resistance to your tooth.
But well done with mustard and extra
sauerkraut, they're perfect. It's a
dollar-ninety-five lunch: two dogs
and a tropical fruit beverage that is
kind of like an Orange Julius, but with
a quarter of the bicarb, so it's only a
little frothy. Afterward, you don't
have to think about food until dinner.

JOE'S SHANGHAI

Multiple locations, including:
9 Pell Street (between Bowery and
Mott Streets), Manhattan
(212) 233-8888
24 W. 56th Street (between Fifth
Avenue and Avenue of the Americas),
Manhattan
(212) 333-3868

I love Joe's Shanghai! I took some
friends here recently, and everyone
was rocking—they all loved the crab
soup dumplings. When you order, you
want to make sure you get a mix of light
and heavy dishes. The lion's heads are
made from pork belly—it's like emul-
sified fat that's textured like meat. It's
amazing, but you can't eat all four of
them. The little turnip pancakes are
good, too. If I have time, I'll get a whole
fish, which is prepared very simply—
just some black beans, garlic, scallions, hot chiles, and it's perfect.

UNION PACIFIC

111 E. 22nd Street (between Lexington
and Park Avenues), Manhattan
(212) 995-8500

Rocco DiSpirito's food is inspirational. He's always pushing the edge.
It's fusion, but his fusion makes
sense. I love that when I eat here,
there's always an ingredient that I
don't know, and I'm hard to stump.
For instance, he'll make the lemongrass soup served in Thai restaurants—with kaffir lime and galangal
[a light yellow root that is similar to
ginger]—but he'll put tripe in it,
cook it all together, and make a little
stew out of it, and then he'll put a
piece of cod on top. There's always
something I can learn when I eat
here. (See also p. 186.)

"*Babbo has phenomenal pastas, and we try to eat
there whenever we're in New York.*"

ANNE QUATRANO AND CLIFFORD HARRISON

BACCHANALIA (ATLANTA)

His Personal Interpretation of Italian Cuisine

How do you evolve your own cuisine? I don't think you start by setting out with that as your goal. What I've done is started with the ideology of a regional Italian cook: that you cook exclusively with local ingredients. I happen to be a regional Italian cook in a region that isn't Toscano and isn't Emilia-Romagna—it's New York.

If you're a cook in Venice, you would never use an ingredient from Calabria, because it's not part of the local repertoire. The traditional dishes in each region are based on what comes out of the dirt in that region. That's what really drives Italian regional distinction: what grows in their soil, what it tastes like, and what the climatic conditions are.

If you are in the area of Italy near the Alps, you'll traditionally see a lot of heavy food, but if you're in Amalfi, on the coast, in the summer, you might eat just a small portion of linguine with a little piece of grilled fish and that's it. Respecting those differences is what drives great Italian restaurants.

If a Roman cook moved to Milan, he or she would use Milanese ingredients—and certainly wouldn't ship things in from New York. Similarly, I am certainly not going to import many things from Milan because the cooking is all about proximity to the soil. That's what drives great food anywhere: the fact that it's out of the ground and onto the plate, after being only very minimally fussed with.

So the cooking we're doing in my restaurants in New York—or my cuisine, if you want to call it that—is regional Italian food, using local ingredients.

However, there are five particular ingredients that any Italian cook anywhere has to use:

- **REAL IMPORTED ITALIAN PASTA.** They just don't take the time to dry it correctly in the United States.

- **EXTRA-VIRGIN OLIVE OIL.** There are great extra-virgin olive oils being made in California, including my favorite right now, which is Da Vero. It's a great oil, big and light.

- **REAL BALSAMIC VINEGAR.**

- **PROSCIUTTO FROM ITALY**, either San Daniele or Parma.

- **PARMIGIANO-REGGIANO CHEESE.**

My list might be a bit skewed because I used to live in Emilia-Romagna, in northern Italy. Someone who lived in Milan might have a different list of five ingredients. But in any part of Italy, when there's a question of a luxury experience, it's going to involve prosciutto and parmigiano. They've been making it right for five hundred years, and everybody has it in their house!

That is really how I developed my style—I'm using the time-tested ideology of Italian cooks, which is to say take things from the soil, then get them as quickly and as simply as possible onto the plate. This is how any Italian cook would probably cook in New York—at least the ones who are not trying to heed the whim of every customer who wants spaghetti with meatballs and risotto with spaghetti on the side. And I've been fortunate enough to be able to do it my way.

Franklin Becker is executive chef of Local. He earned a degree in marketing from Brooklyn College before devoting himself to the culinary arts and attending The Culinary Institute of America. He cooked at Mesa Grill and the Penn Club before becoming Revlon chairman Ron Perelman's personal chef. After a stint at the James Beard House in the capacity of demonstration chef, he was recruited by owner David Napolitan as the chef of Local.

Franklin Becker

LOCAL
224 W. 47th Street
New York, NY 10019
Phone: (212) 921-2005
Fax: (212) 921-1200
www.localnyc.com

MY FOOD I think of my food as imaginative American cuisine. All my dishes emphasize a particular ingredient and try to capture the essence of a particular flavor. They have a central focus, and everything else on the dish supports that. Sample dishes from Local's menu include grilled lamb rack with Brussels sprouts and celery root purée, and pan-roasted chicken with chanterelles and asparagus.

FRANKLIN'S PICKS

DOMINICK'S
2335 Arthur Avenue (at 187th Street), Bronx
(718) 733-2807

There is no menu at this southern Italian restaurant; your waiter tells you what's available that day. You sit at community tables, and people you don't know will stick a fork in your food as it's passed over to you! The check is determined by whether he thinks you enjoyed your meal or not. The waiter will tell the guy what you had and he will look you over and decide the price. Depending on how much he likes you, you can pay fifteen dollars or fifty dollars. At any price, the stuffed artichoke here is the best I have ever had in my life!

IL BAGATTO
192 E. 2nd Street (between Avenues A and B), Manhattan
(212) 228-0977

This is my favorite Italian restaurant. It is simple, with no fuss. If you are late for your reservation, the owner throws you out. Otherwise, she believes in satisfying and making people happy. She has beautiful Pugliese cuisine. Her spaghetti with marinara sauce and her bruschetta are the best in the city. Her tomatoes are vibrant and fresh, and she uses just the right amount of basil, garlic, balsamic vinegar, and olive oil. It is perfectly balanced. You can walk out for under sixty dollars for two, with wine.

OCEAN PALACE SEAFOOD RESTAURANT
5423 Eighth Avenue (at 55th Street), Brooklyn
(718) 871-8080
1418 Avenue U (between 14th and 15th Streets), Brooklyn
(718) 376-3838

It is a huge place, with close to five hundred seats. On Sundays they come around with about a hundred and twenty-five varieties of dim sum. It is great because you get to see so many influences you don't always see in Chinese food. For example, shrimp stuffed inside a pepper, or shrimp paste stuffed inside a Japanese eggplant and served with a mixture of hoisin and oyster sauce, so it has a slight spicy edge with the richness of the oyster sauce. They also have the classics. Eating here has helped me solidify my understanding of Chinese cuisine. It is not all about soy sauce, oyster sauce, ginger, garlic, and scallions.

SAHARA

2337 Coney Island Avenue (between
Avenues T and U), Brooklyn
(718) 376-8594

They have the best *shawarma*. They layer turkey and lamb fat onto a spit, and flavor it with Middle Eastern spices and sumac. Slices of meat are carved off like a gyro, and then put in a pita with lettuce, tahini, and a little harissa. It is the meat alternative to falafel. An order will only set you back about four dollars and fifty cents.

SUSHIKO

40-09 Bell Boulevard, Queens
(Bayside)
(718) 229-1200

There are probably two thousand or three thousand types of sushi rolls listed on the wall at this place, including John's Roll and Rocky V's Roll. Some of the combinations, such as the American Dream, which features fried shrimp, avocado, cucumber, grilled eel, and cream cheese, are pretty wild.

New York Food Field Trips

WITH Franklin Becker

Subway Field Trip #1: Brooklyn

Take the number 2 or the number 4 subway train out of Manhattan, and get off at Borough Hall/Court Street in Brooklyn. From here, you can walk west to **Fatoosh** (330 Hicks Street at Atlantic Avenue; (718) 243-0500), which has the best falafel and great baba ganouj. Or you can go to **Teresa's** (80 Montague Street at Hicks Street; (718) 797-3996) for Polish food, including terrific blintzes, borscht, and tremendous pierogis, which I like fried, with sour cream and applesauce.

Then walk three blocks to the Promenade (which overlooks Manhattan) for a romantic walk along the water. Then walk to Atlantic Avenue, making a left from Hicks Street, where you can hit a number of restaurants, like **Acadia Parish Cajun Café** (148 Atlantic Avenue, between Clinton and Henry Streets; (718) 624-5154), which features inexpensive Louisiana specialties such as fried catfish, gumbo, and jambalaya.

You can see a number of Yemeni places or shop at **Sahadi** (187-89 Atlantic Avenue, between Court and Clinton Streets; (718) 624-4550), which is a Middle Eastern market with all these ingredients you haven't seen before as well as staples like couscous, harissa, olives, spices, and tea. Make a right on Smith Street, where you'll find a bunch of Thai restaurants as well as **Patois,** a well-regarded French restaurant serving bistro fare; it's owned by chef Alan Harding (255 Smith Street; (718) 855-1535). Then hop on the F train at Carroll Street to take you back to Manhattan.

Subway Field Trip #2: Flushing, Queens

Take the number 7 train from Grand Central Station in Manhattan to Main Street. It takes about forty minutes and is the last stop, so you can't get lost.

You will be a block from a strip of Malaysian and other Asian restaurants, such as **Penang,** 38-04 Prince Street; (718) 321-2078. You can shop at various markets in the area, and make it a great day trip.

There is a nameless dumpling shop on 41st Street, off Main Street. Look for a little window with a hundred Chinese people standing outside and a little old woman folding dumplings in back. They are the most unbelievable pork and scallion, and cabbage and scallion, dumplings. They're cooked in a big flat wok, so the dumpling bottom gets nicely seared and caramelized, while the top stays soft. They sell some for twenty-five cents, and the fifty-cent ones are as big as your hand!

Daniel Boulud

RESTAURANT DANIEL
60 E. 65th Street
(between Park and
Madison Avenues)
New York, NY 10021
Phone: (212) 288-0033
Fax: (212) 737-0612
www.danielnyc.com

DANIEL BOULUD is chef-owner of Restaurant Daniel and Café Boulud. His other endeavors include Feast and Fêtes, the exclusive catering department of Restaurant Daniel, and his Private Stock line of caviar and smoked salmon, available by mail. Restaurant Daniel, reopened in a new location in 1999, has been recognized as one of the Ten Best Restaurants in the World by the *International Herald Tribune; Gourmet* ranked it number one in New York in their 1999 Top Tables feature, and *Esquire* cited Restaurant Daniel and Café Boulud as two of the nation's Top Twenty-five New Restaurants in 1999. Among Boulud's many honors are the 1992 James Beard Award as Best Chef: New York, and the 1994 James Beard Award for Outstanding Chef of the Year. He is the author of *Cooking with Daniel Boulud* and *The Café Boulud Cookbook*.

MY FOOD My dream is to give my guests a dining experience that awakens all the senses. At Daniel, I want them to leave the outside world behind and indulge in fine cuisine, the beauty of the setting, and the personalized experience they have come to expect from us. I strive to celebrate each season's best ingredients and reveal their delicious flavors.

With our tasting menu we try to build a menu that matches the food with the wines. We might start with a sweet wine—a late harvest Riesling or a Sauternes or a sweet wine from the Loire Valley—and pair it with a terrine of figs and foie gras. This combination of food and wine creates a certain richness and privilege for the beginning of the meal. It's not something you would want to have between the white wine and the red wine—you want to start with it, be teased with it, and then go to a more dry and serious wine.

We might follow this with a lighter wine, such as a Semillon or a Sauvignon. This will be paired with something like vichyssoise—straightforward and easy to understand, but original in flavor once you taste it. After this, the menu will build to larger flavors, such as seafood with Chardonnay. Perhaps we will prepare a vegetarian course, too.

Then we decide whether we want to continue with the white-wine pairings, or move to red wine. We might prepare a fish and red wine course before moving on to game or meat and cheese. We may start with a Burgundy and finish with a Rhône Valley, or start with a young Rhône Valley and finish with a Cabernet or a Syrah. It all depends on the menu we are building, and the season of the year.

We prepare different dishes for each guest, but the dishes will be compatible for each course. That's how I like to compose a menu and how

"When I come to New York, I almost always eat at Daniel. Daniel's food is simple and exceptionally well executed. It's not an intellectual experience; it's really, really great technical cooking. All the sauces are beautiful; the fish and meats are all cooked perfectly."

TRACI DES JARDINS
JARDINIÈRE (SAN FRANCISCO)

I like to express myself with tasting menus. We try to exhibit a very large palate of tastes and presentations of food—it's almost as if the whole restaurant menu is sampled by the table.

I think first-time visitors should have a tasting menu, but they can create their own menu, too, by talking to the maître d'—sometimes it's nice to share a couple of appetizers, then two main courses. It all depends on how they want to approach it.

DANIEL'S PICKS

BELLA BLU

967 Lexington Avenue (between 70th and 71st Streets), Manhattan
(212) 988-4624

Bella Blu is a lively, crowded northern Italian restaurant with unique décor. It's open on Sundays [Daniel's most frequent day off] and serves very nice simple and light Italian food, including thin-crust pizzas and pastas [such as veal ravioli or lobster with linguine and spiced tomato sauce]."

CAFÉ BOULUD

20 E. 76th Street (in the Surrey Hotel, between Madison and Fifth Avenues), Manhattan
(212) 772-2600

On Sunday, I'll eat early, at around six-thirty or seven P.M., and let them order for me—just two courses. I don't eat at Daniel, but at Café Boulud I like to see the staff's progress, and I can relax and stay in control at the same time.

LOMBARDI'S

32 Spring Street (between Mott and Mulberry Streets), Manhattan
(212) 941-7994

There is a lot of history at Lombardi's [which is often cited as the first pizzeria in New York City; reportedly, Lombardi himself taught John of John's Pizzeria how to make pizza!] I love the thin, smoky-crusted coal oven-baked pizza made with fresh clams and lots of garlic. (See also p. 162.)

NOBU

105 Hudson Street (at Franklin Street), Manhattan
(212) 219-0500

Nobu reworks traditional Japanese recipes and incorporates new ingredients into them. I love his dish of three tunas on ice, with a light marinade.

OYSTER BAR AND RESTAURANT

42nd Street at Park Avenue (in Grand Central Station, lower level), Manhattan
(212) 490-6650

There are lots of reasons to go to the Oyster Bar, including the location, in the newly refurbished Grand Central Station; more than thirty kinds of fish; standard seafood classics such as clam chowder, pan roast, and smoked sturgeon and salmon; the extensive selection of more than two hundred forty wines and more than twenty beers—but I go for the oysters, as the Oyster Bar offers more than twenty different kinds daily.

"Daniel Boulud is my hero. His food is rustic in a sophisticated way."

TODD ENGLISH
FIGS AND OLIVES (BOSTON)

"Daniel is my favorite restaurant for French food."

STEPHAN PYLES
AQUAKNOX (DALLAS)

"Daniel Boulud has lived in the United States as long as he has in France, and he puts both countries' ideals forward in 'French-American' French food."

NORMAN VAN AKEN
NORMAN'S (MIAMI)

serving daniel boulud at café boulud

Andrew Carmellini and Stephen Beckta

When Daniel Boulud mentioned that he likes to eat at his three-star restaurant Café Boulud on Sunday nights, we decided to talk to chef Andrew Carmellini and sommelier Stephen Beckta on what it's like to cook and choose wines for the boss on his night off.

ANDREW CARMELLINI ON COOKING FOR DANIEL

"Daniel will come in early on a Sunday night with his wife [Mickey] and daughter, Alix. If they are not eating family-style, Alix usually eats at the bar and will have pasta, while Daniel likes to see what we are doing on the 'Le Voyage' menu [which celebrates the cuisines of countries other than France]. He likes to have a pasta course and a meat course—especially a [stew-like] meat dish during the winter. He doesn't eat much fish.

"I have to admit I was nervous the first couple of times Daniel came in. But now I just let it flow. The first time I cooked his dinner, I served him a dish I just threw together. He had come in very late, so we were all cleaned out. But I had made gnocchi that day, and we also had some leftover lentil soup. So I put the lentil soup purée with some whole lentils, diced lardons, mirepoix, and diced truffles over the gnocchi—and he loved it! Now it's a dish we serve a lot."

STEPHEN BECKTA ON SERVING WINE TO DANIEL

"When Daniel is in the restaurant, everyone on the staff becomes a little more serious. Not only is the boss in the house, but he is dining in the house and thus able to critique everything—even though he doesn't. It is fun for me the same way it's fun having any other VIP in the restaurant, in that there's a certain excitement and a certain pressure to really be on top of your game.

"Daniel is so down-to-earth. He goes for simplicity, both in his food and in his wine. He just wants a nice glass of Pinot Noir, or something fun. He likes Pinot Noirs from Oregon, like Cristom, that are full of flavor and really luscious with fruit and raspberry. I've served him big, brooding wines, like Priorato from Spain, which has a lot of tannin and alcohol, but he prefers a wine with more elegance. I will also serve him wines I am excited about, like something from Canada [of which Steve is a native]. I found that Daniel really liked the Cave Spring Indian Summer Riesling. He also gets a kick out of the classics. Someone may have a twenty-year-old white Burgundy or a Petrus [which sells from $500 to $21,000 on the restaurant's list], and he is fascinated by it. We recently had a party whose host opened up a 1945 Latour and poured Daniel and me each a glass, and we all sat around talking about it. He gets total joy from tasting a great wine like that.

"When Daniel comes in for dinner on a Sunday night, I'm sensitive to the fact that it's his money, and I don't want to spend too much of it! So I will typically recommend a wine that's a great value, because there are so many on our list. I can easily find a fifty-dollar bottle of wine that will blow him away. For someone like Daniel, whose food and wine knowledge runs deep, it is even more gratifying recommending a great wine at fifty dollars rather than at three hundred dollars a bottle.

"I recently got a bottle of Baco Noir, which is a French hybrid grape that used to be planted widely in Canada. The vintner had found hundred-year-old vines and bottled an incredible reserve wine from them. It turns out that Daniel's father had had some of the same vines on his land in France. So I served Daniel and his father this bottle of wine when they came in, and his father was so surprised and touched that he got tears in his eyes. Wine, like food, can be tied up with great memories and pride."

Terrance Brennan

PICHOLINE
35 W. 64th Street
New York, NY 10019
Phone: (212) 724-8585
Fax: (212) 875-8979

ARTISANAL
Two Park Avenue
New York, NY 10016
Phone: (212) 725-8585

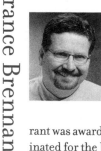

Terrance Brennan is chef-owner of Picholine and Artisanal. He spent several years in Europe working in such places as Taillevent and La Tour d'Argent before returning to New York. *Food & Wine* named him one of America's Best New Chefs in 1995, and that same year Picholine was voted Best Restaurant in New York in *Conde Nast Traveler*'s readers' poll. His restaurant was awarded three stars by the *New York Times*, and he has been nominated for the James Beard Award as Best Chef: New York.

MY FOOD When I was working in Europe, I learned the most in French three-star restaurants. Their kitchens are intense because food is so much a part of their lives—it's fully integrated, not an afterthought. I love that. Because I cook seasonally, the influences at Picholine vary throughout the year—ranging from Mediterranean to French, especially on our fall and winter menu, which features foie gras and truffles. The flavors at Picholine are primarily Mediterranean: sunny, bright, and intense, but interpreted for an adventurous American palate. I was first introduced to these flavors while working at Le Moulin de Mougins in the south of France, and I've been in love with them ever since.

TERRANCE'S PICKS

CAFE MEZÉ

20 North Central Avenue, Hartsdale
(914) 428-2400

Cafe Mezé is considered a fine-dining restaurant in this area for its warm ambiance, good wine list, and really good food. The last time I was in, chef Mark Filippo made a braised rabbit canneloni that was served with a portobello mushroom bolognese that was very good. My wife likes the tartare of portobello with goat cheese salad served with warm bread. We also like their tuna salad of rare peppered tuna served room temperature with sliced potatoes, haricots verts, and pinenut-currant dressing.

CITY LIMITS DINER

200 Central Avenue, White Plains
(914) 686-9000
125 Westchester Avenue, White Plains
(about 20 miles north of Manhattan)
(914) 761-1111

The owners of City Limits, the Livanos family, also own Oceana, a three-star restaurant in Manhattan. This is a place I go with my family, because they have good selections for both kids and adults. It's a high-quality diner serving breakfast, lunch, and dinner; everything is made on the premises, including the breads and pastries and the smoked fish. I had a good roast chicken with Swiss chard and a potato cake recently. My kids really like the pancakes and the corn bread.

JOHN'S PIZZERIA

Multiple locations, including:
48 W. 65th Street (between Columbus Avenue and Central Park West), Manhattan
(212) 721-7001

I love a good pizza, and sometimes I will go to John's and have one at the bar, or I'll even order a pizza to the restaurant. I like the classic margherita pizza or a pizza with just mushrooms. They have a great crust. They put cheese on the dough first, then the sauce. That way, the cheese bubbles up through the sauce, and that keeps the crust crisper. My dad had a family restaurant pizzeria, and he also knew that technique. The other thing I like is that they don't put too much sauce on. They know how to make it right.

TERRANCE'S PICKS

LE BERNARDIN

155 W. 51st Street (between Avenue of the Americas and Seventh Avenue), Manhattan
(212) 489-1515

I always think in terms of the guests I am with. If I am eating out with older relatives, I think of the sound level, the chairs, and the general level of comfort. I took some relatives to Le Bernardin because they probably wouldn't have "gotten" the food at Jean Georges. Everything was very civilized—from the posh setting to the low-key ambiance to the very good dinner we all enjoyed.

VONG

200 E. 54th Street (between Second and Third Avenues), Manhattan
(212) 486-9592

My wife and I like to go to Vong, where the food melds Thai ingredients with French technique. My wife loves everything from the food to the dazzling décor. I'll order the black plate, which is an assortment of five different appetizers, to start. The lobster with curry is a favorite entrée of mine. The wine list is also very good, and I'll usually order a Gewürztraminer, Pinot Blanc, or Condrieu.

---

andrew carmellini is executive chef of Café Boulud. He has traveled widely and worked with several top chefs in Europe. In New York, his résumé includes stints at Lespinasse and Le Cirque, where he was the sous chef. In 2000, he was awarded the James Beard Award for Rising Star Chef of America, and was named one of the ten Best New chefs in America by *Food & Wine* magazine.

MY FOOD At Café Boulud, we pay homage to the food Daniel Boulud grew up with in France and celebrate the food he loves in America. We offer our favorite dishes, drawn from family recipes, regional specialties, and haute cuisine. The menu is presented under the headings of Daniel's four culinary muses: "La Tradition" (French classics), "La Saison" (the seasonal specialties of the market), "Le Potager" (a celebration of the vegetable garden), and "Le Voyage" (the exotic flavors of world cuisines). Guests are encouraged to sample courses from as many of these mini-menus as they wish.

Andrew Carmellini

CAFÉ BOULUD

20 E. 76th Street
New York, NY 10021
Phone: (212) 772-2600
Fax: (212) 772-7755
www.danielnyc.com/cafe.html

"Andrew Carmellini has a lot of talent."

ERIC RIPERT
LE BERNARDIN

BLUE RIBBON BAKERY

33 Downing Street (at Bedford Street), Manhattan (212) 337-0404

This restaurant [a Blue Ribbon spin-off that serves breads baked in the restaurant's huge oven downstairs] is where I seem to find myself the most. The food is great; it is always just what you want to eat. They have really good marinated beets, pâtés, and sandwiches; I especially like the pulled pork sandwich. I always get a pint of Paulaner Weiss beer with a little lemon. We like to sit downstairs, which has the feeling of an Italian *osteria* because it's all brick and arched.

GAM MEE OK

43 W. 32nd Street (at Broadway) (212) 695-4113

This is a twenty-four-hour Korean place where we go after work. *Sul long tang* [oxtail soup] comes with everything. The soup is plain [milky colored broth], but then you add sea salt and scallions from little bowls on the tables, and it is very comforting. They also have *bin dae dok*, which are big Korean-style fried mung bean pancakes. They also have *yook hwe*, a wild dish of shredded raw beef with pears and crisp lettuce to which raw egg yolk is added. Then you have a couple of OBs [Korean beers] or *baekseju*, which is a fermented rice drink.

GENNARO

665 Amsterdam Avenue (between 92nd and 93rd Streets), Manhattan (212) 665-5348

The chef used to be at Bice and other midtown Italian restaurants. Gennaro is a tiny place that serves Italian classics like carpaccio and osso bucco as well as dishes such as orecchiette with broccoli and provolone, and grilled quail, and I especially like the lamb shank and the ravioli. It's only open for dinner [starting at 5:30 P.M.], it's casual, and they don't take credit cards or reservations, but if you have to wait, it's worth it.

SRIPRAPHAI

64-13 39th Avenue, Queens (Woodside) (718) 899-9599

This is a tiny and very nice family-run Thai café and bakery. It is out of the way, but worth seeking out because the food is of extremes. It is salty and sweet at the same time, or it is smoky and really sour at the same time—but they really get the balance right. I like the barbecued beef salad, because the meat is really crispy, and it has sour, spicy sauce with a lot of mint. They also have a great duck in green curry. There is this incredible Thai smoked catfish soup with bamboo, and when it comes to your table, the whole restaurant knows you ordered it! It smells so wild that to like it, you have to be a certain type of person—either Thai or like me!

UNION PACIFIC

111 E. 22nd Street (between Lexington and Park Avenue South), Manhattan (212) 995-8500

If I were to go out for a special occasion and could choose the restaurant, this is where I would go. Chef Rocco DiSpirito has great products and a great wine list. His food has a broad range of influences, and I eat a different style every time I go—from Asian to French to Mediterranean. Not only are his ingredient combinations great, but the execution of the dishes is both innovative and intense. I had a mushroom sherry soup, and it was an intense, clear mushroom broth. Another time I had Arctic char, potatoes, and truffles. It sounds very commonplace, but the char was in a salt dough and was very tender and flavorful. (See also p. 186.)

VIET-NAM

11-13 Doyers Street (between Bowery and Pell Street), Manhattan (Chinatown) (212) 693-0725

When we did our first "Le Voyage" menu at Café Boulud I was nervous, because I didn't want it to taste like a bunch of white kids trying to cook Asian food. I didn't want it to be fusion and I didn't want it to be too authentic, because it wouldn't translate to the Upper East Side. In our research, Viet-Nam in Chinatown was our favorite Vietnamese restaurant. I bet we tasted sixty different things there. The sweet-and-sour shrimp soup was great, with a real balance of flavors. Mint, fish sauce, and shrimp shells are used in the broth, and you get crunch from the bamboo, sweetness from the pineapple, and spice from the chile—it was all there. They also do the best summer rolls, but you have to get them at lunch when they are fresh. We also really liked the caramel pork.

STEPHEN BECKTA OF CAFÉ BOULUD

On Wine Service

Both of Daniel Boulud's restaurants—Restaurant Daniel and Café Boulud—were mentioned by chefs around the country as among the places where they most liked to dine. So, sommelier Steve Beckta finds himself selecting wines for some of the country's most discriminating palates almost nightly. Another aspect of Steve's work is matching wines and spirits to "Le Voyage" (the menu of world cuisines) as well as to "La Tradition" (the menu of traditional French dishes), "Le Potager" (the vegetarian menu), and "La Saison" (the menu of seasonal dishes), all of which are offered daily at Café Boulud.

SERVING WINE TO INDUSTRY INSIDERS

I love it when chefs and other people in the business come in, because they tend to let me have fun. They usually order tasting menus, where our chef, Andrew Carmellini, chooses the foods and I choose the wines to match. I typically serve wines by the glass to complement each course and show a wide variety. We recently had the pastry chefs in from Eleven Madison Park, Gramercy Tavern, Tabla, and Union Square Cafe, and they were great fun! Since our pastry department went crazy on their desserts, we decided to do so with their wines as well, because I suspected that dessert was the course that would get the most attention! So I paired four different wines with their fruit soup course, then another set of different wines with their main desserts.

Some chefs who dine here don't want to give up control to the sommelier or to the kitchen. Usually they are not New York chefs. If they are from out of town, I think they might feel intimidated by being in a New York restaurant, or by the price, or by the idea that the food might be too adventuresome.

New York chefs will typically leave things in my hands or will let me know that they want a certain type of wine, so I can recommend one. Generally, New York chefs want to experience different things, so that will be my primary goal. I love to turn someone on to a weird, obscure wine from an odd place. I like to recommend a wine they would never select themselves, or to bring out a wine and see if they can guess where it is from. Of course, there are other chefs who just want to dine without a "show," or without hearing about the twelve wines you are pouring.

It is all a matter of building up some trust with the table, and you have about ten seconds in which to do that. But determining whether I am going to be a small or a large part of a table's experience is all about reading that customer correctly.

SERVING OTHER CUSTOMERS

The biggest challenge is not matching wine to food; it is matching wine to the personality and taste of the table. While the wine should match the food, it should also be a wine that the guest will enjoy. This is easier said than done. The first thing I do is decide whether or not a table is adventurous. The first clue is to look at what they have ordered. On any menu, you will find more and less challenging dishes. For Café Boulud and many other restaurants, the least challenging dish is typically the chicken. A more challenging dish at Café Boulud would be the salad of frisée, chicken livers, chicken gizzards, country bacon, and poached quail egg! To match that, you need an incredibly high-acid red wine, like a Pinot Noir with soft tannin and piercing acidity.

WINE AND FOOD-PAIRING GUIDELINES

Any guidelines for matching food to wine or wine to food are "typical" or "most often" guides. There are important exceptions to every rule, so it's essential to always double-check with the person with whom you order, to ensure that the wine and food will pair well. Another thing to keep in mind is matching the intensity of the food with the intensity of the wine, because you want to keep them as close as possible. If a wine is too big, you won't be able to taste the food, and food that is too big won't let you taste the wine.

One basic guideline is that if the area a dish is from produces wine, it will be a good match with the food, because the people growing the grapes and cooking the food are essentially the same people.

If you have an area that is not known for wine, there are some other general guidelines. One is that high-acid wines typically complement food better than low-acid wines, because acid will cleanse your palate of salt, sugar, and fat. There are some particularly food-friendly varietals—Barbera, Pinot Noir, Riesling. If you have a low-acid wine and high-acid food, the wine will seem very flabby and boring in your mouth. A Zinfandel, for instance, is very low-acid, so it will seem weak with a high-acid dish, like a salad with a vinaigrette, or a dish with a sherry vinegar sauce. The reverse is also true: If you drink a high-acid wine with a neutral food, the wine will seem out of balance.

Sauvignon Blanc is a high-acid grape that is very food-versatile. In France, Sancerre and Pouilly-Fumé produce good Sauvignon Blancs, and those from New Zealand and California are quite good as well. Among red wines, a Chianti is a natural complement to tomato sauce, as both are high-acid.

Some of the foods that I might pair with particular wines:

- **CHARDONNAY** The Chardonnays grown in certain parts of Burgundy—Chablis, Mâcon, Puligny-Montrachet, and Meursault—are high-acid wines that work well with food. New World Chardonnays from places outside France—like California and Australia—tend not to be the most food-friendly wines, because the acids generally tend to be low. The wines can be big with a lot of oak, which can sometimes overwhelm food. What I do love with a glass of big, oaky Chardonnay is a roasted pork chop. It is a beautiful match. The textures work off each other really well.

- **YOUNG CABERNET OR BORDEAUX** These wines are great with a rare piece of beef. The tannins in Cabernet bond with the uncoagulated proteins of the meat. It then makes the meat seem less fatty and the wine seem less tannic. So, in the end, the flavors help each other go to greater heights.

- **MERLOT (CALIFORNIA)** The new best-seller. The reason people enjoy Merlot so much is because it is generally unchallenging. And it is easy to pronounce, which is not unimportant in restaurants where sometimes diners are intimidated. There is only one way to mispronounce "Merlot," while there are twelve ways to mispronounce "Cabernet Sauvignon"! Merlot is simple, so it should be paired with simple food—like a simple pasta or pizza.

MATCHING WINES TO WORLD CUISINES

When I match wines to dishes from Chef Andrew Carmellini's "Le Voyage" menu, each region offers its own individual challenges.

- **VIETNAM** The food has a lot of spicy flavors, which call for aromatic whites that are off-dry with a little residual sugar and a floral element. I associate Pinot Blanc with melon, Gewürztraminer with lychee, and Viognier with mango and papaya. We also brought in a lot of beer for our Vietnamese "Le Voyage" menu. We featured Chimay, which is a very rich red beer from Belgium that goes great with caramel pork with ginger—the bitterness plays off the sweetness of the pork and the spice of the ginger. Another was Le Fin du Monde, which means "the end of the world"—a triple-fermented ale from Quebec, Canada. It is a little heavier in alcohol than most beers, so it can stand up to more powerful flavors, and it works well with chiles. We also brought in some Red Tail Ale, but I suspect that was because it also happens to be Andrew Carmellini's favorite beer.

- **MARDI GRAS AND MEXICO** You have a lot of spice in southern food, so you want a soft, luscious wine. For a red wine, look to a Zinfandel or a Shiraz. They both have some spice to them, and generally have soft tannins and big-fruit flavors. Beers and off-dry white wines also work. The thing you want to avoid at all cost with this kind of food is a wine high in tannin, which magnifies the spice in your mouth. Tannin and spicy food make the worst combination. Young wines from Côtes du Rhône, Cabernets from California, and red Burgundies are typical wines to avoid with this type of food.

- **GREAT WHITE NORTH** When we focused on Canada and the Nordic countries, we featured Copper River salmon, which may be the greatest fish on the planet. Salmon is very oily, so you need a wine to cleanse your palate, like a non-oaked Chardonnay. I used a Canadian Riesling. Prince Edward mussels done in an herb-cream sauce went well with a Sancerre. And I paired a lobster from Nova Scotia with a demi-sec Vouvray or a Chenin Blanc with tropical fruit characteristics.

- **ITALY** With a risotto with white truffles, my first choice would be an earthy white Burgundy. If you wanted a red, you could do a Barbera from the Alba region, where Italian truffles grow. The earthiness of the wine will go with the earthiness of the truffles. Or you could do a Pinot Noir, because they have many of the same attributes of being earthy and lighter in nature.

- **SPAIN** This is a good example of the wine from the country going with the food. Sherry pairs so well with tapas because the high alcohol goes with the big flavors of tapas. On a tapas plate, you may have seafood salad next to ham next to spicy sausage. You need that high alcohol, which adds body to wine, to cut through it all. I also find that sherry is great with soups because it cuts through the richness and provides a contrasting texture.

PALATE OF THE PEOPLE

Some diners are dedicated "ABC" drinkers—"anything but Cabernet or Chardonnay." These are the people who don't want to drink what everyone else is drinking, and Cabernet and Chardonnay both fall into that category. Chardonnay can often be a little sweet and heavy in its feel.

Everyone wants to drink what makes them comfortable. Palate in general is based upon your native culture and what you were raised on.

- **NORTH AMERICA** In North America, we are raised on sweet, rich food items: We drink Coke, eat Big Macs, and snack on popcorn with lots of butter at the movies. Because we eat a lot of sweet, rich food, we look for wines that reproduce that.

- **ASIA** Most Asians grow up drinking lots of very strong tea, which has a lot of tannin flavor. So it's really no surprise that the latest boom in the Bordeaux market has been in Asia. They like their Bordeaux young, with lots of tannin.

- **ITALY** Southern Italians use a lot of tomato, so they tend to prefer high-acid wines like Chianti, Barbera, and Sangiovese.

- **FRANCE** If you look to France, there are areas with lots of olives and savory ingredients. So the French look for savory qualities in their wines. That is also the way the French "build" them, reflecting their palates.

PEARL OYSTER BAR

18 Cornelia Street
New York, NY 10014
Phone: (212) 691-8211
Fax: (212) 691-8210

Rebecca Charles

REBECCA CHARLES is chef-owner of Pearl Oyster Bar. While living in Maine, she twice earned four stars from the *Portland Press Herald* for the restaurants where she served as chef. Before opening Pearl Oyster Bar, she was Anne Rosenzweig's sous chef at Arcadia for five years, and later executive chef of Cascabel. *Gourmet* called Pearl "a major discovery," and it was ranked one of Manhattan's top thirty restaurants in the 2001 *ZagatSurvey*.

MY FOOD Pearl is a sliver of the Maine coast in Greenwich Village—fried oysters, steamers, lobster rolls. I have an affinity for, and a belief in, traditional American cuisine. I like the intimacy of our space because I like being able to interact with customers. New Yorkers have become obsessed with and savvy about food and restaurants, and at Pearl, the customers get a chance to talk to us. On most nights, the result is a lively discussion up and down the bar about food, sharing recipes, what's good where, that kind of thing.

REBECCA'S PICKS

BLUE RIBBON BAKERY

33 Downing Street (at Bedford Street), Manhattan
(212) 337-0404

I go to Blue Ribbon Bakery, a café-bakery hybrid, about once a week. It satisfies a lot of different cravings, because they always have an eclectic menu. They have great stuff, like beef marrow bones and steak tartare. Like the creature of habit I am, I order the same thing every time. Right now, I'm into their onion soup, which has a really good stock with tons of onions and really good Gruyère cheese slathered all over it. They have great charcuterie. I get a plate of Serrano ham, which I'm very fond of and think is much more interesting than prosciutto. They also have terrific breads. Their rye bread is probably the best I ever had. They have challah in the basket sometimes, and their challah is fierce!

BOND STREET

6 Bond Street (near Broadway), Manhattan
(212) 777-2500

I really like the sushi bar at Bond Street. I don't like to eat in the dining room, which serves inventive Japanese cuisine, because I find that I don't have the clothes for it: I don't have enough black! I don't normally like to eat at sushi bars, because I find them a little too temple-like, in that you're supposed to be hushed and humble and wait for the great master to make this or make that. These five sushi chefs are like the Harlem Globetrotters! They're hysterical—they throw food to each other, and every time someone comes in the room that they know, they all start yelling at the same time. It's like a party! They paint the plates with all kinds of wonderful sauces in squeeze bottles that really enhance the food. They have a lot of cooked things served in rolls that are

really delicious. I'm typically a tuna or fluke kind of gal, but they have all kinds of great combinations of sushi that are really the thing here.

GRAMERCY TAVERN

42 E. 20th Street (between Broadway and Park Avenue South), Manhattan
(212) 477-0777

Gramercy Tavern is definitely one of my favorite restaurants. Whenever I don't know where to go, I go to Gramercy, because there's a level of quality here that I know I can depend on. Whether I'm in the tavern or in the dining room, there's just something about it that I love. (See also p. 184.)

REBECCA'S PICKS

'INO

21 Bedford Street (between Avenue of the Americas and Downing Street), Manhattan
(212) 989-5769

'Ino is short for *panino*, and Jason Denton, who is also involved with Lupa, opened this tiny little sandwich nook. It's just big enough for a five-seat bar and four or five tables. They only serve Italian-style pressed sandwiches and bruschetta. They have an asparagus and truffle oil bruschetta that I really like. They also do tramezzini, the sort of crusts-cut-off white-bread Italian sandwich. Sometimes they have a chicken liver special that's quite good. Then they have the pressed sandwiches with three different cheeses. They're open quite late, too.

JOHN'S PIZZERIA

Multiple locations, including:
278 Bleecker Street (between Avenue of the Americas and Seventh Avenue), Manhattan
(212) 243-1680

Very often on my day off, I'll wait too long to make a decision, then get too tired to go anywhere. And at that point I pick up the phone and call John's Pizzeria. I probably eat John's pizza once a week, and always get it with sausage and mushrooms. They do pastas and other stuff, too, but I don't think I've ever seen anyone order anything else. The pizza is definitely the thing. (See also p. 161.)

LUPA

170 Thompson Street (between Bleecker and Houston Streets), Manhattan
(212) 982-5089

This is my new favorite restaurant. They have pastas there that are like really being in Italy. We ordered a fettucini alfredo that was perfect. It was beautiful, perfectly white, as it should be, in a deep white bowl, and a small portion. I had gnocchi made with ricotta, and they were pillowy and light, not heavy. The sauce was ground sausage and fennel. And it was a lick-the-bowl kind of deal. We had a really good deep-fried baccalà [salt cod] with a fennel salad on top. Lupa has a lot of really Italian stuff on the menu, which is in Italian. Even I had five questions! Mario Batali does his homework; he doesn't coast on his success. (See also p. 168.)

PETROSSIAN

182 W. 58th Street (at Seventh Avenue), Manhattan
(212) 245-2214

We go to Petrossian for anything celebratory. We sit at the bar and eat caviar, blinis, toast, and smoked salmon, and drink vodka or Champagne. It's enormously expensive, but we love it.

Rebecca Charles at Petrossian

GRAMERCY TAVERN

42 E. 20th Street

New York, NY 10003

Phone: (212) 477-0777

Fax: (212) 477-1160

www.gramercytavern.com

CRAFT

43 E. 19th Street

New York, NY 10003

Phone: (212) 780-0880

TOM COLICCHIO is the executive chef and co-owner of Gramercy Tavern and Craft. He was named one of the Ten Best New Chefs of 1991 by *Food & Wine*. In 1999, he was nominated for the James Beard Award as Best Chef: New York, which he won in 2000. Prior to opening Gramercy Tavern, his résumé included stints at The Quilted Giraffe, Gotham Bar and Grill, Rakel, and Mondrian. He is the author of *Think Like a Chef*.

MY FOOD Over time, you find the customers who like what you do. Some people get upset that we have people dining at Gramercy Tavern who are not wearing jackets or ties. Lighten up! This is who we are. I'm glad every dining experience in the city isn't the same. We are in the position we are in because we offer an alternative to that. From day one, we wanted to do food that was top-notch, and service that was as exacting as possible, but with a warmth that was a different hospitality paradigm for a fine-dining restaurant. We have a ninety-two-dollar check average in the dining room. So for us, we have to do something different—and it is fun finding your niche.

I took a two-year break from cooking before opening Gramercy Tavern, during which time I didn't read any cookbooks and ate out very little. The reason? I wanted to see what my food was. It was like packing for a two-week trip where you could only take one bag—I kept discarding until finally only my favorite flavors were left. I also really focused on not interfering with the products.

I once received a letter from a couple who had not been happy with their meal at Gramercy, and called them to follow up. They explained, "When we go out to eat, we look for fireworks and big presentations. We love Gotham Bar and Grill and Aureole. But the food we had at Gramercy, we could have made at home. We had the salmon, and it tasted just like salmon. We had the baby lamb, and it tasted just like baby lamb. And the chocolate tart was bitter!"

Normally, I would have invited them back for dinner, but in their case, if they came back, their reaction would have been exactly the same—because I realized that they had experienced exactly what I had intended! So I told them that I didn't think I could please them, and that I was going to refund their bill.

Body temperature is the perfect temperature at which to taste food. Anything that is too cold, you can't taste; anything too hot has the same problem. If a chef makes some kind of frozen, molded pedestal to put food on, it will never be as good as a quenelle that is just cold enough to hold together.

"I love Tom Colicchio's food—it's amazing."

JEAN-GEORGES VONGERICHTEN

JEAN GEORGES, JO JO, MERCER KITCHEN, AND VONG

There is a lot that goes into presentation, but it starts by treating things right. If you treat a piece of fish correctly, it will be beautiful unto itself. If you take a product and beat it up, fillet it the wrong way, and throw it on the grill, it will never look good. I never want to sacrifice flavor for presentation. I believe a blind person should be able to enjoy their meal.

TOM'S PICKS

BLUE RIBBON SUSHI

119 Sullivan Street (between Prince and Spring Streets), Manhattan
(212) 343-0404

It's next to impossible to get into Blue Ribbon Sushi. They have a great assortment of fish, and I like the way that the menu is broken up into East Coast and West Coast fish. The guys behind the sushi bar are friendly and fun. I like to order horse mackerel, or just some sashimi and a bowl of rice.

DANIEL

60 E. 65th Street (between Madison and Fifth Avenues), Manhattan
(212) 288-0033

JEAN GEORGES

1 Central Park W. (between 60th and 61st Streets), Manhattan
(212) 299-3900

I love eating the food of Daniel Boulud and Jean-Georges Vongerichten. It is always exciting to see what the top chefs are doing. It is also a great experience to have a three- or four-hour meal and get pampered the whole time. (See also pp. 173, 203.)

ETATS-UNIS

242 E. 81st Street (between Second and Third Avenues), Manhattan
(212) 517-8826

More often than not, when people ask me where I want to go, it's here. Etats-Unis is an honest family-run restaurant with thirty-one seats and a handwritten menu that changes daily with the market and the chef's whim. They get ingredients from the Greenmarket and prepare them simply. I once had a roasted striped bass there that was served with cranberry beans and heirloom tomatoes, with a little olive oil drizzled on top. That was it—and it was wonderful! I like it when chefs have the confidence to do that. (See also pp. 193, 196.)

THE RED CAT

227 Tenth Avenue (at 23rd Street), Manhattan
(212) 242-1122

I would go back to The Red Cat in a second! It always strikes me as having exactly what I want to eat, and the atmosphere is stylish and relaxed. The American bistro food is simple and very flavorful. I recently had razor clams in a light white bean broth, and a steak—and everything was great!

UNION SQUARE CAFE

21 E. 16th Street (between Fifth Avenue and Union Square West), Manhattan
(212) 243-4020

At Union Square Cafe, I like to sit at the bar and order pasta. Michael Romano, the chef, makes some wonderful pastas. Last time I was there, I had a wonderful dish of hand-rolled pasta served with some mushrooms and peperoncini that was simple and nice. (See also p. 194.)

UNION PACIFIC
111 E. 22nd Street
New York, NY 10010
Phone: (212) 995-8500
Fax: (212) 460-5881
www.unionpacificrestaurant.com

ROCCO DISPIRITO is chef of Union Pacific. He was featured on the cover of *Gourmet*'s 2000 restaurant issue, and has appeared on David Letterman. In 1999, he was nominated for a James Beard Award as Best Chef: New York, and named one of America's Best New Chefs by *Food & Wine* magazine. He is a 1986 graduate of The Culinary Institute of America, and previously worked with chef Gray Kunz.

"Rocco DiSpirito is creative on the level of the Michelin-starred chefs."

MARIO BATALI
BABBO, ESCA, AND LUPA

MY FOOD I combine classic French techniques with both domestic and international ingredients. I like to use unusual ingredients from around the world. The interplay and balance between the four taste components—sweet, salty, bitter and sour—is at the heart of each of my dishes.

"I think Union Pacific is the best restaurant in the world. It's creative, the portions are perfect, and it has impeccable service."

CINDY PAWLCYN   MUSTARDS GRILL (NAPA)

ROCCO'S PICKS

BABBO
110 Waverly Place (between Avenue of the Americas and MacDougal Street), Manhattan
(212) 777-0303

I love Babbo. I've probably been there more than to any other three-star restaurant. The food is so innovative and well executed. I think Italian food is so simple that it's underestimated sometimes. People don't get the idea that because it's so simple, you really need to pay a lot of attention to the two or three ingredients on the plate, especially when it comes to pasta. Babbo has really, really good pasta. A lot of restaurants don't handle pasta well—they overcook it or undercook it, don't season it enough or season it too much. But not at Babbo. I like to get the beef cheek ravioli, which is served with crushed squab livers and black truffle. I also like the mint love letters, which are ravioli filled with a mint and pea purée, and served with a lamb ragout and fresh mint. Any pasta he's making, whatever it is, it doesn't matter—it's always good. They are very into wine pairings, as we are. I will typically drink whatever the sommelier recommends, a quartino [quarter-liter jug] of something or other. (See also p. 168.)

DANIEL
60 E. 65th Street (between Park and Madison Avenues), Manhattan
(212) 288-0033

CAFÉ BOULUD
20 E. 76th Street (between Madison and Fifth Avenues), Manhattan
(212) 772-2600

I don't go to three- and four-star restaurants often, but these experiences stick out in my mind. I don't worry about anything when I eat at Daniel Boulud's restaurants, because I know that whatever I order, it's going to be good and it's going to make me happy. I remember having amazing veal tongue at Café Boulud, served on a big cutting board. It was perfectly cooked, just acidic enough, and the flavor of the tongue came through. The desserts at Daniel Boulud's restaurants are always really good; their flavors are consistently phenomenal. I think a lot of restaurants can't really do that, or don't do that well. He seems to manage it somehow. (See also pp. 173, 177.)

ROCCO'S PICKS

NHA TRANG

87 Baxter Street (between Bayard and Canal Streets), Manhattan
(212) 233-5948

The first time I ate at this Vietnamese restaurant, it was an epiphany. I couldn't believe how good the food was, or the degree and intensity of the flavors. It really humbled me. The restaurant is basically a dive, but the food, in my opinion, in terms of the flavor combinations and executions, is on par with any four-star restaurant. I have this great sense of joy when I eat there, and when I walk out, I feel like I really need to learn how to cook again. They've kind of achieved what I am trying to do—these wonderful combinations of sweet, salty, and savory flavors. I recommend the barbecued pork chops, which are very thinly sliced and marinated in the typical things—sugar, honey, fish sauce, garlic, limes—and then quickly caramelized in a wok. I have tried to reproduce them, but I can't. I also recommend the "shrimp with little salt." Some of their clam dishes are excellent. Their soups, especially their noodle soups, are really good—especially the one with beef tendon. They've also got all these great exotic Vietnamese drinks made with coconut milk, tapioca, and all kinds of weird stuff. They look really cool, but I usually drink beer.

UNCLE GEORGE'S GREEK TAVERN

33-19 Broadway (near 34th Street), Queens (Astoria)
(718) 626-0593

Uncle George's is an authentic Greek restaurant where the food is consistently good. I like their spit-barbecued lamb, and their simple, grilled fish. They serve retsina [Greek wine], which is fun, and they have the best Greek salads and great feta cheese. I also like the ambiance: There's Greek music playing in the background, the waiters could take you or leave you, and Mama's at the cash register. It's kind of cute. It's like Milos [a restaurant in Manhattan], but for a tenth of the price: Here, four people can have a great meal for fifty or sixty dollars. It's open twenty-four hours, too, which is key—especially for a chef!

Bobby Flay

BOBBY FLAY is chef-partner of Bolo and Mesa Grill. A graduate of the French Culinary Institute, he received the school's first Outstanding Graduate Award in 1993. In 1991, *New York* magazine named Mesa Grill Restaurant of the Year, and it continues to be among the top twenty-five restaurants in the New York *ZagatSurvey*. Likewise, Bolo is continuously voted the top Spanish restaurant in the New York *ZagatSurvey*. In 1993, Flay won the James Beard Award as Rising Star Chef of the Year. He is the host of the Food Network show *Hot Off the Grill with Bobby Flay* and is the chef correspondent for the *Early Show* on CBS. His cookbooks include *Bold American Food*, *Boy Meets Grill*, and *From My Kitchen to Your Table*.

BOLO
23 E. 22nd Street
New York, NY 10010
Phone: (212) 228-2200
Fax: (212) 228-2239

MESA GRILL
102 Fifth Avenue
New York, NY 10011
Phone: (212) 807-7400
Fax: (212) 989-0034

MY FOOD My food is about really big flavors. Especially at Mesa Grill, it's often about using chile peppers. Chiles are part of the American pantry now. It has been proven that they are fabulous to use for flavor, and not just for heat. I try to get people to understand that through my food. Chiles are for accents, not injuries, I like to say. They're not about burning your mouth out.

BLUE RIBBON

97 Sullivan Street
(Prince and Spring Streets),
Manhattan
(212) 274-0404

A lot of New York City chefs have made this restaurant [which serves eclectic American cuisine, such as oxtail marrow, steak tartare, and turkey burgers] their hangout. I used to go there all the time, but now I have a four-year-old daughter, so I don't get there as often as I used to—but when I do, it's still great. (See also pp. 150, 157, 159.)

CHIN CHIN

216 E. 49th Street
(between Second and Third Avenues),
Manhattan
(212) 888-4555

Chin Chin is a throwback to my New York roots. In the 1970s, New York families went out to Chinese restaurants on Sunday nights. In my family, my grandfather would preside. He would take care of everything, from ordering to paying the bill. Chin Chin really reminds me of those times. A guy named Sal, whom I've known now for thirty years, is running Chin Chin, so I'll go there about one Sunday a month during the winter. I just let Sal order for us. We might eat clams steamed in fermented black bean sauce, or a whole fish, or something as simple as sesame chicken. They also make lobster egg rolls that are amazing!

DANIEL

60 E. 65th Street (between Park and Madison Avenues), Manhattan
(212) 288-0033

LESPINASSE

2 E. 55th Street (in the St. Regis Hotel, between Fifth and Madison Avenues), Manhattan
(212) 339-6719

When I'm in the mood or the occasion calls for it, these are the fine-dining restaurants I enjoy most. (See also Daniel on p. 173.)

J.G. MELON

1291 Third Avenue (at 74th Street), Manhattan
(212) 744-0585

I've been eating J.G. Melon's cheeseburgers since I was a kid. They have the best cheeseburger of all time. I think it has to do with the fact that they use a griddle. I usually go with my business partner, Laurence Kretchmer, and we'll order three cheeseburgers, so each of us has one and a half. I like extra cheese, pickles, Dijon mustard, and a lot of black pepper, and cottage fries and a Beck's. They are open until three A.M. Melon's was my first watering hole. It's like my Cheers— the same people have worked there for twenty years, and when I walk in, I know everybody. It's a comforting place to go.

NOBU

105 Hudson Street
(at Franklin Street), Manhattan
(212) 219-0500

Nobu Matsuhisa, the chef, has a vision of inventive Japanese cuisine that no one else in his genre has. I think it has a lot to do with his having lived in Peru, which is why he uses things like chile peppers. He is a great master of balance, especially with tart flavors. At Nobu, they serve a plate of very thinly sliced raw fish with a warm sauce of vinegar, different oils, and fresh chives. The fish cooks a little bit on the plate. The dish has only four ingredients, but it's incredible. There are other great things about Nobu, like the fact that it's a two-million-dollar restaurant where you can drink out of bamboo containers. The whole thing works. It's very upbeat. (See also p. 202.)

BOBBY'S PICKS

RAO'S

455 E. 114th Street
(at Pleasant Avenue), Manhattan
(212) 722-6709

They have reverse reservations at Rao's—their regular customers have permanent tables, and they only call if they're not going to make it! You want a New York experience? Rao's is a New York experience. Now, is the food the best in the world? I don't know. It's some of the best southern Italian food I've ever had.

It's one of those places where there are no menus; instead, your waiter tells you, "Well, we have manicotti, we have sausage and peppers, we have . . ." this or that. I order whatever kind of pasta they're making, and when the food comes out, it's great. There's a great jukebox with old Italian favorites on it. It's in East Harlem, but you can leave your car running right outside the restaurant—nobody's going to touch it. (See also p. 194.)

DIane FOrLeY graduated from Brown University before becoming chef-owner of Verbena. Her culinary training included stints with Michel Guérard and at Lenôtre in France, and at Gotham Bar and Grill, Petrossian, and the River Cafe in New York. In 1995, *Esquire* named Verbena one of the Top Twenty-five New Restaurants in America.

Diane Forley

VERBENA

54 Irving Place
(between 17th and 18th Streets)
New York, NY 10003
Phone: (212) 260-5454
Fax: (212) 260-3595

BAR DEMI

125½ E. 17th Street
New York, NY 10003
Phone: (212) 260-0900

MY FOOD My food is a culmination of my culinary training, my travels, and my interests in nutrition, the history of food, and culinary techniques. I've tried to encourage the idea of seasonality on our menu, and bring in ingredients that represent the time of year. Fortunately, customers are growing more aware of seasonality, of when to eat asparagus and when not to. You can get asparagus all year, but you feel funny eating asparagus in the middle of winter. I like to offer ingredients that people may not normally see on menus. As a contemporary chef, I think that part of my role is to introduce people to new ingredients, and I enjoy using them. But I am sensitive to balance. There are a lot of different kinds of people who come here, so not everything can be esoteric. To me, that's what going out to a restaurant is: a chance to be exposed to new ingredients, new preparations, new techniques. Yet it also depends on what mood I'm in. I don't always want to eat crazy things; sometimes I want something simple.

KEENS STEAK HOUSE

72 W. 36th Street (between Fifth Avenue and Avenue of the Americas), Manhattan (212) 947-3636

Keens has a great ambiance: It just is what it is. It's New York. Their porterhouse steak is really good. They have creamed spinach, and iceberg lettuce with blue cheese dressing. You can't really go wrong. They have a great wine list, too—I usually order a Pinot Noir, because you need something spicy to go with the steak.

L'EXPRESS

249 Park Avenue South (at 20th Street), Manhattan (212) 254-5858

This bistro is always open—twenty-four hours a day, seven days a week—and the food is surprisingly good. In fact, I'm always shocked, really, by how good the food is. I like the mushroom ravioli and the mussels, and their quenelles are delicious. The service is touch and go, however, depending on how busy it is.

RECTANGLES

159 Second Avenue, Manhattan (212) 677-8410

Rectangles is a Middle Eastern place that has great mezze, falafel, and kibbeh. They also have a great flatbread with roasted egg and all the condiments. It's consistently really good, plus it's very informal and inexpensive.

SUGIYAMA

251 W. 55th Street (between Broadway and Eighth Avenue), Manhattan (212) 956-0670

Sugiyama is a small Japanese restaurant that offers a variety of *kaiseki* meals, where you indicate how much you'd like to spend, up to two hundred dollars or more per person, and how many courses you'd like to have, from five to fourteen. I had an amazing meal there recently. They use interesting Japanese ingredients you don't normally see—like different types of savory jellies, and unusual Japanese plums. They grill some things right at your table, and they offer steak cooked on a hot rock. We had a delicious dessert—a tangy and citrusy grapefruit jelly with a little cream on top. It was simple but amazing. If you think about Jell-O with whipped cream, it's a classic combination, right?

TRIPLE EIGHT PALACE

88 E. Broadway (between Division and Market Streets), Manhattan (212) 941-8886

Triple Eight is great for dim sum. It's fun to go to Chinatown, and to just sit in the restaurant and watch while an amazing variety of food passes by on carts. They have a dumpling filled with spinach and leeks that is really good, and I also like the rolled rice noodles. And it's always surprisingly inexpensive. There are various stations that you can go to and order certain specialties, like steamed clams with a pungent sauce or steamed dumplings, which are great, too.

François Payard is chef-owner of Payard Pâtisserie and Bistro. Previously, he was the pastry chef at two three-star Michelin restaurants in France, and at Le Bernardin and Restaurant Daniel in New York. He won the 1995 James Beard Award as Outstanding Pastry Chef of the Year, and the 1998 *Bon Appétit* Food and Entertainment Award as Pastry Chef of the Year.

François Payard

PAYARD PÂTISSERIE AND BISTRO

1032 Lexington Avenue
(at 73rd Street)
New York, NY 10021
Phone: (212) 717-5252
Fax: (212) 717-0986
www.payard.com

MY FOOD It is very easy to understand the food here: We are a bistro. People may know me for the four-star desserts I did before I opened Payard, but now that I am at a bistro I cannot do the more elaborate desserts. My desserts here are simpler.

I wish people would talk more about the restaurant than the pastry shop at Payard. [Executive chef] Philippe Bertineau's food is a big part of the attraction—he's the one behind the food every night, and he's an extraordinary chef. Why do I love him? He's consistent, and nobody makes foie gras or terrine like Philippe. Plus, you have to scream at him to take a day off! I am lucky to have him here.

We have people come in daily for coffee and breakfast in the front room, then come for dinner twice a week in the dining room. I believe we strike a balance. We serve a lot of ladies who lunch, who like to eat something light—a chicken salad and a lemon tart, for example. But dinnertime is different—then, people just want to have a good time!

FRANÇOIS'S PICKS

BALTHAZAR

80 Spring Street (between Broadway and Crosby Street), Manhattan
(212) 965-1414

BLUE RIBBON

97 Sullivan Street
(between Prince and Spring Streets),
Manhattan
(212) 274-0404
Late at night, I'll go with Philippe Bertineau, Payard's chef, to Blue Ribbon or to Balthazar. Why? Because they're both open late, and serve really good food that you want to eat at that hour, everything from oysters to hamburgers and french fries. (See also pp. 150, 157, 159.)

HARU

1329 Third Avenue (at 76th Street), Manhattan (212) 452-2230
433 Amsterdam Avenue
(between 80th and 81st Streets),
Manhattan (212) 579-5655
If you like sushi, you'll love Haru, which has really good, fresh, big sushi. It tends to be crowded, but it's worth the wait.

MONSOON

435 Amsterdam Avenue
(at 81st Street), Manhattan
(212) 580-8686
When I lived on the West Side, my favorite restaurant was Monsoon. I think the French love Vietnamese food. In Paris, there are a lot of Vietnamese restaurants in the 13th arrondissement, and I used to go crazy at them. Vietnamese food is a nice mélange of Asian flavors. Thai food is too spicy for me sometimes, but Vietnamese food is more delicate. I love the Vietnamese spring rolls with beef, pork, and shrimp inside, and the bean sprouts and julienne of carrots with mint leaves. I go crazy for it!

PETER LUGER STEAK HOUSE

178 Broadway (at Driggs Avenue),
Brooklyn
(718) 387-7400
I like having a steak. We'll go to Peter Luger [a New York institution that opened in 1887, and dry ages its steaks on premises] at least once or twice a year for a great steak. They also have good sides, such as tomato and onion salad, creamed spinach, and french fries. (See also p. 164.)

ROSA MEXICANO

1063 First Avenue (at 58th Street),
Manhattan
(212) 753-7407
We are lucky to have such a nice upscale Mexican restaurant, run by Josefina Howard, near us in Rosa Mexicano. They make their delicious guacamole right at your table, so it's very fresh-tasting. Other specialties include taquitos made with blood sausage and cilantro, and pomegranate margaritas.

Eric Ripert

LE BERNARDIN

155 W. 51st Street
(between Sixth and
Seventh Avenues)
New York, NY 10019
Phone: (212) 489-1515
Fax: (212) 265-1615
www.le-bernardin.com

ERIC RIPERT is chef of Le Bernardin in New York, a restaurant credited with revolutionizing seafood in America. Born in Andorra, he worked with chefs Joel Robuchon and Jean-Louis Palladin before joining Le Bernardin as executive chef in 1991. Upon the death of chef-owner Gilbert LeCoze in 1994, he took over the kitchen completely. In 1998, Le Bernardin won the James Beard Award for Outstanding Restaurant, and that same year Ripert won the James Beard Award as Best Chef: New York.

MY FOOD For many years, I sometimes compromised what I cooked. I was trying to please the customer by adding things to my food just to make it look bigger, or better, or more colorful, or whatever. If someone comes to Le Bernardin, where our prix fixe is seventy-two dollars, what are they going to say if I just serve an oyster with one drop of lemon oil on top? I was afraid that customers wouldn't be impressed if it was too simple. Always, though, I tried to get the maximum flavor out of the main ingredient.

Today I am much more confident than I was in the beginning. I have a philosophy that is very simple: If I cook halibut, I cook "for" the halibut. I do not cook "with" halibut. I think that makes a big difference in cooking. To me, it's exciting to cook that way.

When I say I cook for the halibut, it means I respect the fact that halibut is not like tuna, or salmon, or eel. We are trying to really identify, what is the halibut? What kind of a fish is it? What kind of texture does it have? What is the best way to serve it—rare, well done, medium? What kills the flavor of the halibut—too much acidity? Pairing it with something too rich? Over time, you know exactly what will enhance the flavor of a particular product. I think that's what makes the difference for us.

"I think Le Bernardin has one of the best service experiences because it's so fluid. There are a lot of people working there, but everybody has a role, and everyone seems to follow through so well. There is a continuity to the entire experience."

DIANE FORLEY   VERBENA

ERIC'S PICKS

BALTHAZAR

80 Spring Street (between Broadway and Crosby Street), Manhattan
(212) 965-1414

To me, the best thing about Balthazar is that it feels like such an authentic brasserie. When I go there, I am always amazed that the restaurant is only three years old. It could be twenty—it feels like it's been there forever. It is simple food, always nicely done. Nothing is crazy, but then I'm someone who likes to know what I am eating. I like to go for lunch and have the steak frites—and sometimes I have an egg on top of my steak frites, which is vicious! I also like the brandade of cod.

CAFÉ BOULUD

20 E. 76th Street (between Madison and Fifth Avenues), Manhattan
(212) 772-2600

Café Boulud [the three-star restaurant owned by four-star chef Daniel Boulud] is more than a café, obviously! The concept is that they are not stuck in four-star cuisine, or in a category that is strictly French—they can play with whatever ingredients and cuisines they want. In fact, part of the menu is called "Le Voyage," so they can feature food inspired by other cuisines. I like that kind of freedom, and chef Andrew Carmellini does it with a lot of talent. (See also p. 177.)

ETATS-UNIS

242 E. 81st Street (between Second and Third Avenues), Manhattan
(212) 517-8742

Etats-Unis is the best-kept secret in New York. It is a tiny place run by a father-and-son team that serves simple, homey food that is very, very good. The menu features four appetizers, four entrées, and four desserts, all of which change daily. I love it. (See also p. 185.)

JEAN GEORGES

1 Central Park West (between 60th and 61st Streets), Manhattan
(212) 299-3900

I don't want to call Jean-Georges Vongerichten a genius, because I can't define that. But he is one of the most talented and innovative chefs cooking in this country today. I also like the décor at Jean Georges very much, and the service is great, too. (See also p. 203.)

PEACOCK ALLEY

301 Park Avenue (in the Waldorf-Astoria, at 50th Street), Manhattan
(212) 872-4895

Chef Laurent Gras is doing an amazing job with a French menu that changes frequently, without distinctions between appetizers and entrées in offerings such as tuna with caviar and cream of cauliflower or wild turbot with prawns and seaweed. As a chef, I am always amazed by the perfection and precision of his cooking. It is a place I like to go just for the taste! I had turbot here once that was made with a wine called Vin Jaune from the Jura area in France. They take the grapes and dry them a little over dried herbs in the sun to make the wine. It was amazing.

SERAFINA FABULOUS PIZZA

1022 Madison Avenue (at 79th Street), Manhattan
(212) 734-2676

I like to go here for lunch. I love their pizza! It is thin-crust style and my topping is always very simple: tomato and cheese, that's it. They use good ingredients, and it is fast—you don't have to wait forever. The quality is the same every time, and I like that.

UNION SQUARE CAFE

21 E. 16th Street (between Fifth
Avenue and Union Square West)
New York, NY 10003
Phone: (212) 243-4020
Fax: (212) 627-2673
www.kerrymenu.com/
union-square-cafe.htm

MICHAEL ROMANO is executive chef and partner (with restaurateur Danny Meyer) of Union Square Cafe, for which he earned three stars from the *New York Times*. In 1997, Union Square Cafe won the James Beard Award for Outstanding Restaurant. Romano has been nominated several times for the James Beard Award as Best Chef: New York, and was named one of *Food & Wine* magazine's Top Ten Chefs in the USA in 1991. He is co-author of *The Union Square Cafe Cookbook*. He is an alumnus of New York City Technical College, and cooked with Michelin three-star chef Michel Guérard.

MY FOOD Union Square Cafe serves robustly flavored, seasonal American cuisine with an Italian accent in a relaxed setting of casual elegance. Menu specialties include iced oysters on the half shell, grilled marinated filet mignon of tuna, hot garlic potato chips, and warm banana tart. Union Square Cafe is famous for welcoming guests with extraordinary value and warm hospitality.

MICHAEL'S PICKS

CENT'ANNI

50 Carmine Street (between Bedford and Bleecker Streets), Manhattan
(212) 989-9494

Danny Meyer first took me to Cent'anni many years ago, before I started cooking at Union Square Cafe. I always return for the same two items: the pappardelle with rabbit, and the roast pork loin. When the kitchen is on top of its form, the rabbit is sublime and the pork so tender you can eat it with a spoon! I usually order a nice bottle of Italian red wine when I'm here, like a Brunello or a Chianti.

JEAN GEORGES

1 Central Park West (between 60th and 61st Streets), Manhattan
(212) 299-3900

DANIEL

60 E. 65th Street (between Park and Madison Avenues), Manhattan
(212) 288-0033

Jean-Georges Vongerichten and Daniel Boulud are two chefs at the top of their game—the contemporary successors of former Lutèce chef-owner André Soltner and former La Caravelle chef-owner Roger Fessaguet. Their creativity is nicely grounded in solid technique, good sense, and good flavors. Maybe I'm just conservative, but I'm not one for wild creativity for

its own sake, or crazy stuff being put together just to be different. While these two chefs dazzle, their food is just so solid, and their flavors are so good. I admire them. At Daniel, we recently had a dessert that was basically a beer ice cream. It might sound gross, but it was really good and very refreshing. (See also p. 203 and p. 173.)

MAVALLI PALACE

46 E. 29th Street (between Madison Avenue and Park Avenue South), Manhattan
(212) 679-5535

There's been a whole new resurgence of Indian restaurants in Manhattan. This southern Indian vegetarian restaurant does a nice job with *samosas* [deep-fried pastries filled with meat and/or vegetables] and *dosai* [Indian-spiced crispy crêpes made from ground rice and lentils with various fillings].

PAOLA'S

245 E. 84th Street (between Second and Third Avenues), Manhattan
(212) 794-1890

I return to this Italian restaurant fairly consistently, because I always have a good time here. Chef-owner Paola Marracino does wonderful fresh pastas that are not your typical dishes. She has one ravioli that's stuffed with beets and served with beet greens. Another great dish is a little twist pasta with pesto, green beans, and potatoes.

RAO'S

455 E. 114th Street (at Pleasant Avenue), Manhattan
(212) 722-6709

The beauty of Rao's is that while the restaurant is almost always chock-full of celebrities, it remains the quintessential "neighborhood joint." The food reminds me of the Neapolitan fare I ate growing up at home, just five blocks from the restaurant. But the main reason to go is Frank Pelligrino—a consummate restaurateur who enlivens the place with his warm and generous hospitality. It may not be easy to get in, but the food and atmosphere make it worth the try. (See also p. 188.)

Michael Romano and
Frank Pellegrino at Rao's

Anne Rosenzweig

anne rosenzweig is chef-owner of the Lobster Club. She served as chef-advisor to the White House during the Clinton administration, and helped found the International Association of Women Chefs and Restaurateurs in 1993. She has been nominated several times for the James Beard Award as Best Chef: New York.

THE LOBSTER CLUB
24 E. 80th Street (between
Madison and Fifth Avenues)
New York, NY 10021
Phone: (212) 249-6500
Fax: (212) 396-0829

my food The Lobster Club is named after my signature dish at Arcadia [Anne's first restaurant, which she ran from 1984 to 1998], which is a whole lobster served on three slices of toasted brioche with bacon and homemade mayonnaise. Some people have described my food as "eclectic home cooking for Manhattan's Upper East Side." Our menu is sometimes playful, and features dishes ranging from *matzoh brei* [a matzoh omelet, which is a traditional Jewish dish] to Mom's meat loaf. Because I started out in the restaurant business as a pastry chef, I take special pride in the Lobster Club's desserts, which include homemade ice creams and sorbets. And my husband [Andrew Freeman] goes to great lengths to find unusual wines for our wine list.

I still never get tired of lobster. Personally, I like the claws, knuckles, and legs. I love eating lobster out with other people, and getting to trade my tail for their claws. The claws are sweeter and more tender, and they have the flavor of the sea. Even when a lobster is overcooked, the claws are still more tender. At the Lobster Club, we cook the tails and claws separately because they cook at different rates. That way, nothing gets overcooked. I like my lobster female, one and a half pounds—the optimal size for sweetness and tenderness—and steamed. I like to eat them straight, without sauce; it is like caviar. If I had to choose a condiment, it would be lemon mayonnaise. If I find myself snacking in the kitchen, that is what I will dip my bites of lobster in.

One of the things I enjoy about eating out is having food that's not at all similar to what I make. If you look at my list of restaurants, they're all places that serve food that's totally outside of what I do. I prefer something that provides a whole different palette of flavors. To go out to have somebody's food that's of the same ilk as mine is so boring. I'd rather stay at home and eat—or I'd rather get hot dogs from Papaya King!

ETATS-UNIS

242 E. 81st Street (between Second and Third Avenues), Manhattan
(212) 517-8826

I love Etats-Unis. They've got kind of a wacky way of looking at food—it's very particular. The new American menu is tiny, just four appetizers and four entrées. It changes so much that it's not possible to have a favorite dish, but when something here is right, it's perfect. They've also got a really interesting wine list, and they're interested in the same sorts of wines that we are, which are mainly Austrian wines, so it's fun to talk to the sommelier. (See also p. 185.)

GABRIELA'S

Multiple locations, including:
685 Amsterdam Avenue (at 93rd Street), Manhattan
(212) 961-0574

For me, finding restaurants that are kid-friendly has never been an issue, because taking our seven-year-old

daughter, Lily, out is like taking along another adult. For me, it's more about convenience. We go to this Mexican restaurant two or three times a week because Lily goes to tae kwon do practice right next door. Usually I get the chicken with the fried plantains, or any of the specials. Lily likes anything on the kids' menu, especially the enchiladas.

JEAN GEORGES

1 Central Park West (between 60th and 61st Streets), Manhattan
(212) 299-3900

Our daughter, Lily, is as comfortable at Jean Georges as anywhere else I've mentioned. When I'm working, she and Andy will often go to Jean Georges. I like to keep Jean Georges as a special place, but they like to think of Jean Georges as a neighborhood restaurant. I complain to Andy, "Honey, she's seven—when she's twenty, where is there going to be for her to go?" When we go and Jean-Georges Vongerichten cooks a meal for us, it's just so spectacular. To me, he's the most exciting chef in New York. (See also p. 203.)

SHANGHAI CUISINE

89 Bayard Street (at Mulberry Street), Manhattan
(212) 732-8988

If you've been to Joe's Shanghai [which is well known for its signature soup dumplings], this is the nicer, better version. The place is fairly new, and it has some ambiance, which is really rare for Chinatown. It was actually introduced to me by a friend, Han Feng, who's a fashion designer from Shanghai. They're really nice to my daughter, Lily—they don't recognize us, but they always recognize her. Order anything that's Shanghainese, like the soup dumplings, the crab tiny buns, and their wonderful noodle dishes. The other great thing about this place is that under the glass top on each table they have a little cartoon that shows you how to eat a soup dumpling without pouring the hot broth inside all over yourself.

SHUN LEE WEST

43 W. 65th Street (between Columbus Avenue and Central Park West), Manhattan
(212) 595-8895

Whenever Michael Tong [the owner of Shun Lee West] comes to eat at the Lobster Club, he brings a Peking duck. If Michael is at Shun Lee West when I'm there, I eat whatever he suggests. If he's not, I'll order whatever I want. We like the Peking duck a lot, and the Chan-Do Chicken. We usually order the spicier dishes: prawns with garlic and scallions, spicy chicken sung, and Singapore-style rice noodles with curry. We just went a couple of weeks ago for dim sum, and they now have soup dumplings. When I lived on the West Side, Shun Lee was our local take-out, so it's kind of like "Mom's food" to me, and anytime we're at Lincoln Center, we go there.

amy scherber is baker-owner of Amy's Bread. After a brief career in marketing, she attended the New York Restaurant School to pursue her passion for cooking and baking. She worked as a line and pastry cook at Bouley and baked bread and pastries at the now-closed Mondrian before opening Amy's Bread. The 2000 New York *ZagatSurvey* ranked Amy's Bread third in its Top One Hundred Bangs for the Buck. In addition to retail sales, the bakery also provides breads to over a hundred restaurants in New York. She serves on the boards of both the Bread Bakers Guild of America and Women Chefs and Restaurateurs. In 1997, *Crain's* selected her as one of Forty Under Forty Rising Business Stars, and in 1999 she was featured in *Entrepreneur* magazine as one of thirty rising business owners. She was selected as the 1999 New York Woman Business Owner of the Year by the National Association of Women Business Owners. She is the author of *Amy's Bread*.

MY FOOD If you're trying Amy's Bread for the first time, you should start with the basics: our French baguette, which has a crispy, golden brown crust; and our signature semolina raisin fennel bread, which has a nicely balanced flavor and a chewy yet cakelike texture. For fun, our black olive twist is a great snack. It's olivey, salty, toasty, and rich. I'm not able to use only organic ingredients because it's expensive, and I want to respect the price-sensitivity of my clients, but I do make four breads that are completely organic. I think all of my breads are typified by a toasty smell, a chewy crumb, and lots of holes that are big and open. And we just started to offer home-style cakes, including Definitely Devil's Food Cake and Red Velvet Cake.

Amy Scherber

AMY'S BREAD
Chelsea Market
75 Ninth Avenue
(between 15th and 16th Streets)
New York, NY 10011
Phone: (212) 462-4338

672 Ninth Avenue
(between 46th and 47th Streets)
New York, NY 10036
Phone: (212) 977-2670
Fax: (212) 977-2282
www.amysbread.com

AMY'S PICKS

FLORENT
69 Gansevoort Street (between Greenwich and Washington Streets), Manhattan
(212) 989-5779
Florent [which is located in the meat-packing district and open twenty-four hours on weekends] has good French-American food that's not very expensive, and a fun environment with an interesting-looking crowd. The people-watching at this retro diner is half the fun! I like ordering simple, quick things, like vegetarian chili or mussels and frites. They've also got a nice French salad with lentils.

MARKT
401 W. 14th Street (at Ninth Avenue), Manhattan
(212) 727-3314
This Belgian brasserie in the meat-packing district is a huge, open space that is a great place to go for mussels, the house specialty, which are served four different ways: steamed in white wine, in Belgian beer, with garden vegetables, or with tomato and basil and frites. I love the combination of fries with mayonnaise—fat on fat! And I'll usually order a basic white wine, not too dry, to drink with a meal here.

PEARL OYSTER BAR

18 Cornelia Street (between Bleecker and W. 4th Streets), Manhattan
(212) 691-8211

I love the people who run Pearl, including chef-owner Rebecca Charles —they really put their heart and soul into this cozy and comfortable place. I think I have every music CD they play there, so it's always a comfortable place to hang out at the bar—there are twenty bar stools but only one table for four! And I've liked everything I've ever had there, from the steamed clams to the mussels to the daily fish specials. (See also p. 182.)

PHO VIET HUONG

73 Mulberry Street (at Canal Street), Manhattan (Chinatown)
(212) 233-8988

I'll usually order something simple and quick at this Vietnamese restaurant, like the *pho* [beef noodle soup]. And I'll usually start with one of the chicken or shrimp rolls that you wrap in lettuce leaves and mint and dip in *nuoc cham*, a tangy Vietnamese sauce.

SAPPORO

152 W. 49th Street (between Eighth and Ninth Avenues), Manhattan
(212) 869-8972

MENCHANKO-TEI

Multiple locations, including:
43-45 W. 55th Street (between Fifth Avenue and Avenue of the Americas), Manhattan
(212) 247-1585

I love Japanese noodle shops, and these are two of my neighborhood favorites. At Sapporo, which also has great dumplings, I like to order the special ramen. At Menchanko-tei— the name means "house of mixed noodles" in Japanese—I like the noodles with pork in white soup.

MICHAEL JORDAN'S STEAK HOUSE

23 Vanderbilt Avenue (in Grand Central Terminal, at 44th Street), Manhattan
(212) 655-2300

THE TEA BOX

693 Fifth Avenue (in Takashimaya, between 54th and 55th Streets), Manhattan
(212) 350-0180

When I have visitors from out of town, I'll try to judge whether they're adventurous or not. If I think they're not, I'll take them somewhere like Michael Jordan's Steak House, which has the appeal of the celebrity name, the location in the middle of Grand Central Station, and great steaks! If they seem more adventurous, I'll take them somewhere like The Tea Box, for unconventional yet beautiful tea sandwiches in a very comfortable setting.

Jacques Torres

FORMERLY EXECUTIVE
PASTRY CHEF,
LE CIRQUE 2000
New York Palace Hotel
455 Madison Avenue
New York, NY 10022
Phone: (212) 303-7788
Fax: (212) 303-7712

**JACQUES TORRES
CHOCOLATE**
66 Water Street
Brooklyn, NY 11201
Phone: (718) 875-9772
Fax: (212) 489-0142
www.mrchocolate.com

For eleven years, Jacques Torres had been executive pastry chef of Le Cirque 2000, which earned four stars from the *New York Times*. In France, he spent eight years working with Jacques Maximin, and in 1986 became the youngest chef to ever earn the Meilleur Ouvrier de France award. He serves as dean of pastry arts at New York's French Culinary Institute, and is the host of the PBS series *Dessert Circus with Jacques Torres*. He is the author of *Dessert Circus: Extraordinary Desserts You Can Make at Home*, and *Dessert Circus at Home: Fun, Fanciful, Easy-to-Make Desserts*. He won the 1994 James Beard Award as Outstanding Pastry Chef.

MY FOOD I like to think of pastry as an art form, and at Le Cirque I had the opportunity to make dessert the focal point of the dining experience through presentations that were always creative, often whimsical, and sometimes even architectural.

You always want what you don't have. If you do gourmet food all day like I do, you want family food when you go out. The restaurants I mention below tend to do one-pot cooking—dishes that have been cooked a long time.

Jacques's picks

CAFÉ FÈS
246 W. 4th Street (at Charles Street), Manhattan
(212) 924-7653
This is one of our favorite restaurants. It is small, but they do Moroccan food like no one else in New York. The owner is not a professional chef—she learned to cook with her mom. She does a very good couscous, *tajine*, *merguez*—which is a hot sausage that the French love—and grilled sardines. They serve a nice Vin Gris, which the French call Vin Rose, and it goes really well with the food. For dessert, they have an assortment of Moroccan desserts, which are sweet and good.

EL AZTECA MEXICAN RESTAURANT
783 Ninth Avenue (at 52nd Street), Manhattan
(212) 307-0616
Everything is good at El Azteca. The *mole* is very good, as are the fajitas. They also have a good banana margarita made with Cuervo Gold—have that, and you are all set! The owner works there with her family, and it is so nice.

RENÉ PUJOL
321 W. 51st Street (between Eighth and Ninth Avenues), Manhattan
(212) 246-3023
René Pujol is a classic French restaurant that has been around for more than twenty-five years. You go in and you'll find linen tablecloths and

flowers on every table, a great staff, and very reasonable prices. So you think, "At this price, something must be wrong with the food." Yet it comes out, and it is fantastic! The chef [Claude Franques] is a friend of mine, and he puts even more attention than I do into his work! Everything is done by the book. He reduces his stock in the oven, so when you taste it you just put your spoon down and go, "Wow!" I like to go there when they cook lamb shank—when he has it as a special, he calls me. They also have a good pastry person who makes some nice desserts.

SEPPI'S

Le Parker Meridien
123 W. 56th Street (between Avenue of the Americas and Seventh Avenue), Manhattan
(212) 708-7444

Seppi's is a French bistro that is uptown, but it feels like downtown. It is owned by the same people who own Raoul's, another French bistro in the Village. Seppi's has a great *tarte flambée* [an Alsatian pizza, typically made with bacon, onion and crème fraiche] and steak *au poivre*. They also do very nice vegetarian dishes, such as gratin of penne with chanterelles, and a *dégustation* [chef's tasting] menu is available upon request. It is interesting food, and you can go in your jeans.

VICTOR'S CAFÉ

236 W. 52nd Street (between Broadway and Eighth Avenue), Manhattan
(212) 586-7714

This Cuban restaurant is relatively inexpensive. The food is different and interesting; they mix picante and sweet. We love it! I like to get the oxtail, but we also like the pulled beef that has been simmered a long time and is served with plantains. And they have the best sangria!

"I love going to Le Cirque. There's definitely a magic to it. The owners—Sirio Maccioni and his sons—are so good, and it's both beautiful and well run. And the food is always really, really good. I love everything about the place. I think that if I had to pick my favorite restaurant in the country, this would be the one."

LYDIA SHIRE

BIBA AND PIGNOLI (BOSTON)

LAURENT TOURONDEL is chef-partner of Cello in New York. He trained with three-star French chef Joel Robuchon and at the Michelin three-star restaurant Troisgros in France, among other places. Previously, he was executive chef at C.T. in New York and the Palace Court in Las Vegas. He was voted one of America's Ten Best New Chefs by *Food & Wine* magazine in 1998.

Laurent Tourondel

CELLO

53 E. 77th Street (between Madison and Park Avenues)
New York, NY 10021
Phone: (212) 517-1200
Fax: (212) 517-1251
www.cellorestaurant.com

MY FOOD The *terroir* for me is not using any frozen products. Recently, a guest was upset that I had no turbot, but I am not going to put turbot in the freezer to make one person happy. I would prefer to have a hundred people leave happy and one upset. To best experience our restaurant, I encourage people to have the tasting menu. It is always changing, depending on the availability of particular ingredients, particularly seafood, in which we specialize, and I can customize it to the guest's taste, depending on how many courses they want to have and what they like to eat. I did one with three different *amuse-gueules*, a cold appetizer, a hot appetizer, shellfish, two fish, and two desserts—because we like to do a pre-dessert, followed by another dessert. I also serve a lot of caviar here. I get the best caviar, but I cannot give the source—it comes directly from Russia! I cooked in Russia for more than a year and learned a lot about caviar.

"I still get really excited to see something new and different. My dinner at Cello, where everything was right on, really knocked me out."
BOB KINKEAD   KINKEAD'S (WASHINGTON, DC)

"The last amazing meal I had was at Cello. Laurent Tourondel is a chef who really understands food."
FRANÇOIS PAYARD   PAYARD PÂTISSERIE AND BISTRO

DANIEL

60 E. 65th Street (between Madison and Fifth Avenues), Manhattan
(212) 288-0033

I eat at Daniel and Jean Georges to experience their part in the evolution of French cooking: from the use of seasonal products to creativity and progress in classic dishes. I go to Daniel to eat the new classics of French cuisine at their perfect best. I don't have favorite dishes there; everything is good. The restaurant is very warm and comfortable, and the bar is beautiful, with a lot of wood. (See also p. 173.)

JEAN GEORGES

1 Central Park West (between 60th and 61st Streets), Manhattan
(212) 299-3900

I like how simple the food is here. Jean-Georges Vongerichten keeps his traditional French technique, yet his food is very modern, with an Asian touch. Compared to classic French cooking, which can be very heavy, Jean-Georges's food has more of an emphasis on lighter sauces. His cooking reflects the way people want to eat today. The room is very New York, spacious and as modern as the food! (See also p. 203.)

JOHN'S PIZZERIA

Multiple locations, including:
408 E. 64th Street (between First and York Avenues), Manhattan
(212) 935-2895

This is my favorite place for pizza, and not only because it's a block away from my apartment! Most pizza places are usually very boring, but they do a really good job here. The most important thing about pizza is the dough, and theirs tastes so good you just want to keep eating it. I like to order their plain margherita pizza, or one with sausage and fresh basil. (See also p. 161.)

NHA TRANG

87 Baxter Street
(between Bayard and Canal Streets), Manhattan (Chinatown)
(212) 233-5948

A Vietnamese friend brought me to this Vietnamese restaurant for the first time. They have the best calamari I have ever tasted in my life! It's crisp and perfect. I asked what the secret was, and they told me, "It's deep-fried." But they wouldn't tell me what kind of oil or what kind of fryer! As an appetizer, I like to order the *nem*, which is the famous Vietnamese dough filled with shrimp and vegetables that is deep-fried and served with mint. And I love their grilled pork chop, which is topped with crushed peanuts and served with lettuce leaves to wrap it in. They also have really great steamed fish. (See also p. 187.)

NOBU

105 Hudson Street (at Franklin Street), Manhattan
(212) 219-0500

I go to Nobu a lot. Nobu Matsuhisa, the chef-owner, has done a lot of research on fish and gets the best products. It is very interesting to see what he does with raw fish, both sushi and sashimi. He draws on both Japanese and Peruvian influences to create a very modern cuisine. l like almost everything about this place: the fish as well as the presentations. And despite the big volume they do here, the service is good, too. (See also p. 165.)

REPUBLIC

37 Union Square West
(between 16th and 17th Streets), Manhattan
(212) 627-7172

In Manhattan, it's hard to eat for less than ten dollars. That's one of the reasons I think Republic is such a good concept: It's a high-volume pan-Asian noodle shop with modern, spare décor and communal tables; they serve very cheap food that's both well made and tasty. I like to go here on a Sunday when I just want to relax because, as a chef, I know I won't get recognized and sent twenty-five courses! I like to order the "broken rice" with grilled pork chop. The duck curry noodles are really good, too. (See also p. 160.)

JEAN-GEORGES VONGERICHTEN is chef-owner of Jean Georges, Jo Jo, Mercer Kitchen, and Vong. He earned four stars from the *New York Times* as chef of Lafayette (now closed) in the 1980s, a distinction he achieved again at Jean Georges. Jo Jo was named *Esquire*'s Restaurant of the Year in 1991. He won the 1996 James Beard Award as Best Chef: New York, and the 1998 James Beard Award as Outstanding Chef of the Year.

MY FOOD I recommend having a tasting menu at Jean Georges, because it's a nice array of what's on the menu. It shows you what kind of food combinations we are doing. We try to get the waiters to help people compose their à la carte menus, because sometimes people order main courses that don't follow their appetizers very well. Some of the appetizers are best followed by fish, some by meat, so I think it's good to let us guide you.

Jo Jo has a Parisian bistro atmosphere, but the food is similar to what I was doing at Lafayette—the vegetable juices, the flavored oils. The setting is casual, and it's more of a neighborhood place. Chris Belcher is the chef there now, and we offer a tasting menu over there, too. I say to chefs all the time, "It is easier to open a new restaurant than to change the menu." Guests come back and say, "Where is the chicken with olives, ginger, saffron, and chickpea fries?" If we take it away, we lose half of the clientele, because they come in once or twice a month to eat that dish! We tried to take it away before, and it didn't work. When you take it away, people say, "Oh, the food has changed, it's going downhill," and you say, "It's just a new chicken dish, take it easy," but they don't want it. If you change a few items, it's okay, but I think sixty to seventy percent of the menu should stay.

Vong is my Asian fantasy. Again—you should let yourself go and have the tasting menu. Or have the Black Plate, which is a selection of five different appetizers for two people to share. Then choose your entrée, maybe the lobster Thai or the tamarind duck. When the restaurant first opened, it was kind of a beer place—we sold fifty wines and twenty beers—but now we sell two hundred wines and twelve beers. I think the first year of any restaurant is difficult. People want to put a label on a restaurant. When we first opened Vong, people would leave saying, "This is not Thai" or "This is not French." Well, it's not supposed to be! Now, though, it's just Vong.

Mercer Kitchen is much more casual, very Mediterranean, almost Italian. It's very different. So you can start with the salads or Alsatian tarte flambée and finish with a grilled lamb chop or braised short ribs. I think it is very homey, with the communal tables; it's like a party every night.

JEAN GEORGES
Trump International Hotel
1 Central Park West
New York, NY 10023
Phone: (212) 299-3900
Fax: (212) 299-3914

JO JO
160 E. 64th Street
New York, NY 10021
Phone: (212) 223-5656
Fax: (212) 755-9038

MERCER KITCHEN
Mercer Hotel
99 Prince Street (at Mercer)
New York, NY 10012
Phone: (212) 966-5454
Fax: (212) 965-3855

VONG
200 E. 54th Street
New York, NY 10022
Phone: (212) 486-9592
Fax: (212) 980-3745

"Jean-Georges Vongerichten's food reinforces the thinking that 'you don't have to make food complicated to make it great.' His presentations are simple and beautiful, and each flavor stands out."

DAVID HOLBEN
SEVENTEEN SEVENTEEN (DALLAS)

DA SILVANO

260 Avenue of the Americas (between Bleecker and Houston Streets), Manhattan (212) 982-2343

I love Da Silvano—that's my Sunday night choice for Italian. Silvano's a great friend of mine, and he's always very jovial. He's trained a lot of cooks. He's a cool guy, and the food is really Italian. It's just so simple and easy: spaghettini with arrabiata [spicy tomato sauce], whole artichokes, and antipasto. It feels and tastes like home.

GRAMERCY TAVERN

42 E. 20th Street (between Broadway and Park Avenue South), Manhattan (212) 477-0777

I love Gramercy Tavern. When I want gourmet food, or when I have people—chefs and friends from Europe—coming into town, I think it's a great place for Sunday nights [which tend to be chefs' most frequent nights off]. I like to go here to treat myself and my guests, and to see something dif-ferent. I love Tom Colicchio's food—it's amazing. I usually order the tast-ing menu. It changes about four times a year, with the seasons, and he has an excellent pastry chef, Claudia Fleming, too. (See also p. 184.)

INDOCHINE

430 Lafayette Street (between Astor Place and 4th Street), Manhattan (212) 505-5111

Indochine has been one of my fa-vorites since it opened. I go at least once a month. My girlfriend is Viet-namese—she craves Vietnamese food, and I do, too. I like all the summer rolls, and the steamed rice paper filled with ground veal, bean sprouts, and scallions. The sweet-and-sour soup made of tamarind, pineapple, and shrimp is delicious. They also have a wonderful lemongrass beef salad. They sear and slice the beef, then mix it with *nuoc mam* [fish sauce] and lemongrass. Delicious! I like that you wrap all your food with lettuce and coriander leaves.

NOBU

105 Hudson Street (at Franklin Street), Manhattan (212) 219-0500

I go to Nobu for inventive Japanese food and innovative sushi one Sunday a month—when they can take me, be-cause I never call in advance. I like the black cod with miso, and all their rolls are amazing, especially the soft-shell crab roll. One of my favorite dishes is the *tiradito*—usually they do it with very thinly sliced fluke and red chile purée. It's marinated in yuzu juice, and the sauce has no fat or oil. Then you wrap it in coriander leaf. It's the cleanest dish. I drink cold sake, then I go off to bed. It's not too much—it's a good Sunday night meal for me.

PHO BANG

Multiple locations, including: 117 Mott Street (between Broome and Grand Streets), Manhattan (212) 233-3947

I like to go to Pho Bang for simple Vietnamese food. By the end of the week, I'm tired of meals that consist of an appetizer, main course, and dessert. I don't want to look at a menu and choose all this stuff—just give me a bowl of spicy soup! That, I'll appreciate. Pho Bang has great *pho*, which is beef broth made with oxtail and spices—star anise, cinna-mon, lemongrass—to which they add rice noodles and very thinly sliced raw beef. They serve a little dish of bean sprouts and lime on the side, and you put everything in the bowl. You can play with it, adding chiles, lime juice, and/or hot sauce. It makes me sweat!

"Jean-Georges Vongerichten once served me a sea urchin soufflé with fennel. The dish was as incredi-ble as its presentation: Jean-Georges actually served the roe soufflé in the sea urchin itself, so it was kind of like eating an egg out of its shell. During this meal, I saw that first approach of modern cooking peeking its head through: the way things were pre-sented, his simple approach, and the direct flavors that are now his hallmark."

GARY DANKO

GARY DANKO (SAN FRANCISCO)

DAVID WALTUCK, who owns Chanterelle with his wife, Karen, and serves as its chef, earned a degree in biological oceanography before devoting himself to the culinary arts. Chanterelle has twice received four-star ratings from the *New York Times*. In 1996, Chanterelle won the James Beard Award for Outstanding Wine Service. In 2000, the restaurant received the James Beard Award for Outstanding Service.

MY FOOD We change our menu about every six weeks in order to keep it seasonal and fresh. I work with local farmers to obtain the freshest seasonal produce and the best sources of seafood and game. My technique remains classically French, but the flavors of my food have been influenced by my interest in other cultures. Some dishes we've featured include zucchini blossoms stuffed with lobster and shrimp, grilled seafood sausage in white butter sauce, and grilled rack of lamb with gingered eggplant confit.

David Waltuck

CHANTERELLE
2 Harrison Street
(at Hudson Street)
New York, NY 10013
Phone: (212) 966-6960
Fax: (212) 966-6143
www.chanterellenyc.com

LE ZINC
139 Duane Street
(between West Broadway and Church Street)
New York, NY 10013
Phone: (212) 513-0001

DAVID'S PICKS

BABBO
110 Waverly Place (between MacDougal Street and Avenue of the Americas), Manhattan
(212) 777-0303
We live right above Babbo, and if we have a date night out, that's usually where we'll go. We've actually been there more than anywhere else in the last year. I think it's a very well run place, and Mario Batali's food is very good. The staff is extremely knowledgeable about the food and the wine, and they are very enthusiastic about it. They're very good at informing you what everything is. The pastas and appetizers are great—they include such dishes as beef cheek ravioli with crushed squab livers, and steamed cockles in red chile and chive broth. The wine list is great, too—I don't know that much about Italian wine, but I always have something new and exciting when I go there. (See also p. 168.)

EJ'S LUNCHEONETTE
Multiple locations, including:
432 Avenue of the Americas (between 9th and 10th Streets), Manhattan
(212) 473-5555
EJ's Luncheonette isn't really all that exciting, but it's good and comfortable, and my kids like it. They have good burgers and sandwiches, and they do nice nightly specials, which are frequently variations on 1950s luncheonette themes. The chef does a really nice job. And it's not very expensive.

GOLDEN UNICORN
18 East Broadway (at Catherine Street), Manhattan (Chinatown)
(212) 941-0911

20 MOTT STREET RESTAURANT
20 Mott Street (between Bowery and Pell Streets), Manhattan (Chinatown)
(212) 964-0380
I really like Chinese food, and I like going to both of these restaurants for their good and inexpensive dim sum. Golden Unicorn opens at nine A.M. and serves Hong Kong–style [from carts pushed from table to table in its huge dining room] such dishes as *cheung fun*, which is rice noodle stuffed with shrimp. The other restaurant, 20 Mott Street, has three floors and serves such standard dishes as spring rolls, fried crab claws, and fish with black pepper sauce.

NATURAL RESTAURANT

88 Allen Street (at Grand Street),
Manhattan (212) 869-8335

This is probably the restaurant I go to most frequently. Two brothers cook there, and I know their father, who used to have a couple of restaurants in Chinatown. It's very homey; they probably have about eight tables. Their food is not anything very elaborate or fancy. They do pork chops with a sweet sauce that my kids like. I always get the salty fish fried rice, and they do a good steamed chicken with black mushrooms. They cook fish in any number of different, simple ways—for example, steamed with hot oil poured on at the last minute. It's very comfortable. There's nothing you've never heard of before, but the food is always very well done.

I'd asked the people at Natural many times to come eat at Chanterelle, and finally the whole family came in last year. I cooked a tasting menu for them, and I think they had a very good time, but I wouldn't let them pay, and they didn't quite know what to do. First they left an enormous cash tip, and then they walked around with little red envelopes full of money that they handed out to the staff. They probably ended up spending more money than they would have if I'd let them pay for the meal!

ZUTTO

77 Hudson Street (between Harrison and Jay Streets), Manhattan
(212) 233-3287

I just order sushi at Zutto, although they have other Japanese dishes. Sometimes they have fatty tuna, which I really like. My daughter eats sushi. She doesn't like anything too bizarre—she eats the rolls, like tuna, California, vegetable, and yellowtail chopped up with scallions. And she loves the dumplings.

sake to me!

AS AMERICAN CHEFS INCREASINGLY TURN TO THE FLAVORS OF ASIA TO inspire their palates, they're also becoming more interested in sake, the traditional Japanese rice wine. A number of fine-dining restaurants are adding premium sakes to their wine lists, from Charlie Trotter's in Chicago to Café Boulud in New York. Riedel, the celebrated manufacturer of fine crystal, recently added a sake glass to its exclusive line of glassware.

Hiromi Iuchi of the Sake Service Institute (Japan's sake exporting board) shared some of her knowledge of and passion for sake with us over glasses of sake at Chibi's Sake Bar (named for the dog of chef-owner Marja Samson, who also owns the Kitchen Club) and Sakagura, both in New York.

A great deal of the sake imported to the United States before 1997 was mishandled during shipping and storage. Sake requires refrigeration, and the lack of it led to a lot of inferior sake in this country. Now that transportation has improved, the United States is getting both better-quality sake and a greater variety of sakes. In Japan, there are over fifteen hundred sake producers.

Sake is made with rice and is classified in two major ways: according to the "polishing rate," or the percentage of the grain's protein and fat that has been removed to aid the process of fermentation as well as to enhance aroma and flavor; and whether or not alcohol has been added in the brewing process. (The term *junmai* means "pure rice," reflecting no added alcohol.)

There are subtle taste differences between sakes. While unpasteurized sakes are delicate and harder to transport and store, their taste tends to be softer and fresher. Pasteurized sakes tend to have a slightly sharper taste. Another distinction is whether the sake is filtered or unfiltered. Unfiltered sakes tend to look "milky." They are slightly heavier and a little harder to match with food. Hiromi recommends them as after-dinner sakes, suggesting they would be perfect with a creamy dessert, such as rice pudding, or a dessert served with whipped cream.

Aged sake is not yet found widely in the United States. Sake is aged in stainless steel and develops a more complex and fuller flavor through the aging process. It tends to take on characteristics of a sherry as it ages, becoming dry, with a slight sweetness in the finish.

DRINKING SAKE

Sake is served cold or warm. As it is refrigerated while transported and stored, sake's flavor changes when it is heated, which tends to make it milder and rounder. (Heating sakes with a polishing rate of 40 percent or higher is not recommended; typically, only ordinary sake, *honjozo*, or *junmai* are served heated.) It is important to heat sake delicately, such as by setting a bottle in a pot of hot water for about three minutes. When serving sake cold, a temperature of 40 to 45 degrees is ideal. If a premium sake such as a *daiginjo* is served too cold, the bouquet will be off and more difficult to smell.

One thing sake connoisseurs don't recommend is drinking premium sake out of a cedar box, the way some ordinary sakes are offered in some Japanese restaurants. While you may enjoy it if you like the taste of cedar, this serving presentation masks the flavor of the sake, believes Hiromi. The cedar box is used to measure rice and was probably a handy vessel for tasting and drinking. Sake is typically served in a three-ounce portion.

FOOD AND SAKE PAIRING

Sake lends itself well to a wider range of foods because, unlike wine, it can be paired with dishes that have a lot of acidity. Vinegar-based dishes do not offer a challenge, as sake stands up to vinegar. Sake also works especially well with fish, as the amino acid content masks any "fishiness" while bringing out the flavor of the fish. In fact, some people greatly prefer sake over Champagne with caviar and oysters, as there are no abrasive bubbles to fight.

Just as with wine, selecting the sake that provides the best match is more dependent on the sauce than on the protein (meat) used in the dish. While a ponzu sauce might pair best with a sake such as *ginjo* or *junmai ginjo*, a heavy steak sauce might call for an aged sake to stand up to the flavor.

When pairing premium sakes with foods, there are a few additional guidelines to keep in mind:

- **DAIGINJO AND JUNMAI DAIGINJO** (greater than 50 percent polished; typically mellow in flavor): Because of their strong aroma, which is very fruity or flowery, these sakes are best served as an aperitif, or with light dishes, such as soft-steamed vegetables and vegetable mousses, mild white fish (such as snapper), or tofu.

- **GINJO AND JUNMAI GINJO OR TOKUBETSU JUNMAI** (40 to 50 percent polished; typically medium in flavor): Because these sakes have lighter aromas, with light and smooth flavors, they pair well with a broader range of foods.

- **HONJOZO AND JUNMAI** (30 to 40 percent polished; typically sharp in flavor): These fuller-bodied sakes stand up well to creamy or buttery dishes, fried foods such as tempura, and stronger fish, including toro, tuna, and salmon.

- **AGED SAKES**, which are aged for three years or more in stainless steel, are more complicated in flavor, with a fuller, heavier mouth feel. They pair well with a surprising number of dishes, such as rich, strongly flavored meat courses, from foie gras to duck; fattier fish, such as salmon and eel; strongly flavored curries; cheeses, especially heavier cheeses such as blue and Camembert; and desserts or sweets, such as chocolate-covered strawberries.

"Why drink sake? There is a beautiful subtlety to its flavor—not to mention two thousand years of history in every sip!"

HIROMI IUCHI
SAKE SERVICE INSTITUTE

CHIBI'S SAKE BAR

(adjacent to the
Kitchen Club restaurant)
242 Mott Street (at Prince Street),
Manhattan
(212) 274-0025
Chibi's Sake Bar offers sixteen different sakes by the bottle or glass, as well
as Yufuin, a Japanese spirit.

SAKAGURA

211 E. 43rd Street
(near Second Avenue),
lower level, Manhattan
(212) 953-SAKE
Sakagura features more than two hundred different kinds of sake.

Marja Samson with her dog,
Chibi, at his namesake bar

"*I think sake has been so hugely popular here because it's a different realm you enter when you drink it. It's exciting for younger people to try because there's no 'snob appeal' tied up with it— everyone can be a connoisseur.*"

marja samson   CHIBI'S SAKE BAR

Craig Shelton

THE RYLAND INN
Route 22 West
P.O. Box 284
Whitehouse, New Jersey 08888
Phone: (908) 534-4011
Fax: (908) 534-6592
www.therylandinn.com

CRAIG SHELTON is executive chef-owner of The Ryland Inn. He won the 2000 James Beard Award as Best Chef: Mid-Atlantic. After receiving degrees in molecular biophysics and biochemistry from Yale University, Shelton devoted himself to the culinary arts—a stint as a dishwasher originally introduced him to the industry. He cooked at Ma Maison in Los Angeles with Gordon Hamersley, and spent time in France studying at Jamin with Joel Robuchon, and at L'Auberge de l'Ill. He also studied pastry at Lenôtre. In New York, he cooked at La Côte Basque and Le Bernardin before becoming chef de cuisine at Bouley, where he helped earn the restaurant four stars from the *New York Times*.

MY FOOD In New York, you go to a restaurant to be highly stimulated and have your mind blown. If we succeed here, it is because you walk away restored. Our country setting is perfect for that. You spend time in the country setting, and you feel a sense of peace. Our goal was to make the entire three-acre garden self-sufficient. We have five hundred different things growing here, all certified organic: two hundred herbs, two hundred vegetables, and one hundred lettuces. We also have our own well water and our own composting. We harvest food just before service each night and alter it as little as possible. Our cuisine shares the deep histories of France and America. We use the most delicate heat possible. Our ovens are set at three hundred degrees, not five hundred like most restaurant ovens. Our attitude is similar to that of Chez Panisse—that the star of the show should be the product. Or, as I was taught by Joel Robuchon, "It's about making a carrot taste like a great carrot."

"If I'm not drinking sake with sushi, I like Alsatian Riesling or Champagne, which absolutely works with sushi. My favorite nonvintage Champagne in the world is Billecart-Salmon—it's such a purist's Champagne, clean and crisp. We pour it by the glass at The Ryland Inn, and it is also dynamite with sushi."

CRAIG SHELTON

THE RYLAND INN

THE DINING ROOM AT THE HILTON AT SHORT HILLS

41 JFK Parkway, Short Hills
(973) 379-0100

The dining room here is small and wood-paneled. It's a nice, well-set-up space. The hotel has two restaurants, and in this one the chef does not have to worry about things like room service and banquets. It's a very protected and safe environment to cook in, one where the chef doesn't have to worry about paying the bills. It's a nice platform for a young chef, where he can make a name for himself. The chef is Jimmy Haurey, who was my second for a number of years. He is especially strong through the middle of the meal: the second through the sixth courses. His meat and fish preparations are strong, and based on solid classical foundations, but executed with a little bit of adventurousness.

RESTAURANT SERENADE

6 Roosevelt Avenue, Chatham
(973) 701-0303

This is probably the best food in the state, after The Ryland Inn. Chef James Laird was my sous chef for a long while. He worked in France, and also with David Burke [of New York's Park Avenue Cafe] and Gray Kunz [formerly of Lespinasse]. He has lots of integrity, and his food is very refined. It's great—from *canapés* to *petit fours*.

STAGE HOUSE INN

366 Park Avenue, Scotch Plains
(908) 322-4224

Chef David Drake originally made a name for himself at the Frog and the Peach, which was the first high-end restaurant in this area. He is self-taught, and he worked at The Ryland Inn for a while to refine his technique. This is the restaurant that probably most emulates our approach. They are not serving steaks and chops; they are trying to do something out of the ordinary in New Jersey, and Chef Drake is really thinking about food. The restaurant is similar to ours in that it is in an old house that has been converted to a restaurant and has lots of little rooms. They have a real commitment to quality, and you see it in the food. They also have a strong commitment to the wine program. Most of the sommeliers and maître d's have come from The Ryland Inn. In fact, almost half the staff can be from here at any given point. That could be said for a lot of restaurants out here, actually.

SHUMI JAPANESE RESTAURANT

30 Doughty Avenue, Somerville
(908) 526-8596

We take every chef who comes to visit us to Shumi, and they inevitably say it is among the best sushi they have had in their life. I've eaten sushi all over the country—including the famous places in New York, like Sushisay and Kuruma Zushi—and I don't think I've had any that has exceeded Shumi. It is my wife's favorite place in New Jersey, and I adore it. It is a tiny storefront in a working-class town. You just sit at the sushi bar and let the chef make things for you. I like to get sweet Maine shrimp, monkfish liver, or eel. His *sudomono*—a little salad with *bâtonnets* of monkfish liver or tuna—is phenomenal, and his fluke sashimi is one of my wife's favorites. His "Dangerous Roll" is not to be missed. He won't say what is in it, but it may include some fugu once in a while. The chef is also so much fun; he is charming, and will make you laugh. The price is about a third of what you would pay in New York, but the quality of the fish is the same.

STAGE LEFT

5 Livingston Avenue, New Brunswick
(732) 828-4444

This is the most urban restaurant, in that it is a storefront on a main street of a small town. They are very passionate about gastronomy and wine. The chef is Patrick Yves Pierre Jerome—he is one of the nicest people I have ever met. He cooks with his heart, and puts it on the plate.

"Philadelphia is a large city, but its distinctive neighborhoods give it the feel of a small town. Each neighborhood features its own ethnic grocery stores, bars, and restaurants. The Irish area is known as 'Two Street,' not Second Street. The Italian area is South Philly, and the Mexican/Puerto Rican area is known as the Barrio."

JIM COLEMAN   TREETOPS AT THE RITTENHOUSE HOTEL

BAKERY

L. SARCONE AND SON

758 S. 9th Street, Philadelphia
(215) 922-0445

"South Philadelphia's most famous bakery opens at seven-thirty A.M. and closes when the bread is gone."

—JIM COLEMAN, TREETOPS AT THE RITTENHOUSE HOTEL

COFFEE

LA COLOMBE TORREFACTION RESTAURANT AND COFFEEHOUSE

Multiple locations, including:
130 S. 19th Street (in Rittenhouse Square), Philadelphia
(215) 563-0860

"This is the place for coffee. They are actually a coffee-roasting company, and they supply the best restaurants in Philadelphia and New York, including Daniel and Jean Georges. For breakfast, I have a double espresso on ice and a croissant at their café."

—PHILIPPE CHIN, CHIN CHIN RESTAURANT AND BAR

"For cappuccino or espresso."

—JIM COLEMAN, TREETOPS AT THE RITTENHOUSE HOTEL

"There is no question—this is the best coffee in Philadelphia. I'll order a double espresso."

—JEAN-MARIE LACROIX, THE FOUNTAIN RESTAURANT

CRABS

BONK'S BAR

3467 Richmond Street, Philadelphia
(215) 634-9927

"This place is a dive in Port Richmond, which is not the best part of town, but their crabs are big and perfectly spiced. It's fun to go with a bunch of people and get a couple of pitchers of beer."

—PHILIPPE CHIN,
CHIN CHIN RESTAURANT AND BAR

GREEK

DMITRI'S

795 S. 3rd Street, Philadelphia
(215) 625-0556

"For simply prepared fish."

—JIM COLEMAN, TREETOPS AT THE
RITTENHOUSE HOTEL

HAMBURGER

SASSAFRAS INTERNATIONAL CAFÉ

48 S. 2nd Street, Philadelphia (215) 925-2317

"This small neighborhood bar has been around forever. They have a great burger with blue cheese on a kaiser roll."

—PHILIPPE CHIN, CHIN CHIN RESTAURANT AND BAR

MARKET

THE READING TERMINAL MARKET

12th and Arch Streets, Philadelphia (215) 592-9772

"You've got to get the fresh Amish pretzels [at Fisher's Soft Pretzels and Ice Cream, (215) 592-8510]. They're not too huge or thick, like other soft pretzels are—they're unbelievable. I like them with mustard, steaming hot. There are two great cheese steak places [Rick's Philly Steaks, (215) 925-4320, and Sandwich Stand, (215) 625-0489] in there, too, and a great Mexican place [12th Street Cantina, (215) 625-0321]. In fact, when we have to find something unusual, we normally end up buying it at the Cantina in the Reading Terminal Market. There's a good small sushi place [Tokyo Sushi Bar, (215) 440-7970], and there are great seafood and crab cakes places [such as Kim's Seafood, (215) 925-9028, and Pearl's Oyster Bar, (215) 627-7250]. It's fun to bring people from out of town here because you can get a bunch of different things."

—JIM COLEMAN, TREETOPS AT THE RITTENHOUSE HOTEL

"I could spend a whole Saturday morning here! There are lots of different stands, selling everything from oysters to lobsters to Amish pretzels, plus the best hoagies [such as at Rocco's Famous Italian Hoagies, (215) 238-1223, and Salumeria, (215) 592-8150]."

—JEAN-MARIE LACROIX, THE FOUNTAIN RESTAURANT

HOAGIES

SHANK & EVELYN'S LUNCHEONETTE

932 S. 10th Street, Philadelphia
(215) 629-1093

"Shank's has a meatball sandwich with big ol' slivers of garlic in the meatballs—it's unbelievable!"

—JIM COLEMAN, TREETOPS AT THE RITTENHOUSE HOTEL

NICK'S ROAST BEEF

16 S. 2nd Street, Philadelphia
(215) 928-9411

"Nick's is a roast beef place, and that's all they serve: roast beef sandwiches. You eat one, it's like a Quaalude—you can't eat anything else for the rest of the day, and you have to go take a nap. There are guys playing pinochle in the front, and you can't sit in one of those chairs, because they have been there for years. One time I asked for the recipe, and they yelled at me, 'Get outta here!' That's South Philly."

—JIM COLEMAN, TREETOPS AT THE RITTENHOUSE HOTEL

PIZZA

PIETRO'S COAL OVEN PIZZERIA

1714 Walnut Street, Philadelphia
(215) 735-8090

"They make thin-crust pizza that cooks real fast. When I think pizza, I think beer, so I have a couple of beers to go with it."

—PHILIPPE CHIN,
CHIN CHIN RESTAURANT AND BAR

TACCONELLI'S PIZZA

2604 E. Somerset Street (between Almond and Thompson), Philadelphia
(215) 425-4983

"You have to order your dough in the morning and then you pick your pie up that night. It's unbeliev-able. If you don't preorder, you don't get any pie. It's all good, they use all kinds of homemade sausages—it's quality stuff. It's BYOB and it's packed. You've got to go way ahead of time, but it's worth it. They don't call it 'pizza,' they call it 'pie'—so don't order a pizza."

—JIM COLEMAN, TREETOPS AT
THE RITTENHOUSE HOTEL

"Tacconelli's pizza is excellent!"

—JEAN-MARIE LACROIX,
THE FOUNTAIN RESTAURANT

PUB

BARD'S

2013 Walnut Street, Philadelphia (215) 569-9585

"Bard's is a great Irish pub, and happens to be right next to a place called the Irish Pub, which attracts a somewhat younger clientele. You can find three or four Irish beers on draft."

—JIM COLEMAN, TREETOPS AT THE RITTENHOUSE HOTEL

STEAKS

MORTON'S OF CHICAGO

1411 Walnut Street, Philadelphia (215) 557-0724

THE PRIME RIB

1701 Locust Street, Philadelphia (215) 772-1701

RUTH'S CHRIS

260 S. Broad Street, Philadelphia (215) 790-1515

"They are all good, and the owners and maître d's are all friends of mine. Sometimes after work I walk over to the Prime Rib and have a glass of Cabernet and a steak. I like the rib eye, because I like a little fat on my steak. But I won't touch a filet mignon!"

—PHILIPPE CHIN, CHIN CHIN RESTAURANT AND BAR

SWEETS

ROSE TATTOO CAFÉ

1847 Callowhill Street (at 19th Street), Philadelphia (215) 569-8939

"I don't have a big sweet tooth, but my daughter does. The Rose Tattoo has all kinds of fantastic desserts—pies and huge cakes. It's really, really good."

—JIM COLEMAN, TREETOPS AT THE RITTENHOUSE HOTEL

PHILADELPHIA
LOCAL HIGHLIGHTS

A WOrD ABOUT

Philadelphia Cheese Steaks

GENO'S STEAKS

1219 S. 9th Street (at Wharton Street),
Philadelphia
(215) 389-0659

PAT'S KING OF STEAKS

1237 E. Passyunk Avenue (at 9th Street),
Philadelphia
(215) 468-1546

JIM COLEMAN, TREETOPS AT THE RITTENHOUSE HOTEL

"Cheese steaks are kind of a touristy thing. It's fun to get them when other chefs come into town. But there is something about a cheese steak late at night or very early in the day. If you have drinks the night before, or if you're looking for something to eat at four-thirty A.M., they actually taste pretty good. You have to know how to order them. I like them 'provolone with.' 'With' means 'with peppers and onions.' But you don't say 'with peppers and onions.' They made fun of me the first time I ordered it that way. If you just say 'cheese steak,' you get Cheez Whiz and meat, and if you say 'cheese steak with,' you get onions, peppers, Cheez Whiz, and meat. So if you say 'provolone with,' you get provolone instead of the Cheez Whiz, plus you get the peppers and onions. There's Pat's and there's Geno's; they are right beside each other, and sometimes one tastes better than the other. I can't figure out which is better, so you just go back and forth. They're open twenty-four hours a day, almost every day of the year."

PHILIPPE CHIN, CHIN CHIN RESTAURANT AND BAR

"I am not a big fan of cheese steaks, but for me it is more about the place itself than the actual cheese steak. It's always fun to go to Geno's at three A.M. It is in the heart of South Philly and it's a scene. You see everyone in there, from the kids coming out of nightclubs to the old South Philly mafiosos, and people are screaming from one end of a table to the other. And everyone is having a ball!"

JEAN-MARIE LACROIX, THE FOUNTAIN RESTAURANT

"I have my own 'cheese steak' sandwich on the Fountain's menu, made with sirloin, provolone cheese, mushrooms, and peppers on French bread. But I won't tell you what I charge for it!"

NORMAN VAN AKEN, NORMAN'S (CORAL GABLES, FL)

"When you're in Philadelphia, you've got to go to Pat's for a cheese steak!"

PHILIPPE CHIN is chef-owner of Chin Chin Restaurant and Bar. He has been nominated for a James Beard Award as Best Chef: Mid-Atlantic, and in 1997 he became the youngest chef in the world to be inducted into the Maîtres Cuisiniers de France. His unique French-Asian fare has received accolades in *Gourmet*, *Philadelphia*, and *Travel & Leisure*, as well as the *Wine Spectator*'s Award of Excellence.

Philippe Chin

CHIN CHIN RESTAURANT AND BAR

1614 Locust Street (between South 16th and 17th Streets)
Philadelphia, PA 19103
Phone: (215) 735-7551
Fax: (215) 735-7609
www.philippeonlocust.com

MY FOOD I am French-Chinese, and that is reflected on the plate—my style of food is much like me. It is classic French training and technique, with Asian ingredients. My father was a great cook and always told me, "First, you eat with your eyes." I like very clean and vibrant presentation, and I like the combination of French and Asian because I think they are the two best cuisines in the world. The French classic techniques were the best ever invented, and they have been used in so many cuisines ever since. Chinese cuisine is so old, and yet the taste is so fresh and different. I have been doing this style of cuisine for ten years, and ten years ago no one had even heard of ponzu [the savory citrus-, soy- and vinegar-based Japanese dipping sauce]. People are now so familiar with Asian ingredients that it is no longer a novelty. They used to know what soy sauce was, but not tofu or rice vinegar or kaffir lime leaves. Now they know what wasabi tastes like.

PHILIPPE'S PICKS

BISTRO ST. TROPEZ

2400 Market Street, Fourth Floor, Philadelphia
(215) 569-9269

This is a down-home French bistro, and it's one of the only restaurants around that brings me back to France! I especially like their cassoulet. It is also one of the places where I wish I could go more often. When you work six or seven nights a week, though, it is hard to go everywhere you want as often as you'd like! (See also p. 218.)

CENT'ANNI

770 S. 7th Street, Philadelphia
(215) 925-5558

After being around fine dining all the time, it is very refreshing to go to a place where I can wear jeans and a T-shirt and just relax. This is a little hole-in-the-wall trattoria that I go to very often. The food is always fresh, and the people are very friendly. They do a great spaghetti carbonara and a classic tortellini with alfredo sauce. They have great roasted peppers, olive oil, and a bottle of Chianti on each table. It is such a down-to-earth restaurant, and I like that about it.

THE FOUNTAIN RESTAURANT

1 Logan Square (in the Four Seasons Hotel), Philadelphia
(215) 963-1500

This is where I go for fine dining or special occasions. Jean-Marie Lacroix is a fantastic man and great chef, period. He uses ingredients from around the world and pairs that with his French training. You might start with a scallop in a classic nage, then have foie gras with mango and ginger. When I go there, my fiancée and I eat everything, so it is always a great dining experience, from A to Z. They also have a giant cheese cart, with twenty-five different cheeses. (See also p. 218.)

SHANK & EVELYN'S LUNCHEONETTE

932 S. 10th Street, Philadelphia
(215) 629-1093

When I want a great sandwich for lunch, I'll go to Shank & Evelyn's. It is a tiny Italian place with maybe twenty seats. They also have great roast pork with broccoli rabe, and a delicious chicken Parmesan, in addition to other great Italian stuff. (See also p. 212.)

VIETNAM

221 N. 11th Street (at Race Street),
Philadelphia
(215) 592-1163

This is the best Vietnamese restaurant in town. It is owned by a family who all help run the place. It's down-to-earth, straightforward food that's always fresh, flavorful, and great. If there are three or four of us, I like to order about ten appetizers and then three entrées. I always get the spring rolls. I love the Vietnamese version of carpaccio, marinated in lime with Thai basil, peanuts, carrots, and daikon. The Vietnamese-style beef jerky with thin shredded papaya salad and fish sauce is an absolute winner. Also, the grilled squid with lemongrass is always refreshing.

PHILIPPE CHIN ON
Cheese

My favorite of all the blues is Roquefort. For a creamy cheese, like a triple cream, it would be Explorateur or St. André. For a washed-rind cheese, a Pouillac or a Livarot. Gorgonzola is a great Italian cheese. I love any goat cheese, in any form, in any way—from Coach Farm to Montrachet.

I think you should have a great, strong wine with cheese, like a big Cabernet. I disagree with the pairing of cheese and port, unless you're having a blue cheese. Unfortunately, no wine is very good with goat cheese, because goat cheese is very acidic. The first sip of wine after the goat cheese will be very harsh on the tongue, so I recommend eating something before you taste the wine. Because of that, I typically start with the goat cheese, then work my way to the triple cream—that and a good glass of Cabernet, and I'm all set!

TREETOPS AT THE RITTENHOUSE HOTEL

210 W. Rittenhouse Square
Philadelphia, PA 19103
Phone: (215) 546-9000
Fax: (215) 546-9858

Jim Coleman

JIM COLEMAN is executive chef of the Ritten-house Hotel, which includes Treetops Restaurant, Boathouse Bar, and Cassatt Tea Lounge. He hosts the weekly radio show *A Chef's Table* on public radio and the television series *Flavors of America* on public television. He is the author of *The Rittenhouse Cookbook: A Year of Seasonal Heart-Healthy Recipes* and *Flavors of America*.

MY FOOD At Treetops, we specialize in regional American cuisine, with an emphasis on seasonal ingredients. Boathouse Bar features typical American bar food in a fun, relaxed atmosphere. Cassatt serves afternoon tea and is consistently rated one of the top tea services in town.

JIM'S PICKS

DOCK STREET BRASSERIE

2 Logan Square (at 18th Street),
Philadelphia
(215) 496-0413

For casual dining, we go over to Dock Street. Olivier St. Martin is a great chef and does bistro-type food. It's a really good place to stop in for a quick bite. I love his cassoulet, and I love his sweetbreads. He presses them down to where they're real thick and then gets them nice and crispy, and he's served them with everything, from a traditional brown butter sauce to a salad tossed with a warm vinaigrette, and he does a nice red-wine reduction. They have a full liquor license, which is good, because I'm not always in the mood for a beer. I'm a big wine drinker.

FELICIA'S

1148 S. 11th Street (at Annin Street),
South Philadelphia
(215) 755-9656

Felicia's is an Italian restaurant that has the best gnocchi—their gnocchi are so light, they're like little pillows. Gnocchi is a special, not a menu item, and they change their presentation regularly. Normally, the sauces are pretty light, because the gnocchi's so light. It is unbelievable—it just dissolves in your mouth. They have other things on the menu, but we're in a rut—we just order the gnocchi every time we go. My son is a gnocchi fanatic. We all went to Italy and he ate gnocchi everywhere we went, but Felicia's is still the best. We get antipasto for the table, and my wife will get some salad and order roasted peppers or other small plates to start out with. It's not fancy, but it's really good. The whole south Philly area is great for delicious, hole-in-the-wall Italian places.

FRANKIE'S SEAFOOD ITALIANO

1100 Tasker Street (at 11th Street),
Philadelphia
(215) 468-9989

All they do at Frankie's is Italian seafood, and it's great. It takes all night to eat here because he doesn't start to cook anything until you order it. I love baccalà [salt cod], and he always has it on the menu in the late fall and winter. He'll do it a bunch of different ways—sometimes he'll pan-roast it and stew it with tomatoes, olives, and onions. It's really good. He does crabmeat stuff, and grilled baby squid. It's all fantastic, but it takes forever, so don't plan to have dinner here before a movie.

GENJI JAPANESE RESTAURANT

1720 Sansome Street (at 17th Street),
Philadelphia
(215) 564-1720

I go to Genji quite a bit, because they've got fantastic sushi. During the season, I love their soft-shell crab rolls and spider rolls. I try not to eat too much raw stuff because I know it's not the greatest thing in the world for you, but I love the spicy tuna here, as well as their tuna rolls. They make really, really good tempura shrimp. I like to drink Japanese beer—like a Kirin—when I'm here. My daughter and son love the California rolls. My daughter's a teenager now, but when Katie was in first grade, her teacher had all the students stand up and tell everyone their name and their favorite food, to sort of break the ice. They got to Katie, who said, "I like caviar and sushi." The teacher was like, "Who are you?"

SOM SAK

Multiple locations, including:
2442 Route 38, Cherry Hill, NJ
(just outside Philadelphia)
(856) 482-0377
200 White Horse Pike, Voorhees, NJ
(856) 782-1771

This is a great Thai place. All of their food is unbelievable—the *pad thai* and all the variations on it. All their fried dishes are really light. Their duck is wonderful—they serve it really crispy, and we get it with baby bok choy and water chestnuts. The best thing to order, though, is one of the whole crispy fish. The chef goes to the market and gets five fish every day. If you want one of them, you have to get there early or call to tell them you want it, because after seven-thirty, they're gone.

Jean-Marie Lacroix

THE FOUNTAIN RESTAURANT (AT THE FOUR SEASONS HOTEL)
1 Logan Square
Philadelphia, PA 19103
Phone: (215) 963-1500
Fax: (215) 963-2748
www.fourseasons.com

Jean-Marie Lacroix is executive chef of the Four Seasons Hotel in Philadelphia, where The Fountain Restaurant is located. The restaurant has been recognized as one of the Top Twenty-five Restaurants in America by *Food & Wine* magazine. In 1998, he received the Robert Mondavi Award for Culinary Excellence, and in 1999 he was nominated for the James Beard Award as Best Chef: Mid-Atlantic.

MY FOOD I serve French-influenced cuisine that is oriented to the market and to local and regional produce. One of our signature dishes is a potato risotto with tuna carpaccio, topped with a little caviar. We put more emphasis on the taste of the food than on presentation or anything else. If I could say anything to someone dining here for the first time, it would be, "Trust me! And I will take care of you." The best compliment I ever received as a hotel chef was from a guest who said they thought of the Fountain as "a restaurant with rooms on top"! Philadelphia is a big city with a small group of restaurateurs. If I go out, it will be very simple, typically a brasserie or bistro.

JEAN-MARIE'S PICKS

BISTRO ST. TROPEZ

2400 Market Street, Fourth Floor, Philadelphia
(215) 569-9269

Eating at Bistro St. Tropez is always very nice—if you can find it! It's on the fourth floor of the building, with a great view of the river and the train station. Chef Patrice Rames is from St. Tropez, in the south of France, and if you like French home cooking with some style—anything from a cassoulet to grilled fish—you'll like this place. (See also p. 215.)

BLUE ANGEL

706 Chestnut Street, Philadelphia
(215) 925-6889

Blue Angel is a new brasserie I really like that is along the same lines of Balthazar in New York. It is a little different, with fin-de-siècle décor, a zinc bar imported from France, and a blue glass mosaic ceiling, but the feel is the same. They serve classic French bistro food, such as cassoulet; I like to go for steak frites, but the snails and the bouillabaisse are excellent, too.

BRASSERIE PERRIER

1619 Walnut Street (between 16th and 17th Streets), Philadelphia
(215) 568-3000

The former chef here, Francesco Martorella, used to work with me, and I love his cooking—it has a little Italian influence, and he makes great pasta. His mother is a terrific cook—I think everyone should be influenced by their background and where they came from. You need to stay with your roots and yet still change and adapt a little bit. I still like to go here, and to let the chef [now Chris Scarduzio] choose a menu of three or four courses for me.

jean-marie's PICKS

DMITRI'S

795 S. 3rd Street (near Catharine Street), Philadelphia
(215) 625-0556

The cooking at Dmitri's, which is owned by Dmitri Chimes, is very simple Mediterranean, offering a large variety of fish and other specialties, from octopus to hummus, from around Greece, Italy, and the rest of the Mediterranean. Everything is made with very fresh ingredients. I'll always order simple grilled fish, and it will be perfect.

Note: This small restaurant doesn't take reservations, and doesn't have a liquor license, so bring your own wine.

ROUGE

205 S. 18th Street (near Walnut Street), Philadelphia
(215) 732-6622

Rouge is a little bit of Paris in Philadelphia, right on Rittenhouse Square. They don't take reservations, but if you can get a table, it is nice to sit and enjoy the view and watch the people going by. The restaurant does a really good job with French classics such as oysters, hamburgers with caramelized onions, roast chicken, and steak frites, and it's reasonably priced.

STRIPED BASS

1500 Walnut Street (at 15th Street), Philadelphia
(215) 732-4444

Striped Bass is very beautiful. I go because I like the room, and I always enjoy the fish there. Yes, cooking is always important and it has to be good, but I do enjoy décor. It is a package—food, service, and ambiance—and Striped Bass does a good job with all of them. The building used to be a bank, and the designer managed to add to the décor, not change it. I like to go there for oysters with a little bit of caviar on top. I like to get Belon oysters or East Coast oysters like Malpeques. To drink? Champagne, of course—and preferably Piper-Heidsieck or Krug!

SPICY

LOS DOS MOLINOS

8646 S. Central Avenue, Phoenix
(602) 243-9113

"If you can handle spicy food, head straight to Los Dos Molinos. This place is really like walking into a party! No one visiting Phoenix should miss it."

—CHRISTOPHER GROSS, CHRISTOPHER'S

"This is the place I want to go every time I'm in Phoenix!"

—NORMAN VAN AKEN, NORMAN'S (CORAL GABLES, FL)

Chris Bianco

PIZZERIA BIANCO
623 E. Adams Street
Phoenix, AZ 85004
Phone: (602) 258-8300

BAR BIANCO
609 E. Adams Street
Phoenix, AZ 85004
Phone: (602) 528-3699

CHRIS BIANCO is chef-owner of Pizzeria Bianco, which earned a 29 food rating (out of 30) in the 2000 Phoenix *ZagatSurvey*. The *Arizona Republic* named it for Best Pizza in 2000 and Best Italian Restaurant in 1996. In the 1999 *Gourmet* readers' poll, Pizzeria Bianco was voted the number-one restaurant for food in the Phoenix/Scottsdale area. In 2000, Bianco was nominated for the 2000 James Beard Award as Best Chef: Southwest.

MY FOOD My mom and my aunts were great cooks, so I appreciated good cooking from a very early age. I think the key is definitely to start with the right ingredients. For my food, I use local, organic produce and home-made mozzarella.

CHRIS'S PICKS

BARMOUCHE

3131 E. Camelback Road, Phoenix
(602) 956-6900

Chef Mark Tarbell's restaurant has a late-night bar with a dark, sophisticated interior that serves an upscale European/bistro menu until midnight. I love the look of the bar, and I like the music they play late at night. I can always count on some Miles Davis or John Coltrane. This, along with their perfect french fries and BLT made with local tomatoes and English bacon, is the kind of experience I want at midnight.

LECCABAFFI

9719 N. Hayden Road, Scottsdale
(480) 609-0429

The name means "lick the mustache." The chef is Giovanni Scorzo, and I think his food is so authentic that sometimes it can intimidate the average diner. He will offer lamb's brains, but he has a hard time getting people to order it. He might serve beautiful mussels with white wine, but then people will ask for some cheese on the side, and he'll go berserk! There are some Italian chefs who acquiesce to their customers instead of serving authentic, classic dishes. I think Leccabaffi is doing the latter. I had dinner there the other night, and had an earthy and simple gnocchetti with rapini and home-made sausage that was amazing. (See also p. 222.)

RANCHO PINOT GRILL

6208 N. Scottsdale Road, Scottsdale
(480) 367-8030

If anything is not perfectly right, chef Chrysa Kaufman will not serve it. She uses products of great integrity in her new American cuisine. Ninety percent of the produce she uses is organic and locally grown. I could see her throwing a plate across the room because it was not right. I think she does an especially good job with the vegetable dishes on her menu, and I am not even a vegetarian!

RESTAURANT HAPA

6204 N. Scottsdale Road, Scottsdale
(480) 998-8220

Hapa is a great new restaurant that combines contemporary American cuisine with Asian ingredients and techniques. James McDevitt, the chef, who is half Japanese and half American (the word *hapa* is slang for "mixed ancestry" in Hawaii, where he was born), was recognized as one of the country's best new chefs in *Food & Wine* magazine, and his palate is excellent. His wife, Stacey, serves as the restaurant's pastry chef. He does some inspiring dishes, all simply presented. Everything really stands on its own, like his grilled halibut with greens, soy, and ginger.

RITO'S MARKET AND MEXICAN TAKE-OUT

907 North 14th Street, Phoenix
(602) 262-9842

This is a little family-owned Mexican take-out restaurant that has been around for about twenty-five years. There is no sign in the front, so you could drive by it a thousand times and never see it. It is not in the best part of town. But the food is so sincere. They do the simplest green chile burrito that just has beef and green chiles—no cheese or sour cream, no crap. You order from behind a metal grate, then pick up your food in another place. The burritos are really skinny; you order six of them, and they come in half of a soda box. There are some picnic tables outside where you can eat, washing your burritos down with a can of Fanta or Coke.

CHRISTOPHER'S FERMIER BRASSERIE

Biltmore Fashion Park
2584 E. Camelback Road
Phoenix, AZ 85016
Phone: (602) 522-2344
Fax: (602) 468-0314
www.fermier.com

CHRISTOPHER GROSS is chef-owner of Christopher's Fermier Brasserie. *Travel & Leisure* magazine called Gross "a true master of the kitchen arts." He won the 1995 James Beard Award as Best Chef: Southwest, and the 1997 Robert Mondavi Culinary Award of Excellence. Christopher was also named one of America's Ten Best New Chefs by *Food & Wine* magazine. He was the founding chairman of the American Institute of Wine and Food's Arizona chapter.

MY FOOD My cuisine is dedicated to our local and regional farmers. My dishes are French-inspired, but designed to accent the natural flavors of the food itself. At Christopher's Fermier Brasserie, we have a brewery upstairs, and a wood-burning oven, and we offer dishes ranging from hamburgers to foie gras. It's a good mix of formal and casual.

CHRISTOPHER'S PICKS

BISTRO 24 AT THE RITZ-CARLTON HOTEL

2401 E. Camelback Road, Phoenix
(602) 952-2424

Bistro 24 is a conceptual change for a Ritz-Carlton. It doesn't look like any of their other restaurants; it looks like a nice brasserie. They do a great job, especially at breakfast. I like to get a basket of all the different breads, including pain au chocolat and croissants. They make a good cappuccino and double espresso, which you can't get in a diner for breakfast. They also have good traditional egg dishes and a really good duck hash. It is a very nice setting, yet happily it's not terribly expensive.

CHINA CHILI

3501 N. Central Avenue, Phoenix
(602) 266-4463

I just got back from China, and I think I prefer the Chinese food at this restaurant. The food quality is really good out here, while I found most Chinese food in China a little boring, where they use the same chopped-up vegetables for every dish. Yet at this place, all the dishes are different, and all the flavors are vibrant. One of my favorite dishes here is the Szechuan pork.

DUCK & DECANTER

Multiple locations, including:
1651 E. Camelback Road, Phoenix
(602) 274-5429
3111 N. Central Avenue, Phoenix
(602) 234-3656

We like to go here on Sundays. It is not really a restaurant; it's a gourmet store that sells all kinds of cheeses, salamis, salads, and sandwiches, and has tables inside and outside for enjoying their food and wine. It also has a retail wine department, so you can get a big plate of cheese and a nice bottle of wine and consume it there. What usually happens is that you drink your first bottle of wine, then someone you know comes in and they buy some wine, then you buy some more wine—and you are there for four hours! It is a simple, casual place with a park-like setting, even though it is in the center of the city.

LECCABAFFI

9719 N. Hayden Road, Scottsdale
(480) 609-0429

This is one of the best Italian restaurants in Phoenix. We were in Florence a couple of years ago and fell in love with the simplicity of the food; this restaurant is like that. Any of Giovanni Scorzo's new dishes are great, and he changes the menu pretty often. He has a polenta that is like a flan, the texture is so smooth. His breads are also good, and he uses a really high-quality olive oil. (See also p. 221.)

LOS DOS MOLINOS

8646 S. Central Avenue, Phoenix
(602) 243-9113

We really like this family-run restaurant a lot. The chef is Victoria Chavez, who is about sixty-five going on eighteen. I don't know where she gets her energy! She works her butt off. The food is New Mexican–style, meaning it is really hot. When a wine drinker's palate is fatigued, he drinks a good beer. For me, this restaurant serves the same function as that beer: it resets my palate. We like to order the *carne adovado* [stewed meat] and the *machaca* [Mexican jerky] pizza. Then, to get the heat out of our mouths, we have a *sopapilla* [fried dough] with honey and powdered sugar. It is sort of a Sunday restaurant, because if you go in the afternoon, you are totaled for the rest of the day. (See also p. 220.)

Brewery

MCMENAMINS PUB

Multiple locations, including:
McMenamins on Broadway
1504 NE Broadway, Suite 900, Portland
(503) 288-9498
McMenamins Kennedy School
5736 NE 33rd, Portland
(503) 249-3983

"They own about thirty-five pubs. They acquire old real estate and rehab it—they've even redone an old public school. They don't focus on the food, but the beer is really really good, and it's all made here."

—CORY SCHREIBER, WILDWOOD RESTAURANT AND BAR

BRIDGEPORT BREW PUB

1313 NW Marshall Street, Portland
(503) 241-7179

"The BridgePort Brew Pub is unique and quintessentially Portland. It's a no-frills place in an old ivy-covered building. They just serve beer and pizza. There isn't a beer place that really focuses on food—it's about the beer."

—CAPRIAL PENCE, CAPRIAL'S BISTRO AND WINE

Hamburgers

STANICH'S WEST

5627 SW Kelly, Portland
(503) 246-5040

"This place has been around forever, and their burgers are big and sloppy. It is divey, and one of their specialties is a burger with a fried egg and all the garnishes on top. Talk about cholesterol!"

—CAPRIAL PENCE, CAPRIAL'S BISTRO AND WINE

MCMENAMINS PUB

Multiple locations, including:
McMenamins Tavern and Pool
1716 NW 23rd Avenue, Portland
(503) 227-0929

"If I want really good fries, this is where I go. They hand-cut them here."

—CAPRIAL PENCE, CAPRIAL'S BISTRO AND WINE

CAPRIAL'S BISTRO AND WINE

7015 SE Milwaukie Avenue
(at Bybee Boulevard)
Portland, OR 97202
Phone: (503) 236-6457
Fax: (503) 238-8554
www.caprial.com

caprial pence is chef-owner of Caprial's Bistro and Wine. She won the 1991 James Beard Award as Best Chef: Northwest, and received a 1994 Beard Award nomination for her first cooking show, *Caprial's Café*. She is also the author of six cookbooks, including *Caprial Cooks for Friends* and *Caprial's Bistro Style Cuisine*.

MY FOOD I would never say our food is delicate or pretty. It is a more in-your-face kind of food. I love hearing people say "I can't decide" as opposed to "I guess I'll have …" We cook what we enjoy, hoping everyone else will like it, too. We try to use as much local product as we can. We enjoy other cultures, and we express that on our menu in an eclectic way, incorporating Asian, Indian, and Mediterranean influences. The restaurant started as a retirement project for my husband, John, and me. We wanted a little neighborhood bistro with a chalkboard menu. Then the TV show [*Caprial's Café*, which aired on the Learning Channel, and now *Caprial Cooking for Friends*, which airs on public television] moved us into a place we did not intend. It's evolved quite a bit, and I think that's a good thing.

CAPRIAL'S PICKS

LA IGUANA FELIZ

10834 NE Sandy Boulevard, Portland
(503) 257-0342
This is a funky place on the outskirts of town. It is near the airport, so whenever my husband picks me up, we go there. Nobody speaks English—the menu is in Spanish, and the food is not like you would get in a typical Mexican-American restaurant. It is very fresh and not too heavy. They make the best burritos—they are not overly stuffed with beans and things. Their braised chicken is so good, and they wrap it inside tortillas and serve avocados and stuff on the side. They have this chili sauce that is so good, I swear, I could drink it! It is kind of vinegary and sweet, and made with fresh limes.

LEGIN

8001 SE Division Street, Portland
(503) 777-2823
Legin is a great Chinese restaurant for dim sum, which is one of my favorite things to eat. They are considered to have the largest selection of dim sum in Portland, so at the end of the meal, our dim sum card always looks like a bowling score sheet—they can never believe how much we eat! We also go here for dinner, because our kids like it. My daughter loves the salt-and-pepper squid, and my son likes the crispy chicken. They both like dumplings, which is a taste they must get from me!

LEMONGRASS

1705 NE Couch Street, Portland
(503) 231-5780
In Portland, there is a Thai restaurant and an espresso bar on every corner. Shelly Siripatrapa, the chef at Lemongrass, is very good. She brings her food to a different level. She makes traditional Thai dishes, including curries, but they taste different from anyone else's because they are done so well. She does a beautiful coconut soup with either shrimp or chicken. The layers of flavors are amazing. My husband likes food spicier than I do, so we always compromise.

CAPRIAL'S PICKS

NICHOLAS RESTAURANT

318 SE Grand Avenue (at Pine Street), Portland
(503) 235-5123

We go to this tiny and simple Middle Eastern restaurant for mezze. For about four dollars, you get to choose five different things, and they have meat, vegetarian, and vegan options available—including falafel, grape leaves, hummus, and lentils. Everything is very fresh and made on the premises. They have about ten tables, and you can watch them make their own pita in their ancient oven. They also make terrific Lebanese thin-crust pizzas. We go a lot, because it is so good and cheap.

WILDWOOD RESTAURANT AND BAR

1221 NW 21st Avenue, Portland
(503) 248-9663

We like to go to Cory Schreiber's place if we want something nice or are eating out with another couple. He does lots of things with local ingredients such as mussels and oysters, like we do. The food is always very good. Sometimes we also like to go here just to have drinks and snacks—crab cakes, hamburgers, pizza—at the bar. (See below.)

CORY SCHREIBER is chef-owner of Wildwood Restaurant and Bar. His culinary training includes stints cooking with Lydia Shire and Bradley Ogden. He won the 1998 James Beard Award for Best Chef: Northwest, and is the author of *Wildwood: Cooking from the Source in the Pacific Northwest.*

Cory Schreiber

WILDWOOD RESTAURANT AND BAR

1221 NW 21st Avenue
Portland, OR 97209
Phone: (503) 248-9663
Fax: (503) 225-0030
www.wildwoodrestaurant.
citysearch.com

MY FOOD Portland, and in fact the Pacific Northwest in general, is a very product-conscious market, where chefs look to the farms and the food producers for inspiration for their menus, including such products as local romaine, Pacific shellfish, Washington mussels, and Yamhill County pork. We certainly do the same. Portland is not as competitive as larger cities, so chefs can spend more time focusing on their relationships with customers and purveyors and paying extra attention to the quality of the food. We don't have to be overly concerned about our independent food styles standing out from the restaurant's down the street. Basically, I think the philosophy is this: Let the product speak for itself. Those who handle it in the simplest manner will benefit most.

CAFÉ AZUL

112 NW Ninth Avenue, Portland
(503) 525-4422

Claire Archibold and her sister run Café Azul. Claire's a little bit like Rick Bayless [of Frontera Grill in Chicago] in that she spent six or seven years working in Mexico's Oaxaca region and is now bringing those authentic flavors to Portland. She's also a Chez Panisse alumna, so she has a real understanding of local products and melds the two in dishes like Oregon Chinook salmon roasted in corn husks. I like to have appetizers at their bar. It's a very simple environment, but they do a great job with their handmade tortillas, salsas, and shrimp ceviche.

FULLER'S RESTAURANT

136 NW Ninth Avenue, Portland
(503) 222-5608

This is one of the places I like in the Pearl District—it used to be an industrial area, but now it's a trendy retail district with galleries, shops, and restaurants in the historic buildings. Fuller's was founded in the 1940s and has been in its current site since 1960. It's a great place for breakfast and lunch—you sit on stools at the counter. Their French toast and their omelets are stand-outs. You get a little more grease on the side at Fuller's!

HIGGINS RESTAURANT AND BAR

1239 SW Broadway, Portland
(503) 222-9070

Chef-owner Greg Higgins's cuisine is very much based on what's available locally. The restaurant is in contact with farmers, so they have access to incredible products. I enjoy Higgins. I just had lunch there with another chef, and it was marvelous. I like the smoked seafood platter and his cured meats. He makes great smoked hazelnuts, and people rave about the hamburgers—he grinds the Oregon country beef himself. I especially like to go in and sit at the bar. He took over an older restaurant, and it still has the feel of what it was before, and what it was before that. The place has ambiance. He still allows smoking at the bar, which most of us on the West Coast have nixed. The local newspaper offices are right across the street, so it's sort of a working person's bar.

HOUSE OF LOUIE

331 NW Davis Street, Portland
(503) 228-9898

On New Year's Day, we go to this Chinese restaurant. Their menu includes dishes ranging from sautéed-in-the-shell prawns to congees [rice porridges]. I like the casual service, and they have lazy Susans in the middle of the tables, so you can easily share dishes with others at the table. I love whole foods, whole steamed or fried fish—anything I can eat with my hands.

ORIGINAL PANCAKE HOUSE

8601 SW 24th Avenue, Portland
(503) 246-1049

The "original Original" is in Oregon, where it started in 1953. I take my children here because it's a breakfast house and it's easy for them to understand—nobody complains about pancakes. I've never had a bad meal or a bad experience here. The coffee's good, and they use great, premium ingredients. I'll wait forty-five minutes to get a seat. Everybody waits. They're famous for their "Dutch baby," which is served with lemon and powdered sugar, and of course the four-inch-high apple pancakes. I enjoy it when a restaurant keeps its focus intact, when it is true to itself and what it does, and when it understands that it can't be everything to everybody.

PEARL BAKERY

102 NW Ninth Avenue, Portland
(503) 827-0910

This is a wonderful morning spot, because it has really high windows, like many of the other old buildings in the Pearl District. They make really high-grade breads and pastries. I love their raisin rolls—anytime they infuse their bread recipes with fruit or nuts, the results are great. They make sandwiches with fresh focaccia at lunchtime. Plus, it's only two blocks from Powell's City of Books, which is the largest collection of new and used books west of the Mississippi.

PROVIDENCE

CAMBODIAN

NEATH'S NEW AMERICAN BISTRO

262 Water Street, Providence
Phone: (401) 751-3700

"We have a former staff member who's Cambodian [Neath Pal], and he opened a restaurant called Neath's. It's another husband-and-wife team who met at our restaurant. She worked her way through medical school as a waitress, and he was one of our cooks. She is now a doctor but comes in on the weekends to help him out, and they have a great team. It's Cambodian-French food. His Cambodian specialties are things he remembers from his childhood, so it's a very interesting menu."

—GEORGE GERMON AND JOHANNE KILLEEN, AL FORNO

CHINESE

LUCKY GARDEN DIM SUM

1852 Smith Street, North Providence
(401) 231-5626

"We went here with a Chinese couple, who agreed this place is really impressive."

—GEORGE GERMON AND JOHANNE KILLEEN, AL FORNO

CLAMS

MIKE'S KITCHEN

170 Randall Street, Cranston
(401) 946-5320

"Mike's has a lot of regional specialties, like stuffies, which are quahog clams that are shucked, chopped, and mixed with either bread crumbs or cracker crumbs and other ingredients. Mike's are dynamite!"

—GEORGE GERMON AND JOHANNE KILLEEN, AL FORNO

CLAM CHOWDER

NEW RIVERS

7 Steeple Street, Providence
(401) 751-0350

"This restaurant is in Al Forno's original location, and it's run by Bruce Tillinghast. Bruce sometimes makes what is the true Rhode Island chowder, which is made without cream or tomato. It's a gray chowder made with fresh clams, potatoes, and bacon, which is served with common crackers."

—GEORGE GERMON AND JOHANNE KILLEEN, AL FORNO

LEGAL SEA FOODS

2099 Post Road, Warwick
(401) 732-3663

"Their clam chowder is consistently good."

—GEORGE GERMON AND JOHANNE KILLEEN, AL FORNO

FISH AND CHIPS

YE OLDE ENGLISH FISH AND CHIPS SHOP

Market Square, Woonsocket (401) 762-3637

"The food is fabulous. They do a fish cake that is a piece of fish wrapped in potato slices. It just brings you to your knees because it's so good!"

—GEORGE GERMON AND JOHANNE KILLEEN, AL FORNO

HAMBURGERS

STANLEY'S RESTAURANT

535 Dexter Street, Central Falls (401) 726-9689

"Stanley's burgers are truly delicious. They take what looks like an eight-ounce burger and put it on a big griddle with all kinds of onions on the side. Then they start smashing the burger down, until it becomes almost like a pancake. It's served with a pickle and the griddled onions, and you could eat a dozen of them! They even hand-cut their own french fries."

—GEORGE GERMON AND JOHANNE KILLEEN, AL FORNO

PORTUGUESE

LISBON AT NIGHT

17 Exchange Street, Pawtucket
(401) 723-2030

"It's a fun Portuguese restaurant where we go for the roasted chicken that they serve with unbelievable deep-fried potatoes, rice, bread, and hot peppers—it's delicious. It's impossible to resist the sliced potatoes!"

—GEORGE GERMON AND JOHANNE KILLEEN,
AL FORNO

SWEETS

GRAY'S ICE CREAM

16 East Road (at the junction of Routes 77 and 179), Tiverton (about 15 miles outside Providence)
(401) 624-4500

"Gray's opened in 1922, and they do ice cream really well. Their mocha chip and peppermint ice creams are incredible. It's the smoothness of it, the fat content, and the amazing flavors. I'm actually glad I don't live next door to it!"

—EMILY LUCHETTI, PASTRY CHEF, FARALLON
(SAN FRANCISCO)

GEORGE GERMON and JOHANNE KILLEEN are chef-owners of Al Forno, which they opened in 1980. In 1998, they opened Cafe Louis in Boston, with David Reynoso as chef de cuisine. In the *International Herald Tribune*, Patricia Wells called Al Forno the "world's best restaurant for casual dining." Their many honors include the 1993 James Beard Award as Best Chefs: Northeast. They are the authors of *Cucina Simpatica*.

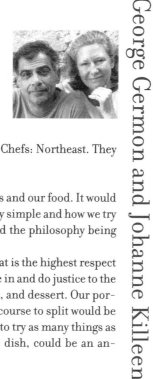

George Germon and Johanne Killeen

OUR FOOD It is really hard to talk about ourselves and our food. It would be easier to talk about the atmosphere being really simple and how we try to bring the Italian philosophy to our shores, and the philosophy being quite different from a direct representation.

We think it is important to come in hungry; that is the highest respect you can pay a chef. I hope first-time visitors come in and do justice to the menu by having an appetizer, pasta, main course, and dessert. Our portions are large, so we encourage sharing. A good course to split would be the pasta and even the main course. We want you to try as many things as possible. A grilled pizza, which is our signature dish, could be an antipasto or its own course.

AL FORNO
577 S. Main Street
Providence, RI 02903
Phone: (401) 273-9760
Fax: (401) 751-7803
Web: www.alforno.com

CAFE LOUIS
234 Berkeley Street
Boston, MA 02116
Phone: (617) 266-4680

"If I was anywhere an hour or more north of New York on the East Coast, I would definitely stop at Al Forno. What an experience, from the pastas to the desserts! It's a very special restaurant for me. The grilled pizza is a must, as well as any dessert. They have about fifteen desserts on their menu, and they're all made to order."

MARIO BATALI
BABBO, ESCA, AND LUPA
(NEW YORK)

"When I was a student at Brown University, in Providence, I remember stumbling onto the original Al Forno. The first time I ate there, it was unlike almost anything I'd ever seen before: It was like an East Coast version of Chez Panisse. I went back the next night and applied for a cook's job. They didn't need anyone, so I waitressed until eventually they gave me a job cooking. I worked there three nights a week during my junior and senior years."

SUZANNE GOIN

LUCQUES (LOS ANGELES)

BASTA! CAFÉ

2195 Broad Street, Cranston
(401) 461-0330

For dinner, there is an extraordinary Italian restaurant that's a block away from our house. The owner has been in the restaurant business for a long time, and then, because of some complication with the chef, who left, all of a sudden he is in the kitchen. The food has never been better! He has some things on the menu like veal parmigiano, but this is like you've never had before—it is so delicious, so pure, so simple. We're hooked on it! He does an appetizer of deep-fried artichokes with artichoke mousse that's unbelievable. Everything on the menu is terrific.

EMPIRE RESTAURANT

123 Empire Street
(at Washington Street), Providence
(401) 621-7911

Two former employees [Loren Falsone and Eric Moshier, who were among *Food & Wine*'s Ten Best New Chefs in America in 2000] opened their own place, and we're minor players in it. We always want people to move on from us and go in their own direction. They are both terrific cooks—two of the best employees we've ever had. They are really making their mark, so there aren't comparisons with Al Forno. It's nice to see they're really growing. They're doing a lot of Italian, some Spanish, and Mediterranean cuisine. I like to order the pizza margherita. They're quite new, so they're still feeling their way into the dishes that will become classics on their menu.

MIKE'S KITCHEN, IN THE VFW HALL

170 Randall Street, Cranston
(401) 946-5320

For lunch, we like to go to Mike's Kitchen, and we recommend it to everybody. They're open for lunch Monday through Saturday, and dinner Monday, Wednesday, Thursday, and Friday nights. It's a funny schedule, but their hours are based on the VFW's needs. One of our customers brought us there once, and we had polenta that first day. Then we started going almost on a daily basis—sort of to escape from Al Forno for a while. We love the sausage there, and the fried squid is delicious. We try different things at different times, but the polenta is still our favorite.

NEW JAPAN

145 Washington Street, Providence
(401) 351-0300

New Japan is a wonderful Japanese restaurant downtown. You can trust the sushi and the sashimi. The chef is a master fryer, and his tempura is without comparison. He is incredibly creative; while he has a menu that will appeal to everyone, there are things that will just take your breath away. He'll make dishes with mushrooms and balsamic vinegar that are almost cross-cultural, but they really work. He does something as simple as avocado with crab meat in the most delicious soy-based sauce. His food has great balance and great integrity. We drink cold sake with his food. He loves sake himself and always puts a bottle down on our table that we have never seen before. So, anytime we can find an unusual bottle of sake, we'll bring it to him.

OLGA'S CUP AND SAUCER

Multiple locations, including:
103 Point Street, Providence
(401) 831-6666
261 W. Main Road, Little Compton
(401) 635-8650

Olga's partner is Becky Wagner, and Becky worked for us for a number of years. She does more of the savory stuff, and Olga [Bravo] is more responsible for the sweet stuff. Becky's pizzas are great: they are little individual pizzas featuring unusual ingredients, like corn, squash, or spinach. It's really good. They have a tendency toward vegetarian cuisine, but with a refreshing point of view. It's primarily a bakery, but they've really expanded their lunch menu in Providence, and it's more than sandwiches. They always have very interesting soups, such as tomato-gorgonzola, in addition to their specialty breads, which are wonderful—they range from raisin fennel to potato dill. Their desserts—including cookies, pies, and tarts—have really gotten extraordinary.

Bar

BIX

56 Gold Street, San Francisco (415) 433-6300

"This restaurant's bar serves great cocktails."

—MARK MILLER, COYOTE CAFÉ (LAS VEGAS AND SANTA FE)

TOMMY'S JOYNT

1101 Geary Street (at Van Ness Avenue), San Francisco (415) 775-4216

"They have a hundred and seventy kinds of tequila and a global selection of beers."

—MARK MILLER, COYOTE CAFÉ (LAS VEGAS AND SANTA FE)

ZUNI CAFÉ

1658 Market Street, San Francisco (415) 552-2522

"For white wine and oysters."

—MARK MILLER, COYOTE CAFÉ (LAS VEGAS AND SANTA FE)

Bread

ACME BREAD

1601 San Pablo Avenue, Berkeley (510) 524-1021

"For the walnut levain—I could eat a loaf of it for lunch or dinner!"

—EMILY LUCHETTI, FARALLON

"The best baguette."

—MARK MILLER, COYOTE CAFÉ (LAS VEGAS AND SANTA FE)

"Their delicious, sophisticated hearth-baked sourdough is top of the line. I always seek it out when I'm in San Francisco."

—AMY SCHERBER, AMY'S BREAD (NEW YORK)

BAY BREAD

2325 Pine Street (at Fillmore Street), San Francisco (415) 440-0356

"Great brioches, croissants, and pain au chocolat."

—GARY DANKO, GARY DANKO

Bread CONT.

BAY VILLAGE BAKERS

40 4th Street, Point Reyes Station
(415) 663-8587

"The best bread in the Bay Area, as far as I'm concerned."

—PAUL BERTOLLI, OLIVETO

CHEESE BOARD COLLECTIVE

1504 Shattuck Avenue, Berkeley
(510) 549-3183

"The Cheese Board makes terrifically crusty baguettes and flawed but delicious handmade bread—their loaves are sort of dome-shaped, but they don't rise evenly, so they puff out at the side. They also have one of the largest selections of cheese anywhere."

—PAUL BERTOLLI, OLIVETO

NOE VALLEY BAKERY AND BREAD CO.

4073 24th Street, San Francisco
(415) 550-1405
2277 Shafter Avenue, San Francisco
(415) 642-8782

"For the fig bread."

—JOYCE GOLDSTEIN, FORMERLY OF SQUARE ONE

BREAKFAST

CAMPTON PLACE HOTEL

340 Stockton Street, San Francisco
(415) 781-5555

"The cook, Scotty, has been there for years, since when I was cooking there, and he still serves an outstanding breakfast!"

—BRADLEY OGDEN, THE LARK CREEK INN AND ONE MARKET

CAESAR SALAD

ZUNI CAFÉ

1658 Market Street, San Francisco
(415) 552-2522

"The Caesar salad at Zuni is nice and big—and perfect."

—CLIFFORD HARRISON AND ANNE QUATRANO, BACCHANALIA (ATLANTA)

CANDY

CHARLOTTE'S CONFECTIONS

1395 El Camino Real, Millbrae
(650) 589-1417
(800) 798-CHAR
www.charlottesconfections.com
Their products are also available at Williams-Sonoma.

"I love their little caramels!"

—EMILY LUCHETTI, FARALLON

CHEESE COURSE

GARY DANKO

800 North Point Street, San Francisco
(415) 749-2060

"Nick Peyton offers great cheese service, featuring cheeses from around the world." (See also p. 246.)

—TRACI DES JARDINS, JARDINIÈRE

ZUNI CAFÉ

1658 Market Street, San Francisco
(415) 552-2522

"They have a nice selection of cheeses."

—TRACI DES JARDINS, JARDINIÈRE

CHEESE, RETAIL

COWGIRL CREAMERY

80 4th Street, Point Reyes Station
(415) 663-8153

"Two Chez Panisse alumnae—Peggy Smith and Sue Conley—are making their own cheese with milk from the Straus Family Creamery, the first organic creamery west of the Mississippi. Their own products include clabbered cottage cheese, crème fraîche, and fromage blanc. They also stock other highly regarded cheeses such as Cypress Grove and Old Chatham Shepherding."

—BARBARA TROPP, FORMERLY OF CHINA MOON CAFÉ

CHINESE

TON KIANG

5821 Geary Boulevard (at 22nd Avenue), San Francisco
(415) 387-8273

"Ton Kiang is a great Chinese restaurant that has tea lunch [dim sum] during the day and excellent Chinese food at night. It's really popular, so be prepared for waits and lines."

—JOYCE GOLDSTEIN, FORMERLY OF SQUARE ONE

COFFEE

CAFFÈ GRECO

423 Columbus Avenue, San Francisco
(415) 397-6261

"For Illy Caffè, which a lot of chefs consider to be the very best espresso."

—JOYCE GOLDSTEIN, FORMERLY OF SQUARE ONE

KLEIN'S DELICATESSEN

501 Connecticut Street, San Francisco
(415) 821-9149

"For a mocha."

—CINDY PAWLCYN, BUCKEYE ROADHOUSE, FOG CITY DINER, AND MUSTARDS GRILL

MR. ESPRESSO

Multiple locations, including:
696 Third Street, Oakland
(510) 287-5200

"The best coffee."

—PAUL BERTOLLI, OLIVETO

FARMERS' MARKETS

ALEMANY FARMERS' MARKET

100 Alemany Boulevard (at Putnam Street) (415) 647-9423
The oldest farmers' market in San Francisco

BERKELEY FARMERS' MARKET

Center Street (on Saturday) or Derby Street (on Tuesday) at Martin Luther King Jr. Way
(510) 548-3333

MARIN FARMERS' MARKET

4th Street between B Street and Cijos, San Rafael (415) 457-2266

*"Berkeley on Tuesdays, Marin on Thursdays, and Alemany on
Saturdays. They're all phenomenal—no one should miss them!"*

—TRACI DES JARDINS, JARDINIÈRE

HAMBURGER

BALBOA CAFÉ

3199 Fillmore Street, San Francisco (415) 921-3944

*"Their delicious hamburger on sourdough bread is perfectly
cooked. Their BLT is good, too, with homemade mayonnaise and
really good bacon. The restaurant has been there for years, and
the menu is simple and classic."*

— JOYCE GOLDSTEIN, FORMERLY OF SQUARE ONE

ZUNI CAFÉ

1658 Market Street, San Francisco (415) 552-2522
Zuni serves its hamburgers on focaccia, and they're available only at lunch.

"It's a great hamburger."

—TRACI DES JARDINS, JARDINIÈRE

"The best burger."

—LORETTA KELLER, BIZOU

INDIAN

INDIAN OVEN

233 Fillmore Street (at Haight Street), San Francisco (415) 626-1628

"*Indian Oven is one of the best northern Indian restaurants in the city. They have a tandoor, in which they cook a wide variety of meats, including chicken, lamb, and prawns, and their vegetarian selections—like lentils with curry—are great. The stuff sounds simple, but it's pretty authentic and really good.*"

—LORETTA KELLER, BIZOU

ITALIAN

DELFINA

3621 18th Street, San Francisco (415) 552-4055

"*Owners Anne Spencer and Craig Stoll are doing a wonderful job with this excellent Mission District Italian.*"

—JOYCE GOLDSTEIN, FORMERLY OF SQUARE ONE

RIVOLI

1539 Solano Avenue, Berkeley (510) 526-2542

"*Worth a trip to Berkeley for their portabella mushroom fritters and other dishes incorporating local and mostly organic ingredients.*"

—JOYCE GOLDSTEIN, FORMERLY OF SQUARE ONE

Japanese

MAKI

1825 Post Street (Kunokuniya Building, in Japan Center), San Francisco (Japantown) (415) 921-5215

"*This is a tiny restaurant—it can seat only about twenty people—that serves very authentic Japanese cuisine. The menu is simple: regular sashimi and bento boxes. We always order the specials. They have almost ten specials a night, and we'll order all ten! When he serves snapper head, you can almost eat the whole thing—cheeks, jaw, eyeballs. He steams it with sake and shiitake mushrooms. They have about twenty different kinds of sake. I like Kubota, which has a nice nose and body, and a rich rice flavor with a good, dry finish that's not sharp.*"

—LISSA DOUMANI AND HIRO SONE, TERRA (ST. HELENA)

OYSTERS

FARALLON

450 Post Street, San Francisco
(415) 956-6969

"Order the plateau [of oysters]."

—MARK MILLER, COYOTE CAFÉ (LAS VEGAS AND SANTA FE)

SWAN OYSTER DEPOT

1517 Polk Street, San Francisco
(415) 673-1101
Open since 1946, and currently run by the third generation of the Sancimino family.

"Great oysters."

—BRADLEY OGDEN, THE LARK CREEK INN AND ONE MARKET

"For Hog Island, Kumamoto, and Belon oysters."

—CINDY PAWLCYN, BUCKEYE ROADHOUSE, FOG CITY DINER, AND MUSTARDS GRILL

"They close at five P.M., and too often we think of it at the last minute. We would go here more if we didn't blow it so often! They have amazingly fresh oysters. Four or five brothers run the place, and they've been there since they were kids. They always have about six kinds of oysters and two kinds of clams, which they shuck for you. Also, they have decent wines by the glass. You just sit there and slurp down oysters with a glass of wine, Champagne, or beer, and you're one happy camper."

—LISSA DOUMANI AND HIRO SONE, TERRA (ST. HELENA)

MUST-GO

YANK SING

427 Battery Street, San Francisco (415) 781-1111

BIZOU

598 4th Street, San Francisco (415) 543-2222

TAQUERIA SAN JOSE #2

2839 Mission Street, San Francisco (415) 282-0283

"When I go to San Francisco, there are three things I wouldn't miss: dim sum at Yank Sing, a meal at Loretta's [restaurant Bizou], and a taco at Taqueria San Jose #2. Why #2? Because it's better than #3. They have tongue and head tacos that will drive you crazy, and their carne asada is perfect. They have bowls of pickled jalapeños and salsas. The whole experience is amazing."

—MARIO BATALI, BABBO, ESCA, AND LUPA (NEW YORK)

ZUNI CAFÉ

1658 Market Street, San Francisco (415) 552-2522

"I think it's a great restaurant. You can go here and feel the real essence of San Francisco."

—CHRIS SCHLESINGER, EAST COAST GRILL (BOSTON)

"Customers always call me and ask me where they should eat when they travel. For anyone visiting San Francisco, I tell them that this is one of the most comfortable restaurants I know. I always get oysters to start, and I love the soups and salads, too."

—SEAN KELLY, AUBERGINE CAFÉ (DENVER)

ZUNI CAFÉ

1658 Market Street, San Francisco
(415) 552-2522

"The best place for oysters."

—TRACI DES JARDINS, JARDINIÈRE;
JOYCE GOLDSTEIN, FORMERLY OF SQUARE ONE;
LORETTA KELLER, BIZOU

PIZZA

TOMMASO'S

1042 Kearny Street, San Francisco (415) 398-9696
Open since 1935, offering the city's first brick-oven pizza.

"The best pizza in town."

—GARY DANKO, GARY DANKO; AND JOYCE GOLDSTEIN, FORMERLY OF SQUARE ONE

"My favorites at Tommaso's are the margherita, sausage, or vegetarian pizzas."

—CINDY PAWLCYN, BUCKEYE ROADHOUSE, FOG CITY DINER, AND MUSTARDS GRILL

CHEZ PANISSE CAFÉ

1517 Shattuck Avenue, Berkeley (510) 548-5525

"Wonderful pizza."

—BRADLEY OGDEN, THE LARK CREEK INN AND ONE MARKET

OLIVETO

5655 College Avenue, Oakland (510) 547-5356

"For pizza, I come to my restaurant." (See p. 244.)

—PAUL BERTOLLI, OLIVETO

ZUNI CAFÉ

1658 Market Street, San Francisco (415) 552-2522

"The thin-crusted pizzas at Zuni are made in a huge wood-burning oven, really true to the Italian style."

—CORY SCHREIBER, WILDWOOD (PORTLAND, OR)

"Their pizzas are great."

—LORETTA KELLER, BIZOU

SHELLFISH

SWAN OYSTER DEPOT

1517 Polk Street [between California and Sacramento Streets], San Francisco
(415) 673-1101

"I go here to eat cracked crab or crab cocktail. I don't usually eat oysters here. I really love it."

—PAUL BERTOLLI, OLIVETO

SAND DABS

SAM'S GRILL

374 Bush Street, San Francisco
(415) 421-0594

TADICH GRILL

240 California Street, San Francisco
(415) 391-1849

"Native foods are one of the things that San Francisco is really all about. Sand dabs should cost ten times as much as they do—and they probably will after this book comes out! They are as delicate as Dover sole, and they cost a fraction of the price. I go to the old places in San Francisco—like Sam's and Tadich Grill—to eat fish like that."

—PAUL BERTOLLI, OLIVETO

SEAFOOD

HAYES STREET GRILL

320 Hayes Street (between Gough and Franklin), San Francisco
(415) 863-5545

"It's fabulous for great local fish, like sand dabs, Dungeness crab, or Petrale sole. Plus, they have great fries!"

—TRACI DES JARDINS, JARDINIÈRE

"Wonderful, simply prepared seafood [owned by local restaurant critic Patricia Unterman]."

—BARBARA TROPP, FORMERLY OF CHINA MOON CAFÉ

SOUPS

CHAVA'S MEXICAN RESTAURANT

3248 18th Street (at Shotwell Street), San Francisco (415) 552-9387

"For caldos [soups]. I really like the chicken and vegetable soup–
if you have a cold coming on, this is the place to go!"

—CINDY PAWLCYN, BUCKEYE ROADHOUSE, FOG CITY DINER, AND MUSTARDS GRILL

LA FOLIE

2316 Polk Street (between Green and Union), San Francisco (415) 776-5577

"This upscale, romantic family-run restaurant does a great job.
The creative food is delicious—especially the soups!"

—BRADLEY OGDEN, THE LARK CREEK INN AND ONE MARKET

THAI

KHAN TOKE THAI HOUSE

5937 Geary Boulevard, San Francisco (415) 668-6654

"I've been eating here for years and always order the Thai crêpe: a
rice flour and turmeric pancake stuffed with tofu, shrimp, pork
and bean sprouts. I could go by myself and have that and a
Tsingtao beer and be happy. All of their appetizers are superb.
They have low Thai tables and a view of the garden."

—JOYCE GOLDSTEIN, FORMERLY OF SQUARE ONE

THEP PHANOM

400 Waller Street (at Fillmore Street), San Francisco (415) 431-2526

"The chef-owner of Thep Phanom is a woman, and her whole
family works here. It's busy all the time. She makes incredible
curries, a great green papaya salad, and this impossible dish:
deep-fried chicken wings stuffed with soba noodles and mushrooms, and served with lettuce and stuff. It's really good."

—LORETTA KELLER, BIZÕU

SOUTHEAST ASIAN

E&O TRADING CO.

314 Sutter Street, San Francisco
(415) 693-0303

"I have a number of favorites
at this Southeast Asian
microbrewery. I always
order the naan with dipping
sauces, the corn fritters, and
a number of satays. I have
to have the Thai fried rice,
because I love fried rice. The
more people I go with, the
more fun it is, because we
get to order more things."

—JOYCE GOLDSTEIN, FORMERLY OF SQUARE ONE

VIETNAMESE

THE SLANTED DOOR

584 Valencia Street, San Francisco
(415) 861-8032

"A great place for Vietnamese
food."

—JOYCE GOLDSTEIN, FORMERLY OF
SQUARE ONE

"When I fly into San
Francisco and land at
lunchtime, I like to go to
The Slanted Door. They use
clean, pure products and
have really flavorful food."

—CHARLIE TROTTER, CHARLIE TROTTER'S
(CHICAGO)

How to Order and Eat in a Chinese Restaurant

Barbara Tropp was chef-owner of China Moon Café in San Francisco for eleven years. She is the author of The Modern Art of Chinese Cooking, *widely regarded as the classic text in English on Chinese cooking techniques, and the* China Moon Cookbook, *winner of the Julia Child Book Award. A China scholar turned Chinese cook, Barbara studied Chinese language, literature, and art at Columbia, Yale, and Princeton. She is the founder and past president of Women Chefs and Restaurateurs, and a recipient of Food Arts' Silver Spoon Award. She currently divides her time between teaching, writing, leading chefs' tours in Asia, and consulting for restaurants, culinary schools, and corporations.*

ACHIEVING A YIN-YANG BALANCE

If you are eating in a Chinese restaurant, the yin-yang guideline—of striving for balance—is perfect. Even if you love all spicy food, or all stir-fried food, it's not appropriate to a Chinese eating experience that every dish be spicy or that every dish be stir-fried. The techniques, the foodstuffs, and the seasonings should all have dynamic opposition.

This is one of my greatest disappointments when I eat Western food: Too often, even in the hands of a gifted chef, every plate will come out with something square in a puddle of sauce, or else every plate will come out with a tower. If you've got four courses of puddles, you've got all yin and no yang; when you have four courses of towers, you've got all yang and no yin. You want to strive for a balance.

CHOOSING A MENU

The basic guideline for ordering in the traditional Chinese way is to order a spicy dish and a mild one, and various center dishes: chicken, fish, red meat, and one vegetable. And the preparations should vary, so you end up with a steamed dish, a deep-fried dish, a stir-fried dish, and a braised dish.

A Chinese restaurant's cold dishes, or what the Chinese call *lung pan*—literally, "cold plates"—are one fabulous indication of a restaurant's acumen, and also are a great part of the Chinese eating experience. So if you see on the menu plates of jellied lamb, or five-spice cold beef, or jellyfish salad, that's an absolutely great way to begin—order several little cold plates.

I think the other place where a Chinese restaurant reveals its acumen is in its stir-fries. Not sweet-and-sour, however, because sweet-and-sour is always doctored to American tastes. And I think that as a general rule, Cantonese food is very poorly presented in your average Chinese-American restaurant. Choose an appealing stir-fry, and it will tell you a great deal.

One of the things that I always do is order stir-fried Chinese greens. A real Chinese restaurant always has stir-fried market greens as a daily special. It might be Chinese spinach, amaranth, or Chinese broccoli, and typically it's stir-fried very simply. That is also a great way to order: cold dishes and a stir-fried green of the day.

The other thing that I almost always order in a Chinese restaurant is steamed fish. A simple purity is valued above all else in Chinese cooking, and there's nothing that better represents that than a steamed fish. If you really want to understand Chinese eating, you have to eat a fish cheek: the meat around the neck is one of the most savory spots of the fish. It also very much gives you the experience of eating in Asian culture, because the fish is presented whole, with its head and its tail on.

One of the things Asian eating has to teach us puritanical Americans is that it's the whole item—whether it's the entire body of the fish or the stems and leaves of broccoli as well as the florets—that has the interesting flavor dynamics. We tend, in our Western culture, to cut off the top and the bottom and eat the middle. The appendages, in Chinese eating in particular, are always very interesting.

The Chinese still think that foreigners are foreigners and won't understand or appreciate their food. For the most part they're right, and that's where it helps to look at the menu for the stranger items. Ask for the simpler preparations, such as, "Can you steam me a fish?" or "What stir-fried greens do you have today?" If someone says, "We have Western broccoli," ask, "Do you have Chinese broccoli?" I think with enough persistence, one can make inroads. See what other people are eating, and go in around staff meal time and ask the waiter, "What's your favorite?" If he says, "Sweet-and-sour pork," ask, "No, what do you yourself like?" Very frequently, a waiter will reply, "You wouldn't like it." Well, then you go ahead and order it anyway. And you may not like it, but at least you'll know what pork kidneys are.

HOW TO BE AN INSIDER

Of course, the advice generally circulated about what to order in a Chinese restaurant is true: Look at what other people are ordering, particularly if you're in a restaurant that's filled with Chinese people. The specials of the day are usually very valid. I also have my own weird law—I always order something that seems preposterously weird, so that I have the experience of what's going to be a very different texture and possibly a foodstuff that I've never had before. This way, you also start scoring points with the establishment, especially if you're going to go back again—ordering weird dishes will earn a diner many points. If you order a dish of stir-fried ducks' tongues, that's very telling.

MIND YOUR MANNERS

If you don't clean your plate, then at least take the leftovers home so that there is no waste. This is absolutely a matter of etiquette: Nothing should be wasted in a Chinese restaurant. It's a famine culture, so the idea that someone wouldn't take food home is seen as scandalous. I do this even in very fancy Western restaurants, and my husband is appalled, but between my Chinese training and my Jewish roots, it's hard not to do that.

EATING CHINESE IN THE UNITED STATES

When you eat a Chinese meal in America, you usually suffer two great indignities: One is the quality of the tea, and the other is the quality of the rice. Chinese restaurants almost uniformly serve inferior tea and rice.

Finding a Chinese restaurant in America that serves even a decent Chinese tea is like finding a needle in a haystack—almost all of them serve truly wretched tea. And tea in China is not drunk with the meal, it is drunk as a between-meals refresher. What's drunk at the meal is a very light soup, which is why we think of Chinese soups as being so insubstantial, because they're used as digestives. That's also why a light, clear broth, maybe with something floating in it, is served at the end of the meal; that's what makes all the food go down and settles your stomach. The Chinese feel that having a caffeinated drink at the end of the meal is very bad for digestion—except in the case of dim sum, where the oiliness of the food is cut by the tannin in the tea.

The general quality of Chinese food in the United States is appalling. This wasn't always the case, but in the last twenty years it has gone steadily downhill. I think, though, that there is now much better Cantonese cooking than there ever was. Thanks to the influx of Chinese people from Hong Kong, we now have lots of large Hong Kong–style Chinese restaurants, but their quality goes up and down depending on who's cooking. We do have some wonderful dim sum, including a couple of very good dim sum restaurants here in San Francisco.

DIM SUM

One of the best places for dim sum in San Francisco is a perennial favorite called Ton Kiang. Like almost all dim sum restaurants, you should go at eleven or eleven-thirty in the morning, because that's when there's the greatest variety of dim sum coming out of the kitchen and they are all very, very fresh. The trick with dim sum is to not order everything at once. This is very difficult and takes patience, but you need to draw out the meal in order to see what's presented to you.

I would say most everything at Ton Kiang is good, and the restaurant is very dependable. However, when you're at a truly good dim sum place, you'll have your own favorites, and the kitchen will have its own strong suits.

There is another good dim sum restaurant called Koi Palace, which is in the outskirts of San Francisco in Daly City, and is very easy to get to.

Dim sum is something that I don't make at all, so eating it is a very special experience. Here again, one has to be aware of ordering yin-yang style, so that you have steamed foods as well as fried foods. You should look beyond the usual northern Chinese favorites, like pot stickers. In fact, I'd never order pot stickers at dim sum because dim sum is all about southern Chinese food, and pot stickers are very northern. Ideally, when I go to a dim sum restaurant it's to have all of the wonderful rice noodles and rice-based doughs that the Cantonese do so exquisitely. *Har gow*, the shrimp dumplings, are a classic, and with them I'll always order chrysanthemum tea, which is a digestive and goes beautifully with the flavors of the seafood while cutting the grease.

I order almost all the rice-noodle-wrapped dumplings, and at a great dim sum place, they'll have dumplings that are stuffed with chives—yellow Chinese chives, green Chinese chives, or pea sprouts—and almost all kinds of seafood.

NOODLE ETIQUETTE

Is it proper to slurp noodles in a Chinese restaurant? Absolutely. Making noise with Chinese food is totally appropriate. Food is served very hot in China, so a certain amount of inhaling is necessary to cool the food enough so that it can be eaten. In fact, that's the *raison d'être* behind slurping—it's the technique of eating hot food in order to cool it down on its way into your mouth. It's not about showing your appreciation, as some mistakenly say.

The Chinese habit is to bring the bowl directly to the mouth, which is so important for the appreciation of aromas. That's why the Chinese will drink soup directly from a bowl rather than from a spoon. I'll often tell my classes, 'Just try to drink wine with a spoon—imagine what you would lose. The Chinese feel that way about food!' In addition, Chinese food often arrives at the table much, much hotter than Western food, as it is usually coming out of a wok fired with 175,000 BTUs rather than the 20,000 or 30,000 BTUs of a Western stovetop burner. All of this means that slurping and blowing is necessary so you don't kill yourself!

CHINATOWN, USA

I think that there is a difference between Chinatowns in American cities where there are newly arrived immigrant populations and Chinatowns that have become tourist meccas. For example, the Chinese restaurants in San Francisco's Chinatown are, by and large, dreadful. Their glory days are long past, but the places in the Bay Area where newly arrived Chinese have settled and opened restaurants are always the more promising places to eat.

I think that's why, for example, one might be disappointed with New York's Chinatown but might be thrilled with the Chinese food in Brooklyn, and that's said from the perspective of somebody who really doesn't know

New York very well. But if you follow New York restaurant critics whom you respect, their rave reviews are almost always written about someplace out in Queens or in Brooklyn. Similarly, maybe Los Angeles's Chinatown is old and tired, but Monterey Park is vibrant.

Usually, the most exciting and interesting food is being made by people who have recently arrived in the United States. Established Chinatown restaurants are often run by people who immigrated to the States a long time ago, and they have either forfeited their standards or they've forgotten their standards or they never had standards to begin with. The time-line of Chinese adaptation to life in America is crucial in determining the authenticity of a restaurant.

DIM SUM

KOI PALACE

365 Gellert Boulevard, Daly City
(650) 992-9000

"Terrific dim sum."

—BARBARA TROPP, FORMERLY OF CHINA MOON CAFÉ

TON KIANG

5821 Geary Boulevard (at 22nd Avenue), San Francisco
(415) 387-8273

"It's a perennial favorite."

—BARBARA TROPP, FORMERLY OF CHINA MOON CAFÉ

"I love dim sum, and at Ton Kiang they also serve dim sum at night—at other places it's often served only in the morning and afternoon."

—LORETTA KELLER, BIZOU

YANK SING

427 Battery Street, San Francisco
(415) 781-1111

"The best dim sum."

—PAUL BERTOLLI, OLIVETO

"It's always extraordinary."

—TRACI DES JARDINS, JARDINIÈRE

"I have been a regular here for the last forty years!"

—JOYCE GOLDSTEIN, FORMERLY OF SQUARE ONE

"They do so much volume that their dim sum is always really fresh."

—LORETTA KELLER, BIZOU

Paul Bertolli

OLIVETO

5655 College Avenue
(at Shafter Street)
Oakland, CA 94618
Phone: (510) 547-5356
Fax: (510) 547-4624

PAUL BERTOLLI is chef-owner of Oliveto. Previously he was executive chef of Chez Panisse, where he co-authored the *Chez Panisse Cookbook* with Alice Waters. In 1997, *Wine Spectator* included Oliveto in its Top Ten Italian Restaurants. Among Bertolli's honors are the 1989 *GQ* awards for Favorite Chef and Golden Dish, and the 1999 James Beard Award as Best Chef: California. He is a contributing editor for *Fine Cooking* magazine and runs his own wine, food, and restaurant consulting company, Agradolce.

MY FOOD I hope that people who eat at Oliveto "get it" on some level. I have noticed that as our cooking has gotten really consistent, people respond to this idea that the Japanese call *umami*. When a dish is seasoned right, or when a dish is all that it can be, it hits the bliss point. It can happen with some in-season vegetable or fruit that we've been waiting to get perfectly ripe. When we finally serve it, people "get it." Somehow in people, there is a nostalgia for this goodness, savoriness, and balance. When you hit the right note across the board, people really start responding. At Oliveto, we try to win our customers one at a time. We win them on the basis of what they learn by coming here, which is to love great food.

PAUL'S PICKS

CHEZ PANISSE

1517 Shattuck Avenue, Berkeley
(510) 548-5525
You can always count on getting really wonderful, up-to-the-moment food there. For me, it is kind of a nostalgic return, since I used to work there. I like to see how the restaurant is developing over time; I think it's done really well. It has become less about one person and more about a diversity of different viewpoints about food. I love to go there and eat oysters, for instance. Not a lot of restaurants serve really great oysters anymore, but Chez Panisse does. I like some of their simple Monday night dinners. The last thing I ate there was a first course of grilled, slightly bitter white escarole with shards of Parmesan cheese, a little bit of lemon, garlic, olive oil, and real pancetta. It was served with garlic toast and some olives. It was delicious.

PHO LAM VIEN

930 Webster Street, Oakland
(Chinatown)
(510) 763-1484
We really like this little Vietnamese noodle house. The food is really clean and filling. There is a lot of variety in taste, and they use all these fresh things, like piles of basil and bean sprouts. But what I think they really know how to do is the broth. I especially love their beef broth. It has boiled tendon in it, and it has a little clove and cinnamon. But it's subtle. You have to reach for it a little bit. It's full of noodles, and we usually get some combination of beef parts in there. They also have a wonderful fresh lotus root salad with shrimp.

RISTORANTE MILANO

1448 Pacific Street, San Francisco
(415) 673-2961
This is a small, neighborhood restaurant off Larkin Street. Its two owners are from Rome, and they really understand authentic northern Italian cooking—their dishes range from handmade gnocchi to grilled veal chop with rosemary and sage. My wife and I really like their mushroom risotto. We even had our wedding here!

"*This is one of the best Italian restaurants in California, if not the United States.*"

GARY DANKO

GARY DANKO

PAUL'S PICKS

THE SLANTED DOOR

584 Valencia Street (at 17th Street), San Francisco

(415) 861-8032

The chef, Charles Phan, is really grounded. He's a Chinese guy who was born and raised in Vietnam. He's wonderful, a natural-born cook who's making authentic Vietnamese dishes, ranging from fried shrimp and pork rolls wrapped in lettuce leaves to green papaya salad, from scratch. He uses really interesting combinations of fresh, local ingredients and is skilled at putting them together, with contrasting flavors, textures, and temperatures in each dish.

TACO TRUCK

The taco truck, whose standard corner is on High Street near East 14th Street in Oakland

Go for the tacos *al pastor*, which are delicious pork tacos.

PAUL BERTOLLI on

One of the Best Meals of His Life

It was a really rainy night, and we just sort of stumbled on a small osteria in the hills above Verona in Italy. I can't remember the name of it, but I can remember the experience vividly.

The osteria was the original stopping station, sort of the progenitor of restaurants. People would stop by and get refreshed—with food, water, and sometimes sleep—before moving on. Osterias tend to be smaller than trattorias, but they're sort of indistinguishable these days because now people don't use restaurants the way they did in the seventeenth century.

The fact that it was an osteria impressed upon me what a restaurant should be. Essentially, it is the place where you go to get restored and to feel absolutely comfortable. Everything about it struck me—the way I was received, to the way that the food was utterly simple, yet some of the most sophisticated food I've ever eaten because it had a lot of tradition behind it. I had extraordinarily simple, in-season, local fare that was served without pretentiousness. It made so much sense to me that people should eat this way. I'm not even sure that if you talked to the chef or the owners, they would even know what they had done.

I learned so much about what cooking is. First of all, it is a response to a place, a season, and a moment, really. There was a little lake behind the restaurant, so we had a dish made with freshwater tench; it was a kind of a soup with garlic croutons in it. I had a pasta with snails that they had gotten out of the garden. I had spit-roasted larks, with little bread cubes and chunks of sausage. And I had wine that they had made themselves, which was an Amarone-style wine that married especially well with the spit-roasted dish.

The place was small and was dominated by a fireplace where all of these different foods were cooking on a spit, dripping down on some porcini mushrooms that had been placed underneath the spit.

We had a Prosecco from nearby, not exactly of the zone, but typical of the Veneto. It was fall, so the dessert was a baked carmelized apple tart that had no crust.

If you removed all of this and put it into a four-star location, it would have read just fine. But this was a very simple environment with really friendly people.

The other thing about it was this quality of absolute at-homeness that I felt, and the comfort that comes from people who are serving you right out of their place, or their home, as it were. I felt so taken care of, without any bullshit—just "Here, this is what we have." It was absolutely delicious and transforming, for all those reasons.

Gary Danko

GARY DANKO
800 North Point Street
San Francisco, CA 94109
Phone: (415) 749-2060
Fax: (415) 775-1805
www.garydanko.com

GARY DANKO is chef-owner of Gary Danko in San Francisco, which won the 2000 James Beard Award as Best New Restaurant in America. He was named one of *Food & Wine*'s Ten Best New Chefs in America in 1989, and earned the Dining Room at the Ritz Carlton four stars from the *San Francisco Chronicle*. He has twice received *Esquire*'s Best New Restaurant award, and in 1995 he won the James Beard Award as Best Chef: California.

MY FOOD We've achieved a beautiful, very simple elegance in this restaurant. We serve classic, seasonal things. That's the way I cook, and that's what I like to represent. The menu is user-friendly, in that you can order dishes in any sequence that you want, which means that if you want to have rack of lamb for your first course, it is feasible, or if you want to order everything from the first section—oysters, seared foie gras, and a salad—that's feasible, too. Pricewise, we feel we are at the low end of the high-end market. We don't have any surcharges on the menu, so foie gras costs the same as salad.

GARY'S PICKS

JARDINIÈRE

300 Grove Street, San Francisco
(415) 861-5555
Traci Des Jardins, the chef, does some really good lamb dishes, and her pâtés and other charcuterie are also very good. (See also p. 247.)

OLIVETO

5655 College Avenue, Oakland
(510) 547-5356
Chef Paul Bertolli makes his own salami, mortadella—all that stuff. He even makes his own balsamic vinegar. I usually order his pastas, and if he has any pork on the menu, I definitely order it! He does a whole pig sometimes, which is delicious. Or get one of his mortadella platters. It's amazing stuff. Recently he made a great dandelion salad. He has a really good selection of wine that complements his cooking. I love to go here. (See also p. 244.)

ZARZUELA

2000 Hyde Street, San Francisco
(415) 346-0800
This Spanish tapas restaurant is one of my favorite places. Zarzuela is the name of a Spanish fish stew. My favorite dish in the city, hands down, is their warm octopus and potato dish. They peel potatoes and cook them until tender, then slice them and layer them on a plate. Then they slice poached octopus, lay it on top, warm it, drizzle a little bit of olive oil on it, and sprinkle it with coarse rock salt and paprika. Their tripe, chorizo [spicy pork sausage], stuffed squid, and croquettes are all great, and I like to drink sherry with them.

ZUNI CAFÉ

1658 Market Street, San Francisco
(415) 552-2522
For great oysters [as Zuni has a large and constantly changing menu of oysters] and perfectly roasted chicken [which is first marinated and then served on a bread salad with pine nuts, currants, and greens, which all absorb the juices from the chicken]. (See also pp. 248, 249, 251.)

"ANY CORNER THAI RESTAURANT, USA"

I joke that Thai red curry is my new Jewish penicillin—it's a very comforting thing for me. I love the flavors, the little bit of sweetness, the richness of the coconut milk. I don't really have any favorite Thai restaurant because the cooks change so frequently. I like to order vegetarian, and I like all the vegetables to be really well cooked through. If they are crunchy, it changes the flavor.

Traci Des Jardins

TRACI DES JARDINS is chef-owner of Jardinière. Her culinary training included stints cooking with Michel and Pierre Troisgros, Alain Ducasse, and Alain Passard. She was opening chef de cuisine at Joachim Splichal's Patina and executive chef at Rubicon before opening her own restaurant in 1997. The *San Francisco Examiner* and *San Francisco Chronicle* proclaimed her "one of the best chefs in the city." Among her honors are the 1995 James Beard Award as Rising Star Chef of the Year, and being named one of *Food & Wine*'s "Best New Chefs" that same year. In 1997, Jardinière was nominated for a James Beard Award as Best New Restaurant, and in 1999 and 2000 Des Jardins as Best Chef: California.

JARDINIÈRE
300 Grove Street
San Francisco, CA 94102
Phone: (415) 861-5555
Fax: (415) 861-5580
www.jardiniere.com

MY FOOD Jardinière is certainly a fine-dining restaurant, but the way that it feels to be sitting in the dining room is anything but stuffy. The space is very open and structured around the central bar, so it invites interaction—it just makes people feel like celebrating. The front door is designed to look like a cocktail glass, and the ceiling above the mezzanine is covered in hundreds of miniature lights, so that it appears to be a huge, inverted champagne glass. With live jazz emanating from the mezzanine and the bar area full of a great mix of people, the atmosphere is very elegant and also very festive.

My cuisine is grounded in traditional French techniques, and the raw ingredients I use are mostly from California, so it is essentially French-Californian cuisine. I create my menus in order to offer a wide range of choices to my guests so they can have something simple or more complex. The tasting menu is a great way to experience how I put food together—each item is prepared in relation to the course before and after it, so there's a real progression. I keep it balanced; they don't get six courses of butter sauces. At the end of the meal, I want people to feel satisfied, but never overly full. I have a fabulous pastry chef who is absolutely passionate about desserts. I think it's crucial that desserts stand up to the rest of the meal.

I love cheese and wanted to take away some of the fear associated with choosing exotic cheeses. I know from dining in France that it can be an anxiety-provoking experience—they wheel out a cart, and it can have a hundred different cheeses on it. For our cheese service I choose a selection of cheeses that doesn't overchallenge the diner—they can order anything and trust that it's going to be top-quality and accessible to their palate. I try to stay away from really strong, overpowering cheese, but I'll have some around in case people request them. I choose cheeses that I feel are sort of pushing the limit as far as their strength and assertiveness, but are still user-friendly.

"Traci Des Jardins is doing the best food in the city."
LORETTA KELLER
BIZOU

"I love Traci's food."
GARY DANKO
GARY DANKO

BIZOU

598 Fourth Street, San Francisco
(415) 543-2222

I go to Bizou a lot, because I like the simplicity of this bistro. Loretta Keller, the chef, cooks very seasonally, too, which is important to me. I like to know that I'm not going to eat tomatoes in January. Loretta gets mad at me because I always order her braised beef cheeks dish. She breads them in mustard and bread crumbs and then pan-fries them, so they've got this great crust on the outside and this succulent, moist beef cheek on the inside. She changes the garnish to reflect the seasons—in winter, they were served with horseradish and beets. (See also p. 250.)

CHEZ PANISSE

1517 Shattuck Avenue, Berkeley
(510) 548-5525

I always like to go to Chez Panisse. Alice Waters's food is simple, but it's so inspiring. It's not so much what she does to the food but the quality of her ingredients to begin with. Everything she's using is from small, sustainable farms. (See also p. 255.)

LA TAQUERIA

2889 Mission Street, San Francisco
(415) 285-7117

This is my favorite taqueria! It's fantastic, every time. I usually get a tongue or carnitas [fried and seasoned meats] soft taco. It's just great.

THEP PHANOM

400 Waller Street, San Francisco
(415) 431-2526

This is my favorite Thai restaurant. I could go here once a week! Their curries are phenomenal, especially any of the seafood or duck curries. Because I don't know a lot about Thai cooking, it's interesting to taste things and not know how they're made—part of the enjoyment of it for me is the mystery. I usually drink beer, but I think that the food here also pairs really well with Alsatian and German wines, like Rieslings. They really stand up to the spice. (See also p. 237.)

ZUNI CAFÉ

1658 Market Street, San Francisco
(415) 552-2522

The restaurants I gravitate toward are really more ingredient-driven, with really simple preparations. Zuni is the place I probably go to the most. I always love the food and I love the environment. It's just a really pleasant place to sit. They've got a great wine list, and I like Judy Rodgers's style—her food is really true. They're known for their Caesar salad, which is great, and they've got a great selection of oysters. I also always love their gnocchi. Her food is very seasonally based. It's inspiring to see what products and ingredients she's using, because you know that they are the best available. (See also pp. 246, 249, 251.)

JOYCE GOLDSTEIN, the former chef-owner of Square One, which closed in 1996 after a twelve-year run as one of the top restaurants in San Francisco, is a founding board member of Women Chefs and Restaurateurs, and a founder of the California Street Cooking School. She has written numerous cookbooks, including *Back to Square One*, which won a 1993 James Beard Award for Best General Cookbook. *Festive Occasions*, co-authored with Chuck Williams, won a 1993 James Beard Award for Best Entertaining Cookbook. Her many culinary honors include being named the 1994 James Beard Award as Best Chef: California.

Joyce Goldstein

FORMERLY OF
SQUARE ONE
San Francisco, CA

JOYCE'S PICKS

BIZOU

598 Fourth Street, San Francisco
(415) 543-2222
Everything Loretta Keller serves at her bistro is good. She has wonderful salads that are flavored perfectly. The things she does with shellfish, squid, and octopus are all superb. Her flatbread is also very good. I've never had anything there that wasn't good—Loretta can cook! Whatever's on the menu, I go for it! She has an impeccable palate, and her food is just gorgeous. (See also p. 250.)

BOULEVARD

1 Mission Street, San Francisco
(415) 543-6084
Chef Nancy Oakes does wonderful things with duck and pork, and they're perfect on the plate. I like her appetizers, too. They are always changing, so I order different things all the time.

HAYES STREET GRILL

320 Hayes Street, San Francisco
(415) 863-5545
Hayes Street is a civilized dining experience. They've been around for a while, so they know what they are doing. Their sautéed and braised dishes are nicely done, and they have a good wine list. It's an affordable restaurant, and I like it. It's not trendy, it's not hot, it's not noisy, and there's not a lot of people screaming at you. It's a grown-up restaurant for grown-ups, and I need that every once in a while. (See also p. 236.)

JARDINIÈRE

300 Grove Street, San Francisco
(415) 862-5555
At Jardinière, I always let Traci Des Jardins plan my menu. It's nice to see what they are proud of and what she's been playing with. Last time I was there, I had crab with a little tomato water that was clean and delicious, and a fabulous quail that was perfectly cooked. And I had cheese, because she always has good cheeses. To certain people, like Traci, I just say, "You do it," and then sit back and enjoy what they serve me. (See also p. 247.)

ZUNI CAFÉ

1658 Market Street, San Francisco
(415) 552-2522
At Zuni, I almost always have anchovies, oysters, and the Caesar salad. Last time I was there, we had all oysters, split a Caesar salad, then had foie gras. I thought, "Why not?" It was a strange dinner, but it was perfect. (See also pp. 246, 248, 251.)

Loretta Keller

BIZOU

598 Fourth Street
San Francisco, CA 94107
Phone: (415) 543-2222
Fax: (415) 543-2999

LOReTTa KeLLer is chef-owner of Bizou. She began her career in New Orleans, cooking with Susan Spicer. She went to Paris in 1985 and apprenticed with Philippe Groult, who was named a Meilleur Ouvrier de France in 1982. Settling in San Francisco, she made a name for herself at Jeremiah Tower's Stars restaurant, as chef of its Grill Room and the original Stars Café. In 1993, she opened Bizou, which Caroline Bates of *Gourmet* praised as "a bistro of integrity and charm."

"I love Loretta's cooking."

CINDY PAWLCYN

MUSTARDS GRILL

MY FOOD My cooking is defined by the seasons and by respect for local farming and fishing. At Bizou, there are a whole bunch of ingredients that I don't use—not because I don't like them, but because I really want my food fairly well defined in certain ways. I think it's important for the public to know what they are going to get when they come to Bizou. The idea of Bizou was to create a local and contemporary equivalent of the great French bistros and Italian trattorias—a place with personality, that's candid, friendly, comfortable, animated, and affordable.

LoReTTa'S PICKS

GLOBE RESTAURANT

290 Pacific Avenue, San Francisco
(415) 391-4132

Globe is run by a very friendly couple, and the food here is very honest. The menu is fairly limited, which I actually find refreshing because I know that whatever I order is going to be perfectly executed. They use really wonderful, fresh, seasonal ingredients supplied by local farmers. You can just tell when the food arrives at the table that it's been handled carefully. They have a spit that they use for chickens, which they usually serve with mashed potatoes, and they do a leg of lamb that they slice really thinly and serve with artichokes. They also have a wood-burning oven for pizzas, so there's this fire thing going on that I really like. And I really like their shellfish version of escargot. Plus, it's open late.

JARDINIÈRE

300 Grove Street, San Francisco
(415) 861-5555

I think Traci Des Jardins is doing the best food in the city. Her cooking is seasonal, very, very creative and bold, but refined as well. Her terrines are great, especially the foie gras terrine and the rabbit terrine with apple salad and horseradish. I also enjoy and admire her commitment to domestic artisan cheesemaking. She's an extremely gifted chef. (See also p. 247.)

SAM'S GRILL

374 Bush Street (at Belden Alley),
San Francisco
(415) 421-0594

Sam's is an institution. It's mostly a lunch place—there are a lot of bankers and lawyers who eat here. It's small, and they have booths with buzzers for calling the waiters and curtains for privacy. They don't buy anything frozen. The owner is on a crusade to save the salmon and the steelhead in all these rivers. He's really pretty extraordinary. I'll go there to eat Dungeness crab when it's in season. They do it real well—no frills. I usually order the Petrale sole, which they serve with a piece of boiled potato and tons of tartar sauce. They have great sand dabs, and the Olympia oyster cocktail must come with over forty oysters, all in a little parfait glass. They give you the condiments—fresh horseradish, ketchup, lemon—and you make your own cocktail sauce. The waiters are old Italian guys in tuxedos. They play cards in the afternoon and then come back for the dinner shift. It's cheap, and they do a huge business.

LORETTA'S PICKS

STARS

555 Golden Gate, San Francisco
(415) 861-STAR

Stars is still a great place. It's comfortable, it's open late, and it's a bit of an institution in San Francisco. It's a great brasserie. The vision of Jeremiah Tower, the founding chef and former owner, was so strong and so well-defined that the restaurant still has some of his energy and electricity. He had the personality to keep a really talented group of people together. There's nostalgia there for me; it was an amazing time to work there.

ZUNI CAFÉ

1658 Market Street, San Francisco
(415) 552-2522

I have great respect for Zuni. It's been very important to locals for twenty years, and it has remained consistent. I crave some of the classic, signature dishes, like the ricotta gnocchi. And yet they always manage to surprise me with new things, too. There's an ingenuity to the design as well—it's both appealing and functional, from the copper at the bar to the glasses. They're geniuses. It's a great example of a restaurant that has evolved in an extraordinary way. (See also pp. 246, 248, 249.)

"I've never had anything at Bizou that wasn't good. Loretta can cook!"

JOYCE GOLDSTEIN
FORMERLY OF SQUARE ONE

Emily Luchetti

PASTRY CHEF, FARALLON

450 Post Street (between Mason
and Powell Streets)
San Francisco, CA 94102
Phone: (415) 956-6969
Fax: (415) 834-1234
www.farallonrestaurant.com

EMILY LUCHETTI is executive pastry chef of Farallon, a restaurant specializing in seafood, which is owned by her former Stars colleague Mark Franz. She was formerly the pastry chef of Stars Restaurant and is the author of *Stars Desserts* and *Four Star Desserts*, which was nominated for a James Beard Cookbook Award in 1995. She was the president of Women Chefs and Restaurateurs from 1994 to 1999. Her many honors include being named one of the Top Ten Pastry Chefs of 1994 by *Chocolatier* magazine, and receiving several nominations for the James Beard Award as Best Pastry Chef.

MY FOOD I believe that desserts increase the social interactions and experiences of friends and family, as they linger around the table to eat that last course. Beauty is only skin deep. Desserts' primary focus should be on flavor. They exist to taste great, not necessarily to entertain us. Desserts should be emotionally fulfilling.

EMILY'S PICKS

ARAWAN

47 Caledonia Street, Sausalito
(415) 332-0882
This is a great place for Thai food in Sausalito, not far from where I live. Their *pad sai roong* is great, and so is their pork with eggplant.

BIZOU

598 Fourth Street, San Francisco
(415) 543-2222
Bizou is a casual bistro, but the food is fabulous and not too refined. [Chef-owner] Loretta Keller's palate is great, and her food is full of flavor and perfectly seasoned. She does really wonderful, slow-simmering dishes, like beef cheeks. (See also p. 234.)

FENG NIAN

2650 Bridgeway, Sausalito
(415) 331-5300
I love their moo shu pork and shrimp fried rice. After a long day in the pastry department, I've had so much sugar that my body craves carbohydrates and protein!

JARDINIÈRE

300 Grove Street, San Francisco
(415) 861-5555
I love going there, and I love Traci Des Jardins's food. Her portion size is great, and her flavor balance is incredible. Her food is always different, so if there's some special thing that she's trying out, I'll order that. When I go out, I'm apt to order meat.

Her lamb dishes are incredible, and she always serves foie gras in really interesting ways. All her salads have intense flavor. All of her food is very intense and full of flavor, but it's not too heavy. (See also p. 247.)

RIVOLI

1539 Solano Avenue, Berkeley
(510) 526-2542
Chef-owner Wendy Brucker has really nice food and a menu that changes about every three weeks, with Italian and French influences. It's very flavorful and well seasoned, yet simple and straightforward. I also like the casualness of this place. (See also p. 250.)

BRADLEY OGDEN is chef-owner of the Lark Creek Group, whose restaurants include One Market Restaurant, the Lark Creek Inn, and Lark Creek Cafes in San Mateo and Walnut Creek. His many honors include the 1993 James Beard Award as Best Chef: California, and an IACP Award for his cookbook, *Breakfast, Lunch and Dinner*. He is a 1977 graduate of The Culinary Institute of America.

MY FOOD I emphasize farm-fresh ingredients and high standards, for my food as well as for service and hospitality. My cooking is American, but with an added level of gutsiness and sophistication. I also like to showcase American wines in my restaurants.

Bradley Ogden

THE LARK CREEK INN

234 Magnolia Avenue
Larkspur, CA 94939
Phone: (415) 924-7766
Fax: (415) 924-7117
www.larkcreek.com

ONE MARKET RESTAURANT

1 Market Street
San Francisco, CA 94105
Phone: (415) 777-5577
Fax: (415) 777-4411
www.onemarket.com

BRADLEY'S PICKS

BOLINAS BAY BAKERY AND CAFÉ

20 Wharf Road, Bolinas
(415) 868-0211
The restaurant uses only organic flour in its baked goods, and also features organic produce throughout its menu, which ranges from salads to pizzas. I love coming here for steamed clams and barbecued oysters. They also carry a large selection of northern California wines.

CHEZ PANISSE

1517 Shattuck Avenue, Berkeley
(510) 548-5525
I go to both the Café upstairs and the more formal dining room downstairs. The Café, which has an à la carte menu, is great for snacks like pizza—a recent version featured spring onions, Parmesan, prosciutto, and an egg—and a glass of wine. The Café just started accepting reservations. Downstairs, which serves one prix fixe menu that changes nightly, for dinner only, is more for special occasions. This is a place I like to bring out-of-town guests. (See also p. 255.)

HAWTHORNE LANE

22 Hawthorne Street (off Howard Street), San Francisco
(415) 777-9779
I love the California-Asian food here. The menu changes daily because of the restaurant's focus on locally available ingredients, while its techniques are drawn from Europe and Asia. Anne and David Gingrass offer dishes such as salmon tartare with a dill crème fraîche, or tuna tartare with fried nori chips. I also love the service here. They really know how to treat individuals, and they have such a great attitude: They make you feel appreciated. I really like to bring people from out of town here. Be sure to save room for the desserts—they are great!

POSTRIO

545 Post Street (between Taylor and Mason Streets), San Francisco
(415) 776-7825
The energy at Postrio, which serves breakfast, lunch, and dinner, is great. I know everybody there, so it is fun to visit. The cuisine is influenced by California, Asia, and the Mediterranean, and features local ingredients from more than forty local farms. Everything is made in-house, including breads, smoked fish, and charcuterie.

YUET LEE SEAFOOD RESTAURANT

1300 Stockton Street (at Broadway), San Francisco (North Beach)
(415) 982-6020
Credit cards are not accepted, and you can bring your own wine or beer.
This Chinese restaurant serves good seafood dishes and is popular among chefs as a great late-night spot, because they serve food until three A.M. It's inexpensive, and the sauces are surprisingly light and delicious. When you're there, don't miss the chili squid with black bean sauce.

MUSTARDS GRILL

7399 St. Helena Highway
Napa, CA 94558
Phone: (707) 944-2424

Cindy Pawlcyn

CINDY PAWLCYN, chef-owner of Mustards Grill, was also the original creative force behind Buckeye Roadhouse, Bix, Fog City Diner, Roti, and the Rio Grill. She has been nominated twice for a James Beard Award for Best Chef: California, and is the recipient of a Robert Mondavi Award for Culinary Excellence. She is also a charter member of Women Chefs and Restaurateurs, and the author of *The Fog City Diner Cookbook.*

MY FOOD At Mustards the food needs to be especially wine-friendly because we are in Napa and people are there to drink wine. We look at food from places all over the world that share the same latitude as Mustards. We also look at food from places that have the exact opposite latitude, such as Argentina or Chile, which are both wine-producing regions. Flavors from places with similar weather go together. Mustards provides an inviting, fun-spirited environment.

CINDY'S PICKS

BIZOU

598 Fourth Street (at Brannan),
San Francisco (415) 543-2222
I love Loretta Keller's cooking—especially her flatbreads, which are made in the restaurant's wood-burning oven, and her fish dishes, which range from local sand dabs to scallops with wild mushrooms, endive, and balsamic vinegar. While the menu changes frequently, when rabbit is offered, it is very good. (See also p. 250.)

THE DINER

6476 Washington Street, Yountville
(in Napa Valley) (707) 944-2626
I love going here for breakfast. I usually order the specials, which are often south-of-the-border-inspired —anything from scrambled eggs on a tortilla to cornmeal pancakes.

TIMO'S

842 Valencia Street
(between 19th and 20th Streets),
San Francisco (Mission District)
(415) 647-0558
Timo's is a Spanish and south Central American restaurant [run by Carlos and Theresa Corredor], serving more than a hundred different tapas dishes. They serve great little plates of food, such as ceviche, salt cod, and tortilla, and also offer a nice selection of wines from Spain and California.

CINDY'S PICKS

YANK SING

427 Battery Street (between Clay and Washington), San Francisco
(415) 362-1640

Yank Sing only serves dim sum, and their dim sum is considered some of the best in San Francisco. They have especially good dumplings, which come filled with shrimp, pork, or vegetables. It's a great place to take the kids, especially since the staff tends to be very patient. Yank Sing has even served Peking duck in dim sum portions. (See also p. 243.)

YUET LEE SEAFOOD RESTAURANT

1300 Stockton Street (at Broadway), San Francisco (North Beach)
(415) 982-6020

Yuet Lee is a Chinese restaurant that's great for late-night eating. It's casual, inexpensive, and filled with lots of characters. You feel like you're in a different world when you're there. They have great fish and squab as well as hot-pot specialties. (See also p. 253.)

CHEZ PANISSE, 1971–PRESENT

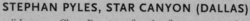

Inspiring a Generation of American Chefs

There was a time when aspiring chefs made pilgrimages to the Michelin three-star restaurants of France in order to experience the potential of dining. But over the last thirty years, it seems every self-respecting American chef has, for the same reason, made a pilgrimage to an American restaurant with no parking, no bar, and a menu with no choices.

Is Chez Panisse the most influential restaurant in America? We asked leading chefs about some of the most important meals of their lives, and Chez Panisse was the single most frequently mentioned restaurant. What was it like to visit Chez Panisse for the first time? What has kept them going back? How have their visits affected their cooking philosophies?

STEPHAN PYLES, STAR CANYON (DALLAS)

"I ate at Chez Panisse for the first time in the late 1970s, and I've continued to have great meals here throughout the years. There's a group of about twelve chefs who consult for American Airlines, of which Alice Waters, Chez Panisse's chef-owner, is a part. We have a conclave each year in one of the chefs' home cities, and this year it was in San Francisco at Chez Panisse. It was like being in Alice's home. She was actually delivering plates, and she moved from table to table tasting things to make sure everything was all right. I'm awed to think that I've been eating here for thirty years, and it's still inspirational!"

SEAN KELLY, AUBERGINE CAFÉ (DENVER)

"It's been a guiding light for me. There's no greater restaurant— I've eaten at Chez Panisse at least twenty-five times. I bought the Chez Panisse Menu Cookbook when I was twenty, and it took me ten years to get everything out of it."

JIM BECKER, RAUXA (SOMERVILLE, MA)

"I first went to Chez Panisse at a stage in my career when I really thought more was more. I was intrigued by chefs who piled tons of different ingredients onto a plate. I knew that the food at Chez Panisse was extremely simple, and the menu sounded almost boring to me. But it was impeccable. Everything was perfectly prepared and seasoned, from the bread to the dessert. I had lobster with spring vegetables in broth, a French cheese-and-onion tart, and a custard for dessert. It was the first time I realized that sometimes less is more. The current trend among chefs is to simplify, and Chez Panisse is responsible for putting me on that path."

EMILY LUCHETTI, PASTRY CHEF AT FARALLON (SAN FRANCISCO)

"One of the most memorable desserts I've ever eaten was at Chez Panisse. I remember reading it on the menu and saying, 'Big deal—it's just vanilla ice cream with caramel sauce and candied walnuts.' But in fact it was one of the most sublime desserts I've had in my life. The vanilla ice cream and the sauce were both perfect. Even though it was simple, it was heaven. It's a pretty rare experience to be eating food that you're so focused on that while you're eating it, you're thinking, 'If anyone tries to take this away from me, I'll kill them!'"

JOHANNE KILLEEN, AL FORNO (PROVIDENCE)

"The single meal that has had the biggest impact on me was our dinner at Chez Panisse in 1981. An artist friend of ours lived in California, and whenever he came to Al Forno, he would talk about Chez Panisse. I was just insane about getting there, and that's why we—or I—planned our honeymoon in California. It was the first meal we ate in the Bay Area, and it was the turning point for me in terms of the direction I wanted to go with our food and restaurant. We wanted to do Italian food, but we always felt that customers would want fancy things with bells and whistles. Our experience at Chez Panisse gave me the courage to say, 'What's important is ingredients. What's important is integrity. What's important is purity.' It's the kind of food that I love, and it's the kind of food we had experienced in Italy. It gave me the courage to pursue a purer approach to my own cooking. Our meal started with prosciutto served with several different fruits, including melon and berries—all of which were perfect. We could hear this chucka, chucka, chucka *coming from the kitchen, which turned out to be the cooks shucking individual Pigeon Point oysters for the oyster soufflé! I thought, 'Oh, my God—this is incredible.' It was pure and simple. The main course was grilled quail with baby lettuces, and George could not believe that that was the main course until he tasted it. The lettuces were beautiful, and the quail was perfectly cooked. We had a Ridge Cabernet that was suggested by our waitperson. Dessert was a glass of Sauternes and an olive oil cake with an apricot mousse on the side. Of course, I had stars in my eyes anyway because I was on my honeymoon, but the meal had an enormous impact on me."*

GEORGE GERMON, AL FORNO (PROVIDENCE)

"I will never forget our first dinner at Chez Panisse. Even with all our trips all around the world, it is the only meal that has ever changed my approach to cooking. I actually remember seeing Alice Waters in the kitchen, with a little scarf on her head. What's ironic is that I was furious with Johanne for bringing me there. I was upset that my whole meal had been chosen for me. Looking at the menu, I kept thinking, 'Well, I'm not really interested in these things.' Then, one course after another, I was completely won over. I don't think it really hit me until the next day that something important had been triggered there. I would always refer to that dinner at Chez Panisse as a reference point and say, 'Is this as honest? Is this as straightforward?'"

SANFORD D'AMATO, SANFORD (MILWAUKEE)

"You don't realize how good the meal is until you leave. It is a very retrospective place, because it is so low-key. We had a tiny appetizer of lamb tongue and salad. Up to that point, it was the best salad I had ever had. I had never tasted lamb like that before—it was the technique and the product. I remember leaving Chez Panisse thinking it was very good, and then later in my trip, after having eaten at other places, realizing just how good it had been. It is something that builds up."

CINDY PAWLCYN, MUSTARDS GRILL (NAPA)

"I go to Chez Panisse once a month with my pastry chef friends. We love it, because we don't have to choose. I will order wine that goes with the menu, and then all we have to do is sit back, enjoy ourselves, and see what is in season. To me, it is better than a massage or a facial; I always come out rejuvenated. I will come out thinking, 'I never thought of that,' or 'What a nice sauce.' It is pure heaven. There is nothing more difficult than going into a restaurant you haven't been to in a while, reading four appetizers and entrées, and having to choose! It is torture. Downstairs at Chez Panisse, they take the torture out of it."

RICK BAYLESS, FRONTERA GRILL AND TOPOLOBAMPO (CHICAGO)

"When you recommend Chez Panisse to some people, they'll come back to you and say, 'Yes, we went there, but we didn't think it was so great.' The problem was that they just didn't get it,

because they couldn't get on the wavelength of perfect resonance with local ingredients. Some people just don't have the perspective to be able to appreciate the absolutely perfect peach that was lying on the plate at the end of their meal."

ROBERT DEL GRANDE, CAFÉ ANNIE (HOUSTON)

"I just had dinner there, and it was the first time I ever had the Chez Panisse experience. It was incredible. I understand how people can completely miss it. It is so highly refined; it is a doorway to another side. If you had just come from a three-star restaurant in France, I can see how you would miss the point. Alice has told me she gets letters from disappointed guests who go there because they know the reputation of the restaurant, not because they know what it is about. I was there for a Bandol wine dinner, and saw what they call in France a ferme auberge—a farm and restaurant together. If you don't get the farming aspect of Chez Panisse, you won't get the restaurant. I have always admired Alice because she believes in this, despite all odds."

PAUL BERTOLLI, OLIVETO (OAKLAND)

"At Chez Panisse [where Paul was formerly the chef], people used to come from quite a wide distance to eat. Customers had grand expectations of what the restaurant should be, but every night was an experiment. Some nights it was brilliant, some nights it was good, and some nights it was... Well, after a certain point, I don't think it ever failed, but there were nights when it did in the early years. I might have five hours to get dinner ready for a hundred people—with a menu that changed every night! Over the years, I got better at it, of course, but there were nights when I said to myself, 'This is not as good as it could be.' One night I had eighty squiggling eels in the kitchen, and I couldn't kill them. I mean, they are just primordial, these things. You have to beat them over the head or slit their throats. I called a Japanese friend and he said, 'Salt them. That works—it's a Roman trick.' So I wasn't able to kill them until around a quarter to six that evening. When the first customers were coming in at six, the eels were in rigor mortis, and I didn't really have anything else to serve. If that happened to me now, I would say, 'Sorry, I'm making a different menu.' But then, I was young and insistent, so I did things like that."

BISTRO

BISTRO JEANTY

6510 Washington Street, Yountville
(707) 944-0103

"I had a phenomenal meal here. Philippe Jeanty is doing really great, classic French bistro food like pigs' feet terrine, and things you just don't see that often."

—TRACI DES JARDINS, JARDINIÉRE

"You can always find something good here. I especially like his lamb tongue salad, his pigs' feet salad, and his rabbit terrine. The steak tartare is also excellent."

—HIRO SONE, TERRA

"Who else serves steak tartare anymore? And I love steak tartare!"

—LISSA DOUMANI, TERRA

BreakFast

GORDON'S CAFÉ AND WINE BAR

6770 Washington Avenue, Yountville
(707) 944- 8246

"In addition to being a café and wine bar, Gordon's also has a bakery and charcuterie and is a local breakfast hangout with communal tables. It's a great breakfast place that serves fresh baked goods [dinner is served on Fridays only]. The food is really clean, fresh, and simple, and everyone seems comfortable here."

—LISSA DOUMANI, TERRA

FINe DInInG

THE FRENCH LAUNDRY

6640 Washington Street, Yountville
(707) 944-2380

"The way Thomas Keller presents his food is very dramatic—and his passion shows in each dish."

—LISSA DOUMANI, TERRA

"The quality was amazing, and the pacing was excellent. It was magical."

—JEAN-MARIE LACROIX, THE FOUNTAIN RESTAURANT (PHILADELPHIA)

"The best meal I've had in the United States was here. Out of fifty-four dishes that the table of six I was with was served, I thought fifty-three of them were perfect."

—MARK MILLER, COYOTE CAFÉ (SANTA FE, LAS VEGAS)

"It's great—if you can get in!"

—HIRO SONE, TERRA

HAMBURGER

TAYLOR'S REFRESHER

933 Main Street, St. Helena
(707) 963-3486

"They've got a great burger, which they cook on a griddle and serve on an egg-sesame bun."

—CINDY PAWLCYN, MUSTARDS GRILL
(SEE ALSO P. 262.)

ITALIAN

TRA VIGNE

1050 Charter Oak Avenue, St. Helena
(707) 963-4444

"If we are in Napa, we have to go here. The Tuscan-style food is so delicious and pure. It is great just sitting outside and eating and drinking wine. Chef Michael Chiarello feels cuisine in his heart. He wants food to be brought into people's lives."

—GALE GAND AND RICK TRAMONTO,
BRASSERIE T AND TRU (CHICAGO)

"I think Tra Vigne has great risotto. The food is innovative, and the menu changes a lot. Michael Chiarello is there a lot, which helps to ensure that the food is consistently good."

—BRADLEY OGDEN, THE LARK CREEK INN AND
ONE MARKET

MARKET

NAPA VALLEY OLIVE OIL COMPANY

835 Charter Oak Avenue, St. Helena
(707) 963-4173

"Visiting this store is a great food experience. We get dried porcini mushrooms and borlotti beans from them. You can get really good things either to snack on or to take home. It's family-run and it's unbelievably quaint inside. They have thousands of business cards on the walls. It's a very nice and comfortable place to hang out."

—LISSA DOUMANI, TERRA

WINERY

SCHRAMSBURG WINERY

1400 Schramsburg Road, Calistoga
(707) 942-4558

"You can tour the cave, which is over a hundred years old and was carved out by hand by Chinese laborers. They'll also show you how they make their sparkling wine, and you can taste a couple of different vintages."

—HIRO SONE, TERRA

napa valley
LOCAL HIGHLIGHTS

Hiro Sone and Lissa Doumani

TERRA

1345 Railroad Avenue
St. Helena, CA 94574
Phone: (707) 963-8931
www.terrarestaurant.com

HIRO SONE and LISSA DOUMANI are chef-owners of Terra in St. Helena. They have received *Wine Spectator*'s Award of Excellence, and Terra is consistently mentioned in the Bay Area *ZagatSurvey*'s Top Ten for food, service, and décor. Hiro Sone won the 2000 Robert Mondavi Award of Excellence. They are co-authors of *Terra: Cooking from the Heart of Napa Valley.*

OUR FOOD We cook from our hearts. We consider our restaurant an extension of our home, and each patron an invited guest arriving for dinner. We try to reflect this feeling in the menus we compose, the way we prepare and serve the food, the ambiance of the dining room, and the hospitality of our staff.

Our cooking is also a reflection of who we are—our heritages, our travels, our memories and our own tastes. Each dish contains traces of Hiro's Japanese ancestry and his French and Italian culinary training, and of Lissa's Lebanese and European background and her Napa Valley roots. Each dish is also inspired by our love of the Napa Valley and the fine wines produced here.

HIRO AND LISSA'S PICKS

BOUCHON

6534 Washington Street, Yountville
(707) 944-8037

Lissa Doumani: One Wednesday a month a girlfriend and I go to Bouchon, an upscale bistro serving classic bistro fare such as steak frites and tarte Tatin, opened by the French Laundry's Thomas Keller and his brother Joseph. We'll have oysters and clams and drink real drinks, like Negronis and sidecars, instead of wine. Randy, the bartender here, is the best!

THE GRILL AT MEADOWOOD

900 Meadowood Lane, St. Helena
(707) 963-3646

Meadowood is a distinguished resort that serves breakfast, lunch, and dinner in the Grill; we like to go there for breakfast. We can sit outside, right above the golf course. Neither one of us knows how to golf, so we find it very amusing to watch the golfers. We'll sit outside and drink very strong coffee and laugh—but not loudly. While they have really nice pancakes, French toast, and omelets, Hiro is addicted to their *huevos rancheros!*

HANA JAPANESE RESTAURANT

101 Golf Course Drive, Rohnert Park
(just south of Santa Rosa)
(707) 586-0270

Sometimes we'll go to this restaurant twice in one day. We'll go for lunch, and then later, we'll ask each other, "Where are we going to go for dinner?" And we'll agree, "Let's go back to Hana!" He has great fish that's so fresh—he gets amazing tuna, *toro*, and good local *uni*. Lissa orders an assortment of sashimi, and Hiro just eats whatever the chef makes for him.

TAYLOR'S REFRESHER

933 Main Street, St. Helena
(707) 963-3486

This is a local burger joint that a friend of ours just rebuilt. Hiro loves their blue cheese burgers, medium rare, that are really juicy and made with tons of blue cheese. Lissa had a cheeseburger that she really liked because they would cook it blue [very rare], along with a huge cup of lemonade. We recently saw noted wine writer Robert Parker in line, ordering a double cheeseburger! (See also p. 261.)

TRIPLE-S RANCH RESORT

4600 Mountain Home Ranch Road, Calistoga
(707) 942-6730

This is a small old-fashioned steak house in the Triple-S Resort. We usually order rib-eye steak, which starts with a plate of green onions and black

HIRO AND LISSA'S PICKS

olives, and sliced salami and peper- oncini with crackers. You get your choice of soup or salad; we usually have salad with blue cheese dressing. With the steak, you get a choice of baked potato or fried potato. We like the baked, and get sour cream on the side. For dessert, the portion of ice cream is bigger than the bowl! The whole meal costs seventeen-fifty. It's outside, so you also have a view of the mountains, a pool, and chickens running around.

LISSA DOUMANI on

What to Drink with Oysters

I actually don't care for wine with oysters all that much. I like a lot of lemon with oysters, and I just don't find that the acidity and the brininess of oysters goes well with wine. Oysters with Champagne is a huge fallacy to me. The liquid from the oysters fights with the acidity of the Champagne. To me, it makes the oysters taste more metallic and the Champagne taste slightly bit- ter, depending on which is the stronger. Sake, however, can handle the brini- ness of oysters. It has a richness, but it's not too rich. The acidity is lower, so it allows you taste the oyster without upsetting the flavor of the sake. [For more on sake, see p. 206.]

ELIZABETH TERRY on
Savannah Highlights

We are on the coast, and therefore we have access to lots of great seafood. If you come to Savannah, you shouldn't miss simple boiled crab or steamed shrimp. They are a really great experience!

In February, we get shad from the Ogeechee River. September is flounder and blue crab season. At the restaurant, we do flounder stuffed with blue crab and served with butter beans, new little lady peas, country ham, and grilled mushrooms. Oysters are in season from the end of October through the end of February. They are at their best when it is very cold. We make oyster stew, and oysters with country ham and pastry. At the restaurant, we use Bluffton oysters, which are harvested right across the river from us. They are little tiny oysters with a wonderful salty flavor—they're just heaven.

Other local fish include scamp, which is similar to flounder; American red snapper; and black grouper. Every once in a while, we have real treats like cobia and bluefish. People are always asking, "Is bluefish fishy?" But no fish is fishy if it is right out of the water—fishy is not a taste I want to cook!

We also have specific local fruit seasons in Savannah. June is blueberry season, and peaches are at their peak in July. In September, the pears are just coming in.

ELIZABETH TERRY is chef-owner of Elizabeth on 37th in Savannah. She is the co-author of *Savannah Seasons: Food and Stories from Elizabeth on 37th*, which she wrote with her daughter Alexis Terry. She won the 1995 James Beard Award as Best Chef: Southeast. In 1999, the restaurant received a Silver Spoon Award from *Food Arts* magazine, and was named one of the top forty restaurants in America by *Forbes* magazine.

Elizabeth Terry

ELIZABETH ON 37TH

105 E. 37th Street
Savannah, GA 31401
Phone: (912) 236-5547
Fax: (912) 232-1095
www.savannah-online.com/
elizabeth

MY FOOD We are in the deep South in a very small city, in a real mom-and-pop restaurant. The heat and the sea are very much a part of Savannah, and therefore a part of my cooking and the restaurant experience. If someone says they never have had grits, black-eyed peas, okra, or country ham, we certainly bring them some!

There is a real tradition here of a gentle pace, not only in dining but in going about daily life. When people come from other parts of the country, they are a little surprised by the pace. When our restaurant was named one of *Food & Wine* magazine's top twenty-five restaurants in the country, we had a couple who flew all the way from New York specifically to have dinner in our restaurant. They wanted French bread with their meal and were very upset that we only serve biscuits. To them, French bread was part of the dining experience. I am certain that they felt they had just selected another restaurant in New York. They just got here too fast. It took us all night to woo them into the pace and style of our restaurant. I always hope that people have spent at least one night in Savannah and come to our restaurant the second night, once they've had a chance to get into the pace of the South.

We are in a little town, and most of my favorite restaurants are casual. If I want something fancier, I like to go to my own restaurant for a nice bottle of wine and a piece of fish.

ELIZABETH'S PICKS

CAFÉ METROPOLE

109 Martin Luther King Jr. Boulevard, Savannah
(912) 236-0110
Café Metropole is kind of funky. I know that is not a very modern word, but that is exactly what this place is. It is our great, chic, weird lunch place. Their salads are wonderful, and they have a brie, apple, and basil bread plate that is great. They also have a bakery and make wonderful breads and fruit tarts. It's run by a young fellow from New York and California. The space used to be an old bus station, and they don't have air-conditioning. It's also an art gallery. It is very relaxed.

DESPOSITO'S

Macceo Drive, Thunderbolt (just across the Wilmington Island Bridge)
(912) 897-9963
This is another place where I have been going for about twenty years. The restaurant is in an old building overlooking a marsh. It's a newspapers-on-the-table kind of place. They have great blue crabs and shrimp, and cold beer. You buy the crabs by the dozen and the shrimp by the pound. As for beer, I like whatever is on draft.

JOHNNY HARRIS

1651 E. Victory Drive, Savannah
(912) 354-7810

This is a great place for barbecue. In Savannah, the barbecue isn't dry-rub—it is usually wet, with a tomato base. At Johnny Harris, I like to get either the pork or the chicken.

MAI WAI

2130 East Victory Drive, Savannah
(912) 234-6778

We have been going to Mai Wai for about twenty years. It's my favorite Chinese restaurant, and it's on the way to the beach. I get the ping pung shrimp, hold the shrimp, so it is vegetarian—just broccoli, onions, snow peas, and mushrooms in a light lobster sauce with rice. The moo shu pork is also great.

NORTH BEACH GRILL

Vanhorne Drive, Tybee
(912) 786-9003

North Beach Grill is a casual, kick-back sort of place, right on the beach. Their food is simple and has lots of Caribbean influences, and everything is served on paper plates. They do great things with pineapple and mango, and they have a great grilled fish with black beans and salsa.

VINNIE VAN GO GO'S

317 West Bryan Street, Savannah
(912) 233-6394

Vinnie's is a great pizza place. I love their pizza with sun-dried tomato, spinach, and feta. They also have a great spinach salad.

Bar

PALACE KITCHEN

2030 5th Avenue, Seattle
(206) 448-2001

"For really good margaritas."

—THIERRY RAUTUREAU, ROVER'S

Breads

GRAND CENTRAL BAKING CO.

Multiple locations in Seattle and Portland, including:
Grand Central Bakery
214 1st Avenue S., Seattle
(206) 622-3644

"We get the bread for our restaurant at Grand Central [which sells its rustic Italian loaf, rosemary rolls, olive bread, cinnamon rolls, and sticky buns at wholesale and retail]."

—THIERRY RAUTUREAU, ROVER'S

LA PANZARELLA

1314 E. Union Street, Seattle
(206) 325-5217

"For Italian country bread."

—THIERRY RAUTUREAU, ROVER'S

LE PANIER

1902 Pike Place (in Pike Place Market), Seattle
(206) 441-3669

"For the almond croissants, and the ham and cheese croissants."

—THIERRY RAUTUREAU, ROVER'S

MACRINA BAKERY AND CAFÉ

2408 1st Avenue, Seattle
(206) 448-4032

"Macrina rotates its bread selections, which include herb wheat walnut bread and cinnamon monkey bread. They are not to be missed!"

—CHRISTINE KEFF, FLYING FISH

"Macrina has excellent breads." (See also p. 274.)

—THIERRY RAUTUREAU, ROVER'S

Breakfast

CAFÉ CAMPAGNE

1600 Post Alley, Seattle
(206) 728-2233

"Café Campagne is a great breakfast spot. I love their big coffee, and they've got great granola, yogurt, and fruit."

—CHRISTINE KEFF, FLYING FISH

SAZERAC RESTAURANT

1101 4th Avenue, in the Hotel Monaco, Seattle
(206) 624-7755

"For southern-inspired cuisine. The restaurant is overseen by executive chef Jan Birnbaum of Catahoula in Napa Valley."

—CHRISTINE KEFF, FLYING FISH

CHOCOLATE

FRAN'S CHOCOLATES

Multiple locations, including:
2594 N.E. University Village, Seattle (206) 528-9969
10305 N.E. 10th Street, Bellevue (425) 453-1698
www.franschocolate.com

"Fran's are the best chocolates—they're just out of this world! They are beautifully wrapped, and the taste is soul-satisfying. I especially like the espresso truffle and the hazelnut cream truffle. Fran [Bigelow] also makes her own ice creams [which are sold only at the University Village location], including a burnt-sugar ice cream that is unbelievable."

—LESLIE MACKIE, MACRINA BAKERY

COFFEE

CAFFÈ LADRO

600 Queen Anne Avenue N., Seattle (206) 282-1549
2205 Queen Anne Avenue N., Seattle (206) 282-5313

"The espresso here is beautifully made. I like a double tall Americano, which is two shots of espresso plus hot water. They have incredible milk, which they steam perfectly, so it has a velvety frothiness. It is luscious!"

—LESLIE MACKIE, MACRINA BAKERY

TULLY'S

Multiple locations, including:
2000 1st Avenue, Seattle (206) 443-6871

"Seattle has no shortage of coffee places, but I like this one—where I always order a double espresso."

—THIERRY RAUTUREAU, ROVER'S

CORNED BEEF SANDWICH

PARK DELI

5011 S. Dawson Street (near Wilson Avenue), Seattle
(206) 722-6674

"A really good corned-beef sandwich."

—THIERRY RAUTUREAU, ROVER'S

FISH AND CHIPS

ANTHONY'S PIER 66

2201 Alaskan Way, Seattle
(206) 448-6688

"For batter-fried fish with tartar sauce."

—CHRISTINE KEFF, FLYING FISH

CHINOOKS AT SALMON BAY/LITTLE CHINOOK'S FISH AND CHIPS

1900 W. Nickerson Street, Seattle
(206) 283-4665

"I love their fish and chips."

—LESLIE MACKIE, MACRINA BAKERY

Hamburgers

MAGGIE BLUFF'S GRILL

2601 W. Marina Place, Seattle
(206) 283-8322

"I love their hamburgers, which they make with Velveeta cheese!"

—CHRISTINE KEFF, FLYING FISH

RED MILL BURGERS

312 N. 67th Street, Seattle
(Phinney Ridge)
(206) 783-6362
1613 W. Dravus, Seattle
(206) 284-6363

"Their hamburgers are so juicy that the juice will run down the sides of your mouth! They grill them to order, and serve them with their own sauce. There's always a long line!"

—THIERRY RAUTUREAU, ROVER'S

"Red Mill Burgers are old-fashioned hamburgers, in that they have shredded lettuce and a great sauce. The special sauce is the key. They also have fabulous fries and cumin onion rings."

—LESLIE MACKIE, MACRINA BAKERY

Ice Cream

SCOOP DU JOUR ICE CREAMERY

4029 E. Madison Street, Seattle
(206) 325-9562

"It's right next to Mad Pizza [see p. 276], so pizza followed by ice cream here is a great treat!"

—THIERRY RAUTUREAU, ROVER'S

Lemon Tart

MACRINA BAKERY

2408 1st Avenue, Seattle (206) 448-4032

"Don't miss Macrina's lemon tart!" (See also p. 274.)

—CHRISTINE KEFF, FLYING FISH

Market

PIKE PLACE MARKET

85 Pike Street, Seattle (206) 682-7453

"You have to see it, especially in the summer and fall."

—THIERRY RAUTUREAU, ROVER'S

UNIVERSITY DISTRICT FARMERS MARKET

N.E. 50th Street and University Way N.E. (University Heights School), Seattle
(206) 633-1024

"A great place to get produce and other food items."

—THIERRY RAUTUREAU, ROVER'S

Late Night

SEA GARDEN

509 7th Avenue S., Seattle
(International District)
(206) 623-2100

"They're open until three A.M. You've got to order the black bean crab, which is terrific. I also had shark fin soup there, and it was awesome!"

—THIERRY RAUTUREAU, ROVER'S

SEATTLE LOCAL HIGHLIGHTS

OYSTERS

ELLIOTT'S OYSTER HOUSE

1201 Alaskan Way, Seattle (206) 623-4340

"It is right on the water, and they have a huge selection of oysters, which are crisp and cold and not overly salty. Bay Water Sweets and Snow Creek are my two favorites. They also have a great selection of wines. My favorite accompaniment is either a Sauvignon Blanc or a crisp Pinot Grigio."

—LESLIE MACKIE, MACRINA BAKERY

MCCORMICK & SCHMICK'S

1103 1st Avenue, Seattle
(206) 623-5500

"Their oysters are tremendous!"

—CHRISTINE KEFF, FLYING FISH

SALUMERIA

SALUMI

309 3rd Avenue S. (off Pioneer Square), Seattle
(206) 621-8772

"My dad [Armandino Batali] just retired from Boeing after more than thirty years and opened a one-table restaurant and a salumeria where he makes salami, sopressata, and prosciutto by hand in his own curing room, and sells them by the quarter pound in little sandwiches. He is open four days a week for that, and then offers dinner once a week for ten: a set menu only, with no choices. A lady was in for lunch in November, and she was just glowing because she got a reservation at Salumi for the third week in April. She said he didn't want to give it to her—he was really brusque with her on the phone. Then he realized that she'd been there the week before for a sandwich and they'd talked, and so he said, 'All right, I'll let you have the third week in April.' I said, 'I've got to call Dad—he can't book out that far! What if he wants to go somewhere?' Plus, booking five months in advance makes New York waits look like a joke!"

—MARIO BATALI, BABBO, ESCA, AND LUPA (NEW YORK)

PIZZA

PEGASUS PIZZA

2758 Alki Avenue S.W., Seattle
(206) 932-4849

"Hands-down, the best pizza in town."

—CHRISTINE KEFF, FLYING FISH

PIECORA'S

1401 E. Madison Avenue, Seattle
(206) 322-9411

"I like the sweet Italian pizza, which has Italian sausage, roasted peppers, and lots of cheese. It is also thin-crust and not too saucy."

—LESLIE MACKIE, MACRINA BAKERY

TAPAS

HARVEST VINE

2701 E. Madison Street, Seattle
(206) 320-9771

"I love this little, informal neighborhood café celebrating Basque regional cooking that opened a block away from me a couple of years ago. Chef-owner Joseph Jimenez de Jimenez is a native of the region, and serves outstanding tapas ranging from stuffed piquillo peppers to rabbit casserole. If you don't get one of the few tables, you can sit at the bar and watch him cook. And he's also got a great little wine list featuring some very nice Spanish wines."

—THIERRY RAUTUREAU, ROVER'S

seafood

ANTHONY'S

2201 Alaskan Way, Seattle
(206) 448-6688
(Anthony's Pier 66, located on the
second floor, serves dinner, while
Anthony's Fish Bar is a sidewalk
walk-up.)

*"They have their own fishing
boats and are always
showcasing the best fish
they can get. They cook it in
a simple fashion, or with a
little twist like serving it
cedar-planked. Sometimes
I want a simple piece of fish
without a red pepper beurre
blanc or all kinds of garnishes on it, and this is
where I go."*

—LESLIE MACKIE, MACRINA BAKERY

ETTA'S SEAFOOD

2020 Western Avenue, Seattle
(206) 443-6000

*"This is another fabulous
place for fresh seafood.
Since it is also just north of
the [Pike Place] Market,
you get to have that experience as well. The food is
nicely prepared, and it is in
the midst of all the action."*

—LESLIE MACKIE, MACRINA BAKERY

sushi

HANA RESTAURANT

219 Broadway E., Seattle
(206) 328-1187

"Hana has great sushi."

—CHRISTINE KEFF, FLYING FISH

*"Hana is my favorite sushi place. It is a simple little restaurant,
but the food is fresh and delicious. The spicy tuna rolls are fabulous, and so is the smoked eel sushi. I am not a beer person, so I
like cold sake to drink."*

—LESLIE MACKIE, MACRINA BAKERY

wine

CHINOOK WINES

Wine Country Road at Wittkopf Road, Prosser
(509) 786-2725

*"Kay Simon is the winemaker, and she makes a fabulous
Chardonnay, Sauvignon Blanc, Merlot, and recently a Cabernet
Franc. They are all consistently delicious. Her wines go perfectly
with the food out here."*

—LESLIE MACKIE, MACRINA BAKERY

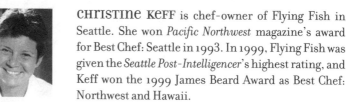

Christine Keff

FLYING FISH

2234 1st Avenue

Seattle, WA 98121

Phone: (206) 728-8595

Fax: (206) 728-1551

www.flyingfishseattle.com

CHRISTINE KEFF is chef-owner of Flying Fish in Seattle. She won *Pacific Northwest* magazine's award for Best Chef: Seattle in 1993. In 1999, Flying Fish was given the *Seattle Post-Intelligencer*'s highest rating, and Keff won the 1999 James Beard Award as Best Chef: Northwest and Hawaii.

MY FOOD Our menu is divided into small plates, large plates, and platters, which are for sharing. Sometimes people don't know quite where to go with it, so the waiters are very careful to get there early in the diner's experience to guide them through it. A lot of times, starting with a platter puts people at ease: because it's food that is usually eaten with the hands, everybody digs in and licks their fingers, and has fun.

We've got about twenty-five different species of seafood on our menu at any time, between shellfish and fin fish. We want people to try different things. It took us a long time to find fresh squid, believe it or not, and we pay about three times as much as other people pay for squid. It's worth it, because it makes a huge difference. We serve a simple little calamari dish, but people go ape over it! I keep telling them, "It's not the dish, it's the squid." They can tell that something's different and that they really like it, but they can't tell what it is.

We don't use any frozen products or farmed fish, like farm-raised salmon. Sometimes in the winter when the weather's really bad in Alaska, we don't get any salmon for a day or two. While an out-of-town guest might find it hard to understand when we don't have salmon available, if a Seattlite can't have salmon for a day, she'll live.

CHRISTINE'S PICKS

CAFÉ LAGO

2305 24th Avenue E., Seattle
(206) 329-8005

The pasta served at Café Lago is easily the best in Seattle. One of the owners—it's a husband-and-wife team, Jordi Viladas and his wife, Carla Leonardi—is from Lucca in Italy, so the food is very authentic. The pasta, from gnocchi to lasagna to ravioli, is all made daily by hand, and it's extraordinary. Their Italian red sauce is wonderful. It's a small, noisy place, with hard chairs, paper-covered tables, and great wines by the glass. The menu is small, and it hardly ever changes. They have three pastas that do change, a few different pizzas that they make in a wood-burning oven, a steak, some simple desserts—biscotti, lemon tart—and that's about it.

LA MEDUSA

4857 Rainier Avenue S., Seattle
(206) 723-2192

Columbia City is an area that is culturally and ethnically quite diverse, and it's very fun. La Medusa is a Sicilian restaurant run by two gals [Sherri Serino and Lisa Becklund], one of whom is Sicilian. They have these greens that are cooked in a broth, and I don't know what they do to them, but they are incredible. It's an appetizer, but I like to order a double plate of them as an entrée. They have certain things you can't find in other places in Seattle. The dry shaved tuna on linguini with olive oil is very strongly flavored and probably not for everybody, but I think it's delicious. We're kind of a conservative food town, and people need to be coaxed into eating new things. I think those gals do a good

CHRISTINE'S PICKS

job of that. I'm glad to see them doing that, because that's how a dining public becomes a little more sophisticated and adventuresome, and then all chefs get to try even more new things.

LUSH LIFE

2331 2nd Avenue, Seattle
(206) 441-9842

Lush Life is right around the corner from my restaurant, and I eat there a lot. The food is really good—and they are open late, so I can eat at the bar by myself. It's fun. They serve rustic Italian food, little pizzas and pastas, and a few entrées. I like to order their baby spinach salad, and one of my favorite pizzas there is the sausage, tomato, and garlic. I typically order a gin martini, because I'm usually there at the end of the night!

THE PAINTED TABLE

92 Madison Street (in the Alexis Hotel), Seattle
(206) 624-3646

If I want something special, I go to the Painted Table—which is so named because the restaurant commissions local artists to paint their serving plates. The chef, Tim Kelley, is a friend of mine, but I really think he's one of the best chefs in Seattle. He's a major flavor guy: His food is beautiful, and complicated, too, but the flavor is always perfect in dishes such as squab with roasted squash ravioli and dates. His menu changes all the time but features Northwest cuisine. I remember a deconstructed beet salad that had all this beet stuff on it: beet, beet greens, oil, all put together in a tower, which tasted a lot better than most towering dishes ever taste.

PHO BAC

1314 S. Jackson, Seattle
(206) 323-4387

We have a great International District in Seattle with a lot of Vietnamese and Thai influences. Pho Bac is a Vietnamese noodle house, and all they serve is the one dish, *pho* [beef noodle soup]. Your only decision is large or medium. I order the medium, although both are less than six dollars. My guess is that they cook the brisket in the water to make the broth, and then they slice it and put it in the broth with rice noodles, bean sprouts, basil, and very thin slices of raw beef, and you add chile sauce to taste. It makes a great meal, even at ten in the morning! It's always good and filling, and I probably eat it about twice a week. It's Vietnamese comfort food.

**MACRINA BAKERY
AND CAFÉ**

2408 1st Avenue
Seattle, WA 98121
Phone: (206) 448-4032

Leslie Mackie

LESLIE MACKIE is baker-owner of Macrina Bakery and Café. A graduate of the California Culinary Academy, she honed her skills in Boston at the Bostonian Hotel and Biba before returning to her native Northwest to open her own bakery and café. Both the *Seattle Times* and the *New York Times* have written about Macrina Bakery. She is an active member of the Bread Bakers Guild and Les Dames d'Escoffier and was recently included in the *Baking with Julia* television series and companion book.

MY FOOD People call our pastries and desserts "European" because they are not overly sweet or gigantically portioned. They can also fall into the category of "rustic," in that they're more homey and not overly frosted. We have both a shop and a café, so in the morning you get things at the counter and sit down. At lunch, we convert the café into a dining room. The room seats about twenty-five, and the menu changes daily. We offer fresh seasonal food. We do a small number of salads, entrées, pizza, a mezze plate, and sandwiches. We also serve brunch. The impetus for what we do came from a place I ate at in Italy called Barni, just outside of Luca. You walked in, and the menu was written on a board. The place was staffed with these beautiful Italian women who were round and robust; you just knew they made fabulous food! Everything they did was roasted, not sautéed, without garnishes. The feeling you got there was that you were eating at home, only in a public place. That is the feeling we try to convey here: the comfortableness of home, only with someone else preparing your food. We have a lot of regulars, and the restaurant is kind of a meeting place for them.

*"Leslie Mackie
makes really good
bread."*

AMY SCHERBER

AMY'S BREAD (NEW YORK)

"Leslie Mackie's bakery in Seattle has become a must-have breakfast scenario for coffee cake and muffins. She's done an incredible job with Macrina. I love the 'bones,' which are her crackers. But she also makes an amazing braided bread with pumpkin seeds, and any time one of my cooks is driving through Seattle, their mission is to bring one back so we can all share it!"

CORY SCHREIBER   WILDWOOD (PORTLAND, OR)

LESLIE'S PICKS

FLYING FISH

2234 1st Avenue, Seattle
(206) 728-8595

Flying Fish is a great place to go and share dishes, which they call "large plates" and "platters." You can get salt-and-pepper crab, which is down and dirty because you have to get dirty opening it. They are also good for light appetizers. All the entrées are delicious because they only feature what is fresh. I also like the Thai crab cakes and their Caesar salad with fried oysters instead of croutons. (See also p.272.)

IL FORNAIO

600 Pine Street (in Pacific Place), Seattle
(206) 264-0994

I like it for its simple Italian food. The place transports you to New York. They have seasonal pastas, and I recently had ricotta-filled tortellini tossed with artichokes and peas in some olive oil, which was delicious. Their bread is also very good.

MALENA'S TACO SHOP

620 W. McGraw Street, Seattle
(Queen Anne)
(206) 284-0304

Malena's is a taqueria, and their *carne asada* tacos are out of this world! It's less than six dollars for a number one, which is two tacos, rice, and beans. The food is very fresh, and seasoned beautifully. The flour tortillas are great, and so is the guacamole. They also have "Jamaica," which is a housemade hibiscus drink that is so good.

PALACE KITCHEN

2030 5th Avenue, Seattle
(206) 448-2001

You have to start a meal at the Palace Kitchen with *plin*, which is little tortellini with a Swiss chard and pork filling, in olive oil with Parmigiano Reggiano and sage. It's really good. They also do a nice job with roasted meats, such as duck or goat, that change daily, so ordering roasted meat is always a good bet.

PASEO CARIBBEAN RESTAURANT

4225 Fremont Avenue N. (at 43rd Avenue), Seattle
(206) 545-7440

Paseo is a Cuban restaurant with only four seats. The serve red shrimp, which is done in a Cuban red sauce. They also have the best black beans in the world—they are spicy and sweet at the same time. Since they are so good, people usually get an extra order of black beans to take home for the next day.

LESLIE MACKIE OF MACRINA BAKERY ON
The Best Bread She's Ever Tasted

At a pizza restaurant in Rome, I saw this bread on another table which had gorgeous structure to it, so I had to seek it out. The restaurant gave me the number of the place that made it, then with a little help we got the address. So Susan Regis [of Biba, in Boston] and I trekked over there. The baker turned out to be Arnese Giuseppe (of Paneficio Arnese Giuseppe, Via del Politeama, 27 Roma; 58-17-265).

The funny thing was when we got there, at eleven in the morning, he was sitting in front of his oven reading the paper and smoking a cigarette. He kept saying, "It is just bread," and meanwhile, I was just going out of my mind! He has two ovens, one gas and one wood, and he fires his wood oven with hazelnut shells. His bread was out of this world! When we got there, he jammed a piece of it in some unbelievable extra-virgin olive oil and presented it to me.

This bread had a golden look to it, as opposed to a bleached white look. It is so rustic and bumpy. The loaves all stick next to each other in the oven, which we call "kissers." I even have pictures of it.

It is the best bread I have ever had. We have a bread here at the bakery we have named after Giuseppe. It is based on the technique he uses, but it does not yet have the complexity that his has. Eventually, I hope it will be that way.

THIERRY RAUTUREAU is chef-owner of Rover's in Seattle, which has been praised in media ranging from the *New York Times* to the *Seattle Times* to *Gourmet*, whose readers awarded Rover's top-choice honors for Seattle. He won the 1998 James Beard Award as Best Chef: Northwest.

ROVER'S

2808 E. Madison Street
Seattle, Washington 98112
Phone: (206) 325-7442
Fax: (206) 325-1092
www.rovers-seattle.com

MY FOOD When you come in to Rover's, you are basically coming into our house. The restaurant looks like a house—we have a small lobby and no bar—and the idea is that we treat you like a guest. I am a chef and I will cook for you, and it has to be good, or I will not be happy.

I feel that service is equal in importance to the food. The people serving food must know what it is and be able to explain it to the customer. They also need to be flexible when caring for the customers' needs.

The goal is to provide you with an experience, maybe to teach you or educate you. We offer six- or nine-course tasting menus. It is important to know that we serve no beef, chicken, veal, or pasta. Sometimes a customer will ask, "What is left?" While I use ingredients such as foie gras, lobster, scallops, sweetbreads, and venison, I have only two signature dishes because we change things all the time. I tell people, "It is not just you here, it is us, too—and I need to keep my life interesting." Two of the longer-lasting dishes on our menu are scrambled eggs with white sturgeon caviar and lime crème fraîche, and a spice-infused Pinot Noir sorbet.

THIERRY'S PICKS

AROSA CAFÉ

3121 E. Madison Street, Seattle
(206) 324-4542

An older gentleman named Hans [Riechsteiner] makes beautiful panini here. Two of my favorites are the one with artichoke and mozzarella, and another with ham and Gruyère. They are awesome, and not fattening! In fact, I just ordered an artichoke mozzarella panini during this interview! [They have take-out in addition to seats where you can enjoy panini, waffles, and coffees and mochas.]

CACTUS

4220 E. Madison Street, Seattle
(206) 324-4140

Cactus is a fun, really popular, and really good Mexican café that is worth the wait. I like to order the chicken fajitas when I'm there. My wife, Kathy, likes the Yucatan-style citrus-marinated and roasted pork loin, which comes wrapped in banana leaves. [And the flan is a dessert specialty!]

MAD PIZZA

Multiple locations, including:
4021 E. Madison Street, Seattle
(206) 329-7037

The kids like plain cheese-and-tomato pizza, but my wife and I like to order the Mad Scientist, which is made with pesto, feta cheese, artichokes, and red peppers!

NISHINO

3130 E. Madison Street, Seattle
(206) 322-5800

This is a Japanese restaurant that serves sushi, and my kids love it. My nine-year-old likes sashimi, and my four-year-old orders fried calamari. My wife and I like to order the black cod. My kids will eat the katsu cod, which is marinated and sort of sweet.

PALACE KITCHEN

2030 5th Avenue, Seattle
(206) 448-2001

My kids love the Roy Rogers [nonalcoholic drinks] at Palace Kitchen! They have really good country bread, which we like to dip in the olive oil and vinegar on the tables. Ordering their roast of the day—whether baby goat or pork—is always great. They have good clams or mussels marinara, and banana cream pie. I like the ambiance there as well, especially the booths. The restaurant is just a good friendly place, like a big bistro. (See also p. 275.)

Janos Wilder

RESTAURANT JANOS AND J-BAR

3770 E. Sunrise Drive
Tucson, Arizona 85718
Phone: (520) 615-6100
Fax: (520) 615-3334

JANOS WILDER is chef-owner of Janos. In 1990, he was cited by the James Beard Foundation as a Rising Star of American Cuisine, and he won the James Beard Award for Best Chef: Southwest in 2000. *Travel and Holiday* magazine named Janos one of their Fifty Hidden Treasures in 1998. Wilder is the author of *Janos: Recipes and Tales from a Southwestern Restaurant*.

MY FOOD I would hope that someone would approach eating at Janos for the first time with curiosity and a sense of adventure. We take ingredients from the Southwest and Mexico and prepare them with French technique. That may mean a relleno stuffed with lobster, black beans, and chipotles served on a Champagne sauce with fennel salad, or lamb loin marinated in a red chile recado. Each dish expresses a complete culinary concept, which will often be articulated with a sense of whimsy. When we train the staff, we encourage them to communicate the concept to our guests. The inspiration, the ingredients, and the marriage of French and the Southwest can all be relayed to the customers if they are receptive to it, and understanding that can enhance the experience.

At J-Bar, we take in the breadth of Mexico and the Caribbean. It's really flavorful, gutsy cooking. The source of inspiration for the restaurant was the border town cooking of Nogales, where you go to the *parillas*, or grills, and get simply prepared meat, fish, or poultry served with *frijoles de la olla*, rice, and salsa. We elaborate that notion a bit to encompass a larger Latin tradition and serve *ceviche*, jerked pork, lamb *machaca*, and incredible *chilequiles*. Most of the dishes are served family style to encourage the conviviality of the shared table. We want dining at J-Bar to be a party—and it is.

JANOS'S PICKS

CAFÉ POCA COSA

88 E. Broadway (Clarion Hotel), Tucson
(520) 622-6400

Poca cosa means "little things," which is what you'll find here. Chef Susana Davila cooks very authentic Mexican food, not border food—it's food from farther down in Mexico, Mexico City and beyond. She'll bring up lots of chiles, and works with lots of *moles*, so I recommend any dishes featuring them. Her *platos* [plates of various meats and vegetables] are very good—they're all interesting and out of the ordinary."

MARISCO'S CHIHUAHUA

Multiple locations, including:
1009 N. Grande Avenue, Tucson
(520) 623-3563
3901 S. 6th Avenue, Tucson
(520) 741-0361

The restaurant's name was Marisco's, and after buying the furniture stand next door called Chihuahua, they never took down the sign, so it became Marisco's Chihuahua. They bring really fresh, good quality seafood up from Mexico, and they've got all sorts of seafood cocktails and ceviche [marinated raw fish] and whole cooked fish. It's always tasty and very casual—Formica counters and fluorescent lighting—but a fun, lively atmosphere, where we know we'll get really high-quality fish and we'll always get in. They make great limonada, so I'll have four or five of those. They use Mexican limes, and it's really refreshing. My son Ben loves the *horchata*, which is a Mexican cinnamon-rice drink.

SUSHI HAMA

3971 North Oracle Road, Tucson
(520) 888-6763

I have to preface my recommendation by saying that when we go to sushi bars in Tucson, it's not like going to Nobu [in New York]! I don't want someone from out of town to come here and leave thinking, "Why did he recommend that? We've got better sushi bars at home!" You probably do. You wouldn't come to Tucson to get sushi, but since I live in the desert, when I want sushi, I go to Sushi Hama. The chef is a good, honest guy, and the quality of his fish is always good. His yellowtail and his onagi are really good, and I just let him make whatever he wants for me, putting myself at his mercy.

TACQUERIA PICO DE GALLO

2618 S. 6th Avenue, Tucson
(520) 623-8775

Pico de gallo means "rooster's beak." This is a taco stand that's been expanded over the years. It's very inexpensive, really small, and extremely casual. They make great quesadillas with guacamole, and terrific *tacos de birria* [a meat-and-chile stew]. They don't have a liquor license, so we'll go down the street and get some beers to have with the food. You go across the street for dessert, where they opened a little stand which serves shaved ice with fresh fruit toppings. The watermelon and other flavors are all pretty good.

VIVACE

4811 E. Grant Road, Tucson
(520) 795-7221

The chef and owner, Danny Scordato, grew up in the restaurant business, and he trained in Italy. His food is of uniformly high quality; the products are always terrific, and the execution is always great. The service is good and attentive, and when I'm going out on a date with my wife, that's what we want. We have two or three items that we get every time: a tremendous osso bucco; a great steak with a wine sauce, which is served with mashed potatoes that are unbelievably rich and good; and a seafood soup with grilled bread, which I love.

BAKERY

BREAD LINE

1751 Pennsylvania Avenue NW, Washington, DC (202) 822-8900

"The breads are amazing, but I especially love the brioche. They also have great sandwiches that you can eat there or take out."

—JOSE ANDRES, JALEO

FIREHOOK BAKERY & COFFEE HOUSE

Multiple locations, including:
1909 Q Street NW, Washington, DC (202) 588-9296

MARVELOUS MARKET

Multiple locations, including:
1535 Connecticut Avenue NW, Washington, DC (202) 686-4040

"I think they are the two best [bread] bakers in town."

—RIS LACOSTE, 1789

"I like Firehook's pound cakes and tarts. Their pecan pies are good, too."

—JOSE ANDRES, JALEO

BOUDIN BLANC

MARCEL'S

2401 Pennsylvania Avenue NW,
Washington, DC
(202) 296-1166

"Their boudin blanc [a white-meat sausage] is a knockout—it's absolutely sensational!"

—BOB KINKEAD, KINKEAD'S

BARBECUE

CAPITAL Q

707 H Street NW, Washington, DC
(Chinatown)
(202) 347-8396

"A great place for Texas-style barbecued beef."

—RIS LACOSTE, 1789

ROCKLANDS WASHINGTON'S BARBECUE

2418 Wisconsin Avenue NW,
Washington, DC
(202) 333-2558

"For barbecued pork ribs and chicken, and pork butt sandwiches. Don't miss their Wall of Fire, which is an entire wall of shelves filled with hot sauces!"

—RIS LACOSTE, 1789

BRUNCH

GABRIEL

2121 P Street NW (in the Barcelo Hotel, between 21st and 22nd Streets),
Washington, DC (202) 956-6690

"They have the classic American brunch buffet, but because they're a Spanish hotel chain they also offer great Spanish specialties. Their whole roasted pig is crisp, juicy, and fabulous!"

—RIS LACOSTE, 1789

CHICKEN, TAKE-OUT

EL POLLO RICO

2917 N. Washington Boulevard, Arlington, VA (703) 522-3220

CRISP AND JUICY

4540 Lee Highway, Arlington, VA (703) 243-4222

"They're both great, but El Pollo Rico serves theirs with a delicious green chile sauce."

—RIS LACOSTE, 1789

CRABS AND CRAB CAKES

CANTLER'S RIVERSIDE INN

458 Forest Beach Road, Annapolis, MD
(410) 757-1311

"This is a crab joint on a little estuary on the Chesapeake. You sit out on the deck, drink beer, and eat hard-shell crabs. I like the setting. They usually have 'whales' or 'super jumbos'—to me, the bigger the better. You bang all day for so little meat with small crabs. The big crabs usually sell out in the first hour. The place is strictly T-shirt and jeans—you get dirty, and it is a blast."

—BOB KINKEAD, KINKEAD'S

"When you're in the area, you should not miss crabs—hard-shell, soft-shell, or cakes! Go to Annapolis for steamed blue hard-shell crabs. Sit at a table outside and eat crabs with a hammer and drink pitchers of beer. It's a great experience."

—NORA POUILLON, RESTAURANT NORA AND ASIA NORA

DC COAST

1401 K Street NW (in the Tower Building), Washington, DC
(202) 216-5988

"They've got good soft-shell crabs."

—BOB KINKEAD, KINKEAD'S

1789

1226 36th Street NW, Washington, DC (Georgetown)
(202) 965-1789

"They also do a nice job with soft-shell crabs." (See also p. 287.)

—BOB KINKEAD, KINKEAD'S

DIM SUM

TONY CHENG'S SEAFOOD RESTAURANT AND MONGOLIAN BARBECUE

621 H Street NW, Washington, DC
(202) 371-8669

"They have the best dim sum—all the wacky stuff, as well as great steamed buns, and their vegetables are really fresh."

—RIS LACOSTE, 1789

ETHIOPIAN

MESKEREM ETHIOPIAN RESTAURANT

2434 18th Street NW, Washington, DC (Adams Morgan)
(202) 462-4100

ZED'S ETHIOPIAN RESTAURANT

1201 28th Street NW (at M Street), Washington, DC
(202) 333-4710

"Whenever I have friends in town from Europe, I take them out for Ethiopian food. Everyone eats from the same platter. I love the injera bread—you tear off pieces and use them to pick up your food. I love the lentils and split peas, and I also like wat, which is spicy. It is healthy food. You do need to be careful with the bread, because if you eat too much, you bloat up like a balloon! I like to drink African beers with this food."

—NORA POUILLON, RESTAURANT NORA AND ASIA NORA

FRENCH

BIS

15 E. Street NW, Washington, DC
(202) 661-2700

"Bis is a bistro that I really like."

—BOB KINKEAD, KINKEAD'S

GÉRARD'S PLACE

915 15th Street NW, Washington, DC
(202) 737-4445

"Chef-owner Gérard Pangaud serves modern French, but not nouvelle, cuisine. He does a great job."

—BOB KINKEAD, KINKEAD'S

HAMBURGER

CLYDE'S OF GEORGETOWN

3236 M Street NW, Washington, DC
(202) 333-9180

TOMBS

1226 36th Street NW, Washington, DC
(202) 337-6668

"They both make great burgers."

—RIS LACOSTE, 1789

PASTA

GALILEO

1110 21st Street NW, Washington, DC
(202) 293-7191

"I love eating at the bar. You will laugh, but I don't think there is anything better than spaghetti with tomato sauce and good Parmesan!"

—JOSE ANDRES, JALEO

PEKING DUCK

PEKING GOURMET INN

6029 Leesburg Pike (in the Culmore Shopping Center, at Glen Carlynn), Falls Church, VA
(703) 671-8088

"Their Peking duck is fabulous. I bet they sell twenty cases of duck a day! It is in kind of a funky area, just outside DC."

—BOB KINKEAD, KINKEAD'S

PIZZA

FACCIA LUNA PIZZERIA

2400 Wisconsin Avenue NW, Washington, DC
(202) 337-3132

"Their pizza has a great crust and is cooked in a wood-burning oven. My favorite is the sausage, ham, and spinach pizza."

—RIS LACOSTE, 1789

PIZZERIA PARADISO

2029 P Street NW, Washington, DC
(202) 223-1245

"They have great combinations of ingredients. I'll order either the tomato and cheese pizza or the potato and pesto pizza."

—RIS LACOSTE, 1789

salvadoran

ATYLACYL

18554 Woodfield Road, Gaithersburg, MD
(301) 670-1674

"At Atylacyl, I like the pupusas [Salvadoran corn tortillas stuffed with meat, beans, and/or cheese] and the sweet-corn-and-flour-pudding tamale topped with Salvadorian crème. The cuisine is not as defined as Mexican or spicy. There are similar ingredients—plantains, masa, queso blanco—and they use a fair amount of cilantro, but not the hot chiles."

—BOB KINKEAD, KINKEAD'S

spanish

TABERNA DEL ALABARDERO

1776 I Street NW, Washington, DC
(202) 429-2200

"The lobster paella is to die for! The people who run this restaurant are very nice, and if you can get into town when they have the flamenco festival [in April] with dinner, it's sensational!"

—BOB KINKEAD, KINKEAD'S

steak

MORTON'S

Multiple locations, including:
3251 Prospect Street NW,
Washington, DC
(202) 342-6258

SAM AND HARRY'S

1200 19th Street NW, Washington, DC
(202) 296-4333

"Both have good steaks, and Morton's also has a good soufflé."

—BOB KINKEAD, KINKEAD'S

sushi

KAZ SUSHI BISTRO

1915 I Street NW, Washington, DC
(202) 530-5500

"Kaz Okochi is doing creative sushi on par with anyone in the United States, and is trying to move sushi slightly ahead. He does a foie gras sushi that is marinated in plum wine and is out of this world! He also does vegetable sushi that is great. Kaz also makes two great hot dishes—sole with truffle oil, and salmon with a mango reduction."

—JOSE ANDRES, JALEO

SUSHI-KO

2309 Wisconsin Avenue NW, Washington, DC
(202) 333-4187

"This is a long-time favorite of mine that does many things well. The sushi is really good."

—JOSE ANDRES, JALEO

SWEET TOOTH

FIREHOOK BAKERY

Multiple locations, including:
1909 Q Street NW, Washington, DC
(202) 588-9296

"I like their pound cakes and
tarts. Their pecan pies are
good, too."

—JOSE ANDRES, JALEO

TAPAS

JALEO

480 7th Street NW, Washington, DC
(202) 628-7949

"Jose Andres does a really
nice job, and he brings
Spanish and Catalan
influences into the food."
(See also p. 284.)

—BOB KINKEAD, KINKEAD'S

TAQUERIA

MIXTEC

1792 Columbia Road NW,
Washington, DC
(202) 332-1011

"This is a great taqueria. My
favorites here are the tacos
al carbón [tacos with
charcoal-grilled meat] and
tacos al pastor [pork
tacos], and their salsas."

—BOB KINKEAD, KINKEAD'S

VIETNAMESE

HUONG QUE

6769 Wilson Boulevard,
Falls Church, VA
(703) 538-6717

"This Vietnamese restaurant
is owned by a family with
four daughters, who all
work there. The food is terrific, and a lot of chefs eat
here frequently." (See also
p. 289.)

—BOB KINKEAD, KINKEAD'S

JALEO

480 7th Street NW
Washington, DC 20004
Phone: (202) 628-7949
Fax: (202) 628-7952
dc.diningweb.com/
restaurants/jaleo

JOSE ANDRES is chef-partner of Jaleo. He studied in Barcelona, and trained at several Michelin-rated restaurants, including the three-star El Bullí in Spain. In 1998, he was named one of *Wine Spectator*'s Rising Stars. In 1999, he was nominated for the James Beard Rising Star Chef of the Year Award, and in 2000, he was nominated for Best Chef: Mid-Atlantic. He was also formerly the executive chef of Café Atlantico, which *Wine Advocate* selected as one of its Most Memorable Meals of 1999 during his tenure.

MY FOOD I believe authenticity and tradition can handle a little creativity, and that is what I do here. Jaleo is a Spanish restaurant. Too often, other Spanish restaurants Mexicanize their food, which is not good for Spain or Mexico. However, we don't use any jalapeño peppers or avocado, because they're not used in Spanish cooking. For me, Jaleo re-creates the food from back home perfectly. I do a lot of research about traditional Spanish food, as well as the trends happening there now.

"Ethnic," to me, is cooking what people eat at home. It is cooking at its deepest level. Jaleo is the food that I remember my father, mother, aunts, and uncles cooking for me. It is also the food of family-run restaurants, where you see the father and mother cooking in back and the kids serving. I want to provide a high-end gastronomic experience in a fun and casual atmosphere. Anyone is welcome—for an entire meal, or just a snack.

JOSE'S PICKS

CASHION'S EAT PLACE

1819 Columbia Road NW,
Washington, DC
(202) 797-1819

I love Cashion's, which is a great American bistro. Chef Ann Cashion analyzes dishes and ingredients very well. I like the Catalan spinach with sweetbreads—it's amazing. Since her name is Ann, she does Pommes Anna, which are very good, and her soft polenta with mushrooms is also nice. Everything is well executed; she has a great sensibility with food. I always learn something here.

FULL KEE

509 H Street NW (Chinatown),
Washington, DC
(202) 371-2233

Lots of restaurant professionals in DC—including my manager, Tony Yelamos, head chef Wayne Combs, and I—love to come here for really good Chinese food after work [as the restaurant is open late: until 1 A.M. Sunday through Thursday, and 3 A.M. Friday and Saturday]. Our favorite dishes are the clams in fermented black bean sauce, the lobster in ginger, and the snow pea shoots when they're in season. It's a great place to get a delicious yet inexpensive meal.

JALEO

480 7th Street NW, Washington, DC
(202) 628-7949

In all honesty, I like to come in to Jaleo with my wife on a Sunday. My relatives are not always open to new food—that is, anything other than their native Spanish cuisine—and it is also a way for me to check on the quality. I often slip in and out very quickly.

KINKEAD'S

2000 Pennsylvania Avenue NW,
Washington, DC
(202) 296-7700

I love this restaurant, especially the oyster bar. It is great because the oysters are close to you, you order as many as you want, and you can have a good bottle of white wine with them. I

bring lots of people here. I brought the chef of El Bullí [see p. 18] here once. Now he is coming to visit again, and he's already asked if we are going back! I also like the fried clams with lemon—I order it every time. (See also p. 285.)

PESCE

2016 P Street NW (between 20th and 21st Streets), Washington, DC
(202) 466-3474

We visit Pesce often. Régine Palladin runs the place, and has very talented chefs in the kitchen. They only serve fish, and they get top product. They will sometimes serve them very creatively, but always with respect for the fish. They are always changing the menu.

JOSE ANDRES on
Tapas for First-Timers

The best thing about tapas is that you're free to order what you feel like at that moment.

The first thing I would start with is *croquetas*, because every mother makes them in Spain. Then have tomato bread and anchovies. They are separate dishes, but order them together.

On our menu we wrote, "Eat anchovies and your life will change forever." A good big anchovy that has been well pressed, salted, and preserved in good olive oil is as good as caviar!

Then I would order some Spanish ham to put on the tomato bread. I would also order some tripe, which we stew with pigs' feet, chorizo, *morcilla* [blood sausage], and chickpeas. It is earthy and homey. I have tripe on the menu just for me.

To drink, I would have white wine—like an Albariño.

In terms of food and wine pairing, I think you should feel free to put anything with anything else. I know that sounds drastic, and I am sure some people will think I am crazy, but I think everything in the right measure goes well with anything else. If you want seafood tapas and red wine, go ahead— it is just a different flavor!

BOB KINKEAD is chef-owner of Kinkead's. In 1993, Kinkead's was selected one of the Twenty-Five Best New Restaurants by *Esquire*, and it has been awarded Mobil's four-star rating, one of only two restaurants in DC to have earned this distinction. Among Bob Kinkead's many honors is winning the 1995 James Beard Award as Best Chef: Mid-Atlantic.

MY FOOD Kinkead's is an American brasserie with a heavy emphasis on seafood and fresh ingredients. I don't let myself get restricted by boundaries; my signature dishes include Portuguese-style roast monkfish with chorizo, and pepita-crusted salmon with crab, corn, and chiles. I adapt dishes from around the world to American ingredients and tastes, creating light but intense and full-flavored dishes.

Chefs tend to go to restaurants that are consistent. They tend to go to restaurants that are not at a really high level, but where they know what to expect and where the chef's grasp is not going to exceed his or her reach. They go where the chef is not going to do a big "woo-woo" on them, but where they can get a great steak frites. I say, "Make it good, make it simple, don't fuss with it. And don't reinvent the wheel on me!"

Robert Kinkead

KINKEAD'S
2000 Pennsylvania Avenue NW
Washington, DC 20006
Phone: (202) 296-7700
Fax: (202) 296-7688
www.kinkead.com

*"Every time I'm in DC,
I go to Kinkead's."*

CHRIS SCHLESINGER
EAST COAST GRILL (BOSTON)

BISTRO FRANÇAIS

3128 M Street NW (at Wisconsin Avenue), Washington, DC (Georgetown)
(202) 338-3830

Bistro Français has been here forever, and is open late at night. It has great onion soup, minute steak, and frites. It is the type of restaurant that chefs love, and almost every chef in the city comes here at some juncture. The owner, Gérard Cabral, is a sweetheart of a guy—everyone in the city loves him. The food is straightforward; with a decent bottle of wine, you are a happy guy!

CASHION'S EAT PLACE

1819 Columbia Road NW (at 18th Street), Washington, DC
(202) 797-1819

It is not very fancy, but Ann Cashion does nice work. She does a buffalo hanger steak with béarnaise sauce that is excellent.

PIZZERIA PARADISO

2029 P Street NW (at 20th Street), Washington, DC
(202) 223-1245

They have very authentic Italian pizza. It is not a New York pie; it is smaller and more artisanal. They use really good, fresh mozzarella. It has large chunks of tomatoes, not sauce. The margherita pizza is good. They also have a nice salad, but the reason you are here is for a pie. It is not cheap, but it is, without question, the best pizza in the city. (See also p. 292.)

THE PRIME RIB

2020 K Street NW (at 21st Street), Washington, DC
(202) 466-8811

This is basically a beef place. They have the best prime rib I have ever had, bar none. They also have a great crab imperial, which is a Mid-Atlantic dish of crab folded into a mayonnaise/white-sauce sort of base, then put into the broiler to bake. When it is made right, it is terrific—and when it is not, it is a gloppy, pasty mess.

1789

1226 36th Street NW, Washington, DC
(202) 965-1789

The chef, Ris Lacoste, was my sous chef for thirteen years, but I would have named this restaurant to my list even if she hadn't been. It's a sensational restaurant, definitely one of the five best restaurants in the city. They do everything well here. She works only with what is in season. She does a great tomato and feta salad, but the big deal here is the rack of lamb, which most restaurants don't even offer anymore because it is so outrageously expensive. For rack of lamb to be profitable, restaurants have to charge forty dollars for it—which they don't—so every rack of lamb is a money-loser. (See also p. 287.)

Ris Lacoste

ris lacoste is executive chef of 1789. Previously, she cooked with Bob Kinkead for several years. In 1992, Lacoste and Kinkead were voted Restaurateurs of the Year by *Washingtonian* magazine. She won the 2000 Washington Restaurant and Hospitality Award for Best Restaurant, and was nominated for a James Beard Award as Best Chef: Mid-Atlantic. She serves on the National Board of the American Institute of Wine and Food.

my food Our menu features classical renderings of American food, and changes seasonally. Additionally, we support local farmers as much as possible, and search out indigenous American ingredients, such as cottage industry cheeses, Nantucket scallops, and Colorado lamb.

1789
1226 36th Street NW
Washington, DC 20007
Phone: (202) 965-1789
Fax: (202) 337-1541
www.1789restaurant.com
E-mail: drisdeveau@aol.com

RIS'S PICKS

FIO'S

3636 16th Street NW, Washington, DC
(202) 667-3040

This is a little Italian joint run by a husband and wife, Fio and Jean Vasaio. The restaurant is on the ground level of an apartment building, and it feels like a VFW hall. It is low-ceilinged, with Formica tables. The wine is served in juice glasses. Jean is the waitress and Fio cooks. The food is delicious. His treatment of vegetables is fabulous. He makes the best braised fennel. It is classic, simple Italian fare. I like to get the white pizza because the dough is unbelievable. He makes his own pasta, so I will usually have one of the pasta specials. This place is heaven to me!

KINKEAD'S

2000 Pennsylvania Avenue NW, Washington, DC
(202) 296-7700

I have been gone from Kinkead's for five years, but it is still home to me. They have such high standards, it suits any occasion, and it is my favorite restaurant in town. I have always loved his seared tuna on flageolet beans, portobello mushrooms, and red wine sauce, and his fried clams are the best! (See also p. 285.)

LEBANESE TAVERNA

2641 Connecticut Avenue NW, Washington, DC
(202) 265-8681

Lebanese Taverna is run by a Lebanese family named Abi-Najm. They own several restaurants and a market. The food is delicious. My favorite dish is the lamb stew with chickpeas, yogurt, mint, and pine nuts. The hummus and the dolmas are the best I have ever had. They also have a fabulous roast chicken served with a thin pita and a great aioli: You rip off the chicken, wrap it in the bread, and dip. Then you're home! The market carries great olives and cheese, and I go there often just to learn about ingredients.

OBELISK

2029 P Street NW, Washington, DC
(202) 872-1180

Obelisk is my favorite place to go for a special occasion. The food is wonderful at this simple Italian restaurant. It is a five-course prix-fixe menu, which changes daily: There are two choices for each course, and one course is always cheese. The plates are sparse, but the quality is flawless, and the seasonality unmistakable in dishes such as roast pigeon and beet-stuffed ravioli. I am envious of the kitchen for being able to be back there making everything by hand. When you have twenty things on your menu, like I do, you can't do that. I really love the simplicity, quality and the personal attention it takes to prepare this style of food. (See also p. 292.)

OLD EBBITT GRILL

675 15th Street NW, Washington, DC
(202) 347-4800

After work, I like to go here [another restaurant that is part of Clyde's Restaurant Group, which owns 1789]. In addition to modern "saloon food," they have a huge oyster selection that is half price some nights after eleven P.M. I love to get Wellfleets when they are available, Chincoteague, and Watch Hill oysters from Rhode Island. The place is hopping, and it is fun to get a booth, order some oysters, hang out, and watch the DC scene.

THE INN AT LITTLE WASHINGTON

Middle and Main Streets
P.O. Box 300
Washington, VA 22747
Phone: (540) 675-3800
Fax: (540) 675-3100

Patrick O'Connell

PATRICK O'CONNELL is chef-partner of the Inn at Little Washington. After pursuing speech and drama at the Catholic University of America, he dedicated himself to the culinary arts. The Inn has received the Relais Gourmand classification from Relais and Châteaux, and was voted Best Inn in America in the *ZagatSurvey*. It is consistently rated number one in all categories of the DC-area *ZagatSurvey*, and was the first establishment to ever win Mobil five-star awards for both restaurant and accommodations. The Inn has also received five-star awards from AAA, and won James Beard Awards for Restaurant of the Year (1993), Outstanding Service (1997), and Outstanding Wine Service (1998). In 1992, O'Connell won the James Beard Award as Best Chef: Mid-Atlantic. He is the author of *The Inn at Little Washington: A Consuming Passion*.

MY FOOD What started as a catering business developed into a little restaurant in an abandoned garage and then finally evolved into the Inn. Our menu changes daily and highlights local delicacies and the best of each season's bounty, and the restaurant—the décor, the fresh flower bouquets, the crystal stemware—is designed to showcase the menu.

We want our guests to feel truly pampered and yet completely comfortable. If they're staying at the Inn, they can curl up with a book in a cozy corner, explore the countryside—whatever they like. Our staff is trained to attend to their needs. If they want a picnic, we'll pack a delicious lunch and suggest a beautiful route. No request is unfulfilled.

Our newly renovated kitchen is a continuation of the fantasy that the Inn was once a grand old private residence. The intent is that the kitchen should feel at least seventy-five years old and evoke the feeling of a film set from another era. We've included two chef's tables, and the entire rear wall is a bay of paned glass that looks out onto our herb and cutting gardens.

PATRICK'S PICKS

BURGER KING

Multiple locations

Where do I eat most often on my day off? I'll stop at Burger King on my way into Washington, DC, for two plain grilled chicken breasts, with or without the bun.

HUONG QUE

also known as
THE FOUR SISTERS

6769 Wilson Boulevard, Falls Church, VA
(703) 538-6717

I don't like eating what I've been cooking all week. Having a grand meal is not always a relief from cooking professionally. In a way, you're still working. When you're visiting another city, or someone's taking you to a new place, then it's different. But when you are just trying to escape your daily reality, it becomes a diplomatic occasion! You have to clean your plate and order dessert, or three or four. When I want a relief, a total departure, I like to go to ethnic restaurants. One of our favorites is a Vietnamese restaurant in the Eden shopping mall in northern Virginia. It is called Huong Que, but it is also called the Four Sisters. We've convinced them to adopt this new name for the Americans, so they have two names now. They put a new neon sign up and everything. Their mom is in the kitchen and the father sort of manages things, and the four daughters wait tables. The daughters are very chic, young American girls, and they are very beautiful. The place is very casual—shoes are suggested, and most people wear flip-flops. When we first started going there it was especially nice, because nobody knew us, so nobody was trying to impress us. Several months after we started going regularly, one of the sisters came over, asking us to sign her mailing list. She asked, "You live in Washington, Virginia? Have you been to the famous Inn there?" Our cover was blown, and Mom began fixing us special desserts. We always order the garden rolls right away, because when we get there, we're ravenous. Then we have this wonderful noodle soup: You drop raw beef in the boiling soup and sort of stir it around. I think they slice the beef while it's frozen in order to get it paper thin. It's very satisfying and clean. Then we have marinated chicken on vermicelli noodles, or sometimes shrimp that are wrapped around sugar cane sticks. Then they usually suggest that we have green worms for dessert, which the mother makes. They're tapioca noodles that look like worms, and they're kind of fun. I'll have beer—like 33, which is Vietnamese—with dinner. (See also p. 283.)

JALEO

480 7th Street NW, Washington, DC
(202) 628-7949

If I'm downtown, I like to get tapas [a selection of Spanish appetizers]. Jaleo is usually open late, and you don't have to think of it as a serious meal. The chef, Jose Andres, is enjoying a bit of time in the spotlight right now—he's a great guy. I like to order as I go along, having a little of this and a taste of that. I think it's nice to let them send you a bunch of things. It's hard to relinquish control on your one night off to someone who says, "Let me feed you," but I know there's nothing I wouldn't enjoy there. (See also p. 284.)

RAKU, AN ASIAN DINER

1900 Q Street NW (at 19th Street), Washington, DC
(202) 265-7258

If I'm stuck in traffic downtown and can't get out of the city, I'll slip into Raku, Mark Miller's noodle place. I sit at the counter and have a very satisfying bowl of noodles. I love their sticky-rice-and-mango dessert, which they cook in coconut milk. Sometimes I can't stop eating it once I start, and then I have to order another one to eat in the car on the drive back to the Inn.

WENDY'S

Multiple locations

I love baked potatoes. As I mentioned, on my way into Washington, DC, I stop at Burger King. I'll eat a meal in town, and then on my way back to the Inn I'll stop at Wendy's. I always order two plain baked potatoes, which are a dollar and three cents each, so they think I am very poor. I can see the face of the girl who gives them to me, and I know she's thinking, "Oh, that poor man, that's all he's going to have for dinner tonight." I try to get them not to cut the potatoes, because they are much easier to eat whole when you're traveling: I just unwrap them and eat them like ice cream cones. They're very nourishing. When you live in such an odd place [like Washington, Virginia], you've got to make do.

In Search of Excellence

PATRICK O'CONNELL OF
THE INN AT LITTLE WASHINGTON

WHEN WE OPENED IN 1978, THERE WERE VERY FEW ROLE MODELS in the United States for what we wanted to do. So we closed the restaurant for the month of January, broke the piggy bank, and went on a pilgrimage to the great restaurants of France.

[Noted food writer and editor] Bill Rice had just left the *Washington Post*, and he wrote a couple of letters of introduction for us to the great chefs of France, who at that time were in their heyday. Bocuse—who had just been on the cover of *Newsweek*—the Troisgros brothers, and Alain Chapel had just achieved incredible stardom. It seemed as though all our wealthy clients had been to at least one Michelin two- or three-star restaurant in order to be able to hold their heads up and give them bragging rights, so it seemed totally essential that we establish those reference points as well.

We were surprised to find that the greater the restaurant, the kinder, warmer, and more human they were. Naturally, we felt it would be the opposite—you know, that we'd drive up in our rusty Volkswagen rental and be shunned. However, our welcomes were surprisingly warm. Of course, a letter from Bill Rice broke some ice, but I think they were also able to intuit how spongelike our interest was in general.

We were fascinated by every detail. I soon learned that a great restaurant has to exude a certain electricity from the instant you come into contact with it. This is rooted in having the staff understand and identify with the potentially life-changing quality that the experience might have for a diner. The staff at the restaurants we visited never forgot that for a moment. They also fully understood how important their role was in terms of participating in that experience and being catalysts for making it happen.

Ultimately, I realized that it was not just about the food, which was certainly a key component. It was about everybody working toward creating the ultimate potential of what the experience could be. I then realized that a lot of people had never had one of those experiences, where, as Hemingway says, "the earth moved." That's what an aspiring chef needs to have in order to know what he's aiming toward.

You know, of course, that you can't achieve that every night for your guests. But aiming toward it and knowing that the possibility is there is what it's all about.

NORA POUILLON is chef-owner of Restaurant Nora and Asia Nora. In 1997, she was honored with the International Association of Culinary Professionals (IACP) Award of Excellence as Chef of the Year. She has published *Cooking with Nora*, and is a founding board member of Chefs Collaborative 2000. She is also an active member of Les Dames d'Escoffier, and serves on the board of Women Chefs and Restaurateurs as well as the international advisory board for the National Foundation for Alternative Medicine.

RESTAURANT NORA
2132 Florida Avenue NW
Washington, DC 20008
Phone: (202) 462-5143
Fax: (202) 234-6232

ASIA NORA
2213 M Street NW
Washington, DC 20037
Phone: (202) 797-4860
Fax: (202) 797-1300
www.noras.com

MY FOOD My food represents everything that is important to me; it is organic, wholesome, seasonal, and flavorful. At my restaurants, I try to educate my customers to live in a healthier way by eating food that is delicious, satisfying, and, at the same time, good for them. The balance of the menu, each individual dish and its presentation, is essential to satisfy their appetites and visual needs.

On the back of my menu, I inform diners about the seasons and the provenance of the food they are eating. I list the different organic farmers and producers who supply us, providing their background and information on how they raise their livestock or grow their crops. Some of our wild foods are in danger of becoming extinct, so I explain why certain things are not available on the menu (e.g., swordfish) and should be avoided. As my customers learn more about my philosophy, I hope they can begin to understand the importance and value of the food I choose to serve, not only for their own good but also for that of the environment.

The décor of the restaurant also plays an important role. Amish antique crib quilts decorate the walls to underline my new American cuisine, and architectural pieces from old buildings are used in the dining room to create an informal setting. Our staff are trained to be friendly and unpretentious, as well as knowledgeable about the wines and food we serve. All this is so important in order to create an elegant restaurant without the fuss. We want everyone—from famous politicians to a family celebrating a reunion—to feel welcome, comfortable, and well looked after.

NORA'S PICKS

FIREHOOK BAKERY

Multiple locations, including:
3411 Connecticut Avenue NW,
Washington, DC
(202) 362-2253
214 N. Fayette Street, Alexandria, VA
(703) 519-8020
This is the result of a great partnership between Kate Jansen, a pastry chef, and Gene Garthright, a baker. Kate introduced Washington to Mediterranean pastries, and Gene introduced the city to organic sourdough breads from European countries. You can find many different types of breads here, from dark rye Swiss bread—it is very dense, and delicious sliced thinly with butter!—to roasted garlic black olive bread from the Mediterranean, all made with organic flour and a natural sourdough starter. We go here on the weekends for muffins or bread. (See also p. 283.)

JOHNNY'S HALF SHELL

2002 P Street NW, Washington, DC
(202) 296-2021
Johnny's is a simple and unpretentious place, with a local-hangout feeling. It offers seafood, as the name implies. Their crab cakes, fried oysters and corn bread are now famous in Washington, DC. Ann Cashion, the chef and owner, is very talented, and this reflects in her food. Ann's other restaurant, Cashion's Eat Place, is another great neighborhood restaurant.

MAKOTO RESTAURANT

4822 MacArthur Boulevard NW,
Washington, DC
(202) 298-6866

This is another very small, unpretentious restaurant in a residential neighborhood of Washington, and could easily be overlooked. You step down into the restaurant, but as soon as you enter you are transported into a Japanese atmosphere, from the welcoming scream of the Japanese sushi chef to the cubbyholes of slippers. Makoto only seats twenty—it is very personal—and they offer *omakasi* [chef's tasting menu] dinners of ten courses; that's the choice! It is wonderful, unusual, and always full of surprises. The presentation is very imaginative, and each course has a completely different texture and

look—once the chef served a broth in a conch shell that was sitting on sand! It is quite reasonable for what it offers.

PIZZERIA PARADISO

2029 P Street NW, Washington, DC
(202) 223-1245

The owners, Peter Pastan and Ruth Gresser [who also own Obelisk, a highly regarded upscale Italian restaurant], have a wood-burning pizza oven from Italy and make pizzas to order from scratch. As a result, their pizzas are wonderful, and I think they're the best in town. The crust is crunchy and the toppings run from simple cheese and tomato to more elaborate combinations such as gorgonzola cheese and pancetta. It is a very small space, so it is perfect for carry-out. (See also p. 286.)

TEAISM (A TEA HOUSE)

Multiple locations, including:
2009 R Street NW, Washington, DC
(202) 667-3827 or (888) 8TE-AISM

Teaism is a retreat from all the coffeehouse chains in DC! Linda Orr and Michelle Brown, the owners, serve their great selection of teas, as well as chais and lassis, along with breads cooked in a tandoori oven. Lunches are often served in bento boxes and are wonderful. It is a great stop for breakfast, a light lunch, or afternoon tea.

MICHEL RICHARD is the chef-owner of Citrus and Citronelle. His culinary training began in a restaurant-run pastry shop at the age of fourteen, and by the time he was seventeen he was quickly moving up the ranks at Gaston Lenôtre's pastry shop. He has owned and operated several pastry shops and restaurants in the United States, including Citrus, which *Traveler's Magazine* voted Best Restaurant in the United States in 1987. In 1992, he won the James Beard Award as Best Chef: California, and he was nominated for the 1996 James Beard Award for Best Chef of the Year. Citronelle was recently named one of the World's Most Exciting Restaurants by *Condé Nast Traveler*. He is the author of *Michel Richard's Home Cooking with a French Accent*.

MY FOOD What might people expect from me? They should expect freshness and simplicity—it's not fussy food. People can expect some texture in my food, and less fat, as well as seasonality. For example, we

Michel Richard

CITRONELLE

The Latham Hotel
3000 M. Street NW
Washington, DC 20007
Phone: (202) 625-2150
Fax: (202) 339-6326
www.citronelledc.com

CITRUS

6703 Melrose Avenue
Los Angeles, CA 90038
Phone: (323) 857-0034

CITRONELLE

901 E Cabrillo Boulevard
Santa Barbara, CA 93103
Phone: (805) 963-0111
Fax: (805) 966-6584
www.citronelle.com

don't use any tomatoes in the fall—we're going to wait until the next summer to use tomatoes. We cook everything à la minute—the sauces are finished à la minute, too. I use food from all over the world. In France, we don't grow vanilla or chocolate or bananas. We still do the same thing our grandfathers used to do—go all over the world and bring food to our country. I'm still doing that now. For instance, because of the influence of China I use wonton skins, spring roll skins, and rice papers. I hope I'm cooking the food of tomorrow.

MICHEL'S PICKS

BISTRO FRANÇAIS

3128 M Street NW
(at Wisconsin Avenue),
Washington, DC
(202) 338-3830

Bistro Français is a wonderful restaurant, because they have everything a Frenchman likes! They have good terrines and very good rabbit. It's a very nice menu of classic bistro dishes such as onion soup, pâté, roast chicken, and steak frites, but the daily specials are also excellent. The food is always simple, very good, and not too expensive.

BISTROT LEPIC

1736 Wisconsin Avenue,
Washington, DC (Georgetown)
(202) 333-0111

Bistrot Lepic is a very small, wonderful restaurant serving lunch and dinner. The chef [Bruno Fortin], is cooking like it's a bistro in Provence. It is very charming. He does a good job serving very simple, typical French bistro food, including country pâté, onion tart, calf's liver, and braised veal cheeks—meaning there's no soy sauce anywhere!

CESCO TRATTORIA

4871 Cordell Avenue, Bethesda, MD
(301) 654-8333

This is an Italian restaurant specializing in traditional Tuscan and Piedmontese cuisine, including such dishes as warm baby octopus salad and veal osso buco. It is a collaboration between chefs Francesco Ricchi and Roberto Donna. My kids love pasta—okay, I like it, too! Francesco is my friend, and it's wonderful to get to talk to him when I eat here. The dessert menu features tiramisu made from the chef's own family recipe.

GALILEO RESTAURANT

1110 21st Street NW, Washington, DC
(202) 293-7191

Galileo is another Italian restaurant that I love. The chef, Roberto Donna, is a good friend of mine, and I will happily eat anything he serves me. He almost cooks like a Frenchman—he serves a nice combination of French dishes and Italian dishes that change every day, ranging from braised beef ravioli to risotto. The food here is wonderful. The French usually don't get along with the Italians, but in the world of food, they do!

KINKEAD'S

2000 Pennsylvania Avenue NW,
Washington, DC
(202) 296-7700

Kinkead's is very nice, especially when you're in the mood for seafood. They have clam bellies from Boston that they fry, which taste so wonderful. [Chef] Robert Kinkead always gives me something different to eat, and I love everything that he sends me. When I go to a restaurant, I always trust the chef—I ask them to serve me whatever they want. (See also p. 285.)

LOCAL HIGHLIGHTS

Barbecue

PIERCE'S PITT BAR-B-QUE

447 Rochambeau Drive, Williamsburg (757) 565-2955

"This is a famous barbecue place right on the outskirts of town. The man who started it passed away, and now his son runs it. Their specialty is pork barbecue—not the dry Texas style, but Carolina-style: with a vinegar-based sauce on a bun, with cole slaw."

—MARCEL DESAULNIERS, THE TRELLIS

Hamburger

YORKTOWN PUB

540 Water Street, Yorktown
(757) 886-9964

"The Yorktown Pub is right on the York River, and it's kind of a gritty place. My wife loves going there—we'll sit at the bar and have burgers and a couple of beers. I like to have a fairly plain burger with some ketchup. With an ice-cold Budweiser, which is the beer of choice around here, I'm pretty happy."

—MARCEL DESAULNIERS, THE TRELLIS

Sushi

SUSHI YAMA

11745 Jefferson Avenue, Newport News
(757) 596-1150

"We actually have a pretty good sushi restaurant in Newport News, which is about twenty miles from Williamsburg. Sushi Yama, in the great tradition of some sushi bars, has a chef who is not very tolerant of the uninitiated. I'm not very adventuresome when it comes to sushi, so I let my wife, Connie, do the ordering."

—MARCEL DESAULNIERS, THE TRELLIS

Soft-Shell Crab

THE FROG AND THE REDNECK

1423 E. Cary Street, Richmond
(804) 648-3764

"Chef Jimmy Sneed, who owns the Frog and the Redneck, is a fanatic about the quality of soft-shell crabs, and he seems to have the best sources for them."

—MARCEL DESAULNIERS, THE TRELLIS

Marcel Desaulniers is chef/co-owner of The Trellis in Williamsburg. A graduate of The Culinary Institute of America, he has twice won James Beard Book Awards for his cookbooks—in 1992 for *Death by Chocolate*, and in 1995 for *The Burger Meisters*—and he is the author of eight books in all. In 1993, he won the James Beard Award as Best Chef: Mid-Atlantic, and he won the 1999 James Beard Award as Outstanding Pastry Chef of the Year.

Marcel Desaulniers

THE TRELLIS
403 Duke of Gloucester Street
Williamsburg, VA 23185
Phone: (757) 229-8610
Fax: (757) 221-0450
www.thetrellis.com

MY FOOD Our menu is seasonal and eclectic, and it spotlights the best of what's available year-round. We focus on Virginia's pantry: lots of peanuts, country ham, grains, root vegetables, and seafood indigenous to the Chesapeake Bay, such as blue crabs and sea scallops.

On our menu, we've tried to use words that people are most apt to understand. If we say something is oven-roasted, what are people going to take that to mean? *Crispy* or *warm* or *chilled* are good words that elicit strong responses from customers. We try to keep it simple, although sometimes our passion does get the best of us. October through December is the height of the tourist season because the climate is great and the leaves are in full force. There are fewer extended families, fewer children, and the people coming in are more sophisticated diners.

MARCEL'S PICKS

ACACIA

3325 W. Cary Street, Richmond
(804) 354-6060

Chef Dale Reitzer is a young guy who used to work for Jimmy Sneed, and he was one of *Food & Wine* magazine's picks for the best new American chefs of 1999. He has an interesting menu: lamb, beef, and four different types of fish are on the menu all the time. However, every day the garnishes change, so essentially there's a new menu every day. I had an incredible cold tomato soup there, made with the tiniest little tomatoes I've ever seen, and served with fresh crab. The restaurant also has a good wine list, with international selections as well as wines from Virginia.

BOBBYWOOD

7517 Granby Street, Norfolk
(757) 440-7515

A guy by the name of Bobby Huber has an outlandish place in Norfolk called Bobbywood, à la Hollywood. He's kind of a character. His cooking is in the same vein as Todd Jurich's [see p. 296], although probably a little more esoteric as far as including some Asian and other ethnic influences and offering dishes such as lump crabcakes with garlic grits as well as up to fifteen types of bread made in-house. It's really excellent.

LE YACA

Route 60, Williamsburg
(757) 220-3616

Williamsburg doesn't have a lot of diversity, but there's a nice little French restaurant here called Le Yaca that was started the same year The Trellis opened. They don't have a very extensive menu, but one of their specialties is a very simple leg of lamb roasted over an open fire. It's terrific. And the roast chicken is always good.

RIVER'S INN

8109 Yacht Haven Road,
Gloucester Point
(804) 642-9942

This is a good place for seafood—and a water view! It's just across the York River from Williamsburg. There's lots of great seafood here because we're on a peninsula. They are pretty well known for their soft-shell crabs, which are especially good. The chef serves them all kinds of ways, from pan-seared to grilled to tempura-battered and fried. My favorite way is pan-seared—in a really hot pan with a squirt of lemon juice, salt, and pepper. That's also the way I fix them when we go down to the beach.

TODD JURICH'S BISTRO

210 W. York Street, Norfolk
(757) 622-3210

A little further afield, in Norfolk, there's a chef named Todd Jurich who is one of a handful of really excellent chefs in our region. He specializes in seafood and regional American ingredients [e.g., salmon glazed with molasses, cayenne, and cinnamon] and puts an emphasis on freshness in preparation, without creating things that run too far amok. Don't be surprised to find as many specials offered as regular menu items.

THE WILLIAMSBURG INN

136 E. Francis Street, Williamsburg
(757) 229-1000

The Williamsburg Inn is still a really wonderful place for afternoon tea or a romantic dinner. It serves classics such as lobster bisque and rack of lamb, and it has an award-winning wine list. The service and the surroundings are both very nice.

CHEFS' RECOMMENDATIONS

Some chefs' recommendations fell outside the leading cities where we interviewed them. Here are some of their favorites across the United States.

California
San Rafael

MULBERRY STREET

101 Smith Ranch Road, San Rafel
(415) 472-7272

"They have great pizza that is always made with top ingredients, including artichokes, fennel, and different cheeses."

—BRADLEY OGDEN, THE LARK CREEK INN AND ONE MARKET (SAN FRANCISCO)

Colorado
Aspen

MATSUHISA

303 E. Main Street, Aspen
(970) 544-6628

"When we were in Aspen for the Food & Wine festival this year, we went to Matsuhisa, and we just let chef Nobu Matsuhisa rock us. And he rocked us! I thought, 'We're two thousand miles from any piece of open sea, and they're rocking me with sushi—this is a serious place!' Having sushi in Aspen is like having barbecue in Nova Scotia—it makes you ask, 'What are you doing here, man?'"

—MARIO BATALI, BABBO, ESCA, AND LUPA (NEW YORK)

Connecticut
New Haven

FRANK PEPE PIZZERIA NAPOLETANA (PEPE'S)

157 Wooster Street, New Haven
(203) 865-5762

"I love their white clam pizza—it's the best. Pepe's is high on my list of favorite places anywhere."

—TODD ENGLISH, FIGS AND OLIVES (BOSTON)

"Pepe's clam pizza with bacon is the best!"

—ANDREW CARMELLINI, CAFÉ BOULUD (NEW YORK)

LOUIS' LUNCH

263 Crown Street, New Haven
(203) 562-5507

"This place claims to be the home of the original hamburger. They have been there for one hundred years. I don't know how to describe how they cook them—they use gas broilers, but they're vertical. They put the burgers into a grill clamp and then place it sideways between two rows of vertical flames. It is just great. They yell at you and give you a hard time. It's not Burger King—you can't have it your way. You have the choice of with cheese or without, but that's it. They put the burger between pieces of white Pepperidge Farm toast and then give it to you in a little mitt so you can eat it right away. It's great."

—TODD ENGLISH, FIGS AND OLIVES (BOSTON)

Hawaii
Honolulu

ALAN WONG'S

1857 S. King Street, fifth floor, Honolulu
(808) 949-2526

"I think Alan Wong is one of the top five chefs in America today. His Hawaiian regional food is very complex—it blows me away." (See also p. 103.)

—MARK MILLER, COYOTE CAFÉ (LAS VEGAS AND SANTA FE)

Illinois

Mundelein

BILL'S PIZZA

624 South Lake Street, Mundelein
(847) 566-5380

"Every time I'm in the Chicago area, I've got to drive the thirty miles to Bill's for either an Italian beef sandwich or a pizza. I could eat here three times in two days!"

—NORMAN VAN AKEN, NORMAN'S
(CORAL GABLES, FL)

Maine

Brunswick

FAT BOY DRIVE-IN

111 Bath Road, Brunswick
(207) 729-9431
Open mid-March through mid-October.

"This is an old-fashioned drive-in, and when you drive up you put your lights on to order. It is the real thing— and the burger is great!"

—SUSAN REGIS, BIBA (BOSTON)

Massachusetts

Cape Cod

CHATHAM SQUIRE

487 Main Street, Chatham
(508) 945-0945

"They have the best fried clams on the Cape!"

—LYDIA SHIRE, BIBA AND PIGNOLI (BOSTON)

PATE'S

1260 Main Street, Chatham
(508) 945-9777

"It's a steakhouse, and I like to order steak and clams casino."

—LYDIA SHIRE, BIBA AND PIGNOLI (BOSTON)

Quincy

KELLY'S (THE ORIGINAL KELLY'S FAMOUS SEAFOOD)

35 Cottage Avenue, Quincy
(617) 745-0202

"For the lobster roll. It's great hangover food, and it's on the beach!"

—TODD ENGLISH, FIGS AND OLIVES
(BOSTON)

Westport

BACK EDDY

1 Bridge Road, Westport
(508) 636-6500

"I've been to the Back Eddy quite a few times. Chris Schlesinger [of the East Coast Grill in Cambridge] put it together, and it sits right along the water. Get a big bowl of steamed clams and dip the clams in the broth. You'll really feel like you're eating seashore food. They have the best stuffed clams I've ever had; usually they are just kind of wet and soggy and gross, but these are really good—they have corn in them, and they are crusty on top. I love this place for its simplicity and its great food, and because you're right on the water." (See also p. 70.)

—EMILY LUCHETTI, PASTRY CHEF, FARALLON
(SAN FRANCISCO)

BUTLER'S COLONIAL DOUGHNUTS

459 Sanford Road, Westport
(508) 672-4600

"Their doughnuts are amazing! They make a whipped-cream-filled doughnut that I have to keep George away from. It's impossible to eat just one—they're light and they're delicious, and the whipped cream is done to order. This is state-of-the-art doughnut making! They also do a glazed doughnut that is just as amazing. When we hear people talk about Krispy Kreme, we're very smug, because if they only knew…"

—JOHANNE KILLEEN
(PROVIDENCE)

"There's a dairy right next door where they get the cream to whip fresh. It's great—they just cut the doughnut in half, leaving it on a hinge, and they whip the cream to order with a little powdered sugar, and pipe it into the doughnut. The owner works like a demon, and when he runs out of doughnuts, he shuts down."

—GEORGE GERMON, AL FORNO (PROVIDENCE)

Michigan
Ann Arbor

ZINGERMAN'S

422 Detroit Street, Ann Arbor
(734) 663-3354

"Zingerman's is a real shrine. It's a gourmet store that has great cheeses and food products from around the world, as well as great sandwiches. They are on a par with Balducci's in New York, only on an Ann Arbor—college—hippie sort of scale. They do a really great job."

—JIMMY SCHMIDT, THE RATTLESNAKE CLUB (DETROIT)

"They have great balsamic vinegar and olive oil."

—TAKASHI YAGIHASHI, TRIBUTE (DETROIT)

Nevada
Las Vegas

THE JOYFUL HOUSE

4601 Spring Mountain Road, Las Vegas
(702) 889-8881

"This is a Chinese restaurant that serves whole steamed fish with various dipping sauces. It's terrific!"

—NORMAN VAN AKEN, NORMAN'S (CORAL GABLES, FL)

New Jersey
Elizabeth

SPIRITO'S

714 3rd Avenue, Elizabeth (908) 351-5414

"Anyone who grew up there knows Spirito's. It is an institution. They make fried veal cutlet and ravioli that I have to have every other month."

—TOM COLICCHIO, GRAMERCY TAVERN (NEW YORK)

New York
The Hamptons (Eastern Long Island)

HENRY'S IN BRIDGEHAMPTON

2495 Montauk Highway, Bridgehampton 631) 537-5665
[A French bistro with American twists]

"It's excellent—I think it's the best food in the Hamptons."

—BOBBY FLAY, BOLO AND MESA GRILL (NEW YORK)

DELLA FEMINA

99 N. Main Street, East Hampton
(631) 329-6666

"Always very good—they've got some of the better food out in the Hamptons."

—BOBBY FLAY, BOLO AND MESA GRILL (NEW YORK)

GOSMAN'S DOCK

500 W. Lake Drive, Montauk
(631) 668-5330
[Founded in 1943 as a lobster roll and clam chowder shack, it now serves other seafood dishes as well.]

"A huge place for lobsters on the dock, located on the tip of Montauk. It's fantastic."

—BOBBY FLAY, BOLO AND MESA GRILL (NEW YORK)

DELLA FEMINA

99 N. Main Street, East Hampton
(631) 329-6666
[A contemporary American/Italian restaurant that favors the unusual, e.g., sturgeon, antelope]

NICK AND TONI'S

136 N. Main, East Hampton
(631) 324-3550
[An eclectic Mediterranean restaurant dedicated to local farmers and fishermen, with a wood-burning oven]

"Both these places are very close to my home. They are pretty consistent, and I can get a table, which helps."

—MICHAEL ROMANO, UNION SQUARE CAFE (NEW YORK)

across the usa

New Hyde Park

UMBERTO'S

633 Jericho Turnpike, New Hyde Park
(516) 437-7698

"*The best pizza I've ever had in my life!*"

—ROCCO DISPIRITO, UNION PACIFIC
(NEW YORK)

Ohio

Cleveland

HONEY HUT ICE CREAM

Multiple locations, including:
4674 State Road, Cleveland
(216) 749-7077
6250 State Road, Cleveland
(440) 885-5055

"*Their maple pecan ice cream is very good. Honey Hut is located in an old, cute little white building. All their ice cream flavors [which range from strawberry to honey nut] are made with honey, giving them a distinctive taste. I always stop by when I'm home in Cleveland.*"

—ANDREW CARMELLINI, CAFÉ BOULUD
(NEW YORK)

WEST SIDE MARKET

Corner of West 25th Street and Lorain Avenue, Cleveland (216) 664-3386
www.westsidemarket.com

"*This market, which opens at seven A.M. [on Mondays and Wednesdays, when it's open until four in the afternoon, and Fridays and Saturdays, when it's open until six], is a great place to go on Saturday mornings. It's housed in a historic terminal that was built in the 1920s, with ceramic tiles in an Art Deco mosaic. You'll find more than a hundred different vendors selling meats—including goat, rabbit, and cured meats—on one side of the market and vegetables on the other. Everything is really great—it's all high-quality stuff. Don't miss the peanut butter at the Peanut Gallery—it's pressed on the premises.*"

—ANDREW CARMELLINI, CAFÉ BOULUD
(NEW YORK)

Texas

Austin

JEFFREY'S

1204 W. Lynn Street, Austin
(512) 477-5584

"*Chef David Garrido's creative cuisine—which features dishes such as duck and shrimp black bean ravioli with porcini mushroom sauce—is worth seeking out.*"

—STEPHAN PYLES, STAR CANYON (DALLAS)

Round Top

ROYERS ROUND TOP CAFÉ

Round Top, Texas: "80 miles from Austin and 80 miles from Houston"
(979) 249-3611: "Call us if you get lost."
(877) 866-PIES
www.royersroundtopcafe.com

"*This place is a little over an hour outside of Austin. I discovered it while I was doing my first book, looking for authentic Texas recipes.*"

—STEPHAN PYLES, STAR CANYON (DALLAS)

"*The signature chocolate chip pie [which should be served warm and, Bud Royers recommends, with a scoop of vanilla Häagen-Dazs] is not for the faint of heart! And their pecan pie is one of the best we've ever tasted.*"

—AUTHORS ANDREW DORNENBURG
AND KAREN PAGE

CHEFS' SECRET CRAVINGS

A question we're often asked as culinary authors is whether anything ever passes our lips that doesn't have the word *gourmet* on the label. We don't like to admit it, but on a busy book tour—when our only choice is between going hungry and grabbing fast food—we opt for the latter. Truth be told, Andrew has a soft spot for chocolate-frosted old-fashioned doughnuts from Winchell's, and Karen has had a thing for White Castle hamburgers since childhood.

We wondered whether leading chefs were ever tempted by the national chains as well. Indeed they are . . . and not only when they're in dire straits, either!

BURGER KING

—PATRICK O'CONNELL, THE INN AT LITTLE WASHINGTON (WASHINGTON, VA) (SEE ALSO P. 289.)

IN-N-OUT BURGERS

Multiple locations, including:
798 Redwood Highway (near Belvedere), Mill Valley, CA
Founded in 1948, California's first drive-through hamburger stand has 140 locations in the western United States; for a complete list, visit www.in-n-out.com or call (800) 786-1000.

"Whenever we're driving down to Orange County, we stop by In-N-Out Burger."

—SUSAN FENIGER AND MARY SUE MILLIKEN, BORDER GRILL AND CIUDAD (LOS ANGELES)

"My wife insisted, 'When, we're in Los Angeles, we've got to find an In-N-Out burger.' There's something I call the 'salmon effect':
sooner or later, people have to swim home and do things from their youth that seem absurd, but they do it anyway. This is one of them. So we went and had an In-N-Out Burger, and she had this surge of memories and thought the burger was terrific. I thought it was a good hamburger, even if I didn't have the same wave of memories flooding back."

—ROBERT DEL GRANDE, CAFÉ ANNIE (HOUSTON)

"I'm not one of these people who likes eight ounces of meat. I like smaller burgers like In-N-Out's, with lots of mayonnaise, ketchup, lettuce, and a soft bun, so the whole thing melts together."

—EMILY LUCHETTI, FARALLON (SAN FRANCISCO)

KRISPY KREME DOUGHNUTS

Multiple locations, including:
265 W. 23rd Street (between Seventh and Eighth Avenues), New York, NY (212) 620-0111

"You have to eat them immediately off the conveyor belt, when they're fresh. They'll melt in your mouth—they're so light!"

—DIANE FORLEY, VERBENA (NEW YORK)

Laurent Tourondel

"I love Krispy Kremes! Before I came to America, I had never had a doughnut. I don't know why they don't make them in France. Krispy Kreme is an amazing product; I offered a guy a thousand dollars for the recipe, but he wouldn't give it to me! While other chefs serve petit fours for desserts, I serve warm doughnut holes. We make them twice a day: at eleven-thirty for lunch and five-thirty for dinner."

—LAURENT TOURONDEL, CELLO (NEW YORK)

KRISPY KREME DOUGHNUTS

5640 S. Harlem Avenue, Summit, IL
(708) 728-0500

"We are wild for them right now. They are very light, with not too much glaze. We stockpile them—we usually have about eight dozen in the freezer! Rick likes to microwave his for exactly two seconds, then pound two or three with an espresso. After that, you are ready to rock! Gale likes them straight from the freezer with tea, much the way she used to eat her grandmother's cookie dough."

—GALE GAND AND RICK TRAMONTO, BRASSERIE T AND TRU (CHICAGO)

MCDONALD'S

"A Big Mac is not about the meat; you don't even think about the meat. It is the soft bread, the pickles, and the sauce. This is an example of getting everything in your mouth and finding that it tastes good. The sum is bigger than the individual parts."

—TERRANCE BRENNAN, PICHOLINE (NEW YORK)

POPEYE'S

"I typically hate fast food, and I don't eat burgers or pizza. My one exception, though, is Popeye's Fried Chicken. I like the four-piece spicy chicken dinner with red beans and rice. I don't have it very often, but when I do, it's fabulous!"

—FRANK BRIGTSEN, BRIGTSEN'S (NEW ORLEANS)

WENDY'S

—PATRICK O'CONNELL, THE INN AT LITTLE WASHINGTON (WASHINGTON, VA) (SEE P. 289.)

CREDIT WHERE CREDIT IS DUE...

We asked chefs for their recommendations of the best spots for enjoying favorite dishes, which they were happy to provide—albeit reluctantly and with great modesty when they honestly believed their own restaurants to be the best source for the dish in question! (In our book, a proud chef is the best recommendation.)

Some of the chefs who recommended their own restaurants for particular specialties include:

BREAKFAST

MACRINA BAKERY

2408 1st Avenue, Seattle, WA
(206) 448-4032

"I like our place for breakfast! We do a morning roll that is croissant dough pin-rolled with ground hazelnuts and vanilla sugar, with orange glaze on top. The other thing not to miss is the Budapest coffee cake!"

—LESLIE MACKIE, MACRINA BAKERY

HAMBURGER

RÖCKENWAGNER

2435 Main Street, Santa Monica, CA
(310) 399-6504

"When it comes to a burger, I have to recommend my own—for anything else, I will gladly mention someone else! We do a half-pound burger with melted Swiss cheese, which we put on a homemade pretzel bun. It is a meal for a day. Don't eat breakfast; eat it at lunch and you are done for the day. It is the combination of the pretzel bun with the burger and cheese that is just incredible."

—HANS RÖCKENWAGNER,
RÖCKENWAGNER AND RÖCK

ICE CREAM

BABBO

110 Waverly Place (between MacDougal Street and Avenue of the Americas), New York, NY
(212) 777-0303

"I like ice cream. Our pastry chef, Gina DePalma, makes the best ice creams, of every kind. It's amazing, and the flavors are always changing, but I'd have to say right now my favorite is the Concord grape sorbet."

— MARIO BATALI, BABBO, ESCA, AND LUPA

CELLO

53 E. 77th Street (between Madison and Park Avenues), New York, NY
(212) 517-1200

"I do like Häagen-Dazs's dolce de leche. But my favorite ice cream is the crème brûlée ice cream we serve at Cello. We make crème brûlée in the oven, then turn it in the ice cream maker. It is amazing. Then we put it into a cannoli-shaped chocolate tuille, and top it with cocoa beans and a warm cappuccino sauce."

—LAURENT TOURONDEL, CELLO

MESA GRILL

102 Fifth Avenue
(between 15th and 16th Streets),
New York, NY
(212) 807-7400

"Ice cream is one of my favorite things to eat. I would prefer to eat a bowl of ice cream rather than some really elaborate dessert. My pastry chef, Wayne Brachman, makes some of the best ice cream I have ever tasted. And when I'm not eating his, it's Häagen-Dazs or nothing. I think the texture of Häagen-Dazs is amazing. It's perfect ice cream."

—BOBBY FLAY, BOLO AND MESA GRILL

BIBA

272 Boylston Street, Boston
(617) 426-7878

"I still think Biba makes the best steak au poivre. It's a recipe I've perfected over the years. We don't put cream in the sauce; instead, we use a third of a bottle of red wine per person and really reduce it down. We add a lot of butter to make it really silky, and pepper the steak just enough."

—LYDIA SHIRE, BIBA AND PIGNOLI

GRAMERCY TAVERN

42 E. 20th Street (between Broadway and Park Avenue South), New York, NY
(212) 477-0777

"Anything Claudia Fleming, our pastry chef, makes is fine with me, and I eat plenty of it. I love sorbets; hers are the best in town!"

—TOM COLICCHIO, GRAMERCY TAVERN

farmers' markets

Many of the chefs interviewed strongly recommended visiting local farmers markets in the cities where they're located. While several are specifically mentioned throughout this book, such as in Dallas, Los Angeles, New York, and San Francisco, a worldwide guide to farmers markets can be found at:

www.openair.org

One Last Bite

ANDRÉ SOLTNER ON A LIFETIME OF LEARNING THROUGH EATING

André Soltner is the former chef-owner of Lutèce—arguably New York City's best restaurant for decades under his command—where he was legendary for never leaving the restaurant. Soltner is currently in "semi-retirement" (or what sounds to us like a nonstop schedule of cooking demonstrations and guest chef appearances in addition to his post as senior lecturer at the French Culinary Institute in Manhattan), but we were able to catch up with him to ask him what he's learned over the years through his dining experiences—as well as where he likes to eat now that he's no longer behind the stove night in and night out!

WHILE SERVING MY APPRENTICESHIP from 1948 to 1951, I learned lessons that are still in my blood today. In general, chefs don't change their cooking style—what we do is adapt and absorb ideas along the way. For instance, it was while serving in the army in Tunisia that I learned how to make couscous! You can't come up with enough ideas on your own. So I tell my students that eating out on their days off is the way for them, as well as for more experienced chefs, to continue their educations—because a chef should never stop trying to improve.

Of course, while a chef also goes to a restaurant to enjoy a meal and to be with friends, you can still learn something. If you don't, you're not on the ball. And it is not necessary to go only to the best restaurants in the world, either. Yes, we may want to see what the big guys are doing at the three- and four-star restaurants, but even a little restaurant may have something to teach you, too.

For example, a few years ago I was in Rochester [New York], and my friends took me to a little place that wouldn't even qualify as a diner. That morning, I had the best poached eggs of my life! They were so perfect, I could not believe it. I went back to the kitchen to ask for the chef, and a woman told me, "We have no chef—*I* made them." So I asked her to show me how she did it. Now, that morning I just went out to have breakfast with friends, not to learn something. But if your eyes and ears are open, and your palate is paying attention, you can learn any time and anywhere. As professional chefs, we have to do that all our lives.

It is also important to not limit your learning to restaurants, books, and magazines. You can learn from good home cooks as well. Once, my mother-in-law was making rabbit stew, so naturally I peeked in the kitchen to see how she was doing it. She started her stew by putting in a cube of sugar. When I asked why, she told me that when you do this at the beginning, the meat caramelizes better. Well, that stew was damn good! After that, whenever I made a stew at the restaurant, I put in a cube of sugar.

Taking Note

I keep a notebook for when I go out to restaurants. I have always done this, because if you see ideas and don't write them down, you will forget some of them.

In 1965, before he was famous, I had lunch at Paul Bocuse [in France]. After lunch, he invited me back into his kitchen and he showed me his food processor. Food processors weren't available yet in the United States, so I bought one right away, which became the first "Robo-Coup" in America. By eating out at Bocuse and being curious about what was in his kitchen, I learned about a tool that went on to revolutionize cooking.

The Mother of Invention

At that same lunch, Bocuse asked me to taste a tarte that he'd made. It was just some brioche dough, very thin, with some cream and another ingredient—it was very moist and very tasty. I took a good look at it, but I didn't ask for the recipe or give it another thought.

We were on our way to Alsace, but Bocuse insisted that we stop in to see his friend Troisgros, who—like Bocuse—I did not know and who was not yet famous. Even though we declined, he insisted, and called to make us a reservation for that night! We had a very nice dinner and went to the Troisgros's little café for coffee and brandy afterward. There, Troisgros asked me to taste his new tarte—and it was the same as Bocuse's! I didn't say anything, but I learned that they both got the idea from [another] Michelin three-star restaurant. Once I was back in New York at Lutèce, I adapted the same tarte to my own style of cooking, which is what a chef should do. I made some brioche and rolled it out very thin, as they had done, and added some sliced almonds. I ended up refining the tarte many times, and I served it for years in different variations.

On that same trip, I went to a simple café in Alsace and had something I had never seen before: a beautiful *boudin* baked in pastry, which was served with apple confit. I didn't put it on the menu at Lutèce because it didn't match our food. However, sometimes when I had customers I knew well in the restaurant, I would make it just for them.

When you go out, you don't go to "steal recipes"—you go out to be influenced, and later to do things your own way based on your own style. What you end up making may be different from what you tasted that inspired it.

Eating Out Today

I go all over to eat. To say I have one favorite restaurant is not true: One night I might go to a four-star restaurant, and the next night to a no-star restaurant.

ALAN WONG'S
1857 S. King St., Fifth Floor, Honolulu
(808) 949-2526

Chef Alan Wong worked with me for a few years, and I think his cooking is great. He doesn't cook my style of food—he's completely different. Yet he is a chef with very strong grounding in the basics. Having gone home to Hawaii, he adapted his cuisine to the ingredients there. I think he does a great job.

DANIEL
60 E. 65th Street (between Park and Madison Avenues), Manhattan
(212) 288-0033

I always like to eat whatever chef Daniel Boulud is cooking.

DESTINÉE
134 E. 61Street (between Park and Lexington Avenues), Manhattan
(212) 888-1220

Chef Jean-Yves Schillinger [who earned two Michelin stars in Alsace]'s father had been president of the Maître Cuisiniers de France. He does a very nice job.

JEAN GEORGES
1 Central Park West (between 60th and 61st Streets), Manhattan
(212) 299-3900

Jean-Georges Vongerichten is a very good chef. I don't know how he does it! I never wanted to have more than one restaurant, but it works for him.

L'ABSINTHE

227 E. 67th Street (between Second and Third Avenues), Manhattan
(212) 794-4950

Chef-owner Jean-Michel Bergougnoux used to work with me and has had this restaurant for the past several years. He cooks the food of Lyon—brasserie food, including, sometimes, such dishes as *tête de veau* and tripe.

LA CÔTE BASQUE

60 West 55th Street (between Fifth Avenue and Avenue of the Americas), Manhattan
(212) 688-6525

I'll go here to eat the classic French food [of chef Jean-Jacques Rachou].

LE CIRQUE 2000

455 Madison Avenue (between 50th and 51st Streets), Manhattan
(212) 303-7788

I like the cooking and the ambiance here very much [at the restaurant owned by Sirio Maccioni].

STATE LINE DINER

375 State/Route 17,
Mahwah, New Jersey
(201) 529-3353

I've found that people think professional chefs eat only in three-star restaurants with fancy sauces, truffles, and fois gras! However, I really enjoy stopping at a good diner for a sandwich. On our way back to Manhattan from the Catskills, we'll sometimes stop at the State Line Diner. They have a really good pastrami sandwich that I like, and my wife, Simone, likes the grilled Swiss cheese. This place is always busy. I may not always learn something new here about food, but eating here reinforces the idea that even if you do something simple— but do it better than others—you will be successful.

VONG

200 East 54th Street (at Third Avenue), Manhattan
(212) 486-9592

I love to go to [chef Jean-Georges Vongerichten's Thai-influened restaurant] Vong for dinner. It is a different style of cooking from mine, but the food is not "crazy." They have good technique in the kitchen, and with that as the basis, you can do anything. I don't have favorite dishes here because I just ask them to cook for me, and I'll typically have a nice Alsatian Pinot Blanc to drink.

Where does Soltner find the best of the best in terms of baked goods?

croissant

PAYARD PÂTISSERIE AND BISTRO

1032 Lexington Avenue (between 73rd and 74th Streets), Manhattan
(212) 717-5212

[Chef Francois] Payard's croissants are very good!

bread

L'ECOLE AT THE FRENCH CULINARY INSTITUTE

462 Broadway (at Grand Street), Manhattan
(212) 219-8890

I think the bread we do here at [L'Ecole at] the French Culinary Institute is very good. It is made by our students, and I think it is some of the best in New York City. The baguette is great!

Does Soltner have any secret cravings that might surprise people?

I don't eat fast food like McDonald's, although Mrs. [Joan] Kroc, the owner, was a regular at Lutèce. I do like anything that's deep-fried, as well as all sweets.

We don't eat much dessert at home except for ice cream. We like Häagen-Dazs. For years, our favorite flavor was Rum Raisin, but now we like Dolce de Leche. I used to tell my wife not to buy it, because I was trying to watch what I ate, but then I would end up eating a piece of chocolate instead!

BENCHMARKS OF EXCELLENCE

Since their inception in 1991, the James Beard Foundation Awards have been recognized as the Oscars of the culinary world. Winners of the award are held up as benchmarks of excellence in American restaurant cuisine and service, both nationally and regionally.

THE JAMES BEARD FOUNDATION AWARD FOR OUTSTANDING CHEF

1991	Wolfgang Puck, Spago (Los Angeles)
1992	Alice Waters, Chez Panisse (Berkeley)
1993	Larry Forgione, An American Place (New York)
	Jean-Louis Palladin, Jean-Louis (Washington, DC)
1994	Daniel Boulud, Restaurant Daniel (New York)
1995	Rick Bayless, Frontera Grill (Chicago)
1996	Jeremiah Tower, Stars (San Francisco)
1997	Thomas Keller, French Laundry (Yountville, CA)
1998	Wolfgang Puck, Spago Beverly Hills (Beverly Hills)
	Jean-Georges Vongerichten, Jean Georges (New York)
1999	Charlie Trotter, Charlie Trotter's (Chicago)
2000	David Bouley, Danube (New York)

THE JAMES BEARD FOUNDATION AWARD FOR OUTSTANDING RESTAURANT

1991	Bouley (New York)
1992	Chez Panisse (Berkeley, California)
1993	Inn at Little Washington (Washington, VA)
1994	Spago (West Hollywood)
1995	Le Cirque (New York)
1996	Commander's Palace (New Orleans)
1997	Union Square Café (New York)
1998	Le Bernardin (New York)
1999	The Four Seasons (New York)
2000	Charlie Trotter's (Chicago)

THE JAMES BEARD FOUNDATION AWARD FOR BEST NEW RESTAURANT

1995	Nobu (New York)
1996	Brasserie Jo (Chicago)
1997	Rose Pistola (San Francisco)
1998	Jean Georges (New York)
1999	Babbo (New York)
2000	Gary Danko (San Francisco)

THE JAMES BEARD FOUNDATION AWARD FOR
OUTSTANDING PASTRY CHEF

1991   Nancy Silverton, Campanile (Los Angeles)

1992   Albert Kumin, Green Mountain Chocolate
(Waterbury, VT)

1993   Lindsey Shere, Chez Panisse (Berkeley)

1994   Jacques Torres, Le Cirque 2000 (New York)

1995   François Payard, Payard Pâtisserie and Bistro
(New York)

1996   Sarabeth Levine, Sarabeth's (New York)

1997   Richard Leach, Park Avenue Café (New York)

1998   Stephen Durfee, The French Laundry (Yountville, CA)

1999   Marcel Desaulniers, The Trellis (Williamsburg, VA)

2000   Claudia Fleming, Gramercy Tavern (New York)

THE JAMES BEARD FOUNDATION AWARD FOR
BEST CHEF: NEW YORK

1992   Daniel Boulud, Daniel

1993   Alfred Portale, Gotham Bar and Grill

1994   David Bouley, Bouley Bakery

1995   Gray Kunz, formerly of Lespinasse

1996   Jean-Georges Vongerichten, Jean Georges, Jojo, and Vong

1997   Charles Palmer, Aureole

1998   Eric Ripert, Le Bernardin

1999   Lidia Bastianich, Felidia

2000   Tom Colicchio, Gramercy Tavern (New York)

THE JAMES BEARD FOUNDATION AWARD FOR
BEST CHEF: NORTHEAST

1991   Jasper White, formerly of Jasper's (Boston)

1992   Lydia Shire, Biba and Pignoli (Boston)

1993   Johanne Killeen and George Germon, Al Forno
(Providence)

1994   Todd English, Olives (Charlestown, MA)

1995   Gordon Hamersley, Hamersley's Bistro (Boston)

1996   Chris Schlesinger, East Coast Grill (Cambridge, MA)

1997   Jody Adams, Rialto (Cambridge, MA)

1998   Susan Regis, Biba (Boston)

1999   Melissa Kelly, Primo (Rockland, ME)

2000   Ken Oringer, Clio (Boston)

THE JAMES BEARD FOUNDATION AWARD FOR
BEST CHEF: MID-ATLANTIC

1991   Jean-Louis Palladin, formerly of Jean-Louis (Washington, DC)

1992   Patrick O'Connell, Inn at Little Washington (Washington, VA)

1993   Marcel Desaulniers, The Trellis (Williamsburg, VA)

1994   Patrick Clark

1995   Robert Kinkead, Kinkead's (Washington, DC)

1996   Roberto Donna, Galileo (Washington, DC)

1997   Susanna Foo, Susanna Foo (Philadelphia)

1998   Georges Perrier, Le Bec-Fin (Philadelphia)

1999   Jeffrey Buben, Vidalia (Washington, DC)

2000   Craig Shelton, The Ryland Inn (Whitehouse, NJ)

THE JAMES BEARD FOUNDATION AWARD FOR
BEST CHEF: SOUTHEAST

1991   Emeril Lagasse, Emeril's (New Orleans)

1992   Mark Militello, Mark's Las Olas (Fort Lauderdale)

1993   Susan Spicer, Bayona (New Orleans)

1994   Allen Susser, Chef Allen's (North Miami Beach)

1995   Elizabeth Terry, Elizabeth on 37th (Savannah)

1996   Guenter Seeger, Seeger's (Atlanta)

1997   Norman Van Aken, Norman's (Coral Gables, FL)

1998   Frank Brigtsen, Brigtsen's (New Orleans)

1999   Jamie Shannon, Commander's Palace (New Orleans)

2000   Ben Barker, Magnolia Grill (Durham, NC)

THE JAMES BEARD FOUNDATION AWARD FOR
BEST CHEF: MIDWEST

1991   Rick Bayless, Frontera Grill and Topolobampo (Chicago)

1992   Charlie Trotter, Charlie Trotter's (Chicago)

1993   Jimmy Schmidt, the Rattlesnake Club (Detroit)

1994   Paul Bartolotta, Spiaggia (Chicago)

1995   Jean Joho, Everest and Brasserie Jo (Chicago)

1996   Sanford D'Amato, Sanford (Milwaukee)

1997   Roland Liccioni, Les Nomades (Chicago)
       Gabino Sotelino, Ambria (Chicago)

1998   Sarah Stegner, the Dining Room at the Ritz-Carlton (Chicago)

1999   Debbie Gold and Michael Smith, the American Restaurant (Kansas City)

2000   Arun Sampanthavivat, Arun's (Chicago)

THE JAMES BEARD FOUNDATION AWARD FOR
BEST CHEF: SOUTHWEST

1991 Stephan Pyles, Star Canyon (Dallas)

1992 Robert Del Grande, Café Annie (Houston)

1993 Vincent Guerithault, Vincent's on Camelback (Phoenix)

1994 Dean Fearing, the Mansion on Turtle Creek (Dallas)

1995 Christopher Gross, Christopher's Fermier Brasserie (Phoenix)

1996 Mark Miller, Coyote Café (Santa Fe)

1997 George Mahaffey, Restaurant at Little Well (Aspen)

1998 Alessandro Stratta, Renoir (Las Vegas)

1999 Roxsand Scocos, RoxSand (Phoenix)

2000 Janos Wilder, Janos (Tucson)

THE JAMES BEARD FOUNDATION AWARD FOR
BEST CHEF: NORTHWEST

1991 John and Caprial Pence, Caprial's Bistro (Portland, OR)

1992 Barbara Figueroa, Ivars, Inc. (Seattle)

1993 Roy Yamaguchi, Roy's (Honolulu)

1994 Tom Douglas, Dahlia Lounge (Seattle)
      Monique Andrée Barbeau (Seattle)

1995 Tamara Murphy, Brasa (Seattle)

1996 Alan Wong, Alan Wong's (Honolulu)

1997 Jeem Han Lock, Wild Ginger (Seattle)

1998 Cory Schreiber, Wildwood (Portland, OR)
      Thierry Rautureau, Rover's (Seattle)

1999 Christine Keff, Flying Fish (Seattle)

2000 Jerry Traunfeld, The Herbfarm (Issaquah, WA)

THE JAMES BEARD FOUNDATION AWARD FOR
BEST CHEF: CALIFORNIA

1991 Joachim Splichal, Patina (Los Angeles)

1992 Michel Richard, Citrus (Los Angeles)

1993 Bradley Ogden, the Lark Creek Inn (Larkspur, CA)
      Jeremiah Tower, Stars (San Francisco)

1994 Joyce Goldstein, formerly of Square One (San Francisco)

1995 Gary Danko, Gary Danko (San Francisco)

1996 Thomas Keller, The French Laundry (Yountville, CA)

1997 Hubert Keller, Fleur de Lys (San Francisco)

1998 Julian Serrano, Picasso (Las Vegas)

1999 Paul Bertolli, Oliveto (Oakland)

2000 Judy Rodgers, Zuni Café (San Francisco)

THE JAMES BEARD FOUNDATION AWARD FOR OUTSTANDING WINE SERVICE

1991 Square One (San Francisco)

1992 Bern's Steak House (Tampa)

1993 Charlie Trotter's (Chicago)

1994 Valentino (Los Angeles)

1995 Montrachet (New York)

1996 Chanterelle (New York)

1997 The Four Seasons (New York)

1998 The Inn at Little Washington (Washington, VA)

1999 Union Square Café (New York)

2000 Rubicon (San Francisco)

THE JAMES BEARD FOUNDATION AWARD FOR OUTSTANDING SERVICE

1992 Danny Meyer, Union Square Café (New York)

1993 Ella and Dick Brennan, Commander's Palace (New Orleans)

1994 Joseph Baum

1995 Drew Nieporent, Montrachet (New York)

1996 Piero Selvaggio, Valentino (Los Angeles)

1997 Reinhardt Lynch and Patrick O'Connell, The Inn at Little Washington (Washington, VA)

1998 Julian Niccolini and Alex von Bidder, the Four Seasons (New York)

1999 Maguy LeCoze and Eric Ripert, Le Bernardin (New York)

2000 Karen and David Waltuck, Chanterelle (New York)

BECOMING A GREAT CHEF IN AMERICA TODAY: RECOMMENDED RESOURCES FOR CHEFS' PROFESSIONAL DEVELOPMENT

COOKING SCHOOL

Dornenburg, Andrew, and Karen Page. *Becoming a Chef: With Recipes and Reflections from America's Leading Chefs*, esp. chapter 3.

Kaplan, Dorlene, editor. *The Guide to Cooking Schools: Cooking Schools, Courses, Vacations, Apprenticeships and Wine Instruction Throughout the World* (ShawGuides). Also, see www.shawguides.com, which provides a free online guide to leading professional and recreational cooking schools.

Peterson's Culinary Schools: Find Out Where to Train for a Career in Cooking. The complete guide to U.S. and international professional cooking schools and apprenticeships.

Ruhlman, Michael. *The Making of a Chef: Mastering Heat at The Culinary Institute of America.*

APPRENTICING

American Culinary Federation Apprenticeship. This three-year program offers on-the-job training while earning an income. Contact ACF Apprenticeship Coordinator, American Culinary Federation, P.O. Box 3466, 10 San Bartola Drive, St. Augustine, FL 32085. Phone: (800) 624-9458. E-mail: educate@acfchefs.com.

Dornenburg, Andrew, and Karen Page. *Becoming a Chef: With Recipes and Reflections from America's Leading Chefs*, esp. chapter 4.

Kaplan, Dorlene, editor. *The Guide to Cooking Schools: Cooking Schools, Courses, Vacations, Apprenticeships and Wine Instruction Throughout the World.* See "National Apprenticeship Training Program for Cooks" at the end of chapter 1.

L'Ecole des Chefs. This one-on-one internship program, for a fee, offers restaurant professionals, culinary students, and committed amateurs unprecedented access to the intimate workings of the world's great kitchens. Participating American chefs include Daniel Boulud, François Payard, Georges Perrier, Michel Richard, Eric Ripert, and Jean-Georges Vongerichten; French chefs include Georges Blanc, Guy Savoy, Alain Senderens, Michel Troisgros, and Marc Veyrat. Address: P.O. Box 183, Birchrunville, PA 19421. Phone: (610) 469-2500. Fax: (610) 469-0272. E-mail: info@leschefs.com.

COMPOSING FLAVORS AND DISHES

Dornenburg, Andrew, and Karen Page. *Culinary Artistry*, esp. the chapters "Composing Flavors" and "Composing a Dish."

"Spend a day in different kitchens, take notes, and you will get so much out of it. I have no formal education, so I learned primarily through apprenticing and eating out."

RICK TRAMONTO

TRU (CHICAGO)

"It's important to read restaurant reviews that are written by people who are really good. Find somebody who knows a lot about food, and then see what their perspective on a restaurant is. When I was starting out, I read [former New York Times restaurant critic] Mimi Sheraton every single week. Wherever I was, I would find a copy of the New York Times and read what she had to say. After a year or two of doing it, I understood what her perspective was, and why she valued some things and not other things. While that certainly helped me to become a better restaurateur, I think it really helped me to become a better chef."

RICK BAYLESS   FRONTERA GRILL AND TOPOLOBAMPO (CHICAGO)

Peterson, James. *Sauces: Classical and Contemporary Sauce Making,* esp. chapter 3, "Ingredients."

Rozin, Elisabeth. *Ethnic Cuisine: How to Create the Authentic Flavors of Thirty International Cuisines.*

Sahni, Julie. *Savoring Spices and Herbs: Recipe Secrets of Flavor, Aroma and Color.*

Schmidt, Jimmy. *Jimmy Schmidt's Cooking Class: Seasonal Recipes from a Chef's Kitchen.*

COMPOSING MENUS

Curnonsky. *Traditional French Cooking,* esp. the chapter "The Art of the Table."

Dornenburg, Andrew, and Karen Page. *Culinary Artistry,* esp. the chapter "Composing a Menu," with examples of great menus from leading chefs.

Olney, Richard. *The French Menu Cookbook.*

Waters, Alice. *Chez Panisse Menu Cookbook.*

UNDERSTANDING THE CRITICAL PROCESS

Claiborne, Craig. *A Feast Made for Laughter: A Memoir with Recipes.*

Dornenburg, Andrew, and Karen Page. *Dining Out: Secrets from America's Leading Critics, Chefs and Restaurateurs.*

Greene, Gael. *Bite: A New York Restaurant Strategy for Hedonists, Masochists, Selective Penny Pinchers and the Upwardly Mobile.*

RECOMMENDED READING

Claiborne, Craig. *A Feast Made for Laughter: A Memoir with Recipes*, esp. the chapter "My Recommended Cookbook Library."

Dornenburg, Andrew, and Karen Page. *Becoming a Chef: With Recipes and Reflections from America's Leading Chefs*. Chapter 7 includes a list of the twenty books and authors most highly recommended by America's leading chefs.

TRAVEL

Dornenburg, Andrew, and Karen Page. *Becoming a Chef: With Recipes and Reflections from America's Leading Chefs*, esp. chapter 7.

Dornenburg, Andrew, and Karen Page. *Dining Out: Secrets from America's Leading Critics, Chefs and Restaurateurs*. The book's appendix includes a guide to leading restaurant critics' favorite restaurants across America.

Leff, Jim. *The Eclectic Gourmet Guide to Greater New York City*. www.chowhound.com.

Levine, Ed. *New York Eats (More): The Ultimate Food Shopper's Guide to the Big Apple*.

Plotkin, Fred. *Italy for the Gourmet Traveler*.

Relais and Châteaux International Guide. Updated annually. www.relaischateaux.com.

Sietsema, Robert. *Good and Cheap Ethnic Eats in New York City*.

Stern, Jane, and Michael Stern. *Eat Your Way Across the USA*.

Stern, Jane, and Michael Stern. *Roadfood*.

Unterman, Patricia. *Food Lover's Guide to San Francisco*.

Wells, Patricia. *The Food Lover's Guide to France*.

Wells, Patricia. *The Food Lover's Guide to Paris*.

"With all the culinary scholarships being organized, I think some of the money should be spent having students go to restaurants to taste real food, so that taste is not just a class experience. More of the people aspiring to restaurant kitchens should experience dinners in a variety of restaurants as part of their core education. They'll also find out that way what it's like when somebody is rude, or nice, to you."

MICHAEL BATTERBERRY OF *FOOD ARTS*, IN ANDREW DORNENBURG AND KAREN PAGE, *DINING OUT*

PROFESSIONAL COURTESIES

Recognizing that young cooks often lack the financial means to eat at the restaurants that will give them the very polish they need, many leading chefs extend dining courtesies to their own staff members as well as visiting restaurant professionals. Leading chefs repeatedly stress how important it is for young cooks to dine where they work, and many restaurants encourage their staff to do so by offering them dining discounts or occasional complimentary meals.

"We will send cooks out to eat for their birthdays," says Suzanne Goin of Lucques (Los Angeles), "and sometimes we will organize ourselves to go eat as a gang. It is easy for cooks to lose focus. A cook comes in for a shift, preps like a maniac, works service, which goes on forever, is finally done, goes home, gets some sleep, and then comes back to do it again the next day. They can find themselves thinking, 'Why am I doing this?' Unfortunately, they rarely see how that work plays out in the dining room. So it's important to help them keep the big picture in sight."

DINING OUT IN OTHER RESTAURANTS

When professional cooks go to visit other restaurants, they are sometimes "taken care of," meaning that the host restaurant might offer them special hospitality, ranging from an extra dish to taste to a tour of the kitchen.

Most leading chefs remember what it was like when they were struggling cooks, so this hospitality is often offered out of compassion as well as a sense of pride. It is flattering to have someone from another restaurant in your dining room, and chefs naturally want to make sure that visiting restaurant professionals enjoy themselves!

If you are a restaurant professional and will be dining at another restaurant, it may be helpful to let the restaurant know in advance, either at the time you make your reservation and/or immediately thereafter (such as by dropping a note, or sending a fax or e-mail, that mentions when you'll be dining and where you work).

- Mario Batali of Babbo, Esca, and Lupa (New York) will sometimes try to make an effort to squeeze in a party of restaurant professionals, even on a busy night. He believes that cooks need to maximize the learning done on their limited free time, so it's nice to make it a little easier for them. He encourages his own cooks to eat out on their nights off, and tries to help them get reservations or at least recommends places where he knows they'll be able to enjoy some great food.

- Jonathan Eismann of Pacific Time (Miami Beach) requires all his cooks to eat in the restaurant every six months, and he picks up the tab (excluding bottled wines). All the restaurant's employees receive a 50 percent discount when they dine in the restaurant. If you are a local

"When chefs visit, I sometimes send them a lagniappe—local dialect for 'a little something extra.'"
FRANK BRIGTSEN
BRIGTSEN'S (NEW ORLEANS)

chef, or a chef whom he looks up to as an "elder statesman," he might pick up the check entirely. He says he feels he owes the latter for being great chefs and forerunners. If you are a cook, he might send out extra food, and if you are a local cook who has worked for him in the past, he will still give the 50 percent employee discount.

· Gordon Hamersley of Hamersley's Bistro (Boston) encourages his cooks to eat in his restaurant at least once each menu cycle (the menu changes seasonally), and offers everyone a complimentary dinner for two—including hosts and wait staff.

· At 1789 (Washington, DC), chef Ris Lacoste offers the restaurant's managers complimentary meals to encourage them to come in to dine. She also sends them to eat in other DC fine-dining restaurants and asks them to report their experiences. To make dining at 1789 more affordable for her staff, she offers them specially priced tasting menus and wines. Additionally, she sometimes sets up swaps with other chefs, a you-feed-my-staff-I'll-feed-yours situation, to encourage their staffs to eat at other restaurants. Chefs and cooks from other restaurants who eat at 1789 are frequently treated to extra dishes and invited to visit the kitchen. Lacoste also offers special tasting menus to visiting chefs. She encourages restaurant professionals to identify themselves as such when calling for reservations, so that 1789 will know to expect them.

· Monica Pope of Boulevard Bistrot (Houston) gives her staff dining certificates in exchange for their written reviews of their experience. She has also coordinated dining certificate exchanges with other Houston restaurants in order to offer staff members a wider range of dining experiences. When chefs from out of town visit her restaurants, she often sends some of her signature dishes to their table.

· Norman Van Aken of Norman's (Coral Gables, FL) says, "Since my cooks and staff work so hard for me here, I will make reservations for them when they travel to other cities. I have a file for which I collect information about places I have been or want to go, so if one of my cooks is traveling, I will pull up my file to see what is happening there. I find out how much time they have, and then call some chefs in that city. Like in New York, I might call Georgette Farkas at Daniel or Agnes Deshayes at Jean Georges and let them know one of my cooks is coming, and they will hook them up. Sometimes I'll arrange for my cooks to work in the kitchen during the day and dine in the restaurant later that night. It's a way of kicking them out and throwing them into the pool, so to speak. They love it! I'll also send them to Kitchen Arts and Letters and Kalustyan's, which is an amazing spice store, while they're in New York, so they can get as much out of their trip as possible. When they come home, they are so excited. It's amazing for young cooks to travel and dine out, because they are so young they haven't been to the table that many times. They eat at our restaurant and it changes their hearts and heads, so we almost make them eat here if they've been here six months."

CHEF'S NIGHT OUT DINERSHIPS
AND OTHER SUPPORT FOR DINING

Part of our mission in writing *Chef's Night Out* was to spotlight the importance of dining out to an aspiring chef's professional education, and to encourage efforts supportive of this.

A percentage of the proceeds from *Chef's Night Out* is being used to provide restaurant vouchers to aspiring professional chefs who have not had the experience of dining out in some of America's best restaurants. In addition, *Chef's Night Out* chronicles some of the efforts already under way nationally to support young chefs' education in restaurants.

The authors envision a national effort to support the cultural education of aspiring culinary artists in much the same way as other programs have provided theater and concert tickets to aspiring actors and musicians.

Recipients of *Chef's Night Out* "dinerships" will be asked to write a review of their dining experience and to share it with their co-workers (or fellow students) as well as with the authors. Here is an excerpt from an essay by recipient Renee Schuler, a twenty-five-year-old graduate of Peter Kump's New York Cooking School who is now cooking at the Murphin Ridge Inn in West Union, Ohio, on her first dining experience at Le Bernardin, a four-star restaurant in New York:

> I chose what to wear to Le Bernardin carefully. I didn't want to be underdressed, but on a cook's salary, fancy clothes and jewelry are few and far between. I was too excited to be very concerned about what I was going to wear, anyway. One last glance in the mirror at the outfit I'd selected, and I was out the door, grinning from ear to ear, about the prospect of spending a cold December afternoon enjoying fine food, wine, and company at what I'd long heard and read was one of the finest restaurants in America.
>
> We were warmly welcomed by the staff, and taken to a wonderful table in the middle of the restaurant. Champagne was poured to celebrate the holiday season, and we were left to look through the wine list and the menu. Immediately I sensed how wonderful the meal would be, regardless of how the food tasted. The staff bustled around us, taking care of every detail, but at the same time they managed to be soundless and unobtrusive. Every time I turned to pick something up, there was someone offering it to me.

The first thing I tasted was a salmon spread that was accompanied by grilled crostini. I was surprised to be offered such a simple-looking item at a four-star restaurant. The spread came in an almost rustic-looking crock, with the bread on a small side plate. After the first taste, however, I was in heaven. It was perfect in every way—slightly smoky, but with a clean, rich salmon flavor. The bread was slightly charred and crispy. What an excellent way to begin. I also like how it established comfort around the table, as we all participated in sharing from the same crock. It brought us together as we anticipated our first course.

Mine was a special of lobster bisque with truffles. When it was set before me, the scent of my soup mingling with the fragrance of the truffles was incredible, and I savored the first bite slowly. Chunks of the most succulent lobster meat were nestled in the bottom of the bowl, and the texture and flavor were amazing.

Usually, working in a kitchen, I am used to building elements of a dish and then putting them together. It was an interesting change to have a completed dish placed before me and then work backward to imagine how the dish was assembled, taking the elements apart and analyzing how each complemented the others and why.

The next course, which arrived as a surprise from the kitchen, was a small plate with only two ingredients on it: leeks and yellowtail tuna, glistening under a veil of vinaigrette. How simple, I thought, although the symmetry of the dish and its stark presentation seemed to make it more beautiful. One taste and I realized why those two items were all that the chef had placed on the plate. Meltingly tender, sweet leeks and the cool, rich fish were a perfect complement. I was surprised at what an extraordinary experience it was to be able to taste two perfect ingredients paired together, simply plated, and without any excessive garnish....

I should mention that I grew up in the Midwest hating fish, so eating at Le Bernardin was a revelation to me as a cook. That day, I enjoyed fish prepared to the height of its glory, and I loved every bite.

INDEX

OTHER BOOKS BY ANDREW DORNENBURG AND KAREN PAGE

Becoming a Chef: With Recipes and Reflections from America's Leading Chefs (Wiley; $29.95 paperback; 320 pages; ISBN 0-471-28571-4). Winner of the 1996 James Beard Award for Best Writing on Food. Essential reading for anyone who loves food, *Becoming a Chef* is an entertaining and informative insider's guide to the chef's profession, providing the first behind-the-scenes look into some of the most celebrated restaurant kitchens across America.

"One of the top 20 books of 1995 recommended as holiday gifts."

ANNE MENDELSON   GOURMET

"One of the top 5 Editor's Choice cookbooks of 1995."

SAN FRANCISCO CHRONICLE

"You'll love Becoming a Chef.*"*

MATT LAUER   NBC'S TODAY

Culinary Artistry (Wiley; $29.95 paperback; 426 pages; ISBN 0-471-28785-7). *Culinary Artistry* is the first book to examine the creative process of culinary composition as it explores the intersection of food, imagination and taste. Through interviews with more than thirty of America's leading chefs—including Rick Bayless, Daniel Boulud, Jean-Louis Palladin, Jeremiah Tower, Jean-Georges Vongerichten, and Alice Waters—the authors reveal what defines culinary artists, how and where they find their inspiration, and how they translate that vision to the plate.

"In Culinary Artistry . . . *Dornenburg and Page provide food and flavor pairings as a kind of stepping-stone for the recipe-dependent cook. . . . Their hope is that once you know the scales, you'll be able to compose a symphony."*

MOLLY O'NEILL   NEW YORK TIMES MAGAZINE

"Andrew Dornenburg and Karen Page go where no culinary writers have gone before, exploring what inspires great chefs to create new flavor combinations, dishes and menus."

INTERNATIONAL COOKBOOK REVIEW

"Culinary Artistry receives honorable mention as one of the year's best culinary reference books. . . . [It] offers insights into creative cooking."

WILLIAM RICE   CHICAGO TRIBUNE

Dining Out: Secrets from America's Leading Critics, Chefs and Restaurateurs (Wiley; $29.95 paperback; ISBN 0-471-29277-X). *Dining Out* was a finalist for the two most prestigious awards in American culinary literature—the 1999 James Beard Book Award and the 1999 IACP/Julia Child Book Award—and was cited as one of the world's best culinary books of 1998 at the World Cookbook Fair held in Perigueux, France. It is the first book to demystify the clandestine process of restaurant criticism and to unlock the secrets of a great restaurant experience.

"Fascinating. . . . Illuminating insights."

NEW YORK TIMES BOOK REVIEW

"Anybody who has ever dreamed of joining a restaurant critic's inner circle will thoroughly enjoy this gossipy, insider's view. . . . Thanks to the unexpectedly dramatic lives of the characters involved, the pages buzz with often surprising tension, humor and emotion."

PUBLISHERS WEEKLY (lead starred review)

"An intriguing foray into the secret and powerful world of restaurant criticism."

NANCY NOVOGROD   TRAVEL & LEISURE